M

MACMILLAN LAW MASTERS

Series Editor   **Marise Cremona**

Basic English Law 2nd edition   W. T. Major
Business Law   Stephen Judge
Company Law 3rd edition   Janet Dine
Constitutional and Administrative Law 2nd edition   John Alder
Contract Law 3rd edition   Ewan McKendrick
Conveyancing 2nd edition   Priscilla Sarton
Criminal Law   Marise Cremona
Economic and Social law and Policy of the European Union   Jo Shaw
Employment Law 2nd edition   Deborah J. Lockton
Family Law 2nd edition   Kate Standley
Intellectual Property Law   Tina Hart and Linda Fazzani
Land Law 3rd edition   Kate Green
Landlord and Tenant Law 3rd edition   Margaret Wilkie and
  Godfrey Cole
Law of the European Union 2nd edition   Jo Shaw
Law of Succession   Catherine Rendell
Law of Trusts   Patrick McLoughlin and Catherine Rendell
Legal Method 2nd edition   Ian McLeod
Legal Theory   Ian McLeod
Torts 2nd edition   Alastair Mullis and Ken Oliphant

Company Law

Third edition

Janet Dine
Professor of Law
University of Essex

Law series editor: Marise Cremona
Senior Fellow, Centre for Commercial Law Studies
Queen Mary and Westfield College, University of London

MACMILLAN

First edition 1991
Reprinted once
Second edition 1994
Third edition 1998

Published by
MACMILLAN PRESS LTD
Houndmills, Basingstoke, Hampshire RG21 6XS
and London
Companies and representatives
throughout the world

ISBN 0–333–71095–9

A catalogue record for this book is available
from the British Library.

Copy-edited and typeset by Povey–Edmondson
Tavistock and Rochdale, England

10   9   8   7   6   5   4   3   2
07   06   05   04   03   02   01   00   99   98

Printed in Malaysia

Contents

Preface

In accordance with the intentions behind the *Mastering Law* series, this book is intended as an introduction to the basic principles of company law. Like the other books in the series the book contains features designed to help those studying this subject for the first time. These include *casenotes* at the end of most chapters which give a short account of the facts and decisions in key cases. A number of points for further consideration are included in the *exercises* at the end of each chapter. In addition an attempt has been made to state the law in clear and simple terms. I hope it has succeeded.

JANET DINE

The publishers and authors are grateful to Butterworth Publishers London for the permission to reproduce material as casenotes taken from *Butterworth's Company Law Handbook*.

Table of Cases

Table of Statutes and Directives

1 The Reasons for Forming Companies

'The limited liability corporation is the greatest single discovery of modern times. Even steam and electricity are less important than the limited liability company,' said Professor N. M. Butler, President of Columbia University (quoted by A. L. Diamond in Orhnial (ed.), *Limited Liability and the Corporation* (Law Society of Canada, 1982) p. 42; see also Len Sealy, *Company Law and Commercial Reality* (Sweet & Maxwell, 1984) p. 1.)

Why so important? Well, a huge proportion of the world's wealth is generated by companies.

However, companies are most often used by people as a tool for running a commercial enterprise. Many of these businesses start in a small way, often by co-operation between a small number of people.

If a commercial undertaking prospers the persons involved will wish to expand the undertaking, which will generally require an injection of money. This can be achieved by inviting more people to contribute to the capital sum which the business uses to fund its activities. The alternative is to raise a loan. The latter course has the disadvantage of being expensive because the lender will charge interest. On the other hand, if a large number of persons are involved in a business, then this too may have considerable disadvantages. One is that they may disagree with each other as to how the business should best be run. They may even disagree with each other as to who should make the decisions about how the business is to be run. This is partially solved in a company by the necessity of having a formal constitution (the memorandum and articles of association) which sets out the voting and other rights of all the members (shareholders) of a company.

Another disadvantage of expansion of a business is that as the amounts dealt with increase, so also do the risks. One great advantage of the most widely used type of company is that it has 'limited liability'. This means that if the company becomes unable to pay its debts, the members of that company will not have to contribute towards paying the company's debts out of their own private funds: they are liable to pay only the amount they have paid, or have promised to pay, for their shares. This means that contributors to the funds of businesses which are run on this limited liability basis may be easier to find. Limited liability is also said to encourage greater boldness and risk-taking among the business community, so that new avenues to increasing commerce are explored. The advantage of limited liability may lead quite small businesses to use a company, although this may not be advantageous from a tax point of view and does lead to a considerable number of obligations to file accounts, and so on, which may create a considerable burden for a small concern. Further, if a very small business wishes to raise a loan from a bank, the bank will normally require a personal guarantee from the people running the business. This means that the advantage of limited liability will, practically speaking, be lost.

A further disadvantage of attempting to run a business with a large number of people involved is that there may be considerable difficulties experienced when some of those people die, wish to retire or simply leave the business. There may be great difficulties for a person dealing with the business in deciding precisely who is liable to pay him. In a shifting body of debtors, an outsider may experience extreme difficulty in determining which people were actually involved in the business at the time that is relevant to his claim against the business. This difficulty is solved by the invention of the legal fiction of corporate personality. The idea is that the company is an entity separate from the people actually involved in it. This fictional 'legal person' owns the property of the business, owes the money that is due to business creditors and is unchanging even though the people involved in the business come and go. The importance of the invention was emphasised when in 1971 a team of Canadian lawyers (principally Robert Dickerson, John Howard, Leon Getz and Robert Bertrand) undertook a comprehensive review of Canadian corporation law. Their aim was not piecemeal reform but a fundamental review of company law in order to determine what the purpose behind the existence of the current rules were, whether that purpose was being achieved, and where necessary to suggest improvements to the system. Because the review started from fundamentals it contains many lessons for those who seek to formulate law to govern the behaviour of corporations and their relationship with the public and the state.

The first point made in the Introduction to the Canadian review (*Proposals for a New Business Corporations Law for Canada* (Canadian Government Publications, 1971), authors as above) is the importance of the corporation in the economic system: it can 'scarcely be exaggerated'.

Those reformers came to the conclusion that Canadian companies were subject to too much regulation and proposed a drastic reduction of the number and complexity of rules applying to companies. Their recommendations were largely accepted and became the Canada Business Corporations Act of 1975. As we examine the company law of the United Kingdom it is useful to consider the purpose behind the various rules and whether they are sufficiently effective in achieving their purpose. Also whether they justify the expense which is incurred by companies to ensure that their operations stay within the complicated framework that has grown up. Section 1 of the Companies Act 1985 begins the statute with the declaration:

'Any two or more persons associated for a lawful purpose may, by subscribing their names to a memorandum of association and otherwise complying with the requirements of this Act in respect of registration, form an incorporated company, with or without limited liability.'

If only it were as simple as that . . .! Apart from other complications it is now possible to have a company with only one member. This is discussed further at the end of this chapter.

1.1 The Elements of a Company

The people who provide the money to run the business of the company are called members or shareholders. They put money into the business by buying shares from the company. Their rights and liabilities are governed by the constitution of the company contained in the memorandum and articles of association. It is usual (though not universal) for a share to carry voting rights. Many of the decisions necessary for the running of a company can be arrived at by a majority vote of the shareholders taken at a meeting. However, it would be cumbersome for the everyday running of the business to be conducted in this way, so the company votes that certain people should be 'directors' of the company and should take care of the everyday running of the company. The meeting of shareholders has the right to appoint and remove directors by majority vote. This procedure is not as democratic as it first appears, however, as the person who is suggested as a director may himself hold a majority of the shares and be able to vote himself into office. Alternatively, a director may be able to prevent his removal from office by special multiple voting rights which operate when there is an attempt to remove him (*Bushell* v. *Faith* [1970] AC 1099) or by making it very expensive for the company to get rid of him or her.

If there is a disagreement between the shareholders of the company and the management in the form of the directors, complicated issues arise. This is particularly the case when the directors have a majority of the shares. If they were permitted to use that majority in any way they wished they would be able to authorise themselves to use the company assets for any purpose, perhaps even to deprive other shareholders of any valuable stake they had in the company. This would amount to an unjust expropriation of the property of a minority and the court will intervene to prevent such a thing happening (see Chapter 13). However, the court will be cautious not to intervene too readily in the running of the company, partly because many of the judgments that must be made by directors are commercial ones and the courts have little expertise in making such assessments. Another reason is that the directors would be hampered if they constantly had to look over their shoulders when commercial judgments had to be made, in case an action could be brought against them. Another balancing act has to occur because the directors are similar to trustees in that they are engaged in handling money in which other people have a considerable stake–both the shareholders and the creditors of the company. They should therefore behave honestly and fairly. However, if the rules making them responsible for mistakes or breaches of duty are too strict, directors may become too cautious in performing an entrepreneurial role and the business may fail from that cause.

The law has sought to balance these interests by use of the idea that the company is a thing separate from any of the humans involved in the business (see Chapter 2). If a company is seen as a person, albeit a legal person, the directors owe it a duty to act in the correct fashion. If they do not do so, it is the company's right to sue them. This theory means that the directors will only be sued if a majority vote is in favour of such action. To prevent this from allowing directors too much power, particularly where they have control of the majority of votes, the court will overturn the result of such a majority vote where it feels that in the particular circumstances the result is very unfair to other shareholders (see Chapters 11, 12 and 13). It is very difficult to get the balance between these groups right, but it is important to view the law as holding the line between the various interest groups, as the jargon involved with the law sometimes obscures the reality.

Another tension is created between shareholders and creditors where the subject of disposal of the assets of the company is concerned. The law in this country takes the line that attempts must be made to keep a sum of money in the company which will be available to pay debts if the company fails. To this end an elaborate system regulating the raising and maintenance of capital has grown up (see Chapter 9). Furthermore there are elaborate accounting rules which are expensive for the company to maintain. These may be of use to a potential investor or someone who is contemplating doing business with the company, but are against the interests of current shareholders who would usually prefer either to have the money paid to them or to use it in the business.

There are many other tensions which will appear in a study of this subject. The technicalities of the subject become more comprehensible if the law is seen as struggling to hold a fair line between competing interest groups. The debate as to the proper degree and method of regulating this balance of interests is often referred to as the 'corporate governance debate'. It has been carried on vigorously in recent years (see Chapter 11).

1.2 **Outsiders**

It is important to draw a distinction between the relationships which occur between the inside factions within a company and the relationships between a company and those who are 'outsiders'. Identification of 'outsiders' may be complicated, as a single person may be both a member and an outsider at the same time. Consider someone who is owed money by the company on a commercial transaction; in his capacity as a commercial creditor he is an outsider. If he also owns shares he will have rights as a member, but the two bundles of rights are quite separate and the one will not usually affect the other.

It may be surprising to some that employees are also (in that capacity) outsiders. Until recently directors were not entitled to give any priority to the welfare of the employees unless this could be shown to be in the ongoing interests of the company (*Parke* v. *Daily News* [1962] 2 All ER 929) (see Casenotes). Even now, section 309 of the Companies Act 1985 is generally agreed to be ineffective. This section provides:

(1) The matters to which the directors of a company are to have regard in the performance of their functions include the interests of the company's employees in general, as well as the interests of its members.
(2) Accordingly, the duty imposed by this section on the directors is owed by them to the company (and the company alone) and is enforceable in the same way as any other fiduciary duty owed to a company by its directors.
(3) This section applies to shadow directors as it does to directors.'

Although it appears at first sight that this may make a significant change in the interests of employees, the duty is enforceable only if a majority of shareholders vote to sue the directors for non-compliance, an unlikely event. In fact the letter of the law is often observed by the interests of employees being on the agenda at directors' meetings, the chairman remarking; 'We are now considering the interests of employees' before passing to the next business.

A more substantial change in the law was effected by section 719, which gives the company power to make provision for its present or past employees, or those of its subsidiaries on cessation of the business of the company. This provision will prevent payments to employees made in those circumstances being challenged on the grounds that it is a misuse of money which should have been paid to the shareholders and therefore not in the interests of the company. It was the latter argument which succeeded in *Parke* v. *Daily News* (see Casenotes). This case will not now be followed, because s. 719 permits a company to make these payments. The case is still useful as an illustration of the competing interest groups within a company.

1.3 'Parent' and 'Subsidiary' Company

It may be convenient for different parts of a business to be managed by a separate but connected company. In this case one company may cause another to be formed. If the first company wishes to retain a measure of control over the new company, it will take shares in it. If the shareholding gives the first company control over the new company, the first company will be a 'parent' company and the new company a 'subsidiary'. In certain circumstances the financial affairs of subsidiary companies must be disclosed by the parent company in its accounts. There is now a special definition of 'parent' and 'subsidiary' for determining when this must be done (s. 258 Companies Act 1985). Despite the new definitions, group activities still cause problems and the courts have sometimes ignored the separate personality of companies within a group (see Chapter 3).

1.4 **Single Member Companies**

The EC Twelfth Directive (see Chapter 18) provides that all Member States must allow the formation of single member companies. This Directive has now been implemented in the UK by the Companies (Single Member Private Limited Companies) Regulations 1992, SI 1992/1699 which bring the law into line with a common practice which was to form companies which had two shareholders but where one of those shareholders was a mere nominee who took no part at all in the affairs of the company. Now a single member does not need this extra shareholder and can make all the company decisions. In such companies the usual rules as to the quorum at meetings and voting procedures have been modified since it is clear that a single member does not need to convene a formal meeting with him or herself in order to take a valid decision!

The Regulations apply to all private limited companies. Public companies must still have at least two members.

Where a single member company enters into a contract with the sole member and that sole member is also a director of the company then, unless the contract is in the ordinary business of the company, a record of the contract must be kept. Failure to comply with this restriction renders the company and every officer of it in default liable to a fine but it does not, of itself, invalidate the contract. The contract might be invalid under Part X of the Companies Act 1985 (see Chapter 11).

Summary

Companies are a useful tool for conducting business, particularly when that business has grown bigger than can usefully be managed by a few people and also requires an increase in funding. The laws governing companies seek to achieve a balance between the various interested groups within companies and also between the protection of people dealing with companies and the freedom to act of those managing companies. If too many regulations are imposed on companies, these may be counter-productive in that they may make the organisation inefficient and thus liable to fail.

Casenotes

Parke v. *Daily News* [1962] 2 All ER 929 Ch 927.
The *Daily News* sold a significant part of its business and proposed to distribute the money received to employees who would be made redundant by the sale. Although most shareholders supported this distribution, the plaintiff (who was also a

shareholder) objected. The question was whether the majority vote in favour of the distribution entitled the directors to give away the money of the company (and thus money which would eventually be returned to shareholders, including Mr Parke). The court held that such an action could only be justified if the company would benefit from the distribution. As the company had sold the main part of its business, the kindness to employees could not be justified as having any future effect in securing loyalty or attracting good staff. The distribution was held to be invalid despite the majority vote in favour. Plowman J referred to a previous case which had arisen on similar facts, *Hutton* v. *West Cork Railway Company* (1883) 23 ChD 654. He said:

'That was a case where a company had transferred its undertaking to another company and was going to be wound up. After completion of the transfer, a general meeting of the transferor company was held at which a resolution was passed to apply (among other sums) a sum of 1,000 guineas in compensating certain paid officials of the company for their loss of employment, although they had no legal claim for compensation . . . . In an oft-cited judgement, Bowen LJ said: 'Now the directors in this case have done, it seems to me, nothing at all wrong . . . Not only have they done nothing wrong but I confess I think the company have done what nine companies out of ten would do, and do without the least objection being made. They have paid, perhaps liberally, perhaps not at all too liberally, persons who have served them faithfully. But that, of course, does not get rid of the difficulty. As soon as a question is raised by a dissentient shareholder . . . sympathy must be cut adrift, and we have simply to consider what the law is. In this particular instance the plaintiff is a person who stands prima facie in the condition of those who are bound by the vote of a general meeting acting within the powers of a general meeting, but he complains that the majority purpose to expend certain purchase money which the company are receiving . . . in two ways which he thinks are beyond their powers . . . Now can a majority compel a dissentient unit in the company to give way and to submit to these payments? We must go back to the root of things. The money which is going to be spent is not the money of the majority. That is clear. It is the money of the company, and the majority want to spend it. What would be the natural limit of their power to do so? They can only spend money which is not theirs but the company's if they are spending it for the purposes which are reasonably incidental to the carrying on of the business of the company. That is the general test. Bona fides cannot be the sole test, otherwise you might have a lunatic conducting the affairs of the company, and paying away its money with both hands in a manner perfectly bona fide yet perfectly irrational . . . one must ask oneself what is the general law about gratuitous payments which are made by the directors or by a company so as to bind dissentients. It seems to me you cannot say the company has only got power to spend the money which it is bound to pay according to law, otherwise the wheels of business would stop, nor can you say that directors . . . are always to be limited to the strictest possible view of what the obligations of the company are. They are not to keep their pockets buttoned up and defy the world unless they are liable in a way which would be enforced at law or in equity. Most businesses require liberal dealings. The test there again is not whether it is bona fide, but whether, as well as being done bona fide, it is done within the ordinary scope of the company's business, and whether it is reasonably incidental to the carrying on of the company's business for the company's benefit. Take this sort of instance. A railway company, or the directors of the company, might send down all the porters at a railway station to have tea in the country at the expense of the company. Why should they not? It is for the directors to judge, provided it is a matter which is reasonably incidental to the carrying on of the business of the company, and a company which always treated its employees with Draconian severity, and never allowed them a single inch more than the strict letter of the bond, would soon find themselves deserted – at all events, unless labour was very much more easy to obtain in the market than it often is. The law does not say that there are to be no cakes and ale, but that there are to be no cakes and ale except such as are required for the benefit of the company . . . [*Re Lee, Behrens & Co. Ltd.* [1932] 2 Ch 46 was also cited] . . . The conclusions which, I think, follow from these cases are: first that a company's funds cannot be applied in making *ex gratia* payments as such; secondly, that the court will inquire into the motives actuating any gratuitous payment; and the objectives which it is intended to achieve . . .'

In the event, the distribution in *Parke* was held to be invalid. The case would not be decided in the same way today, as s. 719 of the Companies Act 1985 gives express power to provide for employees where the business is to cease or be substantially lessened as a result of transfer to another party. Some of the comments must also be read with some reservation in view of later case law on *ultra vires* points (see Chapter 4). However, the action could still arise in a similar form, despite the 'reform' of the *ultra vires* rules, since a shareholder was suing in advance of the distribution to prevent it.

Exercises

1 Why are companies a useful form of business association?
2 Identify the different interest groups involved in *Parke* v. *Daily News* (see Casenotes). What is the best method of resolving the potential conflicts between these groups?
3 Explain why the 1989 Act definition of the parent–subsidiary relationship is wider than that in the Companies Act 1985.
4 After reading Chapters 3 and 11 consider the implications of the separate corporate personality of companies within a group on the duties of directors.

---

2   Starting a Company

The first decision that must be made by those considering incorporation of a business is the type of company that will be suitable.

2.1 Limited and Unlimited Companies

An unlimited company has the advantage of being a legal entity separate from its members, but lacks the advantage that most people seek from incorporation, that is the limited liability of the members. Thus, the members of an unlimited liability company will be held responsible for all of the debts of the company without limit. Unlimited companies therefore form only a small proportion of the number of registered companies.

Limited liability companies have the advantage that the members' liability to contribute to the debts of the company have a fixed limit which is always clear. There are two ways of setting the limit, by issuing shares or by taking guarantees from the members that they will contribute up to a fixed amount to the debts of the company when it is wound up or when it needs money in particular circumstances. The first type of company is a company limited by shares, the second is a company limited by guarantee (s. 1(2)(b) Companies Act 1985). No new companies limited by guarantee and having a share capital to provide working money can be formed (s. 8 and Table D Companies Act 1985). This means that a guarantee company formed in the future cannot have any contributed capital (until it is wound up) (s. 1(4)). This form is therefore unsuitable for commercial enterprises although the form has been extensively used to carry out semi-official functions, particularly in the sphere of regulation of the financial services market.

In a company limited by shares, the members know that they will never have to pay more into the company than the full purchase price of their shares. This need not necessarily be paid when they are first purchased. When some money is outstanding on shares, the company may issue a 'call' for the remainder to be paid, but it can never demand more than the full price due to the company for that share. Such a company will be registered as a 'company limited by shares'. By s. 1(2)(a) Companies Act 1985 such a company has 'the liability of its members limited by the memorandum to the amount, if any, unpaid on the shares respectively held by them'.

Section 2 of the Companies Act 1985 sets out basic requirements which must be included in the essential document, the Memorandum of Association. By s. 2(5)(a) a limited company with a share capital must state the maximum amount of share capital which the company is to be entitled to raise. This is known as its 'authorised share capital', 'registered share capital' or 'nominal share capital'. It does not represent the amount actually contributed at the time when the company is formed, which may only be a nominal amount. Section 2(5) also provides that each subscriber to the memorandum must take at least one share.

2.2 **Public and Private Companies**

Where a company is registered as a public company, this must be stated in the memorandum, and the words 'public limited company' (or the abbreviation PLC or plc) must come at the end of its name (Companies Act 1985 ss. 1(3) and 25(1)). All other companies are private companies.

The fundamental difference between public and private companies is that only public companies may invite the public to subscribe for shares. Section 81 Companies Act 1985 prohibits a private company from issuing, or causing to be issued, any advertisement offering securities to be issued by the company. Public companies are therefore more suitable for inviting investment by large numbers of people. A private company is particularly suitable for running a business in which a small number of people are involved. Professor Len Sealy describes the situation as follows:

> 'During the nineteenth century (and indeed for a considerable period before that) the formation of almost all companies was followed immediately by an appeal to the public to partcipate in the new venture by joining as members and subscribing for "shares" in the 'joint stock". . . The main reason for "going public" in this way was to raise funds in the large amounts necessary for the enterprises of the period - often massive operations which built a large proportion of the world's railways, laid submarine cables, opened up trade too distant parts and provided the banking, insurance and other services to support such activities. The promoters would publish a "prospectus", giving information about the undertaking and inviting subscriptions. This process is often referred to as a "flotation" of the company or, more accurately, of its securities.' (Sealy, *Cases and Materials in Company Law*, 6th edn, Butterworths 1996.)

It would now be most unusual for a new enterprise to 'float' immediately. The Stock Exchange controls the rules for flotation and requires an established business record before it will permit it to occur. There are two other markets, whose requirements are similar but not quite so strict. These are the Unlisted Securities Market (USM) and the Alternative Investment Market (AIM). The USM is being gradually replaced by the AIM. No new companies will be listed on the USM. (For further discussion see Chapter 7.)

As one would expect, the regulations governing public companies are more extensive than those governing private companies. In many areas, however, no distinction is made between the two types of company.

2.3 **Minimum Capital Requirements for a Public Company**

We have seen that a private company need have only a very small amount of capital. However, the European Community Second Directive has set the minimum capital for a public company registered in the EC at 25,000 ecu. Section 118 Companies Act 1985 sets the minimum for UK companies at £50,000 and gives the power to the Secretary of State to specify a different sum by statutory instrument. The company is not obliged to have received the full £50,000. However, by s. 101 Companies Act 1985, public companies must receive at least one-quarter of the nominal value of the shares. The amount of capital actually contributed could be as little as £12,500, although the company would have a right to make a 'call' on the shareholders demanding payment of the unpaid capital (that is, the outstanding £37,500).

By s. 117 it is a criminal offence committed by the public company and any officer of it in default, to do business or to borrow money before the Registrar of Companies has issued a certificate to the effect that he is satisfied that the nominal value of the company's allotted share capital is not less than the prescribed minimum and that he has received a statutory declaration which must be signed by a director or secretary of the company and must

(a) state that the nominal value of the company's allotted share capital is not less than the authorised minimum;
(b) specify the amount paid up, at the time of the application, on the allotted share capital of the company;
(c) specify the amount, or estimated amount, of the company's preliminary expenses and the persons by whom any of those expenses have been paid or are payable; and
(d) specify any amount or benefit paid or given, or intended to be paid or given, to any promoter of the company, and the consideration for the payment or benefit (see Chapter 6).

2.4 **Change of Status from Public to Private Company and Vice Versa**

A change of status from private to public company is much more common than registration as a public company on initial incorporation. Section 43 Companies Act 1985 provides for this change of status and s. 53 Companies Act 1985 permits a company to change from public to private status. In both cases the members of the company must pass a special resolution (a resolution passed by at least 75 per cent of the votes cast) to effect the change. In the case of a change from private to public the Registrar must be provided with a statutory declaration that the minimum capital requirements for public companies have been satisfied and that the requisite special resolution has been passed. By s. 47(2) Companies Act

1985, the Registrar may accept this as sufficient evidence that the requirements of registration as a public company have been satisfied and issue a certificate of incorporation. By s. 47(5) such a certificate is conclusive evidence that the company is a public company and that the requirements of the Act as to re-registration as a public company have been complied with.

If the reverse change of status from public to private is undertaken, the members may find that it is more difficult to sell their shares. There are safeguards in the Act aimed at protecting a minority who object to such a change of status. Under s. 54 Companies Act 1985, the holders of 5 per cent or more of the nominal value of a public company's shares or 50 or more members may apply to the court for the cancellation of a special resolution to request re-registration as a private company. The court has an unfettered discretion to cancel or approve the resolution on such terms as it thinks fit (s. 54(5) Companies Act 1985).

2.5 **Groups**

The old definition of this relationship was to be found in s. 736 of the 1985 Companies Act. That read:

'(1) For the purposes of this Act, a company is deemed to be a subsidiary of another if (but only if)–
    (a) that other either–
        (i) is a member of it and controls the composition of its board of directors, or
        (ii) holds more than half in nominal value of its equity share capital, or
    (b) the first-mentioned company is a subsidiary of any company which is that other's subsidiary.'

This definition of the parent–subsidiary relationship caused two main difficulties. The first was that it concentrated on the number of shares held by (1)(a)(ii). This ignores the fact that control is exercised through voting rights, which need have no relationship to the number of shares held.

The second difficulty lay with the reference to the control of the board of directors. Under the original sections in the 1985 Act, a company was deemed to control the composition of the board of directors if it could appoint or remove the holders of all or a majority of the directorships. If one company could appoint less than a majority of the directors, but those it was able to appoint had extra voting rights so that they could outvote the other directors, then control of the board's activities was effectively achieved, while the arrangement was still outside the scope of the section.

By these and other methods it was possible to avoid the intended effect of the section, which was to treat a group of companies as a single business for various purposes, including accounting purposes.

Because of this the Companies Act 1989 introduced new definitions of this relationship. These sections provide one definition for accounting purposes (see Chapter 9) and another, the following one, which applies in all other circumstances (inserted into the 1985 as new s. 736).

'(1) A company is a "subsidiary" of another company, its "holding company", if that other company–
  (a) holds a majority of the voting rights in it, or
  (b) is a member of it and has the right to appoint or remove a majority of its board of directors, or
  (c) is a member of it and controls alone, pursuant to an agreement with other shareholders or members, a majority of the voting rights in it,
  or if it is a subsidiary of a company which is itself a subsidiary of that other company.
(2) A company is a "wholly owned subsidiary" of another company if it has no members except that other and that other's wholly owned subsidiaries or persons acting on behalf of that other or its wholly owned subsidiaries.'

The emphasis will thus shift from ownership of shares to control of voting rights which are further defined by the Act. This should give a more realistic picture of a group of companies. The definition for accounting purposes is even wider (see new s. 258 CA 1985, Chapter 8).

2.6 The Memorandum of Association and Registration

It is essential that a company have a memorandum of association to specify its constitution and objects. This is because s. 1(1) Companies Act 1985 provides:

'Any two or more persons associated for a lawful purpose may, by subscribing to a memorandum of association and otherwise complying with the requirements of this Act in respect of registration, form an incorporated company, with or without limited liability.'

Contents

Companies Act 1985, s. 2 requires the memorandum of a company limited by shares to state:

(a) the name of the company;
(b) whether the company's registered office is to be situated in England and Wales or in Scotland;
(c) the objects of the company (see Chapter 4);
(d) that the liability of the members is limited;
(e) the maximum amount of capital the company may raise and its division into shares of a fixed amount.

The memorandum of a public company must state that it is to be a public company (section 1(3)(a) Companies Act 1985). Each subscriber to the memorandum must take at least one share in the company and the number of shares taken by a subscriber must be shown against the subscriber's name (section 2(5) Companies Act 1985). Precedents for the memorandum of association for a private company are set out in SI 1985 No. 805, Table B, and for a public company in SI 1985 No. 805, Table F (set out below in Casenote 1).

In practice the contents of a memorandum will be much more elaborate than the suggested form, but the essential contents can be discovered from the precedents. The contents and drafting of the objects clause is dealt with in more detail in Chapter 4 below.

Name

The choice of a name for a company is of considerable importance and subject to a number of restrictions. If it is to have limited liability the name must end with 'Limited' (permitted abbreviation 'Ltd') for a private company, and 'Public Limited Company' (Permitted abbreviation 'PLC' or 'plc') for a public company (or Welsh equivalents) (ss. 25(2), 25(1), Companies Act 1985).

By s. 714 Companies Act 1985 the Registrar of Companies is required to maintain an index of the names of companies and a company may not be registered with a name which is the same as a name appearing on the index (s. 26(1)(c) Companies Act 1985). A company may not be registered with a name which, in the opinion of the Secretary of State would constitute a criminal offence or be offensive and the Secretary of State's approval is required for the use of a name which would be likely to give the impression that the company is connected with the government or any local authority, or which includes any word or expression specified in regulations made by the Secretary of State (section 26, s. 29 Companies Act 1985, Business Names Act 1985, SI 1981 No. 1685; see Casenote 2). The peculiar mixture of words can be seen in Casenote 2. A company must have its name outside its place of business and its name must appear on all correspondence: Companies Act 1985 s. 348–9, Business Names Act 1985 s. 4. If a company goes into insolvent liquidation a person who was acting as a director of the insolvent company is not allowed to act as a director of a new company with the same or a similar name. The restriction lasts for 5 years (s. 216 IA 1985). This is to prevent the misuse of limited liability companies by using a series of companies, putting one into liquidation, leaving the debts behind and then starting a new one.

Passing off

One further restriction on the selection of names is imposed by the rules against using a name so similar to the name used by an existing business as to be likely to mislead the public into confusing the two concerns. Thus in

Exxon Corporation v. *Exxon Insurance Consultants International Ltd* [1982] Ch 119 the court granted an injunction restraining the defendants from using the word Exxon in their company's name.

2.7 **Incorporation**

Section 10 Companies Act 1985 requires delivery of the memorandum (and articles, if any (see Chapter 5)) to the Registrar of Companies for England and Wales, if the registered office is to be situated in either England or Wales, and for Scotland if the registered office is to be situated in Scotland.

With the memorandum and articles the following must also be delivered to the Registrar:

a statement of the names and particulars of:
(a) the person who is, or the persons who are, to be the first director or directors of the company; and
(b) the person who is, or the persons who are to be the first secretary or joint secretaries of the company (s. 10 Companies Act 1985. The particulars required are set out in Schedule 1 to the 1985 Act).

The statement must be signed by or on behalf of the subscribers to the memorandum and the intended address of the company's registered office must be stated.

2.8 **Duty of Registrar**

Section 12 Companies Act 1985 provides that the Registrar shall not register a company's memorandum unless he is satisfied that all the statutory requirements have been complied with. Once satisfied, the Registrar has the duty to retain and register a memorandum and articles. At this point the Registrar must give a certificate that the company is incorporated (section 13 Companies Act 1985) and (if such be the case) that it is limited. The effect of this process of registration is set out in the remainder of s. 13 Companies Act 1985:

'(3) From the date of incorporation mentioned in the certificate, the subscribers of the memorandum, together with such other persons as may from time to time become members of the company, shall be a body corporate by the name contained in the memorandum.
(4) That body corporate is then capable forthwith of exercising all the functions of an incorporated company, but with such liability on the part of its members to contribute to its assets in the event of its being wound up as is provided by this Act [and the Insolvency Act 1986].

(5) The persons named in the statement under s. 10 as directors, secretary or joint secretaries are, on the company's incorporation, deemed to have been respectively appointed as its first directors, secretary or joint secretaries.

(6) Where the registrar registers an association's memorandum which states that the association is to be a public company, the certificate of incorporation shall contain a statement that the company is a public company.

(7) A certificate of incorporation given in respect of an association is conclusive evidence–

   (a) that the requirements of this Act in respect of registration and of matters precedent and incidental to it have been complied with, and that the association is a company authorised to be registered, and is duly registered under this Act, and

   (b) if the certificate contains a statement that the company is a public company, that the company is such a company.'

Thus, the company's existence as such is unchallengeable from the date of the issue of the certificate of incorporation.

2.9 Off-the-Shelf Companies

Ready-made companies can be acquired from enterprises which register a number of companies and hold them dormant until they are purchased by a customer. This may save time when a company is needed quickly for a particular enterprise. There used to be a potential problem in that the objects clause of such a company might not precisely cover the enterprise in question, with the result that such a company would be precluded from carrying on the desired business. Contracts made in pursuance of such an enterprise would be of no effect (see Chapter 4). However, many such companies will be formed in the future with the objects of a general commercial company. Section 3A companies Act 1985 provides that such a company may carry on any trade or business whatsoever, and has the power to do all things which are incidental or conducive to the carrying on of any trade or business by it. This will give the company a range of objects and powers sufficient to eliminate any problems which might remain under the *ultra vires* law (see Chapter 4). Further, where a company with a limited objects clause is acquired, the new law on *ultra vires* should ensure that few problems will be encountered.

Summary

1 There are several types of company. The most common company is a limited company, the liability of the members being limited to the amount they have previously agreed. There are some unlimited companies where members are liable to pay the whole of the debts of the company.

2 Companies may have a share capital or be limited by guarantee. In the former case members buy shares. In the latter case members agree to contribute to the debts of the company up to a certain amount.

3 Companies may be public companies (PLCs) or private companies (normally having Ltd after their names). Only public companies can sell shares to the public. Public companies are subject to more regulations than private companies.

4 There is a minimum capital requirement for public companies of £50,000.

5 Companies can change from public to private status and vice versa.

6 A company must have a memorandum of association.

7 The choice of the name of a company is important and subject to a number of restrictions.

8 Incorporation is achieved after the memorandum and articles are delivered to the Registrar of Companies.

9 Ready-made companies can be bought.

Casenote 1

Table B

A PRIVATE COMPANY LIMITED BY SHARES
MEMORANDUM OF ASSOCIATION

1. The company's name is 'The South Wales Motor Transport Company cyfyngedig'.

2. The company's registered office is to be situated in Wales.

3. The company's objects are the carriage of passengers and goods in motor vehicles between such places as the company may from time to time determine and the doing of all such other things as are incidental or conducive to the attainment of that object.

4. The liability of the members is limited.

5. The company's share capital is 50,000 pounds divided into 50,000 shares of one pound each.

We, the subscribers to the memorandum of association, wish to be formed into a company pursuant to this memorandum; and we agree to take the number of shares shown opposite our respective names.

Names and Addresses of Subscribers	Number of shares taken by each Subscriber
1. Thomas Jones, 138 Mountfield Street, Tredegar.	1
2. Mary Evans, 19 Merthyr Road, Aberystwyth.	1
Total shares taken	2

Dated
Witness to the above signatures,
Anne Brown, "Woodlands", Fieldside Road, Bryn Mawr.

TABLE F

A PUBLIC COMPANY LIMITED BY SHARES
MEMORANDUM OF ASSOCIATION

1. The company's name is 'Western Electronics Public Limited Company'.
2. The company is to be a public limited company.
3. The company's office is to be situated in England and Wales.
4. The company's objects are the manufacture and development of such descriptions of electronic equipment, instruments and appliances as the company may from time to time determine, and the doing of all such other things as are incidental or conducive to the attainment of that object.
5. The liability of the members is limited.
6. The company's share capital is 5,000,000 pounds divided into 5,000,000 shares of one pound each.

We, the subscribers to this memorandum of association, wish to be formed into a company pursuant to this memorandum; and we agree to take the number of shares shown opposite our respective names.

Names and addresses of Subscribers	Number of shares taken by each Subscriber
1. James White, 12 Broadmead, Birmingham.	1
2. Patrick Smith, 145A Huntley House, London Wall, London EC2.	1
Total shares taken	2

Dated
Witness to the above signatures,
John Green, 13 Hute Street, London WC2.

Casenote 2

The Companies and Business Names Regulations 1981 (SI 1981 No. 1685) sets out in its schedule a list of words which may not be used in a company's name without permission of the Secretary of State. They include (this list is not complete):

Abortion
Assurance
Benevolent
Breeder
Building Society
Chamber of Trade
Co-operative
Dental
Dentistry
District Nurse
Duke

English
European
Friendly Society
Giro
Great Britain
Health Service
Her Majesty
Institute
Ireland
King
Midwife
Nursing
Patentee
Police
Prince
Princess
Queen
Reassurance
Royal
Scotland
Sheffield
Special School
Stock Exchange
Trade Union
Trust
Wales
Windsor

Exercises

1 What is the difference between the various types of companies?
2 What matters should be considered when choosing a name for a company?
3 What information is needed by the Registrar on the incorporation of a company?
4 When does a company come into existence?

3   Corporate Personality

The essence of a company is that it has a legal personality distinct from the people who create it. This means that even if the people running the company are continuously changing, the company itself retains its identity and the business need not be stopped and restarted with every change in the managers or members (shareholders) of the business. If the company is a limited liability company not only is the money owned by the company regarded as wholly distinct from the money owned by those running the company, but also the members of the company are not liable for the debts of the company (except where the law has made exceptions to this rule in order to prevent fraudulent or unfair practices by those in charge). Members can only be called upon to pay the full price of their shares. After that a creditor must depend on the company's money to satisfy his claim. This limitation of the liability of the members has led to careful rules being drawn up to attempt to prevent a company from wasting its money (Chapter 9). It is one of the disadvantages of incorporation that a number of formal rules, designed to protect people doing business with companies, have to be complied with. A partnership which consists of people carrying on a business with a view to making profits has many fewer formalities to be complied with. On the other hand, the members of a partnership are liable for all the debts incurred by the business they run. If large losses are made they must contribute their own money to clear the debts of the business. In practice this may be a distinction without a difference since, where small businesses are concerned, banks will not lend money to a company without first securing guarantees from those running the business so that if the company cannot pay its debts, such debts will be met from the personal assets of those in charge.

The separate personality of a company creates a range of problems because although the company is regarded as a person in law it can, of course, only function through the humans who are running the business in which the company is involved. The law must regulate the relationships between a company and its creators and members or shareholders as well as the relationship between a company and 'outsiders' who do business with the company.

3.1 **The Legal Basis for the Separate Personality Doctrine**

The case of *Salomon* v. *Salomon* [1897] AC 22 is by no means the first case to depend on the separate legal personality of a company, but it is the most widely discussed in this context. Mr Salomon was a boot and shoe manufacturer who had been trading for over thirty years. He had a thriving business. He also had a large family to provide for. To enable the business to expand, he turned it into a limited liability company. As part of the purchase price he took shares in the company and lent the company money in return for 'debentures', which are paid off preferentially in the event of a liquidation. The company did not last very long. Almost immediately there was a depression in the boot and shoe trade and a number of strikes. Mr Salomon tried to keep the company afloat by lending it money and by transferring his debentures to a Mr Broderip for £5000, which he handed over to the company on loan. However, liquidation was not long in coming. The sale of the company's assets did not realise enough to pay the creditors. The liquidator claimed that the debentures had been fraudulently issued and were therefore invalid. He also denied that the business had been validly transferred from Mr Salomon to the company. The grounds for both these claims were that the business had been overvalued at £39,000 instead of its true worth of around £10,000 and that the whole transfer to a limited company amounted to a scheme to defeat creditors. The judge who heard the case first admitted that the transfer had been legally carried out and could not be upset. However, he suggested (*Broderip* v. *Salomon* [1895] 2 Ch 323) that Mr Salomon had employed the company as an agent and that he was therefore bound to indemnify the agent. He said that the creditors of the company could have sued Mr Salomon despite the existence of the company to whom the business had been legally transferred. In the Court of Appeal, Mr Salomon's appeal was dismissed. However, the House of Lords took a different view. Lord MacNaughten said:

'The company is at law a different person altogether from [those forming the company]: and, though it may be that after incorporation the business is precisely the same as it was before, and the same persons are managers, and the same hands receive the profits, the company is not in law the agent of the subscribers or trustee for them. Nor are the subscribers as members liable, in any shape or form, except to the extent and in the manner provided by the Act . . . If the view of the learned judge were sound, it would follow that no common law partnership could register as a company limited by shares without remaining subject to unlimited liability.'

Thus was established the complete separation between a company and those involved in its operation. As with many principles of English law, having established first the principle we must then look at the problems caused by and the exceptions to that principle.

The fundamental importance of separate personality

The invention of the company as separate is vital as it means that it is free to develop as an instrument of business shaped by both the people involved in its running and those regulating its existence. The fact that different models of companies have come to exist is a direct result of the fact that the company's separate personality sets it apart from the individuals that are running it. The models that have developed say a great deal about the society in which they operate.

What models exist?

The contractual theory

This is usually accepted as the philosophy underlying United Kingdom company law, which generally adheres rather strictly to a contractual theory of companies, regarding a company as primarily if not solely the property of and co-extensive with the owners. This theory is exemplified by the first section of the Companies Act 1985:

> 'Any two or more persons associated for a lawful purpose may, by subscribing their names to a memorandum of association and otherwise complying with the requirements of this Act in respect of registration, form an incorporated company . . .'

Thus, at formation the owners alone are involved. The United Kingdom courts have tended to carry this theory into the period when the company is full operation. This has the major consequence that the wishes of the shareholders are seen as the overriding consideration for management, who are obliged to act 'in the best interests of the company.' Numerous cases equate the interests of the shareholders with the interests of the company. This has the effect of excluding other interests from consideration in the way the company is run, in particular leaving creditors and employees as 'outsiders'. This model is reflected in the structure of UK companies where employee directors are rare and shareholders elect the whole of the management team. Although this model would seem at first sight to be a simple one it has inbuilt complications. For example, shareholders are not an amorphous body. Different shareholders will have different interests at any one time. The interest of an aged shareholder intent on enjoying the good life before departure may differ radically from the young shareholder just starting out in life. Thus attempts by the UK courts to pin down the true meaning of the 'interests of the company', even applying this simple theory, have been fraught with difficulty and division. Much debate centres round whether a dissentient minority of shareholders should be considered when the 'interests of the company' are at stake. The interests of the company have been equated with 'the single individual hypothetical shareholder', but commentators have pointed out that this formulation does not solve the problem, because the hypothetical shareholder could be in the majority or in the minority. A hypothetical future shareholder has been suggested as the benchmark, but even this formulation does not solve the potential conflict between short-term and long-term policies. Thus even the simple model meets difficulties in its application.

Separation of ownership and control

The famous research of Berle and Means (p. 141) showed that the ownership and control of companies was increasingly in different hands. The identification of the shareholders with the company no longer represented reality. This could have led to a re-identification of the company as the creature of its professional managers, but instead the tendency has been to regard the company more and more as a creature in its own right and to struggle to identify what are the interests of the company as an entity clearly distinct from its shareholders. Critical theorists have argued from a Marxist perspective that the separation of ownership and control necessarily leads to a depersonalisation of the relationship between capital and labour, but this need not be the case provided that an inclusive model of this separate legal entity is chosen, rather than a divisive one. What are the alternatives?

The constituency model

In order to read other interested parties into the decision making of directors, some have suggested a move to a constituency or stakeholder model of company law. There are two variants of this model. The adoption of one or the other variant will have little practical effect on the actual decisions made, but the different theoretical underpinning has important implications for determining which parties should have a corporate governance role. The first variant of the model sees the company as run in the interests of shareholders, it being in the interests of shareholders to take account of other interest groups, because to ignore them would damage shareholder interests. This approach is exemplified by legislation which details the interests which must be considered by directors in determining their actions while enforcement is left in the hands of shareholders. The importance of the routing of the constituency interests through the interests of the shareholders is that the logical group to enforce those interests is the shareholders themselves. In the second variant of the model it is accepted that interests of other groups must be taken into account, because such an approach directly benefits the company. In this variant the company is seen as encompassing interests other than those of shareholders. Then 'interests of the company' are seen as including at least the interests of employees and creditors as well as shareholders. The distinction between the two variants is that in the second it is more clearly the company which has the corporate governance role and it is less clear that shareholders should have an exclusive role in acting on behalf of the company to ensure that it is run in its best interests. It could be argued that the company should be able to depend on other interested groups to ensure its proper management. Both variants of this model are able to absorb the tendency of the courts to give different weight to the degree of interest of the constituencies, which will vary at different times in the history of the company, reflecting not least the financial health of the company; thus it is likely that creditors will be considered more important than shareholders when the company is insolvent. This model is hard to control because groups of interested parties are considered relevant since they comprise a described group and not because of any analysis of how closely they are in fact involved with the interests of the company.

The enterprise model

An enterprise model differs from a constituency model in that the directors not only have to take into account the interests of others as well as the shareholders; those interests are also regarded as part of the company, having a corporate governance role of their own inside the decision making process. The contrast can be drawn between the obligation of directors to take account of the interests of employees under s. 309 Companies Act 1985 (which has no enforcement mechanism open to employees, only to shareholders) and the election of employees to the boards of companies. A further example would be the ability of a person named in the articles of association to nominate members of the supervisory board, a provision which would probably be used by banks to involve themselves in corporate decision making. This model is the classic one developed in Germany and Holland and originally reflected by the draft EC Fifth Directive and European Company Statute.

The associative model

At Essex University a team of lawyers are developing an associative model of a company. It is postulated that all who have dealings with a company have potentially two rights. They will usually form a contractual relationship with it, but if their association with it becomes very close (as in many contracts of employment or contracts for loans) then a different relationship, that is, an associative relationship, will arise, and this will give the holder of such a right a corporate governance role. The holder of such a right will be able to argue that the company is not being run in its own best interests because associative rights are being disregarded. The great value of this model is that corporate governance roles are available to particular persons or groups when they can show that their interests should be considered as part of the company's interests rather than because they belong to a particular group. Thus the interested parties have the advantage of the enterprise model in that they become insiders, but their interests are less likely to be institutionalised or frozen at a particular point of time because the associative interests in a company will be constantly changing. Thus the corporate governance right will only be available to a person who can prove that at that moment in the history of the company their interests should be an important element for management to take into account when determining the interests of the company. This right is different from but might complement a right of representation in the corporate governance structure, and may be particularly valuable where, for example, employee representatives on a supervisory board wish to argue that their interests have been totally ignored. So far as UK company law is concerned it would represent a small shift from the mixed contract–constituency model that exists. The courts have, as we have seen, required interests of creditors to be taken into account in certain situations and s. 309 Companies Act 1985 requires managers to take account of interests of employees while other cases equate the interests of shareholders with the interests of the company. Those holding associative rights would not be as powerful as if they had representation on the decision-making body of the company, although it would always be open to a company to adopt the enterprise model as well, ensuring a really tight model of 'insider' governance. The challenge to management decisions would be by derivative action reflecting similar features to a shareholder derivative action. Thus, such an action could only be brought to defend the interests of the company and the eventual 'winner' of any successful action would be the company itself. The action would succeed only where the court was able to determine that the interests of the company had been contravened. Where associative rights had been totally disregarded the action would succeed, but where associative rights had been considered and other interests had prevailed a successful action would be rare indeed.

That the associative model represents only a small shift from the current model is shown by the fact that an employee shareholder would already be in the position postulated, but it may provide a different source of enforcers who by definition have a long-term connection with the company and, unlike the second variant of the constituency model are not defined solely by their membership of a particular group.

One great advantage of this model is that it is immensely flexible and can serve a variety of purposes. Mayer (in *Enterprise and Governance* (Institute of Directers, 1996) made the point that insider or outsider governance structures would serve different purposes. The associative model could be structured by those controlling it, so that if 'outside' governance was the aim then short-term loans and employment as well as diversity of shareholding could be used to prevent a tight structure of corporate governance. If, on the other hand, a really tight corporate governance was required, then the company might move towards an associative plus enterprise structure, reflecting the philosophy embodied in the Commercial Code of the Czech and Slovak Republics, where the definition of an enterprise gives us some clues as to the underlying policy and theory of company law in these countries. Section 5 of the Code (since amended) defined an enterprise as 'the aggregate of all its tangible and intangible assets and the skills applied by its staff to its business activity'. This clearly signalled an inclusive enterprise approach to companies.

3.2 **Problems Caused by the Personality Doctrine and Exceptions**

The first 'personality' problem that can arise is that experienced by those seeking to form a company in order to carry on a business. While they are completing the formalities which will lead to registration of the company and the consequent gain of legal personality for the company, its creators may wish to sign contracts for the benefit of the company when it is formed. The difficulty is that the company does not exist as a legal person until registration and therefore cannot be party to any contract, nor can it employ agents to act on its behalf. The law on such 'pre-incorporation contracts' is explained in Chapter 6.

The second problem was one under discussion in *Saloman*'s case. A limited liability company can be a very powerful weapon in the hands of one determined on fraud and on defeating a creditor's rightful claims. Will the courts make no exceptions to the rule that a company is wholly separate from those who manage and control it?

A survey of the case law shows that the courts do contravene the strict principle of the separateness of the company from time to time. There is general agreement among those who have sought to analyse the relevant cases that the only principle that can be gleaned from them is that the courts will look at the human reality behind the company if the interests of justice provide a compelling reason for doing so. This may sound an excellent principle, but when the huge variety of fact situations that are likely to arise are considered, such a vague notion makes it extremely difficult to predict what a court will do in any given case. When the existence of the company is disregarded, commentators have called it the 'lifting' or 'piercing' of the veil of incorporation. There are a number of cases discussed below which are clearly relevant to the sanctity of the 'veil' of incorporation, but the whole of company law is riddled with examples of the validity of acts depending on the effect they will have on the members of a company.

An example would be where the part of the constitution of a company known as the articles of association are changed, that change can be challenged unless it can be justified as in good faith and for the benefit of the company as a whole. In order to determine the latter, the effect of the decision on the members of the company must be examined.

It is also said that the proper person to sue to redress a wrong done to the company is the company itself. However, there is an exception to this rule to prevent those in charge of the company causing damage to shareholders in a powerless minority, for example by taking the company's property. The examples on pages 28–9 clearly show the difficult task which those seeking to regulate a company have because of the doctrine of legal personality. The company must be given as much independence from its operators as possible, otherwise it would always be subject to interference from a large number of (probably disagreeing) voices and therefore be no less cumbersome than a partnership trying to operate by consensus. On the

5

other hand, the law must always recognise the reality of the fact that the company can do nothing without human operators and that those human operators may wish to hijack the company for their own ends, to the detriment of others who have money at stake.

3.3 Statutory Intervention

The personality of the company is recognised and ignored at will by the legislature. Those drafting legislation do not seem to respect the principle as being sacrosanct in itself and look merely to the end sought to be achieved by particular provisions. This is a highly practical approach. The courts might do well to admit that the only principle running through their decisions is 'justice in the individual case' and thus adopt a similar pragmatic approach. Examples of statutory interference with the principle of legal personality are listed below (see Casenotes). It should be noted that these are only examples. Many more can be found.

3.4 Lifting the Veil

The separate personality of the company can have some unexpected and sometimes unwelcome effects. In Neptune (Vehicle Washing Equipment) Ltd v. Fitzgerald [1995] 1 BCLC 352 the defendant was a sole director of a company. Despite this he was obliged to make disclosure of a personal interest in a resolution which he passed purporting to terminate his contract of employment although the court held that 'it may be that the declaration does not have to be out loud.' Although this sounds strange it emphasises that the contract was one between the director and the company so that in his capacity as an official acting in the interests of the company the director must remind himself of his personal interest before determining a course of action. In *Macaura* v. *Northern Assurance Co* [1925] AC 619 the court refused to ignore the separateness of the company and 'lift the veil' despite the fact that the consequence of so doing was to deny a remedy to someone whose personal fortune had gone up in smoke. Macaura had sold the whole of the timber on his estate to a company. He owned almost all of the shares in the company and the company owed him a great deal of money. Macaura took out an insurance policy on the timber in his own name. When almost all the timber was later destroyed by fire he claimed under the insurance policy. The House of Lords held that he could not do so. He no longer had any legal interest in the timber and so fell foul of the rule that an insurance policy cannot normally be taken out by someone who has no interest in what is insured.

Sometimes other rules of law can be used to mitigate the effects of the strict application of the doctrine. This was done in *Harrods* v. *Lemon* [1931] 2 KB 157. The estate agents division of Harrods was acting as agent in the sale of the defendant's house. A purchaser was introduced and subsequently instructed surveyors to examine the house. The surveyors that were instructed were Harrods surveyors department. The survey disclosed defects as a result of which a reduced price was negotiated. The defendant had been informed prior to this of the fact that Harrods were acting on both sides of the sale. This would normally be a breach of the agency contract between the estate agents department and the defendant. The defendant, however, agreed to Harrods continuing to act for her. The two departments of Harrods were in fact completely separate. The judge (Avory J) agreed that there had been a technical breach of the agency contract between Harrods and the defendant. Although the two departments were completely separate the company in fact was one single person in the eyes of the law. However, he also insisted that the defendant should pay Harrods despite the breach as she had agreed to them continuing to act despite having full knowledge of the breach.

The following two cases provide a prime example of the way the courts will disregard the separate personality of the company if that will achieve a just result, but will equally keep the veil of personality firmly in place where that will benefit someone for whom the court feels sympathy. In *Malyon* v. *Plummer* [1963] 2 All ER 344 a husband and wife had full control of a company. The husband was killed by the defendant in a car accident and the widow was unable to continue the business of the company. An insurance policy had been taken out on the man's life and £2000 was paid to the company on his death. The shares of the company were therefore more valuable than they had been prior to his death. The plaintiff (widow) had received an inflated salary from the company prior to her husband's death. The court had to assess the future financial situation of the widow in order to set the amount of damages payable to her. It was decided that the excess of the plaintiff's salary over the market value of her services was a benefit derived from the plaintiff's relationship as husband and wife. It was therefore a benefit lost by his death and only the market value of her services should be taken into account in assessing her future position. This ignores the fact that she was employed by a company which should in accordance with *Salomon*'s case have been regarded as a completely separate entity from both husband and wife. It did mean, however, that the widow got more. Similarly, the court held that the insurance money was money which should be regarded as having been paid to the wife as a result of the death of the husband. The shares owned by the wife should therefore be valued at the lower value before the £2000 was paid.

It is very difficult to see a distinction in principle between *Malyon* v. *Plummer* where the veil was not just pierced but torn to shreds and *Lee* v. *Lee's Air Farming* [1916] AC 12 where the emphasis was laid heavily on the separate legal personality of the company. In this case the widow would have lost everything if the *Malyon* v. *Plummer* approach had been adopted. In *Lee* the appellant's husband was the sole governing director and controlling shareholder of a company. He held all but one of the shares in the company. He flew an aeroplane for the company which had taken out an insurance policy which would entitle his widow to damages if when he died he was a 'worker' for the company. He was killed in a flying accident. It was held that the widow was entitled to compensation. Lee's position as sole governing director did not make it impossible for him to be a servant of the company in the capacity of chief pilot because he and the company were separate and distinct legal entities which could enter and had entered into a valid contractual relationship. The approach in *Lee* was followed in *Tunstall* v. *Stiegman* [1962] 2 QB 593. There a landlord was unable to terminate a tenancy on the ground that he was going to carry on a business on the premises because the business was to be carried on by a limited company. This was despite the fact that the landlord held all the shares in the company except for two which were held by her nominees and of which she had sole control.

The result in this case would be different if it fell to be decided now, because s. 6 of the Law of Property Act 1969 provides that where a landlord has a controlling interest in a company, any business to be carried on by the company shall be treated for the purposes of s. 30 of the Landlord and Tenant Act 1954 as a business carried on by him. The case remains useful as an illustration of the way in which the courts have approached the question of corporate personality. Further confusion results from the decision of the Court of Appeal in *Williams* v. *Natural Life Health Foods Ltd* [1997] 1 BCLC 131 where a diector of a one man company was held personally liable for negligent misstatements made on behalf of his company. The court stated that a company director was only to be held personally liable where the plaintiff could establish 'special circumstances'. it also said that in the case of a director of a one-man company particular care should be taken 'lest the protection of incorporation should be virtually nullified'. However, the court held that in the case the special circumstances had been established. They were that he had played a significant part behind the scenes in negotiations leading up to the grant of a franchise which the plaintiff purchased on the faith of financial projections furnished by someone introduced by the director and misrepresented as having relevant expertise. A brochure issued by the director's company had placed particular emphasis on the personal expertise and experience of the director. The court held that it was not necessary for the plaintiff to prove that the director and the plaintiff had personal dealings. This strange and unsatisfactory case gives few clues as to what special circumstances will in future be considered relevant for a court considering lifting the veil. It seems once again to be a case of a sympathetic plaintiff and it may well be relevant that the company on whose behalf the statement was made by the director had been wound up at the time of the proceedings. If there was no personal liability the plaintiffs would have been without a remedy.

3.5 **Fraud**

The ability to hide behind the corporate veil could be a powerful weapon in the hands of those with fraudulent tendencies. The courts have therefore always reserved the right to ignore a company which is formed or used merely to perpetrate a dishonest scheme. In *Salomon*'s cases both the Court of Appeal and the judge in the first instance thought that they had before them just such a case of fraud. Since there was no evidence of dishonest intent in that case it seems that these courts were using 'fraud' in a very wide sense. Indeed, they seem to have regarded the formation of the company so that the business could henceforth be carried on with limited liability as sufficient evidence of 'fraud'. To take such a wide view would defeat the whole notion of the separate existence of the company and make it impossible for small private companies to function in any way differently from partnerships. The importance of the decision in *Salomon* in the House of Lords is clear. A mere wish to avail oneself of the benefits of limited liability is not of itself to be regarded as fraudulent. A different view was taken of the conduct in *Jones* v. *Lipman* [1962] 1 All ER 442. In that case the first defendant agreed to sell land to the plaintiffs. When he later wished to avoid the sale he formed a company and transferred the land to it. The court held that the company was a 'cloak' for the first defendant, that he had the power to make the company do as he wished and the court would order the transfer of land to the plaintiff. Similarly, in *Gilford Motor Co.* v. *Horne* [1933] Ch 935 the court refused to allow the defendant to avoid an agreement that he would not compete with former employers. He had attempted to do so by competing with them in the guise of a limited company. Even clearer cases were *Re Darby* [1911] 1 KB 95 and Re H [1996] 2 BCLC 500. In Re Darby the corporation was simply a device whereby a fraudulent prospectus was issued and the directors of the company pocketed the public's money. The directors were prosecuted for fraud and convicted. The court held that the directors were liable to repay all the money that had been received by them via the company. In *Re H and others (restraint order: realisable property)* [1996] 2 BCLC 500 two family companies had been used to defraud the revenue. The assets of the company could be treated as the assets of their fraudulent owners and seized. See also *H. Leverton Ltd* v. *Crawford* (1996) *Times*, Nov 22nd (Casenotes, p. 000).

3.6 **Groups**

The courts have sometimes to make difficult decisions about the circumstances in which a group of companies is to be regarded as one entity. Different jurisdictions have reached different answers. In United Kingdom case-law there is no formal or informal recognition of group interests.

Do companies with a significant cross-shareholding have a special relationship? In the United Kingdom, while for many tax and accounting purposes groups of companies are treated as one unit, the courts are reluctant to admit the reality of interrelated companies acting in any way other than as a number of separate entities tied together by their relationship as significant shareholders in each other. Thus in *Scottish Co-op* v. *Meyer* [1959] AC 324 three directors of a subsidiary company were also directors of the parent company. Lord Denning said:

'So long as the interests of all concerned were in harmony, there was no difficulty. The nominee directors could do their duty by both companies without embarrassment. But, so soon as the interests of the two companies were in conflict, the nominee directors were placed in an impossible position. It is plain that, in the circumstances, these three gentlemen could not do their duty by both companies, and they did not do so. They put their duty to the co-operative society above their duty to the textile company . . .'

The approach of the UK courts is epitomised by Templeman LJ in Re Southard & Co Ltd [1979] 3 All ER 556:

'English company law possesses some curious features, which may generate curious results. A parent company may spawn a number of subsidiary companies, all controlled directly or indirectly by the shareholders of the parent company. If one of the subsidiary companies, to change the metaphor, turns out to be the runt of the litter and declines into insolvency to the dismay of its creditors, the parent company and the other subsidiary companies may prosper to the joy of the shareholders without any liability for the debts of the insolvent subsidiary.'

The approach is confirmed by the cavalier treatment by the courts of 'letters of comfort'. Thus in *Re Augustus Barnett & Son Ltd* [1986] BCLC 170 the company was a wholly owned subsidiary of a Spanish company. The subsidiary traded at a loss for some time but the parent company repeatedly issued statements that it would continue to support the subsidiary. Some of the statements were made in letters written to the subsidiary's auditors and published in the subsidiary's annual accounts for three successive years. Later the parent company allowed the subsidiary to go into liquidation and failed to provide any financial support to pay off the debts of the subsidiary. In deciding the this did not constitute fraudulent trading on the part of the parent company Hoffman J accepted that the assurances of the parent were without legal effect.

Community law and concepts of 'undertaking' or 'enterprise'

The 'economic unit' approach is exemplified by a number of cases concerning Article 85 of the EEC Treaty of Rome which seeks to control unfair competition by *inter alia* outlawing 'agreements between undertakings, decisions by associations of undertakings' the object of effect of which is distortion of competition. It has become necessary on occasion to determine the nature of an 'undertaking' and it is clear that the EC (European Court of Justice or ECJ) will not adopt the somewhat simplistic approach of the UK courts and will investigate the reality of the economic unit rather than rely on the technical boundaries drawn by incorporation. Thus the definition includes non-profit-making associations and the reality of the parent–subsidiary relationship will always be investigated by the court. In *Centrafarm* the court said:

> 'Article 85, however, is not concerned with agreements or concerted practices between undertakings belonging to the same concern and having the status of parent and subsidiary, if the undertakings form an economic unit within which the subsidiary has no real freedom to determine its course of action on the market, and if the agreements or practices are concerned merely with the internal allocation of tasks as between undertakings.

German law and the EC proposed Ninth Directive

In Germany there is a law of groups which has been placed on a statutory footing. It is this *Konzernrecht* which formed the model for the draft EC Ninth Directive on Company law. The *Konzernrecht* is applicable only to stock corporations although a vigorous body of developing law applies it to other companies.

Under this law a distinction is made between contractual and *de facto* groups of companies. In contractual groups the creditors of the subsidiary are protected by a legal obligation of the parent towards the subsidiary to make good losses at the end of the year. Shareholders other than the parent company have a right to periodic compensation payments and must be offered the opportunity of selling their shares to the parent at a reasonable price. They have a right to an annual dividend which is calculated according to (a) the value of their shares at the time of the formation of the contractual group and (b) the likelihood of such dividends without the formation of the group. the board of the subsidiary has to give a report on all transactions, measures and omissions during the past year which result from its membership of the group. The conclusion of the contract between members of the group is encouraged by the ability of the parent company to induce the subsidiary to act against its own interests, thus legitimising the concept of the interests of the group as a whole. However, the concept has been little used. Hopt (Schmittoff & Wooldridge (eds), *Groups of Companies* (Sweet & Maxwell, 1991) observes that most groups have chosen 'cohabitation without marriage certificates'.

Despite problems experienced in the operation of the German law, the draft proposal for an EC Ninth Company Law Directive took a similar route. The proposal would have affected groups of companies and public limited companies controlled by any other undertaking (whether or not that undertaking was itself a company). The proposal was that there should be a harmonised structure for the 'unified management' of groups of such companies and undertakings. The proposal was that rules would be laid down for the conduct of groups which were not managed on a 'unified' basis. Unless an undertaking which exercised a dominant interest over a public limited company formalised its relationship and provided for some prescribed form of 'unified' management', it would be liable for any losses suffered by a dependant company provided the losses could be traced to the exercise of the influence or to action which was contrary to the dependant company's interest. Although loosely based on thee German *Konzernrecht* the proposal would have been less effective. Not only did it rely on a satisfactory definition of dominance or control being found (see below) but it failed to give adequate incentives to persuade companies to adopt a formal 'unified management' approach. The German law on which it was based permits a parent company to induce a subsidiary to act against its own interests if the contractual 'unified Management' approach is adopted.

United States approaches

In the USA it is recognised that dominant shareholders have fiduciary duties towards both the company and other shareholders. Thus, dominant shareholders are distinguished from other shareholders. The latter, as in the UK, are permitted to vote their shares according to their own selfish interests. In *Southern Pacific Co* v. *Bogert* 250 US 483 (1919) the Supreme Court stated:

> 'The rule of corporation law and of equity invoked is well settled and has been often applied. The majority has the right to control; but when it does so, it occupies a fiduciary relation toward the minority, as much so as the corporation itself or its officers or directors'.

The principle is widely, if not unanimously, accepted by states. However the implications of the doctrine vary widely. Two states have adopted by legislation a general principle which authorises contracts between parent and subsidiary companies subject to certain conditions of fairness and procedural requirements for adoption or ratification. In other states a voluminous body of case-law is evidence of the different and uncertain effects of the doctrine. Part V of the *American Law Institute's Principles of Corporate governance: Analysis and Recommendations* deals with the duties of dominating shareholders. Ability to control over 25% of the voting equity would give rise to a presumption of control. It is a strange feature of the definition of control that it focuses solely on control of shareholder votes. In Tentative Draft No. 5 control is defined as:

> 'the power directly or indirectly, either alone or pursuant to an arrangement or understanding with one or more other persons, to exercise a controlling influence over the management or policies of a business organisation through the ownership of equity interests, through one or more intermediary persons, by contract or otherwise'. Transactions between a dominating shareholder and the corporation are valid if:

(i)   the transaction is fair to the corporation when entered into;
or
(ii) the transaction is authorised or ratified by disinterested shareholders, following disclosure concerning the conflict of interest and
the transaction, and does not constitute a waste of corporate assets
at the time of the shareholder transaction.

If the transaction is ratified according to (ii) the burden of proving
unfairness is on the challenging party. Otherwise it is for the dominant
shareholder to prove the fairness of the transaction. A transaction is 'fair'
if it falls 'within a range of reasonableness'.

Conflicting duties of loyalty owed by directors who sit on boards of
parents and subsidiaries are also judged on a 'fairness' scale: 'In the
absence of total abstention of an independent negotiating structure,
common directors must determine what is best for both parent and
subsidiary'.

This rule is intended to reflect the decision in *Jones V. H. F. Ahmanson &
Co.* (1993) 1 Cal 3d in which a majority of shareholders had enhanced
their investments in a scheme which was not open to the minority
investors. Delivering the judgment of the Supreme Court of California,
Chief Justice Roger Traynor determined that the conduct of the majority
had been unfair. Although he emphasised the duty of the majority towards
the corporation as well as to minority shareholders, in fact the relevant
opportunity would not have been available to the corporation so that, on
the facts, only the majority's duty to the minority was an issue. What is
interesting and may provide further insight into a way forward is that the
minority did not suffer a loss but were denied an opportunity which was
available exclusively to the majority.

UK

In many circumstances statutes dictate where groups should act as if they
were one enterprise (see Chapter 8). The matter may be formalised if the
EC Ninth Directive on the conduct of groups becomes law (see Chapter
18). Where there are no statutory rules the principles that will guide the
court are to be found in *Smith, Stone & Knight* v. *Birmingham Corporation*
[1939] 4 All ER 116 (Casenote 1). Atkinson J reviewed previous cases on
the point and said:

'I find six points which were deemed relevant for the determination of
the question: Who was really carrying on the business? In all the cases,
the question was whether the company, an English company here, could
be taxed in respect of all the profits made by some other company,
being carried on elsewhere. The first point was:

Were the profits treated as the profits of the company? – when I say
"the company" I mean the parent company – secondly, were the persons
conducting the business appointed by the parent company? Thirdly, was

the company the head and brain of the trading venture? Fourthly, did the company govern the adventure, decide what should be done and what capital should be embarked on the venture? Fifthly, did the company make the profits by its skill and direction? Sixthly, was the company in effectual and constant control.'

Where these questions can be answered in the affirmative it is likely that the group will be treated as a single entity. However, the answers to these questions can only provide guidelines and the court will determine each case according to its own facts and the context in which the case arises. The background to such cases can be varied. One involved the determination of the residence of a company registered in Kenya but managed by a parent in the UK. The company was held to be resident in the UK (*Unit Construction Co.* v. *Bullock* [1960] AC 351). In *Firestone Tyre Co.* v. *Llewellin* [1957] 1 WLR 464 an English subsidiary was held to be the means whereby the American parent company traded in the UK. A similar decision was arrived at in *DHN Food Distributors* v. *Tower Hamlets Borough Council* [1976] 1 WLR 852. Recently in *Lonrho* v. *Shell Petroleum* [1980] QB 358 it was decided that documents could not be regarded as in the 'power' of a parent company when they were in fact held by a subsidiary (see Casenote 2). In *National Dock Labour Board* v. *Pinn & Wheeler Ltd & others* [1989] BCLC 647 the court emphasised that it is only in 'special circumstances which indicate that there is a mere facade concealing the true facts that it is appropriate to pierce the corporate veil'. Similarly, the rule in *Salomon* was approved and relied on in *J.H. Rayner (Mincing Lane) Ltd* v. *Department of Trade and Industry* (Court of Appeal judgment [1988] 3 WLR 1033) (see Casenote 3). This approach was upheld by the House of Lords in *Maclaine Watson & Co* v. *DTI, Maclaine Watson & Co Ltd* v. *International Tin Council* [1990] BCLC 102 and applied in *Adams* v. *Cape Industries PLC* [1990] BCLC. *Adams* v. *Cape Industries* provides a particularly stark example of the application of the *Salomon* principle. Several hundred employees of the group headed by Cape Industries had been awarded damages for injuries received as a result of exposure to asbestos dust. The injuries had been received in the course of their employment. The damages had been awarded in a Texan court. The English Court of Appeal held that the awards could not be enforced against Cape even though one of the defendants was a subsidiary of Cape's and there was evidence that the group had been restructured so as to avoid liability. Slade J said;

'Our law, for better or worse, recognises the creation of subsidiary companies, which, though in one sense the creation of their parent companies, will nevertheless under the general law fall to be treated as separate legal entities with all the rights and liabilities which would normally attach to separate legal entities . . . We do not accept as a matter of law that the court is entitled to lift the corporate veil as against a defendant company which is the member of a corporate group merely because the corporate structure has been used so as to ensure that the legal liability (if any) in respect of particular future activities of the group . . . will fall on another member of the group rather than the defendant company. Whether or not this is desirable, the right to use a corporate structure in this way is inherent in our law.'

A similar approach was taken in *Re Polly Peck International Plc (in administration)* [1996] 2 AllER 433 where the court held that where companies were insolvent the separate legal existence of each within the group became more, not less important.

Agency and Trust

Other cases that are often cited on this issue are sometimes put into categories such as 'agency' or 'trust' cases. This can give the impression that the reason for interfering with the corporate veil in those cases was because the court made a finding that an agency or trust relationship had developed between the company in question and some other body. In fact it may well be that, as in the *Malyon* and *Lee* cases the interests of justice required the court to ignore the corporate veil. The finding of agency or trust may be a convenient excuse for a refusal to follow the rule in *Saloman*'s case. Thus, in *Abbey Malvern Wells* v. *Minister of Local Government* [1951] Ch 728 the company owned a school which was managed by a board of trustees who were bound by the terms of the trust to use the assets of the company for educational purposes. The company applied to the Minister for Town and Country Planning for a ruling that the land they held was exempt from development charges because it was held for charitable (educational in this case) purposes. The Minister ruled against them but on appeal from that decision the court held (1) that the land was occupied by the company for the educational purposes of the school; (2) that the trusts in the trust deed were charitable; (3) that the company was controlled by trustees who were bound by the trust deed; so that (4) the property and assets of the company could only be applied to the charitable purposes of the trust deed. Accordingly the company's interest in and use of the land were charitable and fell within the exemption provisions of the tax statute. In this case it was because the very strict control over the use of the land that was imposed by the trust deed bound the controllers of the company both as trustees and directors. In consequence the legally separate nature of the trust and the company could safely be ignored. Similarly, in *Littlewoods Stores* v. *IRC* [1969] 1 WLR 1241 it was held that a subsidiary company held an asset on trust for the holding company Littlewoods because Littlewoods had provided the purchase price. Littlewoods could therefore not take advantage of the separate legal identity of its subsidiary to avoid the tax consequences of ownership of the asset.

The decision in *Re F. G. Films* [1953] 1 WLR 483 is sometimes regarded as an instance of lifting the veil where the company concerned is acting as an agent for another. Although the judgment mentions agency, the true basis for the decision is that the interests of justice required the court to have regard to the realities behind the situation. The case concerned an application to have a film registered as a British film. To succeed, the applicant company had to show that they were the 'makers' of the film. Vaisey J said;

> 'The applicants have a capital of £100 divided into 100 shares of £1 each, 90 of which are held by the American director and the remaining 10 by a British one . . . I now understand that they have no place of business apart from their registered office and they do not employ any staff . . . it seems to me to be contrary, not only to all sense and reason, but to the proved and admitted facts of the case, to say or to believe that this insignificant company undertook in any real sense of that word the arrangements for the making of this film. I think that their participation in any such undertaking was so small as to be practically negligible, and that they acted, in so far as they acted at all in the matter, merely as the nominee of and agent for an American company called Film Group Incorporated . . . The applicant's intervention in the matter was purely colourable.'

A similar motive lies behind the decision in *Daimler* v. *Continental Tyre Co.* [1916] AC 307, where an English company was held to be an enemy alien because of the nationality of its shareholders.

It is impossible to find a legally consistent basis for the cases in which the courts have decided to ignore the separate legal personality of the company. All that can be said with certainty is that unless there are compelling considerations of justice and fairness the courts will follow *Salomon* and respect the doctrine which declares a company to be a body quite distinct from its members.

3.7 **The Criminal and Civil Liabilities of Companies**

If a company is to be regarded as a person under the law, it follows that it can incur liabilities as can any other person. The courts have held that a company can be convicted of crimes. There are two ways in which this may happen. A company may be *vicariously liable* for a crime which is committed by an employee. This will occur when the law says that if a crime is committed by an employee the employer will bear criminal liability for that act even though the employer may have known nothing about the action in question. The general rule about vicarious liability in criminal law was laid down in the case of *Huggins* (1730) 2 Stra 883. It was made clear that as a general rule the civil doctrine of vicarious liability was not going to be adopted into criminal law. There are two exceptions to this rule which judges have made. In public nuisance and criminal libel an employer can be liable for his employees' crimes on the basis of the relationship alone. Many statutes also impose criminal liability. However, the courts were not content with this relatively narrow basis for the criminal liability of companies and have found that if the criminal acts were committed by persons of sufficient importance in the company, those acts will be seen as the acts of the company itself. This is the wrongly named *alter ego* (other self) doctrine. Those committing the crime, if of sufficient standing, are said to be the 'other self' of the company. In fact they are the only 'self' as the company has no other physical existence. There are two difficulties:

(1) are there crimes which a company cannot commit? and (2) who are the individuals of sufficient status to be the *alter ego* of the company?

3.8 **What Crimes?**

It seems most likely that a company can only be convicted of criminal offences that can be punished by a fine. This would not exclude many offences. Murder, however, is punishable only by life imprisonment and would therefore be excluded. In their textbook on criminal law, Professors John Smith and Brian Hogan state:

> 'There are other offences which it is quite inconceivable that an official of a corporation should commit within the scope of his employment; for example, bigamy, rape, incest and, possibly perjury.' (*Criminal Law*It is arguable that even these crimes might be committed by an important official in a company who aided or abetted another in the commission of such a crime.

The above seem to be the only limitations on the potential criminal liability of companies. It was at one time thought that a company could not be convicted of a crime involving personal violence (*Cory Bros & Co* [1927] 1 KB 810) but in *P&O European Ferries Ltd* (1990) 93 Cr App R 72 Turner J held that an indictment for manslaughter would be against a company in respect of the Zeebrugge disaster. the company was acquitted on the merits.

3.9 **Why Convict Companies?**

There are three possible justifications for this rather curious procedure. The most convincing one is that the public is thereby informed of wrongdoing by companies. They might read in the press that Mr Smith had been guilty of selling contaminated milk or pies and this would mean little. If it is a well-known supermarket which is convicted the attendant publicity might well affect sales. This possibility might have a significant deterrent effect on the company's controllers. This argument may be significant in the decision to prosecute companies implicated in disasters.

The second justification is that a company can be made to pay a larger fine than an individual so that serious breaches, for example of pollution regulations, can be met with large fines to denote public condemnation. The problem with this approach is that the shareholders are those who ultimately shoulder the burden of the fine, since money leaving the company will cause the devaluation of their shares. As we will see elsewhere (Chapter 13) the idea that the controllers of the company can be effectively disciplined by shareholders is far-fetched, particularly in a large company.

The third justification is that there may be crimes which have obviously been authorised by the controllers of a company but it may be very difficult to prove individual liability. This is unconvincing, as it would be difficult in such a case to establish the mental state necessary for conviction of a crime.

Smith and Hogan find none of these arguments convincing. The present author feels that the first justification has some considerable force. What is unfortunate is that little consideration seems to have been given to the social policy behind conviction of companies.

3.10 **Identification of the Company's** *Alter Ego*

In *H. L. Bolton (Engineering) Co. Ltd* v. *T.J. Graham & Sons Ltd.* [1957] 1 QB 159 Lord Justice Denning said:

'A company may in many ways be likened to a human body. It has a brain and nerve centre which controls what it does. It also has hands which hold the tools and act in accordance with directions from the centre. Some of the people in the company are mere servants and agents who are nothing more than hands to do the work and cannot be said to represent the mind or will. Others are directors and managers who represent the directing mind and will of the company, and control what it does. The state of mind of these managers is the state of mind of the company and is treated by the law as such.'

Examples

In *Tesco Supermarkets* v. *Nattrass* [1972] AC 153 Tesco had been convicted of an offence under the Trade Descriptions Act for selling a product at a price higher than the advertised price. Tesco was entitled to a defence if it could be shown (amongst other things) that the offence was committed by 'another person'. Tesco alleged that the 'other person' in this case was the manager of the branch involved who had been in sole command of that store. It was held that the manager was not the 'brains' of the company so that he was indeed 'another person' for the purposes of the offence. In *DPP* v. *Kent and Sussex Contractors Ltd* [1944] KB 146, the Divisional Court held that a company could properly be convicted of an offence which required proof of an intent to deceive. The intention was that of the transport manager of the company.

Each case will turn on its own facts and depend upon the precise nature of the distribution of power within the particular company. The case of *Moore* v. *Bresler Ltd* [1944] 2 All ER 559 has been criticised on the grounds that the court went 'too far down the scale' in convicting a company of tax fraud where that fraud was carried out by the company secretary and the manager of one branch. (See *Welch* (1946) 62 LQR 385.) In view of the enhanced status of the company secretary (see Chapter 10) that criticism may be of less force today.

3.11 Civil Liability

A precisely similar test is used to determine the civil liability of a company. (see *El Ajou* v. *Dollar Land Holdings Plc* [1994] 1 BCLC 464) It must be remembered, however, that the principle of vicarious liability in civil law is much more widely used and so there may be that route to liability as well as the use of the *alter ego* doctrine. In *Lennard's Carrying Company Ltd* v. *Asiatic Petroleum Co. Ltd* [1915] AC 705, the *alter ego* doctrine was the basis of the company's liability. The question was whether damage had occurred without 'the actual fault or privity' of the owner of the ship. The owners were a company. The fault was that of the registered managing owner who managed the ship on behalf of the owners. It was held that Mr Lennard was the directing mind of the company so that his fault was the fault of the company. (See also *Campbell* v. *Paddington Corporation* [1911] 1 KB 869 and *The Lady Gwendolen* [1965] P 294, but for a different test see *Meridian Global Funds Management Asia Ltd* v. *Securities Commission (PC)* [1995] 2 BCLC 116.

Summary

1 A company has the advantage that it continues to exist despite a change in the persons carrying on the business. A limited company has the advantage that the liability of the members is limited to an amount agreed by them. Companies have the disadvantage that they have to comply with more regulations than do partnerships.

2 A company is a separate legal person, with an existence independent from its members.

3 Because a company does not exist until registered it cannot be a party to contracts entered into before that registration.

4 The courts will 'lift the veil' in cases where a company's separate legal personality is being used unjustly or as a fraudulent device.

5 A company may incur criminal or civil liability as a result of the action of someone important enough in the company to be regarded as the directing 'mind and will' of the company.

Casenotes

1 *Smith, Stone &.Knight* v. *Birmingham Corporation* [1939] 4 All ER 116.
The claim was for compensation for a factory which was to be the subject of a compulsory purchase by the defendants. The plaintiffs had let the premises to a subsidiary company and the question arose as to whether the parent company could claim compensation for what would, in fact, be damage done not to its business but to the business of a subsidiary. The court held that in this case it could.

2 *Lonrho* v. *Shell Petroleum* [1980] QB 358.
The case involved UK companies. However, the plaintiffs sought to obtain documents that were in the possession of wholly-owned foreign subsidiaries of the defendant. The Court of Appeal refused to order this. Lord Denning said:

'These South African and Rhodesian companies were very much self-controlled. The directors were local directors—running their own show, operating it, with comparatively little interference from London.'

That, together with the fact that the foreign companies had in fact refused to give up the documents, led to the conclusion that these companies were separate entities.

3 *J.H. Rayner (Mincing Lane) Ltd* v. *Department of Trade and Industry* [1987] BCLC 667.
This case involved the International Tin Council (ITC) whose members were the UK, twenty-two other sovereign states and the EC. The ITC had corporate status under UK law. Because of this the Court of Appeal refused to hold that the members had personal liability for the debts of thè ITC. This was later affirmed by the House of Lords.

4 *H. Leverton Ltd* v. *Crawford Offshore (Exploration) Services Ltd* (in liquidation) (1996), Times, Nov. 22nd
Garland J held that the director who managed a company should be personally liable for the costs of the action. The director was the sole decision maker, had kept its only records, had been present throughout the action and had improperly caused the company to defend the action and prosecute a falsely concocted counterclaim.

5 *Meridian Global Funds Management Asia Ltd* v. *Securities Commission* [1995] 2 BCLC 116
The Meridian's funds were used by two senior investment managers to provide finance for an attempted takeover of a New Zealand company. The funds were used to purchase shares. The New Zealand legislation required immediate notification of acquisition of more than 5 per cent of the shares of a public company. Meridian was held liable for non-disclosure despite the fact that the investment managers had been acting without the authority of the directors. The court held that the knowledge of the investment managers was to be attributed to the company. The test of 'directing mind and will' was not appropriate in all cases and here would defeat the purpose of the Act, which was to encourage immediate notification of acquisition of substantial shareholdings (Meridian's board met only once a year) and restricting the company's knowledge to the knowledge of those directing the company could encourage the board to pay as little attention as possible to what its investment managers were doing.
As possible examples of statutory 'lifting the veil' consider s. 214 Insolvency Act 1986, s. 459 Companies Act 1985, s. 6 Company Director Disqualification Act 1986.

Exercises

1 What advantages and disadvantages does the doctrine of the separate legal personality of a company have?

2 Is there any purpose in convicting a company of crimes?

3 Would it be possible to formulate satisfactory rules to determine when the courts would lift the corporate veil?

4 The Memorandum of Association

The contents of the memorandum of association were discussed in Chapter 2 above. One problem which caused extensive debate over many years was an issue arising from the setting out of the objects of association in the memorandum. The courts held that the company was unable to create legally binding contracts or act outside the scope of the objects of association as they were set out in the memorandum. The law has been substantially changed following the Companies Act 1989 and it will be in rare circumstances that the old law will be relevant. However, the reforms did not completely get rid of the necessity for an understanding of the common law rules. This chapter will examine first the background and justification behind the common law rules, then the new rules and finally indicate briefly the difficulties which may be encountered by anyone seeking to raise an issue of *ultra vires* in the limited situations where it may still be relevant.

4.1 *Ultra Vires* – The Old Law

By s. 2(1)(c) of the Companies Act 1985 the memorandum of a company is required to 'state the objects of a company'. This simple requirement has been the object of much heart-searching in the past and gave rise to an enormous body of law. This law needs to be briefly examined in order to form a proper understanding of the present law. It also affords an interesting example of the way in which case law can develop.

It was first apparent that the requirement to state objects would cause problems when the courts held that if a company did an act which was outside the scope of the objects as described in the memorandum, that act would be wholly without legal effect (void). This so-called doctrine of '*ultra vires*' is similar to the law concerning public bodies. They are unable to act outside the statutory powers given to them. It was felt that the same should be true of companies. Unfortunately, the law that developed had unhappy results. This is partly because the reason that public bodies should be restricted to the powers given to them by Parliament is in order to safeguard democracy. If a public body takes to itself more power than the elected representatives of the people have chosen to give it, it is setting itself up as more important than the electorate. Similar considerations do not apply when companies are considered. Companies need to respond with a considerable degree of flexibility to changing markets and it is difficult to see who has ever benefited from this doctrine.

4.2 **Constructive Notice**

The doctrine of *ultra vires* only worked in conjunction with the doctrine of constructive notice. By this doctrine everyone is deemed to know the contents of the memorandum of association of the company with which they are dealing because it is a public document. (This doctrine has disappeared on the implementation of Companies Act 1989 which inserted a new s. 711A into Companies Act 1985; see below.)

4.3 **Justification of the Doctrine**

The original justification for its existence was that it would serve as a protection for shareholders and creditors. A company formed for one purpose should not be permitted to pursue other ends which did not have the blessing of the shareholders and creditors, who stood to lose their money if unprofitable adventures were indulged in by the company. However, as will be seen, the element of protection was lost the moment that the court accepted memoranda with objects clauses so widely drafted that they covered almost every activity. After that the doctrine was only of use if a party sought to avoid a contract. The determination of where the loss caused by the application of the doctrine should fall appears to have been a matter of mere chance of circumstances.

Apart from providing an expensive parlour game for lawyers, there appeared to be very little point to this doctrine. Reform was attempted on accession to the European Community but it was badly done. The relevant provision of the EC Directive 68/151/EEC is Article 9 which reads:

'Acts done by the organs of the company shall be binding upon it even if those acts are not within the objects of the company, unless such acts exceed the powers that the law confers or allows to be conferred on those organs. However, Member States may provide that the company shall not be bound where such acts are outside the objects of the company if it proves that the third party knew that the act was outside those objects or could not in view of the circumstances be unaware thereof; disclosure of the statutes shall not of itself be sufficient proof thereof.'

Our law on *ultra vires* remained out of line with the Directive.

4.4 **How to Determine Whether an Act is** *Ultra Vires*

If the validity of a particular act by a company directors being considered, the act must be measured against the company's constitution as follows, bearing in mind that if the statement of objects is too wide the company's main object will be deduced from the name of the company. Thus a very widely drawn clause is in danger of being read in the light of the 'main objects' rule as ancillary to the main objects of the company.

(1) Is the act within the express objects in the light of any possible restrictive interpretation? If so it binds the company; if not:

(2) Is the act within the validly stated ancillary objects or powers which are 'converted' into objects by an independent objects clause? If so the act binds the company; if not:

(3) Is the act within a 'subjective' clause and the directors bona fide believe that the business can be carried on with the other businesses of the company? If so the act is binding on the company; if not:

(4) Is the act done in accordance with an express power of the company and not done *mala fide* with the knowledge of the outsider? If so it binds the company; if not:

(5) Is the act done in accordance with implied powers of the company and done to further the objects of the company? If so it binds the company; if not, the act is *ultra vires*.

4.5 The New Law

As we have seen, the above Directive was not adequately implemented in the UK. Section35 Companies Act 1985 reads:

'35. A company's capacity not limited by its memorandum

(1) The validity of an act done by a company shall not be called into question on the ground of lack of capacity by reason of anything in the company's memorandum.

(2) A member of a company may bring proceedings to restrain the doing of an act which but for subsection (1) would be beyond the company's capacity; but no such proceedings shall lie in respect of an act to be done in fulfilment of a legal obligation arising from a previous act of the company.

(3) It remains the duty of the directors to observe any limitations on their powers flowing from the company's memorandum; and action by the directors which but for subsection (1) would be beyond the company's capacity may only be ratified by the company be special resolution.

A resolution ratifying such action shall not affect any liability incurred by the directors or any other person; relief from any such liability must be agreed to separately by special resolution.

(4) The operation of this section is restricted by s. 30B(1) of the Charities Act 1960 and s. 112(3) of the Companies Act 1989 in relation to companies which are charities; and s. 322A below (invalidity of certain transactions to which directors or their associates area parties) has effect notwithstanding this section.'

However, the 1989 Companies Act further addressed the problem.

The provisions which partially abolish *ultra vires* have the effect that once an act has been done by a company, that act cannot be challenged on the *ultra vires* basis so as to upset the rights of third parties. This is plain from new s. 35(1) Companies Act 1985. Similarly, if a company has committed itself to do an act (affecting third party rights) which it would then be bound to do but for the *ultra vires* question, then acts done in pursuance of that commitment cannot be challenged (new s.35(2) Companies Act 1985). Two remains of the doctrine will be that a shareholder who discovers in advance that the directors are going to act outside the objects clause is entitled to ask for an injunction to restrain them from such action (s.35(2) Companies Act 1985), and the exercise of directors' powers to complete an *ultra vires* transaction will be a breach of directors' duties. The *ultra vires* doctrine may also affect the validity of a contract made between the company and the director. These provisions mean that the whole of the complicated case law remains important for situations which are unlikely often to occur and will become even more unlikely if the objects clause for a 'general commercial company' is increasingly adopted. This objects clause is set out in s. 3A Companies Act 1985. It provides:

'Where the company's memorandum states that the object of the company is to carry on business as a general commercial company–
(a) the object of the company is to carry on any trade or business whatsoever, and
(b) the company has power to do all such things as are incidental or conducive to the carrying on of any trade or business by it.'

It is important to note that these provisions have effect so far as liability of the company to outsiders is concerned. So far as the effect within the company, acting *ultra vires* will remain a breach of directors' duties (s.35(3) Companies Act 1985). This, then, is another instance when the old case law will need to be examined – in order to determine whether directors have acted in breach of duty by completing a transaction which under the old law would have been invalid because it was *ultra vires* the company. The *vires* of a transaction may also be called into question where a transaction involves a director or connected person and involves the board of directors in exercise of a power in excess 'of any limitation of their powers under the company's constitution'. This language is more apt to describe directors' acting in excess of their powers, but could include actions outside the 'limitation' on their powers imposed by the objects clause in the memorandum. This section is discussed further below (s.322A Companies Act 1985).

4.6 Ratification

New s. 35(3) Companies Act 1985 provides that if the directors act in a way which would have been *ultra vires* the company under the old law, the shareholders may vote to ratify (forgive the breach of duty) such action by special (75 per cent majority) resolution. Such a resolution will have a limited effect since the action will be enforceable by a third party under the new law. The section goes on to provide that another and separate special resolution will be needed to alter the liability of directors or others who were involved in the transaction. It would seem that the only effect of the first special resolution will be to alter the status of a contract which would otherwise be voidable under s. 322A Companies Act 1985. This seems to have been inserted in an attempt to prevent directors and connected persons from taking advantage of the new, wider, capacity of companies to act. It provides that where the company enters into what would have been an *ultra vires* transaction with a director of the company or of its parent company or a person or company connected with such a director, that transaction is voidable at the instance of the company. If it is ratified by special resolution, the contract becomes valid (new s. 322A(5) Companies Act 1985). Nevertheless, the director or connected person involved and any director who authorised the transaction remain liable:

'(a) to account to the company for any gain which he has made directly or indirectly by the transaction, and
(b) to indemnify the company for any loss or damage resulting from the transaction.'

A second special resolution passed under new s. 35(3) could relieve a director of this liability.

It is not only the first special resolution to ratify the transaction which will make the contract an enforceable one. The contract will also cease to be voidable if:

'(a) restitution of any money or other asset which was the subject-matter of the transaction is no longer possible, or
(b) the company is indemnified for any loss or damage resulting from the transaction, or
(c) rights acquired bona fide and for value and without actual notice of the directors' exceeding their powers by a person who is not a party to the transaction would be affected by the avoidance (s. 322A(5) Companies Act 1985).'

It is noteworthy that directors are caught by this section whether or not they know they are exceeding their powers. Others are not affected unless they know that the directors' are exceeding their powers. If someone other than a director of the company or of its holding company or persons or companies connected or associated with that director enters into a contract with a company, the contract would normally be fully enforceable even if the directors were acting *ultra vires* according to the old law (because of the effect of new s. 35). However, s. 322A gives such a person the right to apply to the court which 'may make such order affirming, severing or setting aside the transaction, on such terms, as appear to the court to be just' (s.322A(7) Companies Act 1985). This is another area in which the old law will still be relevant, since the right to apply to the court will only arise where the transaction can no longer be called into question by reason of anything in the company's memorandum because of new s. 35 Companies Act 1985, and yet the transaction has involved the directors etc. referred to in s. 322A Companies Act 1985.

4.7 **The old case-law**

In the limited relevant circumstances where the case-law is now relevant all the old complications may need to be examined by the court. The following is a brief consideration of those difficulties.

One of the early cases was *Ashbury Railway Carriage and Iron Co.* (1875) LR 7 HL 653. The memorandum gave the company the power to make and sell railway carriages. The company purported to buy a concession for constructing a railway in Belgium. Later the directors repudiated the contract and were sued. Their defence was that the contract was *ultra vires*, outside the memorandum and had been of no effect from the first. The court held that a contract made by the directors of such a company on a matter not included in the memorandum of association was not binding on the company. Indeed, the court went further than this and decided that such a contract could not be rendered binding on the company even though it was expressly assented to by all the shareholders. This was because of a principle of agency law that an agent (in this case a director) cannot have more power than the principal (in this case the company). It is possible that this part of the decision would not have been laid down in such absolute terms if it were not for the fact that it was in those days impossible to alter the memorandum of association. Such an alteration was possible after 1890 but was made easier after 1948. However, *Ashbury* and cases like it laid the foundation stones of the doctrine of *ultra vires*, these being that a contract made in an area not covered by the objects is of no legal effect and that such a contract cannot be made effective by a vote of the shareholders. Although the doctrine could be advantageous to a company where it was used to avoid a contract which had become onerous, it could also be a burden. For example, banks or other companies might be reluctant to deal with a company where the objects of that company were unknown to the contracting partner, where they were narrowly drawn or of uncertain ambit. The courts had decided in *Re Crown Bank* (1890) 44 ChD 634, that a proper statement of objects had not been made where the objects of the company were expressed in such wide terms as to be (in the words of North J):

'So wide that it might be said to warrant the company in giving up banking business and embarking in a business with the object of establishing a line of balloons between the earth and the moon.'

The courts determined that it was permissible to achieve a similar effect by listing every imaginable kind of business. In *Cotman* v. *Brougham* [1918] AC 514 the company's memorandum had thirty sub-clauses enabling the company to carry on almost any kind of business, and the objects clause concluded with a declaration that every sub-clause should be construed as a substantive clause and not limited or restricted by reference to any other sub-clause or by the name of the company and that none of such sub-clauses or the objects specified therein should be deemed subsidiary or auxiliary merely to the objects mentioned in the first sub-clause.

The last part of this statement of objects was there to avoid a restriction which the courts had been prone to place on statements of objects. They had construed them according to a 'main objects' rule. This meant that the main object of the company could be determined either from the name of the company or from the first named object on the list of objects. All subsequent statements in the objects clause would then be considered to be powers of the company which could only be validly exercised for the purpose of furthering the 'main' object. In *Cotman* v. *Brougham*, the draftsman had drafted the statement of objects to avoid this rule and also sought to avoid the *Re Crown Bank* restriction by the long list of thirty objects. His attempt was successful. It was held that the memorandum must be construed according to its literal meaning, although the practice of drafting memoranda in this way was criticised.

A further extension of the liberty given to companies came with the acceptance of the 'subjective clause' in *Bell Houses Ltd* v. *City Wall Properties Ltd* [1966] 2 QB 656. In that case the company's memorandum of association contained the following clause:

'3(c) To carry on any other trade or business whatsoever which can, in the opinion of the board of directors, be advantageously carried on by [the plaintiff company] in connection with or as ancillary to any of the above businesses or the general business [of the company].'

It must be noted that this clause is more restricted than the one found to be an improper statement of objects in *Re Crown Bank*, particularly because it refers to the business already being carried on by the company and requires that the business justified under this clause must be compatible with business permitted by other clauses in the memorandum. If objects as wide as *Bell Houses* were accepted, the company would be permitted to carry on two competing businesses.

The subjective element in the *Re Crown Bank* clause comes in the reference to the 'opinion of the directors'. With reference to this clause, Danckwerts LJ said in *Bell Houses*:

'On the balance of the authorities it would appear that the opinion of the directors if bona fide can dispose of the matter; and why should it not decide the matter? The shareholders subscribe their money on the basis of the memorandum of association and if that confers the power on the directors to decide whether in their opinion it is proper to undertake particular business in the circumstances specified, why should not their decision be binding?'

4.8 **Objects and Powers**

We have seen that the memorandum should contain a statement of *objects*. We have also seen that sometimes the statement of objects would be construed so as to discern a 'main' object and ancillary objects which could only be exercised in order to further the company's main objects.

There are two further complications to this picture, One is that the 'long list' *Cotman* v. *Brougham* approach may list objects and also ancillary objects or powers necessary for the attainment of those objects. The memorandum may then contain a clause that all the clauses and sub-clauses are 'independent objects' and none of them subsidiary to the others. This raises the question as to whether there is any essential distinction between objects and powers, and if so, what it is and how each may be identified.

The second complication is that all companies are covered by the doctrine of 'implied powers' whereby the law will assume that all powers necessary for the attainment of a lawful objective are possessed by the body seeking to achieve the objective.

In view of these numerous complications it is perhaps unsurprising that the courts seem to have occasionally lost their way in the maze and confused objects and powers.

4.9 *Ultra Vires* **and Objects**

Strictly speaking, the doctrine of *ultra vires* should apply only to objects. However, on numerous occasions the courts have found that the company has acted outside powers and held the act to be *ultra vires*. Many examples of this confusion concerned cases which either involved the company borrowing money in excess of its powers to do so or giving money away. An example of the latter is *Hutton* v. *West Cork Railway Company* (1883) 23 Ch 653. In that case the company was about to be dissolved. A resolution was passed to the effect that money would be paid by the company to its officials as compensation for loss of office and to other directors who had never received remuneration for their work. The Court of Appeal held that payments of this sort would be invalid. Bowen LJ said:

'Most businesses require liberal dealings. The test . . . is not whether it is bona fide, but whether, as well as being done bona fide, it is done within the ordinary scope of the company's business, and whether it is reasonably incidental to the carrying on of the company's business for the company's benefit . . . a company which always treated its employees with Draconian severity, and never allowed them a single inch more than the strict letter of the bond, would soon find itself deserted – at all events, unless labour was very much more easy to obtain in the market than it often is. The law does not say that there are to be no cakes and ale, but that there are to be no cakes and ale except such as are required for the benefit of the company.'

It must be noted that this discussion related to the exercise of a *power* of the company, giving away money was something which the company had the power to do, but the Court of Appeal suggested in this case that such a gift would be invalid if it were not exercised bona fide for the benefit of the company. Similar restrictions were placed on the exercise of a power to give a gift for the furtherance of scientific education in *Evans* v. *Brunner Mond* [1921] 1 Ch 359. It is noteworthy that in that case the 'power' in question was no different from the implied powers a company would be assumed to have, but in this instance they had been enshrined in the memorandum. The court held that it would be for the benefit of the company to increase the 'reservoir' of trained experts by making a gift which would benefit scientific education.

4.10 Knowledge by an Outsider that a Transaction is Outside Objects or Powers

The *ultra vires* problem has also frequently arisen where borrowing powers are at issue. In *Re David Payne & Co. Ltd* [1904] 2 Ch 608 the court held that where borrowing was for an *ultra vires* purpose but this was unknown to the lender, the loan could be recovered. In that case the loan money could have been applied by the directors for *intra* or *ultra vires* purposes. The fact that the directors chose to apply the money to *ultra vires* purposes was a matter for which the directors could be called to account by the shareholders, as being a breach of their duties. It was not a matter which ought to affect the rights of the lender. It would have been different if the lender had notice that the money would be applied for *ultra vires* purposes. That was the situation in *Re Jon Beauforte (London) Ltd* [1953] Ch 131. The company's memorandum authorised the business of dressmaking. However, at the relevant time the business carried on was that of veneered panel manufacture. On notepaper which clearly indicated that this was the current business of the company, a supply of coke was ordered. The court held that as the coke supplier had had notice of the fact that the current business of the company was *ultra vires* business, the contract for the supply of coke was void and he would therefore not be paid. The validity of the contract in this case depends on the knowledge of the outsider. If he knows that the transaction is outside the powers of the company, the transaction will be unenforceable.

4.11 Can Borrowing Ever be an Object?

We have seen that one of the ploys used by draftsmen in order to ensure that a memorandum is as widely drafted as possible, is to insert a clause elevating the long list of clauses to the status of objects. This is added in an attempt to avoid the 'main objects' rule of construction. Despite the finding in *Cotman* v. *Brougham* (see p. 49) that a memorandum should be read literally, the court held that such an 'elevation' clause was ineffective in the case of borrowing. In *Introductions Ltd* v. *National Provincial Bank Ltd* [1970] Ch 199 there was a provision in the objects clause that the company could 'borrow or raise money in such manner as the company shall think fit'. There was also a clause which 'expressly declared that each of the preceding sub-clauses shall be construed independently of and shall be in no way limited by reference to any other sub-clause and that the objects set out in each sub-clause are independent objects of the company'. Harman LJ said: 'you cannot convert a power into an object merely by saying so . . . I agree with the judge that it is a necessarily implied addition to a power to borrow whether express or implied, that you should add "for the purposes of the company".'

In that case the judge found that the borrowing was *ultra vires* and consequently the contract involved in that borrowing could not be relied on. As we have seen, this goes beyond the original doctrine which held that only actions outside the *objects* would be void.

4.12 **Recent Authorities**

Cases decided in the 1980s limited the *ultra vires* doctrine to a considerable extent. In *Re Halt Garage Ltd* [1982] 3 All ER 1016, Oliver J was faced with the task of deciding whether payments made to directors just prior to the liquidation of the company were valid, or whether the money could be recovered by the liquidator. There was a *power* to make payments but the company had been in some financial difficulty at the time when the payments had been made. Oliver J held that if the power to make payments had genuinely been exercised and the payments were not some other transaction in disguise, then they could not be challenged on the grounds that they were *ultra vires*. The judge refused to accept tests which had been put forward in older authorities which would have resulted in the payments being held to be *ultra vires* if they were not made in good faith and for the benefit of the company.

Similarly in *Re Horsley & Weight Ltd* [1982] Ch 442, the question was the validity of a pension which had been purchased by the company for a retiring director. The court held that the grant of the pension could fall within a clause of the memorandum which was capable of describing objects and if that were the case no question of deciding whether or not the action benefited the company arose – it was valid. The judgment of Buckley LJ contains some interesting observations on what can be considered objects and what can only ever be powers no matter that the memorandum contains an 'elevation' clause. He said:

'It has now long been a common practice to set out in memoranda of association a great number and variety of "objects", so called, some of which (for example, to borrow money, to promote the company's interest by advertising its products or services, or to do acts or things conducive to the company's objects) are by their very nature incapable of standing as independent objects which can be pursued in isolation as the sole activity of the company. Such "objects" must, by reason of their very nature, be interpreted merely as powers incidental to the true objects of the company and must be so treated notwithstanding the presence of a separate objects clause . . . *ex hypothesi* an implied power can only legitimately be used in a way which is ancillary or incidental to the pursuit of an authorised object of the company, for it is the practical need to imply the power in order to enable the company effectively to pursue its authorised objects which justifies the implication of the power. So an exercise of an implied power can only be *intra vires* the company if it is ancillary or incidental to the pursuit of an authorised object. So, also, in the case of express "objects" which upon construction of the memorandum or by their very nature are ancillary to the dominant or main objects of the company, an exercise of any such powers can only be *intra vires* if it is in fact ancillary or incidental to the pursuit of some such dominant or main object.

On the other hand, the doing of an act which is expressed to be, and capable of being, an independent object of the company cannot be *ultra vires*, for it is by definition something which the company is formed to do and so must be *intra vires* . . . [counsel] submits that. . .a capacity to grant pensions to directors or ex-directors, is of its nature a power enabling the company to act as a good employer in the course of carrying on its business, and as such is an incidental power which must be treated as though it were expressly subject to a limitation that it can only be exercised in circumstances in which the grant of a pension will benefit the company's business. I do not feel able to accept this contention. Paragraph (o) must be read as a whole. It includes not only pensions and other disbursements which will benefit directors, employees and their dependants, but also making grants for charitable, benevolent or public purposes or objects. The objects of a company do not need to be commercial; they can be charitable or philanthropic; indeed they can be whatever the original incorporators wish, provided that they are legal. Nor is there any reason why a company should not part with its funds gratuitously or for non-commercial reasons if to do so is within its declared objects.'

This case was affirmed in *Rolled Steel Products* v. *British Steel Corporation* [1985] Ch 246 where Slade LJ, after an extensive review of the authorities, set out the following conclusions:

'(1) The basic rule is that a company incorporated under the Companies Acts only has the capacity to do those acts which fall within its objects as set out in its memorandum of association or are reasonably incidental to the attainment or pursuit of those objects.

Ultimately, therefore, the question whether a particular transaction is within or outside its capacity must depend on the true construction of the memorandum.

(2) Nevertheless, if a particular act . . . is of a category which, on the true construction of the company's memorandum, is capable of being performed as reasonably incidental to the attainment or pursuit of its objects, it will not be rendered *ultra vires* the company merely because in a particular instance its directors, in performing the act in its name, are in truth doing so for purposes other than those set out in its memorandum. Subject to any express restrictions on the relevant power which may be construed in the memorandum, the state of mind or knowledge of the persons managing the company's affairs or of the persons dealing with it is irrelevant in considering questions of corporate capacity.

(3) While due regard must be paid to any express conditions attached to or limitations on powers contained in a company's memorandum (e.g. a power to borrow only up to a specified amount), the court will not ordinarily construe a statement in a memorandum that a particular power is exercisable "for the purposes of the company" as a condition limiting the company's corporate capacity to exercise the power; it will regard it as simply imposing a limit on the authority of the directors: see the *Re David Payne* case.

(4) At least in default of the unanimous consent of all the shareholders . . . the directors of a company will not have *actual* authority from the company to exercise any express or implied power other than for the purposes of the company as set out in its memorandum of association.

(5) A company holds out its directors as having *ostensible* authority [for a discussion of actual and ostensible authority, see Chapter 4] to bind the company to any transaction which falls within the powers expressly or impliedly conferred on it by its memorandum of association. Unless he is put on notice to the contrary, a person dealing in good faith with a company which is carrying on an *intra vires* business is entitled to assume that its directors are properly exercising such powers for the purposes of the company as set out in the memorandum. Correspondingly, such a person in such circumstances can hold the company to any transactions of this nature.

(6) If, however, a person dealing with a company is on notice that the directors are exercising the relevant power for purposes other than the purposes of the company, he cannot rely on the ostensible authority of the directors and, on ordinary principles of agency, cannot hold the company to the transaction.'

The practical effect of these decisions seems to be that if an act could be justified by reference to an object of the company, the transaction could not be challenged. If the act could be justified by reference to a power of the company then the transaction would be valid unless the power was being used as a disguise for another purpose and the outsider was on notice of this. An action may also be valid if it can be justified by reference to an implied power, that is, that it was done bona fide in furthering the objects of a company. This interpretation is supported by the recent case of *Halifax Building Society* v. *Meridian Housing Association* [1994] 2 BCLC which also makes plain a further area in which the complex case-law will still be relevant. Many companies in the 'regulated sector', i.e. insurance companies, building societies and friendly societies, have their objects restricted by statute as well as their rules. This case makes it plain that the old rules will be used to determine the validity of acts of such companies, although in most cases the relevant legislation has an equivalent of s. 35 of the Companies Act to protect third parties, so the issue will only arise in rare circumstances. In that case Mrs Justice Arden held that a development of mixed offices and residential accommodation was 'reasonably incidental to the pursuit' of the objects of Meridian, which were 'to carry on the industry, business or trade of providing housing or any associated amenities'.

4.13 **Alteration of the Memorandum of Association**

Section 2(7) Companies Act 1985 prohibited the alteration (except in accordance with the Act) of the conditions contained in a company's memorandum. By s. 17 Companies Act 1985, this did not apply to matters which could lawfully have been in the articles of association rather than in the memorandum, unless the memorandum specifically prohibits the alteration of such conditions. The Companies Act 1989 widened the power to alter the objects of a company by the insertion of a new s. 4 Companies Act 1985. This places no restrictions on the power to alter objects by special resolution. Section 5 Companies Act 1985 sets out the procedure for objection to an alteration of objects. This will remain the same. An application may be made to the court for the cancellation of the alteration which will then not take effect except in so far as it is confirmed by the court. An application may be made by the holders in aggregate of not less than 15 per cent in value of the company's issued share capital or of any class of shares, or by the holders of not less than 15 per cent of the company's debentures.

Summary

1 If an act of a company was not authorised by the objects clause in the memorandum it was *ultra vires* the company and of no effect.

2 The 1989 Act imperfectly abolishes the doctrine, leaving it open to (a) a shareholder who discovers in advance that an *ultra vires* action is planned and seeks an injunction; and (b) a member who alleges that there is a breach of duty by a director because he is acting *ultra vires*, to raise the issue of *ultra vires*, whereupon the whole of the old case law will become relevant.

3 Under the old law the doctrine of constructive notice appplied and everyone was held to know the contents of the memorandum and articles of a company.

4 Various drafting devices were adopted to avoid the difficulties of the doctrine. Many clauses were inserted, a clause 'elevating' all the other clauses to the status of independent objects was included, and a subjective clause referring to the opinion of the directors was inserted.

5 These drafting devices were mostly effective but the courts held that some activities could not be sensible commercial objectives (for example, borrowing) and therefore refused to afford them any higher status than powers.

6 Even before the statutory reform cases showed a tendency to equate objects and powers and to limit the effect of the doctrine.

Exercises

1 Could companies be endowed with the same powers as a natural person?

2 Is the power which remains with shareholders to challenge *ultra vires* actions of directors sufficiently useful to justify the retention of the old case-law?

5 The Articles of Association

The articles of association contain an important part of the constitution of the company. Their contents are not compulsorily laid down by the Companies Act, the approach to regulating their contents being rather by forbidding the inclusion of certain clauses or making them of no effect if they do appear. An example of this appears at s. 310 Companies Act 1985, which prevents a company including a provision in its articles exempting any officer or employer from liability they would otherwise have incurred 'in respect of any negligence, default, breach of duty or breach of trust' in relation to the company.

While the contents are not laid down by the Act, there are attached to the Act a number of schedules known as Tables A, C, D and E. Table A becomes the articles of association of a company limited by shares if no articles are registered, or if the articles that are registered do not exclude or modify Table A. Tables C, D and E perform the same function for:

(a) companies limited by guarantee without a share capital;
(b) companies limited by guarantee with a share capital; and
(c) unlimited companies with a share capital.

The articles will be the chief instrument for regulating the relationship between a shareholder and the company and the balance of power amongst shareholders themselves. The voting rights attached to various classes of shares will be one of the most important things set out in most articles of association. Other important matters will be: the powers exercisable by the board (or boards) of directors, payment of dividends, and alteration of the capital structure of the company.

One of the most difficult questions that arises concerning the articles of association, is the degree to which they form an enforceable agreement between the shareholders and the company itself, and amongst shareholders. If the articles were too rigidly binding, management would be restricted in their actions for fear that their decisions would be challenged as having contravened a small (and perhaps relatively unimportant) provision contained in the articles. On the other hand, the articles are part of the constitution of the company and stand between the shareholders and the otherwise practically unrestricted powers of the management.

The potential misuse of the power to alter articles was well put in the Australian case of *Peter's American Delicacy Company Ltd* (High Court of Australia) (1939) 61 CLR 457. In that case Dixon CJ said:

'If no restraint were laid upon the power of altering articles of association, it would be possible for a shareholder controlling the necessary voting power so to mould the regulations of a company that its operations would be conducted or its property used so that he would profit either in some other capacity than that of member of the company or, if as member, in a special or peculiar way inconsistent with conceptions of honesty so widely held or professed that departure from them is described, without further analysis as fraud. For example, it would be possible to adopt articles requiring that the company should supply him with goods below cost or pay him 99% of its profits for some real or imaginary services or submit to his own determination the question whether he was liable to account to the company for secret profits as a director.'

How has the law held the balance between the various power groups whose privileges and duties are governed by the articles?

5.1 **The Articles as a Contract**

Section 14 of the Companies Act 1985 reads as follows:

'(1) Subject to the provisions of this Act, the memorandum and articles, when registered, bind the company and its members to the same extent as if they respectively had been signed and sealed by each member, and contained covenants on the part of each member to observe all the provisions of the memorandum and articles.'

The precise effect of this provision is most unclear. First of all, it is a peculiarly drafted provision as it provides that the members shall be bound as if they had signed and sealed the articles. It makes no mention of the company being bound by the same fiction. This appears to ignore the fact that the company is said to be a legal person separate and distinct from its members. The courts have ignored this apparent omission. In *Wood* v. *Odessa Waterworks* (1889) 42 ChD 636 Stirling J said: 'The articles of association constitute a contract not merely between the shareholders and the company, but between each individual shareholder and every other.'

A further uncertainty is caused by the fact that, unlike an ordinary contract, the 'section 14' contract can be altered without the consent of one of the parties to it. By s. 9 of the Companies Act 1985 a company may alter its articles by special resolution. Thus, if 75 per cent of shareholders present and voting at a meeting determine that the articles are to be altered, that alteration will normally be effective and thus the 'contract' will be altered, as much for the objectors as for those in favour of the alteration.

5.2 **What Rights are Governed by the Contract in the Articles?**

Section 14 appears to bind the members of the company to each other without the company's involvement in that relationship. As described above, the courts have 'read the company back into' the contract. They have made it clear that the only relationship between members which is governed by this 'contract' in the articles is the dealings which they have with each other because they are shareholders in the company. No contractual relationship outside those confines is created by s. 14. This can be illustrated by *London Sack and Bag* v. *Dixon* [1943] 2 All ER 763.

This case concerned a dispute between two members of the UK Jute Association. The dispute had arisen out of trading transactions between them, and not as a result of shareholder's rights. It was argued by the appellants that there was a binding submission to arbitration by virtue of the fact that both disputants were members of the association. The articles of the association provided for arbitration in the event of a dispute between members. The court held that the appellants had failed to prove that there had been a binding submission to arbitration. Scott LJ said that the contract which was created between the members because the predecessor to s. 14 did not constitute a contract between them 'about rights of action created entirely outside the company relationship such as trading transactions between members'.

An example from the other side of the line, where shareholders were bound to abide by the articles was *Rayfield* v. *Hands* [1960] Ch 1. In that case the plaintiff was a shareholder in a company. Article 11 of the articles required him to inform the directors of an intention to transfer shares in the company. The same article provided that the directors 'will take the said shares equally between them at fair value'. The plaintiff notified his intention of selling the shares but they refused to buy. The plaintiff's claim for the determination of the fair value of the shares and for an order that the directors should purchase the shares at a fair price succeeded. Vaisey J said: 'the articles of association are simply a contract as between the shareholders *inter se* in respect of their rights as shareholders'. Vaisey J also relied on the fact that in this case a small company, somewhat akin to a partnership, had been involved. If he was right to believe that this strengthened the s. 14 contract we can see that this alleged contract affects the 'constitutional' rights of shareholders that are affected by the articles. The contract may be more readily enforced where there are few shareholders.

5.3 Outsiders

The same theme runs through the next topic for consideration. Because shareholders are affected by the 'contract' only in their capacity as shareholders, it is clear that outsiders (non-shareholders) cannot be affected by the contract in the articles. Strangely, however, the rights of such outsiders are often set out in the articles. This may be partly because of the special definition of 'outsiders' in these circumstances. The practice has led to a number of cases. A good illustration of the point is *Eley* v. *Positive Government Security Life Association* (1876) 1 ExD 88. There the articles of association contained a clause in which it was stated that the plaintiff should be solicitor to the company and should transact all the legal business. The articles were signed by seven members of the company and duly registered. Later the company employed another solicitor and the plaintiff brought an action for breach of contract. This action did not succeed. The court held that the articles were a matter between the shareholders amongst themselves or the shareholders and the directors [as representing the company]. They did not create any contract between a solicitor and the company. This was so even though the solicitor had become a member of the company some time after the articles had been signed.

This means that there is a subtlety in the definition of an 'outsider' in these circumstances. He is a person unable to enforce the articles or be affected by the contract in the articles. When the person seeking to enforce the articles has effectively two relationships with the company he may be both an 'outsider' in the sense discussed in *Eley*, but at the same time be a shareholder of the company. This problem was discussed in *Hickman* v. *Kent and Romney Marsh Sheepbreeders* [1915] 1 Ch 881. In that case, the articles contained a clause which provided for a reference to arbitration of any disputes between the company and its members concerning the construction of the articles or regarding any action to be taken in pursuance of those articles. When the plaintiff issued a writ claiming an injunction to prevent his expulsion from the company, the defendant company asked that the dispute be referred to arbitration. Astbury J cited a number of cases (*Prichard's Case* (1873) LR 8 Ch 956; *Melhado* v. *Porto Alegre Ry Co* (1874) LR 9 CP 503; *Eley* v. *Positive Life Assurance Co.* (1876) 1 ExD 88; *Browne* v. *La Trinidad* (1888) 37 ChD 1), and went on to say:

'Now in these four cases the article relied upon purported to give specific contractual rights to persons in some capacity other than that of shareholder, and in none of them were members seeking to enforce or protect rights given to them as members, in common with the other corporators. The actual decisions amount to this. An outsider to whom rights purport to be given by the articles in his capacity as outsider, whether he is or subsequently becomes a member, cannot sue on those articles treating them as contracts between himself and the company to enforce those rights. Those rights are not part of the general regulations of the company applicable alike to all shareholders and can only exist by virtue of some contract between such person and the company, and the subsequent allotment of shares to an outsider in whose favour such an article is inserted does not enable him to sue the company on such article to enforce rights which are . . . not part of the general rights of the corporators as such.'

Having examined a number of other cases (including *Wood* v. *Odessa Waterworks* (1889) 42 ChD 636; *Salmon* v. *Quinn & Axtens* [1909] AC 442;

and *Welton* v. *Saffery* [1987] AC 299), Astbury J found the law clear on the following points:

> 'first, that no article can constitute a contract between the company and a third person; secondly, that no right merely purporting to be given by an article to a person, whether a member or not, in a capacity other than that of member, as, for instance, as solicitor, promoter, director, can be enforced against the company; and thirdly, that articles regulating the rights and obligations of the members generally as such do create rights and obligations between them and the company respectively.'

The conclusion arrived at by Astbury J was reached after consideration of the case of *Salmon* v. *Quinn & Axtens Ltd* (1889) 42 Ch D 636. In that case the articles of association gave a veto to Joseph Salmon which could prevent the board of directors from validly making certain decisions. On the occasion in question in this case, Salmon had used his power of veto. Salmon was a managing director and yet he was able to enforce his right of veto by way of the contract in the articles despite the fact that there was only one other shareholder who held a similar right. This case can be reconciled with *Hickman* on the grounds that every shareholder has the right to enforce the articles of the company and it is irrelevant and coincidental that the article sought to be enforced in any one case stands to benefit the shareholder bringing the action more than others. In other words, a shareholder who also holds a position as outsider (such as managing director, solicitor, etc.) can, wearing his shareholder hat, enforce the contract in the articles, even if the direct result of that enforcement is of benefit to him wearing his outsider hat.

This approach was rejected in *Beattie* v. *Beattie* [1938] Ch 708 (see Casenotes). Sir Wilfred Greene MR said:

> 'It is to be observed that the real matter which is here being litigated is a dispute between the company and the appellant in his capacity as a director, and when the appellant, relying on this clause, seeks to have that dispute referred to arbitration, it is that dispute and none other which he is seeking to have referred, and by seeking to have it referred he is not, in my judgment, seeking to enforce a right which is common to himself and all other members . . . . He is not seeking to enforce a right to call on the company to arbitrate a dispute which is only accidentally a dispute with himself. He is asking, as a disputant, to have the dispute to which he is a party referred. That is sufficient to differentiate it from the right which is common to all the other members of the company under this article'.

The line between 'shareholders' rights and 'outsiders' rights remains, despite the anomalous decision in *Salmon* v. *Quinn & Axtens.*

Section 14 (with other issues) has been the subject of a study by the Law Commission. In Shareholder Remedies (Law Commission Consultation Paper No. 142) the Commission sets out the current law, acknowledges that the law is unclear but provisionally recommends against providing a statutory list of situations which fall within the scope of the section. The author, in responding to the consultation paper, has suggested that rather than providing a statutory list, an attempt should be made to redraft the section making it plain that, rather than seeing s. 14 as a type of contract, it should be clear that it is present to protect constitutional rights which belong to a substantial body of shareholders.

5.4 **The Articles as Evidence of a Contract**

Whereas an 'outsider' may not enforce rights which are in the articles by invoking s. 14 of the Companies Act 1985, he may be able to show that he has a contract with the company apart from the articles, but the articles may provide or be evidence of some of the terms of that contract. An example of this is *Re New British Iron Company, ex Parte Beckwith* [1898] 1 Ch 324. In that case the articles provided (by article 62) that 'The remuneration of the board shall be an annual sum of £1000 to be paid out of the funds of the company, which sum shall be divided in such manner as the board from time to time determine.' Wright J said:

'That article is not in itself a contract between the company and the directors; it is only part of the contract constituted by the articles of association between the members of the company *inter se*. But where on the footing of that article the directors are employed by the company and accept office the terms of article 62 are embodied in and form part of the contract between the company and the directors. Under the articles as thus embodied the directors obtain a contractual right to an annual sum of £1000 as remuneration.'

The same reasoning proved detrimental to the plaintiff in *Read* v. *Astoria Garage (Streatham) Ltd* [1952] Ch 637. The company had adopted the standard form of articles of association set out in the Companies Act in force at the time. The article at the centre of the dispute provided that managing directors could be appointed by a resolution of the directors and for that appointment to be terminated by a resolution of the general meeting. The plaintiff was appointed and dismissed by those procedures. He claimed unfair dismissal, arguing that there was a contract between him and the company, one of the terms of which was that his employment should not be terminated without reasonable notice. The Court of Appeal could find no evidence of a contract between the company and the plaintiff, still less evidence of a contract which contradicted the terms of the articles, so the plaintiff failed.

Still more unfortunate was the plaintiff in *Re Richmond Gate Property Co. Ltd* [1965] 1 WLR 335. In that case the court held that the defendant had been employed by the company as managing director. The court looked to the articles to find what remuneration was due since there was no evidence of a contract term about pay elsewhere. The articles provided that he should be paid such amount 'as the directors may determine'. In fact the directors had made no determination so nothing was due to him. Furthermore because he had a contract with the company he could not recover any money on a '*quantum meruit*' claim, which is a claim for money when work has been done without any formal agreement as to the amount that will be paid in respect of that work. It is, in effect, a claim for a 'reasonable amount' for work done.

The facts of the last two cases considered lead to the question: what would be the situation if a contract had existed and that contract and the articles contained contradictory clauses. In *Read* v. *Astoria Garages* (see above), Jenkins LJ said: 'a managing director whose appointment is determined by the company in general meeting . . . cannot claim to have been wrongfully dismissed unless he can show that an agreement has been entered into between himself and the company, the terms of which are inconsistent with the exercise by the company of the power conferred on it by the article . . .'.

From this it follows that the company can exercise whatever powers the articles specify, but if a contractual right is breached by this exercise of powers, damages must be paid. This was what occurred in *Nelson* v. *James Nelson & Sons Ltd* [1914] 2 KB 770. In that case, the directors tried to terminate the employment of the plaintiff as managing director. He had been appointed as managing director for life provided that he complied with a number of conditions. It was not alleged that he had broken any of the conditions. The articles gave to the directors power to appoint managing directors and power to 'revoke' such appointments. The court held that the power to revoke appointments did not mean that the directors could do so in such a way that contracts entered into by the company would be broken. That was what had happened here and therefore the termination of the plaintiff's employment was unlawful and the company was liable in damages for breach of contract.

5.5 **Alteration of the Articles of Association**

Section 9 of the Companies Act 1985 reads as follows:

'(1) Subject to the provisions of this Act and to the conditions contained in its memorandum, a company may by special resolution alter its articles.
(2) Alterations so made in the articles are (subject to this Act) as valid as if originally contained in them, and are subject in like manner to alteration by special resolution.'

By s. 16 of the Act a member will not be bound by alterations made after he has joined the company in so far as they make him liable to pay extra money to the company. There are special provisions which apply when the rights attached to classes of shares are to be varied (see s. 125 *et seq*. and Chapter 14). This cannot be done simply by special resolution. The general rule is that articles may be altered by a special (75 per cent majority) resolution. This rule can put very considerable power in the hands of the majority. The number of shareholders making up such a majority may be very small, perhaps only one person. Because of this the court has found it necessary to control this power. The rule that has been formulated is that an alteration of articles is valid only if it is in good faith (bona fide) and for the benefit of the company as a whole. At first sight this would seem to be a stringent control, but closer examination of the cases shows a considerable reluctance to intervene in favour of an aggrieved minority, and great confusion as to what is actually meant by 'bona fide for the benefit of the company as a whole'.

In *Allen* v. *Gold Reefs of West Africa Ltd* [1900] 1 Ch 656 (see Casenote 2), Lindley MR said:

> 'the power conferred by [what is now s. 9 of the Act] must, like all other powers, be exercised subject to those general principles of law and equity which are applicable to all powers conferred on majorities and enabling them to bind minorities. It must be exercised, not only in the manner required by law, but also bona fide for the benefit of the company as a whole, and it must not be exceeded. These conditions are always implied, and are seldom, if ever, expressed. But if they are complied with I can discover no ground for judicially putting any other restrictions on the power conferred by the section than those contained in it . . .'

The judge went on to say that shares were taken on the basis that articles were subject to alteration. It would therefore require very clear evidence of an undertaking by the company to treat a particular shareholder differently; an undertaking that a particular article would not be altered. However, where there was an agreement that would be broken by the alteration of the articles of association, the company would be liable for a breach of contract brought about by the change of article:

> 'A company cannot break its contracts by altering its articles, but, when dealing with contracts referring to revocable articles, and especially with contracts between a member of the company and the company respecting his shares, care must be taken not to assume that the contract involves as one of its terms an article which is not to be altered' (Lindley MR in *Allen* v. *Gold Reefs of West Africa*).

5.6 *Bona Fide* for the Benefit of the Company

Given that a resolution to alter articles will be regarded as valid if it is passed '*bona fide* for the benefit of the company', and invalid if this can be shown not to be the case, do the cases throw light on what is meant by that phrase?

In *Brown* v. *British Abrasive Wheel* [1919] 1 Ch 290, the company was in need of raising further capital. The 98 per cent majority were willing to provide this capital if they could buy up the 2 per cent minority. Having failed to effect this by agreement, the 98 per cent proposed to change the articles of association to give them power to purchase the shares of the minority. The proposed article provided for the compulsory purchase of the minority's shares on certain terms. However, the majority were prepared to insert any provision as to price which the court thought was fair. Despite this the court held that the proposed alteration could not be made. Astbury J held that the alteration was not for the benefit of the company as a whole. One reason for this was that there was no direct link between the provision of the extra capital and the alteration of the articles. Although the whole scheme had been to provide the capital after removing the dissentient shareholders, it would in fact have been possible to remove the shareholders and then refuse to provide the capital. Astbury J's judgment seems to determine that two separate criteria must be met: the judgment must be 'within the ordinary principles of justice' and it must be 'for the benefit of the company as a whole'. So far as the latter requirement was concerned, the company seems to have been identified with the shareholders and the reality of the whole plan seems to have been overlooked, for the judge ignored the plan to provide capital on the grounds that there was no formal link between this and the alteration. He also said that the alteration would benefit the majority and not the company as a whole, thus ignoring the company's separate existence as a commercial entity in need of further funding.

Brown v. *British Abrasive Wheel* was not followed in the later case of *Sidebottom* v. *Kershaw, Leese & Co. Ltd* [1919] 1 Ch 290, and the approach taken by the judge in the *Brown* case was criticised. In *Sidebottom* an alteration was approved although it provided for the compulsory purchase of shares. One difference between this case and *Brown* is that the ability to purchase the shares was limited to a situation where the shareholder in question was carrying on business in direct competition with the company. The relationship between this article and the benefit of the company was therefore much clearer. In *Sidebottom* two of the Court of Appeal judges made it clear that they believed that in *Brown*, Astbury J had been wrong to regard good faith and the company's benefit as two separate ideas. The important question was: was the alteration for the benefit of the company as a whole?

Settling the important question and determining its meaning proved to be two different things. In *Dafen Tinplate Co. Ltd. v. Llanelly Steel Co. (1907) Ltd* [1920] 2 Ch 124, the plaintiff company was a member of the defendant company. The defendants realised that the plaintiffs were conducting business in a manner detrimental to their interests. In fact they were buying steel from an alternative source of supply. There was an attempt to buy the plaintiff's shares by agreement but this failed. The defendant company then altered its articles by special resolution to include a power to compulsorily purchase the shares of any member requested to transfer them. It was this alteration which was the subject of the action. The court held that the alteration was too wide to be valid. The altered article would confer too much power on the majority. It went much further than was necessary for the protection of the company. The judge seemed to be using the 'bona fide for the benefit of the company' test in an objective sense, that is, he was judging the situation from the court's point of view.

A different view of the meaning of this important question was taken in *Shuttleworth* v. *Cox Bros & Co. (Maidenhead) Ltd* [1927] 2 KB 9. In that case the company had a board of directors appointed for life. The alteration to the articles provided that any one of the board of directors should lose office if his fellow directors requested in writing that he should resign. The alteration was directed at a particular director whose conduct had not been satisfactory. Again the words 'bona fide for the benefit of the company' were interpreted as one condition. This time, however, the court approached the question from the point of view of the subjective belief of the shareholders. Scrutton LJ said: 'the shareholders must act honestly having regard to and endeavouring to act for the benefit of the company'. Bankes LJ agreed and added:

> 'By what criterion is the court to ascertain the opinion of the shareholders on this question? The alteration may be so oppressive as to cast suspicion on the honesty of the persons responsible for it, or so extravagant that no reasonable man could really consider it for the benefit of the company. In such cases the Court is, I think, entitled to treat the conduct of shareholders as it does the verdict of a jury and to say that the alteration of a company's articles shall not stand if it is such that no reasonable man could consider it for the benefit of the company . . . I cannot agree with what seems to have been the view of Peterson J in *Dafen Tinplate Co.* v. *Llanelly Steel Co.* [see page 65] . . . that whenever the Court and the shareholders may differ in opinion upon what is for the benefit of the company, the view of the court must prevail.'

If this passage is right, the court will only intervene in the most extreme cases – when no reasonable man could believe that the alteration could be good for the company. One of the considerations which caused the courts to withdraw from their more interventionist stand is the fact that shares and the right to vote attached to shares are regarded as property rights. It would be unrealistic, in the words of Dixon CJ in the *Peters'* case (see pp. 56–7): '[to] suppose that in voting each shareholder is to assume an inhuman altruism and consider only the intangible notion of the benefit of the vague abstraction . . . "the company as an institution"'.

A further difficulty is that the alteration of the articles presupposes that there will be conflicting interests to be adjusted. It is therefore very difficult for anyone to determine what will be for the positive benefit of the whole company. It may be that two conflicting rights have been confused.

It can be argued that a shareholder has two rights. One is the right to uphold the value of her shareholding. In defence of this right the shareholder may vote selfishly without any regard to the benefit of the company. If, despite so voting the right is unfairly damaged the shareholder will be entitled to compensation (probably as a result of an action under s. 459 Companies Act 1985 for unfair prejudice). A shareholder defending such a right would not be entitled to set aside a decision of the management or company on such grounds.

However, a decision by the company or the management may be struck down if it is not taken *bona fide* in the interests of the company. This is because decisions which affect the interests of the company must be taken for the benefit of the company as a whole even if some shareholders are damaged in the process. A decision not taken for the benefit of the company as a whole should be challengeable by shareholders seeking to protect the value of the interest they hold in the company rather than the value of the interest they hold in their shares.

The courts have taken a cautious view and retained their power to prevent manifest abuses while fighting shy of interference in the internal affairs of the company. This caution can be seen as part of the whole approach of the law to the principle of majority rule (see Chapter 1).

Two other cases show the reluctance of the court to intervene. In *Greenhalgh* v. *Arderne Cinemas Ltd* [1951] Ch 286 (see Casenote 3), a change in articles which effectively removed the plaintiff's pre-emption rights was approved, despite the reference in the judgment to the factor of discrimination as a factor which would cause a resolution to be disallowed by the courts. It must be clear that *any* discrimination between majority and minority shareholders would not be sufficient to cause a resolution to fail the bona fide test, since many alterations of articles will cause adjustments between classes of shareholders from which some will emerge better off than others. An example of this is to be found in *Rights and Issue Investment Trust Ltd* v. *Stylo Shoes Ltd* [1965] Ch 250. In that case the effect of the alteration was (amongst other things) to halve the voting rights of a number of ordinary shareholders as against the rights held by management. Despite this the resolution was upheld. The management shares had not been voted and the resolution had been passed by the requisite majority. The court refused to interfere. It seems that if discrimination is to be a ground for interference it will have to be some very clear, perhaps vindictive discrimination that is. alleged before the court will be moved to upset the normal voting patterns of the company and declare a resolution invalid.

5.7 Remedies

The remedies that are available to a sucessful challenger when an alteration to the articles has been or is about to be made include the following.

Injunction

An injunction will be available where the alteration does not pass the 'bona fide' test but it is doubtful whether it will be available where the objection to the alteration is that it will cause the company to break a contract. In *British Murac Syndicate* v. *Alperton Rubber Co.* [1915] 2 Ch 186 there was an agreement separate from the articles, by which the defendant company was obliged to accept two directors nominated by the plaintiff syndicate. Two directors were nominated but their appointment was not acceptable to the defendants. The defendant company proposed to delete the regulation that was in the same terms as the external contract. It was held that the company had no power to alter its articles of association for the purpose of committing a breach of contract and that therefore an injunction would be granted to restrain the holding of the meeting which was to be convened for that purpose.

This case must be contrasted with *Southern Foundries Ltd* v. *Shirlaw* [1940] AC 701. In that case the House of Lords held that the company could alter its articles so as to put itself in a position in which it could break a contract. When such powers were used, however, there would be a breach and the other party to that contract would be entitled to damages. Where there was a contract made in the expectation that a state of affairs would continue, it was not open to the company, by using its power to change articles, so to undermine that contract that it became worthless. While leaving a plaintiff a remedy in damages this case throws some doubt on the *British Murac* case, since it implies that the change in the articles could not be restrained by injunction. It was only misuse of the new powers inserted by the alteration that could be questioned. Damages were the remedy asked for, so that it is still uncertain if the use of the new powers could have been restrained in respect of this particular member. It may be that in *British Murac* the injunction should not have been aimed at preventing the meeting to alter the regulation, but at a future use of the altered regulation in order to break the contract that existed independently of the articles. The exact significance of these two cases is still somewhat uncertain.

Damages

There is no doubt that where alteration of the articles, or even use of a power contained in the articles, causes a contract with an outsider to be broken, damages will be awarded. In *Shindler* v. *Northern Raincoat Co. Ltd* [1960] 1 WLR 1038, the defendant company agreed to employ the plaintiff as its managing director for ten years. By using a power in the articles, the plaintiff was dismissed in the first year. He was entitled to damages.

Where the complaint is a breach of the contract in the articles (the s. 14 contract), matters are not so clear. In the old case of *Moffatt* v. *Farquhar* (1878) 7 Ch D 591 a challenger was awarded damages, but where the plaintiff is a member of the company at the time of bringing his action his right to damages might be blocked by the decision in the later case of *Houldsworth* v. *City of Glasgow Bank* (see Chapter 10) (1880) 5 App Cas 317, where it was laid down as a general principle that a member of a company could not recover damages from the company since this would involve a return of capital to the members of the company in contravention of the maintenance of capital provisions. This rule was abolished by Companies Act 1989 inserting s. 111A into Companies Act 1985.

Rectification

This would involve an order of the court altering the document (in this case the articles) so that it will read in the way that was originally intended. In the case of articles of association, the courts have held that this is out of the question because the Registrar approved the document in its original form. It is in that form and no other that the articles become the constitution of the company binding on the members, so it cannot be subsequently altered by the court (see *Scott* v. *Frank F. Scott (London) Ltd* [1940] Ch 794).

5.8 **Power of Directors to Bind the Company**

Even if an action is within the capacity of the company, it may be outside the powers of the individuals who are involved in the transaction. Rules have been formulated, therefore, to determine in what circumstances a company will be bound, notwithstanding that the individual has not the power to carry out the transaction in question. Persons outside a company are entitled to assume that internal procedures have been complied with. This is a consequence of *Royal British Bank* v. *Turquand* (1856) 6 E&B 327. That case involved an action for the return of money borrowed from the plaintiff by the official manager of a company. The company argued that it was not bound by the actions of the official manager in this case. This was because the company's deed of settlement contained the following clause:

'That the Board of Directors may borrow on mortgage, bond or bill in the name of, and if necessary under the common seal of, the Company such sum or sums of money as shall from time to time, by a resolution passed at a general meeting of the Company, be authorised to be borrowed: provided that the total amount of the sum or sums of money so borrowed shall not at any time exceed two thirds of the total amount on the instalments on the capital of the Company paid up or called for, and actually due and payable at the time of, the passing of such resolution.'

No resolution as required by this clause had been passed. The court held that the plaintiffs had no knowledge that the resolution had not been passed, that it did not appear from the face of the public document (the contents of which the plaintiffs were deemed to know) that the borrowing was invalid. The company was therefore bound.

Outsiders are therefore entitled to assume that internal procedures such as the passing of the resolution in *Turquand*'s case have been complied with. New s. 35B Companies Act 1985 reads: 'A party to a transaction with a company is not bound to enquire as to whether it is permitted by the company's memorandum or as to any limitation on the powers of the board of directors to bind the company or authorise others to do so.'

Coupled with the abolition of the doctrine of constructive notice by (new s. 711A Companies Act 1985) and the provisions of new s. 35A, below p. 71, the problem of lack of actual authority by reason of non-compliance with internal procedure has been fairly comprehensively solved save for the remaining difficulties with the construction of the relevant sections. There remains an exception, which is to be found in new s. 322A Companies Act 1985. This section has already been discussed (see Chapter 4). It creates an exception to the general rule where the parties to a transaction include the company and either (i) a director of that company or of its holding company, or (ii) a person connected with such a director or a company with whom such a director is associated (see Chapter 6 for an explanation of these terms). If the parties *include* (emphasis added) such persons (there may be other parties as well), then the situation is as follows:

(a) the transaction is voidable at the instance of the company in respect of persons in categories (i) and (ii) above.
(b) each of the persons within categories (i) and (ii) above and any director who authorised the transaction is liable to account to the company for any gain made or indemnify the company for any loss it suffers as a result of the transaction.
(c) as regards parties to the transaction other than those in categories (i) and (ii), they remain protected by the provisions of s. 35A Companies Act 1985, but in that case the court may, if such a person or the company applies, make an order affirming, severing or setting aside the transaction on such terms as appear to the court to be just.

Article 9 of EC Directive 68/151 was also partially implemented into UK law in the form which appears as s. 35A of the Companies Act 1985 which reads:

'(1) In favour of a person dealing with a company in good faith, the power of the board of directors to bind the company is deemed to be free of any limitation under the company's constitution.

(2) For this purpose –

(a) a person 'deals with' a company if he is a party to any transaction or other act to which the company is a party;

(b) a person shall not be regarded as acting in bad faith by reason only of his knowing that an act is beyond the powers of the directors under the company's constitution; and

(c) a person shall be presumed to have acted in good faith unless the contrary is proved.'

5.9 Protection

One thing that was quite clear from the section is that it is *only* intended to benefit an outsider dealing with the company in question. It cannot be used in any way by the company whose action is in question in order to save a transaction. The section could, of course, be used by a company dealing with another company, but only in order to benefit the company whose action is not questionable on the *ultra vires* ground.

5.10 Transaction and Dealing

The previous law contained an uncertainty about the ambit of the reference to 'transaction' and 'dealing'. There was some doubt about whether a gift would be included. This seems to have been solved by new s. 35A (2)(a) which reads: '(a) a person "deals with" a company if he is party to any transaction or other act to which the company is a party.'

5.11 Decided on by the Directors

The preceding law required a transaction 'decided on by the directors'. It was not clear what degree of delegation was permissible before a transaction became one which was decided on by someone other than 'the directors'. For example, if the directors decided that as a matter of policy they would attempt to move towards making the company environmentally friendly, was it a transaction 'decided on by the directors' when an expensive piece of de-polluting equipment was ordered by a plant manager? A similar problem arose if decisions were taken by a single director. If there was no express delegation of power to him to take decisions in that area, were his acts in pursuance of decisions by the directors? This delegation point has been solved by new s. 35A. The opportunity to explain in statutory form the composition of the decision-making body was not taken. The relevant part of new s. 35A is subsection (1) which reads: 'In favour of a person dealing with a company in good faith, the power of the board of directors to bind the company, or authorise others to do so, shall be deemed to be free of any limitation under the company's constitution.'

5.12 **Good Faith**

The old s. 35 applied 'in favour of a person dealing with a company in good faith'. The outsider was presumed to be in good faith unless the contrary was proved. This meant that a company had to prove the absence of good faith. The meaning of the phrase 'good faith' was not clear. In *International Sales and Agencies* v. *Marcus* (above) Lawson J, referring to the Directive for guidance, came to the conclusion that:

'the defendants had actual knowledge that the payments to them were in breach of duty and trust and were *ultra vires* the companies . . . alternatively, at the lowest, that the defendants could not in all the circumstances have been unaware of the unlawful nature of the payments that they received.'

In these circumstances the allegation that the defendants were not in good faith had been proved. However, this finding did not help where the lack of good faith was less clear. Could behaviour less blameworthy qualify as bad faith? Would suspicion in the mind of the outsider that the transaction was *ultra vires* the company or outside the powers of the directors be sufficient to bring him within the bad faith exception? Did the bad faith relate solely to those issues or would an unconnected allegation be sufficient to prevent recovery? None of these questions had been decided under the old law and these problems have not been satisfactorily solved by new s. 35A.

If anything, the new s. 35A makes slightly more obscure the meaning of 'good faith' by adding s. 35A(2)(b). This reads:

'(b) a person shall not be regarded as acting in bad faith by reason only of his knowing that an act is beyond the powers of directors under the company's constitution.'

This was intended to avoid the possibility that a person would be held to be in bad faith if they had read the constitution but not understood that its provisions made the contemplated action beyond the powers of the company or the officer purporting to complete the transaction. It is far from certain that the courts will construe the provision in this way – they might require proof not only of knowledge and understanding that the action was beyond the relevant powers, but perhaps something more serious, such as fraudulent intent. Further, the section does not address the issue as to whether the bad faith must be connected with knowledge concerning the constitution of the company, or whether a person would be prevented from relying on s. 35A if involved in other skullduggery unrelated to knowledge that the action was outside the powers of the company or the officer involved.

5.13 **Unauthorised Agents**

Despite the reform of the law, a problem remains in that a person purporting to act for a company may actually have no connection whatsoever with the company. In those circumstances it would be wholly unfair to hold the company to a contract purportedly made on its behalf by someone who may be no more than a confidence trickster. If X purports to sell Tower Bridge to Y, should the Tower Bridge Company Limited (supposing that they own the bridge) be bound? Obviously if there is no connection between X and the Tower Bridge Company Ltd, that course would be wholly unfair. However, if Y reasonably believes that X is authorised, because of the actions of the Tower Bridge Company Limited, then the company ought to be bound. Although much complicated terminology is used in the cases, the law seems to achieve this result.

In *Freeman & Lockyer* v. *Buckhurst Park Properties Ltd* [1964] 2 QB 480, the plaintiff was a firm of architects and surveyors. The firm was engaged by a person acting as the defendant's managing director. The claim for fees was repudiated on the grounds that the apparent managing director had not been validly appointed. The Court of Appeal upheld the plaintiff's claim. Diplock LJ said:

'It is necessary at the outset to distinguish between an "actual" authority of an agent on the one hand, and an "apparent" or "ostensible" authority on the other. Actual authority and apparent authority are quite independent of one another. Generally they co-exist and coincide, but either may exist without the other and their respective scopes may be different. As I shall endeavour to show, it is on the apparent authority of the agent that the contractor normally relies in the ordinary course of business when entering into contracts.

An actual authority is a legal relationship between principal and agent created by a consensual agreement to which they alone are parties. Its scope is to be ascertained by applying ordinary principles of construction of contracts, including any proper implications from the express words used, the usages of the trade, or the course of business between the parties. To this agreement the contractor is a stranger; he may be totally ignorant of the existence of any authority on the part of the agent. Nevertheless, if the agent does enter into a contract pursuant to the "actual" authority, it does create contractual rights and liabilities between the principal and the contractor . . .

An 'apparent' or 'ostensible' authority, on the other hand, is a legal relationship between the principal and the contractor created by a representation, made by the principal to the contractor, intended to be and in fact acted on by the contractor, that the agent has authority to enter on behalf of the principal into a contract of a kind within the scope of the 'apparent' authority, so as to render the principal liable to perform any obligations imposed on him by such a contract . . . The representation, when acted on by the contractor, by entering into a contract with the agent, operates as an estoppel, preventing the principal from asserting that he is not bound by the contract. It is irrelevant whether the agent had actual authority to enter into the contract.

In ordinary business dealings the contractor at the time of entering into the contract can in the nature of things hardly ever rely on the 'actual' authority of the agent. His information as to the authority must be derived either from the principal or from the agent or from both, for they alone know what the agent's actual authority is. All that the contractor can know is what they tell him, which may or may not be true . . . The representation which creates 'apparent' authority may take a variety of forms of which the commonest is representation by conduct, i.e. by permitting the agent to act in some way in the conduct of the principal's business with other persons. By doing so the principal represents to anyone who becomes aware that the agent is so acting that the agent has authority to enter on behalf of the principal into contracts with other persons of the kind which an agent so acting in the conduct of his principal's business has normally 'actual' authority to enter into . . . unlike a natural person [a company] can only make a representation through an agent, [this] has the consequence that, in order to create an estoppel between the corporation and the contractor, the representation as to the authority of the agent which creates his 'apparent' authority must be made by some person or persons who have 'actual' authority from the corporation to make the representation . . . the contractor cannot rely on the agent's own representation as to his actual authority. He can rely only on a representation by a person or persons who have actual authority to manage or conduct that part of the business of the corporation to which the contract relates . . . If the foregoing analysis of the relevant law is correct, it can be summarised by stating four conditions which must be fulfilled to entitle a contractor to enforce against a company a contract entered into on behalf of the company by an agent who had no actual authority to do so. It must be shown: (a) that a representation that the agent had authority to enter on behalf of the company into a contract of the kind sought to be enforced was made to the contractor; (b) that such representation was made by a person or persons who had 'actual' authority to manage the business of the company either generally or in respect of those matters to which the contract relates; (c) that he (the contractor) was induced by such representation to enter into the contract, i.e. that he in fact relied on it; and (d) that under its memorandum or articles of association the company was not deprived of the capacity either to enter into a contract of the kind sought to be enforced or to delegate authority to enter into a contract of that kind to the agent.'

As we have seen above, the advent of the Companies Act 1989 has almost certainly caused condition (d) to disappear. The outsider will need to show that the other party to the contract appeared, because of some actions by those actually entitled to represent the company, to be empowered to bind the company to the particular transaction in question. This may be because the company in some way represents that he has authority to enter into the particular transaction in question, or because the company make it appear that he holds a particular position or job within the company (often that of managing director). In the latter case, it is necessary for the outsider to go one step further and show that an officer of that kind 'usually' may bind the company to the type of transaction in question, that is, that the company's alleged agent has 'usual' authority. Where a transaction is questioned on the grounds that the company's representative has no power to enter into it (other than because of limitations under the constitution, unless the outsider was acting in bad faith), the relevant questions are:

(i) Did the person apparently representing the company have the authority to do so? If so, the contract is enforceable. If not:

(ii) Did the company lead the outsider to believe that the person apparently representing the company had the power to complete this particular transaction? If so, the contract is enforceable. If not:

(iii) Did the company lead the outsider to believe that the person apparently representing the company held a particular position in the company? If so *and* if a person validly appointed to that position would usually be able to complete the type of transaction in question, then the contract is enforceable.

5.14 Usual Authority

An illustration of the last point made above is to be found in *Panorama Developments* v. *Fidelis Furnishing Fabrics* [1971] 3 WLR 440. In that case, the secretary of the company hired cars from the plaintiff pretending that they were for the use of the defendant, but in fact they were for for his own use. The Court of Appeal held that the defendant was bound by the contracts. Lord Denning MR said:

'Mr Hames' second point is this: he says that the company is not bound by the letters which were signed by Mr Bayne as 'Company Secretary'. He says that, on the authorities, a company secretary fulfils a very humble role: and that he has no authority to make any contracts or representations on behalf of the company. He refers to *Barnett, Hoares & Co* v. *South London Tramways Co.* (1887) 18 QBD 815, where Esher MR said:

'A secretary is a mere servant; his position is that he is to do what he is told, and no person can assume that he has any authority to represent anything at all.'

But times have changed. A company secretary is a much more important person nowadays than he was in 1887. He is an officer of the company with extensive duties and responsibilities. This appears not only in the modern Companies Acts, but also by the role which he plays in the day-to-day business of companies. He is no longer a mere clerk.

He regularly makes representations on behalf of the company and enters into contracts on its behalf which come within the day-to-day running of the company's business. So much so that he may be regarded as held out as having authority to do such things on behalf of the company. He is certainly entitled to sign contracts connected with the administrative side of the company's affairs, such as employing staff, and ordering cars, and so forth.'

Summary

1 The articles of association regulate the relationship between the shareholders and the company, and the balance of power amongst shareholders.
2 It is difficult to assess the contractual binding force of the articles as a contract.
3 Some authorities require the right sought to be enforced under s. 14 and the articles to be a 'member's right' and not a 'special right'. *Quinn and Axtens* v. *Salmon* appears to contradict this.
4 An alteration of the articles can be effected by a 75 per cent majority of the shareholders but can be challenged on the ground that the alteration was not 'bona fide for the benefit of the company'.
5 The power of any person to bind a company is governed by agency principles and bona fide outsiders will be protected by s. 35A Companies Act 1985 as inserted by Companies Act 1989.

Casenotes

1 *Beattie* v. *Beattie* [1938] Ch 708.
The articles of association contained an arbitration clause. An allegation was made by a shareholder who stated that the defendant had, in his capacity as director, paid himself unjustified remuneration. Sir Wilfred Greene said:

'It is to be observed that the real matter which is here being litigated is a dispute between the company and the appellant in his capacity as a director, and when the appellant, relying on this clause, seeks to have that dispute referred to arbitration, it is that dispute and none other which he is seeking to have referred, and by seeking to have it referred he is not, in my judgment, seeking to enforce a right which is common to himself and all other members . . .

2 *Allen* v. *Gold Reefs of West Africa* [1900] 1 CH 656.
The case concerned an attempted alteration of the articles of association which would have retrospective effect and alter the obligations of a shareholder towards the company. The court held that, provided the alteration could be seen as bona fide for the benefit of the company, the power to alter articles was otherwise unfettered.

3 *Greenhalgh* v. *Arderne Cinemas* [1951] Ch 286.
Eveshed MR said:

'Certain principles can be safely stated as emerging from [the] authorities. In the first place, I think it is now plain that 'bona fide for the benefit of the company as a whole' means not two things but one thing. It means that the shareholder must proceed upon what, in his honest opinion, is for the benefit of the company as a whole. The second thing is that the phrase 'the company as a whole' does not (at any rate in such a case as the present) mean the company as a commercial entity, distinct from the corporators as a general body. That is to say, the case may be taken of an individual hypothetical member and it may be asked whether what is proposed is, in the honest opinion of those who voted in its favour, for that person's benefit.

I think that the matter can, in practice, be more accurately and precisely stated by looking at the converse and by saying that a special resolution of this kind would be liable to be impeached if the effect of it were to discriminate between the majority shareholders and the minority shareholders, so as to give to the former an advantage of which the latter were deprived.'

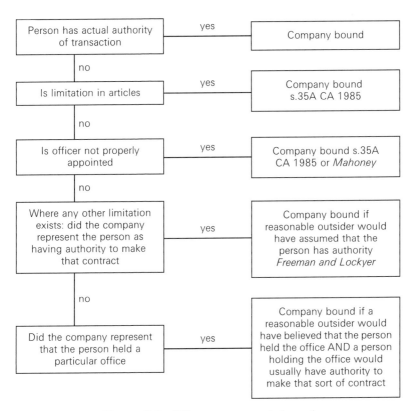

Figure 5.1 *When a company is bound*

Exercises

1 What are the policy factors behind the decisions on enforcement of the articles of association as a contract?

2 What is meant by '*bona fide* for the benefit of the company'?

3 Distinguish the various types of authority which may equip a person to make a binding contract on behalf of a company.

6   Promoters

One of the problems caused by the separate legal identity of the company is that prior to registration it has no existence at all. The persons who are responsible for the company coming into existence are known as 'promoters'. The law imposes duties on them not unlike those owed by directors. This is because the company can be badly cheated at the outset, particularly by those who sell it the assets on which it will found its business. The importance of the law on promoters has been much diminished by the controls exercised over public companies by the various regulatory authorities such as the stock exchange. It is now very rare for a new company to seek money from the public. However the rules remain valid.

6.1 **Who are Promoters?**

In *Twycross* v. *Grant* (1877) 2 CPD 469, Cockburn cj said:

> 'A promoter, I apprehend, is one who undertakes to form a company with reference to a given project and to set it going and who takes the necessary steps to accomplish that purpose. That the defendants were promoters of the company from the beginning can admit of no doubt. They framed the scheme; they not only provisionally framed the company but were, in fact to the end its creators, they found the directors and qualified them, they prepared the prospectus; they paid for printing and advertising and the expenses incidental to bringing the undertaking before the world. In all these respects the directors were passive; without saying that they were in a legal sense the agents of the defendants, they were certainly their instruments.'

This passage gives a clear indication of the actions which will be considered important by the courts when they are determining who was and who was not a promoter of a company. No stricter definition of a 'promoter' has been attempted because the situation can vary so widely. Investment of time or money in the enterprise will always be considered important. However, it is possible for a promoter not to have been obviously active. If he is the real 'power behind the throne' he will be held to have been a promoter. This is one case in which the court is committed to looking at the reality of the situation. Promoters of the type found in the cases are extinct. It is unusual for a newly-formed company to make an issue of shares to the public, and impossible to obtain a stock market listing without having been in business for some time. There is also an enormous body of law and regulation aimed at preventing the abuses that in the previous century only the courts could prevent (see Chapter 8).

Private companies do not issue shares to the public. Although they still have promoters in the sense described in the cases, the fact that they are unable to defraud the public makes control of their activities of less importance. Despite the obsolescence of this body of law it is still valid law, so the present tense will be used throughout to describe it.

6.2 **Duties of Promoters**

Promoters are not trustees or agents of the company but they do stand in a special position in relation to the company. This is called a 'fiduciary' relationship and means that some of the same duties that trustees owe to their beneficiaries will also be owed by promoters to their company.

Promoters are most likely to defraud the company and its future shareholders by selling to the company property that they have previously bought. Because they are usually in control of the company at the outset they are able to determine the price that is paid. The temptation is to overvalue the property and fail to make disclosure of the overvaluation to an independent person. If that occurs, then the company can reverse (rescind) the contract, that is, give back the property and get back the money.

Situation 1 – If property is acquired before promotion commences (See *Erlanger* v. *New Sombrero Phosphate Co.* (1878) 3 App Cas 1218; *Omnium Electric Palace* v. *Baines* [1914] 1 Ch 332).

If someone who subsequently becomes a promoter acquires property that is resold to the company, he may retain any profit that is made on that property provided he has made the correct disclosures (see page 70). This is so even if the property was acquired with the idea that at some time in the future a company would be formed and the property would be sold to it. The vital factor which needs to be identified is the time at which the promotion commences because different rules apply thereafter.

Situation 2 – If property is acquired after promotion commences.

If property is acquired by someone who has already become a promoter and that property is subsequently resold to the company, the courts will assume that the property was acquired for the company. Unless it can be proved that this was not the case the promoter will be unable to make a profit out of that property and the company will have the option of rescinding the contract or keeping the property and requiring the promoter to account for any profit he has made. This latter option is not open to the company in Situation 1 above. It was held in *Omnium Electric Palace* v. *Baines* [1914] 1 Ch 332, that proof that the property was not acquired on the company's behalf could consist of proof that the scheme had throughout been that the property should be bought and then resold to the company. The strange result of this seems to be that a profit may be kept if throughout the promoter had mercenary intentions. This is, of course, provided that the proper disclosures are made (as in Situation 1).

6.3 **Disclosure**

The general rule is that no promoter, whether in Situation 1 or 2, can make a *secret* profit. Thus if any property belonging to a promoter is sold to a company, or if a promoter makes a profit on a transaction connected with the company's formation (see *Gluckstein* v. *Barnes* [1900] AC 240), he will not in any event be permitted to keep that profit unless proper disclosure is made of the transaction. The difficulty is that frequently in this situation the same people are the promoters and the first directors. In *Gluckstein* v. *Barnes* and *Erlanger* v. *New Sombrero Phosphate Co.* (1878) 3 App Cas 1218 it was suggested that the transaction must have the blessing of an independent board of directors before a promoter would be permitted to keep his profit. This would seem to be far too sweeping since it would invalidate all '*Saloman* v. *Saloman*-type' transactions. Nevertheless the court was vehement in *Erlanger*. Lord Cairns said:

> 'I do not say, that the owner of property may not promote and form a joint stock company and then sell his property to it, but I do say that if he does he is bound to take care that he sells it to the company through the medium of a board of directors who can and do exercise an independent and intelligent judgment on the transaction.'

This strict approach was not followed in *Lagunas Nitrate* v. *Lagunas Syndicate* [1899] 2 Ch 392. In that case the company was formed and directed by a syndicate. The company was specifically formed to purchase part of the property of the syndicate which consisted of nitrate works. The syndicate and the board of directors were composed of the same people. The court held that the company was not entitled to recission or damages in respect of the contract to purchase the property of the syndicate. Among the reasons given were:

(1) At the date of the contract the company knew, because it appeared in its memorandum and articles, that its directors were also the vendors or agents of the vendor syndicate. The mere fact that the directors did not constitute an independent board was not a sufficient ground for setting aside the contract.
(2) That there had been no misrepresentation made to, or any material fact concealed from any of the persons who were members of the company at the date of the contract, those persons being the directors themselves.
(3) The defendants as directors had not been guilty of such negligence or breach of trust as would render them liable to the company.

It would seem, then, that disclosure to an independent board *or* to the present and future shareholders via the memorandum and articles will be sufficient disclosure. If this is done and the property was acquired before the buyer became a promoter, or was not acquired on behalf of the company, then the profit may be kept by the promoter.

Two other issues are relevant to this discussion: the loss of the right to recission and the possibility of a remedy in damages.

6.4 The Loss of the Right to Recission

Another reason that was given by the court for the decision in *Lagunas* was that the alteration of the position of the parties as a result of the working of the land had so altered the position of the parties as to make recission impossible. The remedy of recission was not available because the contract could not be reversed. The parties could never be put back into the position that they were in before the contract was made. The loss of the remedy is particularly serious in Situation 1 above. It has been held that where the right to recission is lost, a company has not available the alternative remedy of demanding that the promoter pay his profits to the company, nor is there a right to damages (see *Gover's Case* [1875] 1 ChD 182; *Re Cape Breton* (1885) 29 ChD 795). In the second situation the company has that alternative.

6.5 Actions for Damages

Where a secret profit has been made, the parties may be liable in tort for deceit or negligent misstatement. A difficult case to understand is *Jacobus Marler Estates* v. *Marler* (1913) 85 LJPC, which at first sight suggests that there is an action in damages for the breach of a promoter's fiduciary duty. As Sealy points out (*Cases and Materials in Company Law*, 5th edn (Butterworths 1989), p. 28), it would be unusual to permit an action for damages for the breach of an equitable obligation. He suggests that the damages in this case were awarded against the directors for breach of director's duties. This remedy may often be an alternative course open to the company to pursue where promoters have also acted in the capacity of directors after the formation of the company (see Chapter 11).

6.6 Remuneration of Promoters

Promoters do not have a right to remuneration simply because such a right is included in the articles of association (see Chapter 5, s. 5.1). Any contract purportedly made with the company before it was formed will equally not be binding on the company (see next section). To receive either remuneration, or even recoup preliminary expenses, the promoter must prove the existence of a binding contract with the company (see *Re National Motor Mail Coach Co.* [1908] 2 Ch 515). Section 97 of the Companies Act 1985 is of relevance here but only permits a company to pay underwriting commission to a promoter if the articles so permit. To enforce a right to this and any other remuneration the promoter will need to show that the company is contractually bound to pay him.

6.7 **Pre-incorporation Contracts**

Until a company is registered it has no existence of any kind. Sometimes promoters wish to enter into contracts which are intended to be for the benefit of the company and/or the liability under those contracts is intended to be the company's liability. This may be done in order for the public to see, when they are asked to subscribe for shares, that the company is more than just an 'empty shell'. This would be an unusual situation now, when shares are so rarely offered to the public immediately after a company is formed. It may be done simply to 'get things going'. In any event, the promoter must be careful since it is not possible to act for a non-existent person. The position at common law was confused, but s. 36C Companies Act now provides:

36C. Pre-incorporation contracts, deeds and obligations
(1) A contract which purports to be made by or on behalf of a company at a time when the company has not been formed has effect, subject to any agreement to the contrary, as one made with the person purporting to act for the company or as agent for it, and he is personally liable on the contract accordingly.'
(2) Subsection (1) applies—
    (a) to the making of a deed under the law of England and Wales, and
    (b) to the undertaking of an obligation under the law of Scotland, as it applies to the making of a contract.

The promoter is thus personally liable on any pre-incorporation contract. A wide interpretation of the section was adopted in *Phonogram* v. *Lane* [1981] 3 WLR 736. It was held that the company need not actually be in the process of formation for the section to apply and that there need be no representation that the company is already in existence. Further, it was held that the words in the section 'subject to an agreement to the contrary' would only prevent the operation of the section if there was an express agreement that the person who was signing was not to be liable.

However, in other situations a narrow interpretation of s. 36C has been favoured. In *Oshkosh B'Gosh Inc* v. *Dan Marbel Inc Ltd* [1989] BCLC 507 the Court of Appeal held that the section did not apply when the company was in existence at the time the relevant contracts were made. The promoters were about to buy the company 'off the shelf'. This was held to be the case even though the company had since changed its name. Further, in *Cotronic (UK) Ltd* v. *Dezonie* [1991] BCLC 721 it was held (also by the Court of Appeal) that s. 36C does not apply when a person purports to make a contract for a company which once existed but has been dissolved.

Since the contract is said to have 'effect' as one entered into by the person purporting to act for the company, it would seem likely that the contract will be enforceable by him as well as against him.

6.8 **Liability of the Company**

It is unfortunate that the reform of this area of the law did not go so far as to permit the company to adopt the contract by passing a resolution to that effect in a general meeting. This 'ratification' procedure has been held not to make the company liable (see *Re Northumberland Avenue Hotel Co.* (1866) 33 ChD 16). The company will still not be liable even though all persons concerned act as if the company is bound, and large sums of money are spent in the belief that the contract is binding on the company. In certain circumstances a new contract between the original non-promoter party and the company can be deduced from the circumstances, but this will be rare. It is a new contract that is necessary, either expressed or implied. In *Howard* v. *Patent Ivory Co.* (1888) 38 ChD 156, the circumstances were such that a new contract could be inferred from the circumstances. In that case, the contract was made before the company was formed. After formation the contract was the subject of a resolution passed by the company at a meeting at which the other party to the contract was present. It is significant that the resolution altered the original terms of the agreement. In these circumstances the court could find that there had been a new contract (a novation) formed between the company and the party to the original contract. It is only in this sort of circumstance that a company could be sued on a contract made before its formation by its promoters. It is impossible for a company simply to adopt or ratify a pre-incorporation contract.

Summary

1 Promoters are persons who undertake to form a company and take the necessary steps to set it going.
2 Promoters stand in a fiduciary relationship to the company.
3 If promoters purchase property on behalf of a company they are not permitted to make a profit on it.
4 If promoters make a secret profit they can be forced to disgorge it.
5 Contracts made prior to incorporation do not bind the company but will make those who enter into them personally liable.
6 A pre-incorporation contract will only bind the company if a novation (new contract) occurs.

Exercises

1 Explain the situations in which a promoter may become liable to the company for activities prior to incorporation.
2 If an agreement is made by a person prior to incorporation of a company but the promoter making the contract expressly states that he is not to be liable on that contract, who are the contracting parties?

7   Public Issue of Securities

By the Companies Act 1985, s. 81 it is an offence for a private company to offer shares to the public. The result is that only PLCs can offer shares to the public. However an offer is not made to the public if the only persons who are able to take it up are the persons who receive the offer or if the offer can otherwise be regarded as being a 'domestic concern' of the persons making and receiving it (s. 60(1)). By s. 60(4) an offer is to be regarded as being a domestic concern if it is made to:

(a) an existing member of the company making the offer;
(b) an existing employee of the company;
(c) a member of the family of such a member or employee (as defined in s. 60(5));
(d) an existing debenture holder.

Theoretically it is possible for a company to start life as a public company, but in fact a company is now always registered first as a private company. It will then be converted to a public company when more money than can be supplied by the members needs to be found to fund an expansion of the business. This will require the raising of money by issuing shares.

7.1 Shares

For a discussion of the nature of rights in shares see Chapter 14. In this chapter we shall be concerned with the way in which shares come into the hands of the shareholders, and the rules governing issuing shares to the public. This chapter also contains an overview of the regulatory framework which now governs the carrying on of 'investment business'.

7.2 Direct Offers, Offers for Sale, Issuing Houses

A direct offer of shares to the public is now an unusual method of proceeding, although still possible. If it were used, investors would subscribe for shares which would be allotted directly by the company.

A more common method of issuing shares is by an *offer for sale*. Here the whole of the shares are taken by an 'issuing house' which then offers the shares to the public for purchase. This means that the issuing house, and not the company, will take responsibility for the risk that all the shares may not be sold. It will therefore be the issuing house which will need to take out insurance against this risk.

7.3 **The Three Regimes**

There are three systems, public companies whose shares are listed on the Stock Exchange and two for public companies which do not have such a listing. The latter companies may have their shares traded on the *Unlisted Securities Market* (USM) or the *Alternative Investment Market* (AIM). The USM is being gradually phased out and will not list any new companies.

The rules relating to companies whose shares are listed on the Stock Exchange are to be found in Part 4 of the Financial Services Act 1986 and the 'Yellow' book which contains the Stock Exchange's own rules. Unlisted companies are governed by the provisions of the Companies Act 1985 and the Public Offers of Securities Regulations (POSR) (SI 1995 No.1537) which implement the Prospectus Directive (OJ 32L 124 pp. 8–15).

7.4 **Rights Offers and Public Offers**

If a company wishes to raise money from existing shareholders it may seek to do so via a *restricted rights offer*. This is an offer of more shares made to existing shareholders and capable of acceptance only by existing shareholders. If the shareholder may pass the offer on to others the issue is described as a *rights issue*. In the case of a rights issue the shares will usually be offered in a renounceable letter of right. If the shareholder to whom it is addressed does not wish to avail himself of the offer, he may renounce his right to do so in favour of another person.

A public offer is an invitation to the public at large to buy the shares. When shares are bought for the first time it is said to be a *subscription,* the shares are *subscribed for* and the buyer is known as a *subscriber*.

7.5 **Placing**

An alternative way of disposing of the shares and raising the money is to sell (at the time of first sale of a share this is known as an allotment) the entire issue to an 'issuing house' who will find buyers other than by an offer to the public at large. They are said to 'place' the shares with their clients, hence this method is known as a 'placing' of shares. This type of placing is now also referred to (in the Yellow Book) as 'selective marketing'.

7.6 **Pre-emption Rights**

Sections 89–96 of the Companies Act 1985 set out a procedure which must be followed if the company already has shareholders who own ordinary (equity) shares. Those shareholders have the right to be offered a proportion of the new securities which correspond to the proportion of 'relevant shares' (ordinary shares) already held by them. The shares must be offered on the same or more favourable terms than the eventual offer to the public. The definition of 'relevant shares' excludes shares which have a right to participate in a distribution only up to a specified amount (non-participating preference shares). (See Chapter 14 for a description of the different types of shares a company may issue.)

The shareholders then have twenty-one days in which to accept the offer. This right applies to public and private companies but it may be excluded by the memorandum or articles of a private company. Private companies must not contravene the ban on offering shares to the public. Private companies may thus make restricted rights offers only in respect of equity securities (ordinary shares) provided the offer is limited to its own shareholders or its employees.

In a public company pre-emptive rights may be overridden by a general authority given to directors under s. 80 Companies Act 1985 (see below) or may be removed by a special resolution of the company (see s. 95 Companies Act 1985).

7.7 **Authority to Issue Shares**

Section 80 Companies Act 1985 requires directors who issue shares to have been authorised to do so either (a) by the company in general meeting; or (b) by the articles of the company. An authority may be given for a particular occasion or it may be a general power. The authority must state the maximum amount of shares which must be allotted under it. It must also state the date on which it will expire. This is to be not more than five years from the date of the incorporation where an authority was included in the articles. In any other case it is not more than five years from the date on which the authority is given by resolution. A director who knowingly and wilfully contravenes the section will be liable to a fine. Where directors have a *general* authority under s. 80 they may be given power by the articles or by special resolution to allot shares as if the pre-emption rights granted by s. 89 did not exist. Pre-emption rights also do not apply where the shares are to be wholly or partly paid for otherwise than in cash. This provision makes a large hole in the idea of the protection of the existing shareholders since only a small part of the consideration need be otherwise than cash.

7.8 **Directors' Duties**

Directors must use their powers to issue shares bona fide for the benefit of the company (*Percival* v. *Wright* [1902] 2 Ch 421. The court will examine the reason for the issue and if the 'primary purpose' was not to raise capital the issue will be an abuse of the directors' powers (*Howard Smith Ltd* v. *Ampol Petroleum Ltd* [1974] AC 821). Directors may purchase shares from existing shareholders but must not do so on favourable terms (See *Alexander* v. *Automatic Telephone Co.* [1900] 2 Ch 56) unless the terms have been publicised.

7.9 **The Structure of the Rules**

The issue of shares in a company applying for Stock Exchange Listing is governed by the Financial Services Act and by the Stock Exchange Rules. The Financial Services Act rules which apply to Listing Particulars and the rules in the POSR which apply to prospectuses are very similar.

In the case of both an application for Listing and an issue of a prospectus there will be a very wide duty of disclosure (s. 146 FSA 1986, reg. 9 POSR 1995). In both cases supplementary documents must be issued if there is a change of circumstances (ss. 147 FSA 1986, reg. 10 POSR) and in both cases the provision for compensation for misleading information is very wide (ss. 150 FSA 1986, reg. 14(1) POSR 1995).

7.10 **Admission to Stock Exchange Listing**

Where the shares are to be listed on the Stock Exchange the company must comply with the Stock Exchange rules which set out a number of conditions to be fulfilled by an applicant.

Among the conditions are:

(i)   The applicant must be a public company.

(ii) The expected market value of securities for which listing is sought must be at least £700,000 in the case of shares. Securities of a lower value may be admitted provided that the Committee of the Stock Exchange are satisfied that adequate marketability can be expected. These limits do not apply where the issue is of more shares of a class already listed.

(iii) The securities must be freely transferable.

(iv) A company must have published or filed accounts in accordance with its national law for five years preceding its application for listing. The Committee has a discretion to accept a shorter period provided that it is satisfied (a) that it is desirable in the interests of the company or of investors and (b) investors will have the necessary information available to arrive at an informed judgment on the company and the securities for which listing is sought.

(v)   At least 25 per cent of any class of shares must at the time of admission be in the hands of the public (that is, persons who are not associated with the directors or major shareholders). (vi)
The Bank of England controls sterling issues in excess of one million pounds in value. In such cases application must be made to the government broker for a date known as 'impact day' when the size and terms of the issue are to be made known.

(vii) All offer documents (including listing particulars) must be lodged in final form forty-eight hours before the Committee is to hear the application.

(viii) No offer documents may be made public until they have received the approval of the Department of Trade and Industry.

7.11 **Contents of Listing Particulars**

The required contents for listing particulars is a long list. Included in the mandatory contents are:

(i)   Details of the company and details of any group or company of which it is a part.

(ii) Details of the shares which are to be issued.

(iii) Considerable financial detail of the company and group including an accountant's report for the last five completed financial years.

(iv) Details of the persons forming the management of the company.

(v)   A description of the recent developments and prospects of the company and its group.

7.12 **Continuing Obligations**

Companies that wish to obtain a listing on the Stock Exchange must comply with continuing obligations imposed by the Yellow Book, s. 5. This requires a listed company to notify to the Stock Exchange any information necessary to enable holders of the company's listed securities and the public to assess the performance of the company. The obligation is set out in amendments to the Listing Rules which came into force on 8 January 1995 and require a company to make an announcement where, to the knowledge of the company directors there is a change in the company's financial position, the performance of its business or in the company's expectation of its performance, where knowledge of that change is likely to lead to a substantial movement in the price of the company's listed securities. No guidance is given as to the meaning of 'substantial movement' which will therefore depend on the individual track record of the particular company.

7.13 **Remedies for Defective Listing Particulars**

The remedies available where listing particulars are defective consist of remedies available under the common law (discussed under remedies for defective prospectuses on p. 91) and statutory remedies contained in ss. 146 and 150 of the Financial Services Act 1986. The reason for reserving the discussion of the common law remedies until later is that the relevant statutory and common law remedies apply to defective prospectuses as well as to defective listing particulars. In both cases the remedies afforded by the Financial Services Act (when fully in force) are widely drafted so that it would only be in an unusual situation that a litigant would pursue a remedy under the common law rather than rely on the statute.

Section 146 Financial Services Act 1986 contains a general duty of disclosure. It reads:

'(1) In addition to the information specified by listing rules or required by the competent authority as a condition of the admission of any securities to the Official List any listing particulars submitted to the competent authority under s. 144 above shall contain all such information as investors and their professional advisers would reasonably require, and reasonably expect to find there, for the purpose of making an informed assessment of –
> (a) the assets and liabilities, financial position, profits and losses, and prospects of the issuer of the securities; and
> (b) the rights attaching to those securities.'

The information must be within the knowledge of any person responsible for the preparation of the particulars or it must be information which 'it would be reasonable for him to obtain by making enquiries' (s. 146(2)). In determining what information should be included, the type of investment and the type of persons likely to acquire such investments are to be taken into account (s. 146(3)). Presumably the more unsophisticated the potential purchasers of the securities, the more information should be included, although s. 146(3)(c) tends to limit the ambit of information to be made available by requiring that in determining the information to be included in listing particulars regard shall be had 'to the fact that certain matters may reasonably be expected to be within the knowledge of professional advisers of any kind which those persons may reasonably be expected to consult'. Section 147 Financial Services Act 1986 requires any significant changes or new matter which would be relevant to be the subject of supplementary listing particulars.

Given the long list of matters which must be included (see p. 000) and the general duty of disclosure, the remedy afforded by s. 150 Financial Services Act 1986 is very wide. Section 150 reads:

'(1) Subject to s. 151 below, the person or persons responsible for any listing particulars or supplementary listing particulars shall be liable to pay compensation to any person who has acquired any of the securities in question and suffered loss in respect of them as a result of any untrue or misleading statement in the particulars or the omission from them of any matter required to be included by s. 146 or 147 above.'

Section 151(2) provides that an omission of required material amounts to a statement that there is no such relevant matter. This widens the remedy to include omissions as well as misleading positive statements.

Section 151 contains exemptions from liability to pay compensation:

'(1) A person shall not incur any liability under s. 150(1) above for any loss in respect of securities caused by any statement or omission as is there mentioned if he satisfies the court that at the time when the particulars were submitted to the competent authority he reasonably believed, having made such enquiries (if any) as were reasonable, that the statement was true and not misleading or that the matter whose omission caused the loss was properly omitted and –

(a) that he continued in that belief until the time when the securities were acquired; or

(b) that they were acquired before it was reasonably practicable to bring a correction to the attention of persons likely to acquire the securities in question; or

(c) that before the securities were acquired he had taken all such steps as it was reasonable for him to have taken to secure that a correction was brought to the attention of those persons; or

(d) that he continued in that belief until after the commencement of dealings in the securities following their admission to the Official List and that the securities were acquired after such a lapse of time that he ought in the circumstances to be reasonably excused.'

Section 151 contains other exemptions, for example an exemption relating to statements made on the authority of an expert. A person responsible for particulars will not be liable if they believed on reasonable grounds that the expert was competent and had consented to the inclusion of the statement (s. 151(2)). Similarly there will be no responsibility for the accurate and fair reproduction of a statement made by an official person or contained in a public official document (s. 151(4)). The full list of exemptions in s. 151 is set out in the Casenotes, together with s. 152 which contains the list of persons who are responsible for listing particulars.

Several points must be noted about this remedy:

(i) It applies to omissions as well as positive misstatements.

(ii) The plaintiff need only show that he has acquired the securities and suffered loss as a result of the untrue or misleading statement or omission. After that the burden lies on the persons responsible for listing particulars to exculpate themselves. This reversal of the usual burden of proof could assist a plaintiff considerably.

(iii) The remedy is available to first time purchasers of shares when they are initially issued (subscribers) and to later purchasers. This contrasts with the Companies Act remedy previously available (Public Offers of Security Regulations 1995, see p. 91) to those suffering loss as a result of misstatements in prospectuses.

(iv) The remedy is available as well as the common law remedies discussed below in relation to liabilities for misleading prospectuses. In view of the width of the statutory remedy, however, it would be rarely if ever that the common law remedies would be more beneficial to a plaintiff.

7.14 **Prospectus Issues**

Where the shares are not to be listed on the Stock Exchange, any advertisement of them for sale must be accompanied by a 'prospectus' complying with the requirements of the Prospectus Directive as implemented by the Public Offers of Securities Regulations 1995. A prospectus for unlisted shares must contain the information specified in Schedule 1 to the POSR (reg 8(1)) or equivalent information where Schedule 1 is inappropriate to the issuer's sphere of activity or legal form. Regulation 9 imposes a general duty of disclosure in the same terms as the duty imposed by FSA, s. 146. Regulation (93) follows Article 11(2) of the Directive and requires that the information in a prospectus for unlisted shares should be presented 'in as easily analysable and comprehensible form as possible'.

7.15 Remedies for Defective Prospectuses

Regulations 14 and 15 of the Public Offers of Securities Regulations shadow the Financial Services Act provisions regarding listing particulars very closely and impose the same duties and liabilities in respect of a prospectus for unlisted securities.

7.16 Liabilities for Misstatements in Prospectuses and Listing Particulars

The summary of actions which might arise from an incomplete or misleading prospectus are shown in the table in Casenotes at the end of this chapter. It is incomplete since the issue of the misleading prospectus could also give rise to actions by oppressed minority shareholders, either by way of ss. 459–461 of the Companies Act 1985 or a derivative action. Further, the directors may well be in breach of their duties to the company and be liable for such breaches. Criminal penalties under s. 47 of the Financial Services Act 1986, ss. 1 and 2 of the Theft Act 1978, or under ss. 15 and 19 of the Theft Act 1968, might apply.

In the past a problem was caused by *Houldsworth* v. *City of Glasgow Bank* (1880) 4 App Cas 317 (HL). In that case, the question discussed was whether a person holding shares in a company is entitled to receive damages from that company. In that case it was held that because of the shareholder's special relationship with the company it was not open to him to remain a member of the company and claim damages from the company for fraudulently inducing him to buy the stock. Following that case it was clear that where the company is the defendant in an action for fraud no damages could be awarded to a member of the company. Recission was the only remedy available to him. This case did not, in any event, apply to the remedy under the Financial Services Act because of s. 168(8) of that Act, which provides that where compensation is paid in pursuance of s. 166 of the Act, such compensation is not to be taken into account 'in determining any question as to the amount paid on subscription for those shares or as to the amount paid up or deemed to be paid up on them'. Following the implementation of s. 131 Companies

Act 1989, members have an unrestricted right to claim damages from a company. Section 131 of the 1989 Act introduces a new section, s. 111A into the Companies Act 1985 which provides that a person is not to be debarred from obtaining damages or other compensation from a company simply because he holds or has held shares in the company or has any right to apply or subscribe for shares or to be included in the company's register in respect of shares. The measure of damages for intentional wrongdoing was determined recently by the House of Lords. In *Smith New Court Securities* v. *Scrimgeour Vickers (Asset Management) Ltd and another* (1996) *Times* Nov. 22nd the House of Lords decided that an intentional wrongdoer in an action for fraudulent misrepresentation would be liable for all loss (including consequential loss) directly flowing from the fraudulent misrepresentation and could not benefit from any issues as to foreseeabilty. The plaintiff was entitled to be put into the position as if no misrepresentation had been made.

A number of actions claiming damages for negligence and deceit have left the law in some confusion. Thus in *Al-Nakib Investments (Jersey) Ltd* v. *Longcroft* [1990] 1 WLR 1390, issuers of a prospectus, which was issued specifically to enable shareholders to consider the rights offer, was held not to give rise to a duty of care between the issuers and people who subsequently purchased shares on the market. No duty would arise unless the person responsible for the prospectus was aware, or ought to have known, that the recipient would rely on it for the specific purpose of entering into a particular transaction. However, in *Possfund Custodian Trustee* v. *Diamond* [1996] 2 BCLC 665 Lightman J in the Chancery Court refused to strike out an action for deceit and negligence by purchasers subsequent to the original subscribers. He held that it was arguable that persons responsible for the issue of a company's share prospectus owed a duty of care to, and could be liable for damages to, subsequent purchasers of shares on the unlisted securities market provided that the purchaser could establish that he had reasonably relied on representations made in the prospectus and reasonably believed that the representor intended him to act on them, and that there existed a sufficient direct connection between the purchaser and the representor to render the imposition of such a duty fair, just and reasonable. He also felt that Al-Nakib should be reviewed by a higher court. Until that happens the extent of the duty owed by issuers to subsequent purchasers will remain uncertain.

7.17 The EC Prospectus Directive

This Directive OJ 32 L124, 5 May 1989, pages 8–15, was adopted on 17 April 1989 and has been implemented in the UK by the Public Offers of Securities Regulations 1995 (SI 1995 No. 1537).

Perhaps one of the most notable things about the EC Directive is that it will not in any way affect the laws of Member States regarding liability for misstatements or omissions in prospectuses.

In outline the Directive is not dissimilar from present UK prospectus law in that issuers of securities will be required to produce and make available a prospectus, subject to certain exceptions, when offering securities to the public for the first time.

The Directive also provides for the mutual recognition of prospectuses drawn up in accordance with the Listing Particulars Directive, both as public offer prospectuses and as listing particulars.

Article 9 of the Directive requires the communication of a prospectus 'to the bodies designated for that purpose in each Member State in which . . . securities are offered to the public for the first time'. Even if the measure does achieve some harmonisation in the issue and content of prospectuses the value of the resultant rules will depend on the strength of the internal laws providing a remedy. The designated body is not obliged by the Directive to have a clearing or overseeing role.

7.18 Aims of the Directive

The preamble to the Directive concentrates on the provision of information to investors. An avowed aim is to put investors into a position to make a correct assessment of the risk in investing in transferable securities by the provision of full appropriate information concerning those securities and the issuers of such securities. The provision of such information is seen as having a role in reinforcing confidence in transferable securities and this is expected to contribute to the correct functioning of the securities markets and encourage their development.

By encouragement of markets two aims are sought to be achieved: (l) the interpenetration of national transferable securities markets; and (2) a contribution to the creation of a genuine European capital market.

It must also be noted that the Directive does not provide for two separate regimes dependent on whether the securities are to be listed on an approved exchange or not. Therefore, unless the regimes under ss. 159 and 160 of the Financial Services Act 1986 comply with the Directive they will have to be amended.

7.19 Transferable Securities

The Directive applies to transferable securities which are offered to the public for the first time in a Member State. The ambit of the word 'transferable' is unclear. As noted above, one of the aims of the Directive is 'the creation of a genuine European capital market'. Elsewhere the Directive is seen as an aid to 'the correct functioning of transferable securities market'. Such avowed aims would seem to indicate that the Directive is aimed at the regulation only of securities markets whereas if 'transferable' is given its widest meaning it would also apply where shares were capable of transfer, even if such transfer is subject to restrictions (for example, pre-emption rights). The Directive would thus prima facie apply to all issues of shares regardless of an existence of a market, provided there was an 'offer to the public'.

'Offer to the public' creates the second area of uncertainty in the Directive. It is a concept the English courts found some difficulty in defining. The Directive contains a recital that 'it is not possible or expedient at the present stage to have a common definition of offer to the public'. This basic omission is likely to defeat any value that the Directive might otherwise have as a harmonisation measure. It will be open to Member States to define 'offer to the public' in a wide range of different ways so that similar issues would be subject to the Directive in one jurisdiction and not another.

A further difficulty might arise with the use of the concept 'for the first time'. If a company makes an unsuccessful offer accompanied by a prospectus, that offer could (at any time) be repeated without the need for a prospectus. It might be that unsuccessful offers should be subjected to the most stringent safeguards.

The Public Offers of Securities Regulations 1995

The Public Offers of Securities Regulations 1995 implement the Prospectus Directive in the United Kingdom. These measures came into force on 19 June 1995. The major features of the regulations are that they:

(i)   alter the listing requirements where a UK public offer is to be made before the admission of the securities to the Official list of the London Stock Exchange;

(ii)   Create a new prospectus regime for public offers in the UK of securities which will not be listed;

(iii) Introduce new provisions for the recognition of UK prospectuses in other member states of the EEA by introducing an optional regime under which issuers can apply to the London Stock Exchange for the pre-vetting of prospectuses for unlisted and non-listed securities;

(iv)   replace the existing provisions under which 'incoming' prospectuses from the EEA countries will qualify for mutual recognition in the UK.

The regulations apply to offerings of defined classes of securities. Offers of securities outside the scope of the regulations may still be covered by the general regime on investment advertisements and business in the Financial Services Act 1986.

One of the difficulties with the Directive is the lack of definition of 'offer to the public'. This part of the directive has been implemented by s. 144(2) Financial Services Act and Regulation 4(1). Both written and oral offers are included. This is wider than the regime in the Companies Act 1985 which required a document before the regime was triggered. The offer must be one which is either an invitation to make a contractual offer or is capable of being accepted to form a contract for the sale or issue of securities. This will exclude much warm-up advertising. That type of activity will remain subject to the general advertising restrictions in the Financial Services Act 1986, particularly ss. 56 and 57.)

'Offer'

A person is regarded as offering securities if, as principal:

(i)   he makes an offer which, if accepted, would give rise to a contract for their issue or sale (which for this purpose includes any disposal for valuable consideration) by him or by another person with whom he has made arrangements for their issue or sale; or
(ii) he invites another person to make such an offer but not otherwise and, except where the context otherwise requires, 'offer' and 'offeror' are construed accordingly (S142(7)(a) of the Financial Services Act and regulation 5.

Offer to the public

This is an offer which is made to any section of the public [in the United Kingdom], whether selected as members or debenture holders of a body corporate, or as clients of the person making the offer, or in any other manner is to be regarded as made to the public (s. 142(7) (b) Financial Services Act, para. 1, Schedule 11A and regulation 6.

The new rules require a prospectus where the offer is made to the public 'in the United Kingdom' - thus incoming offers may trigger a prospectus requirement. A prospectus is only required where the offer is being made 'for the first time' in the UK (s. 144(2) Financial Services Act and regulation 4(1)). This is the case even if the first offer was made before these regulations came into force.

There is a long list of exemptions. Most notably in favour of securities which are offered to 'persons whose ordinary activities involve them in dealing in investments for the purposes of their business' or 'persons in the context of their trades, professions or occupations', where the offer is made to no more than 50 persons, to members of a club or association who have a common interest or the total consideration payable is less than 40,000 ECU.

There are also exceptions for private companies, offers to public authorities, large-denomination offers, and exchange and employee share schemes, as well as the expected exemption for Eurosecurities.

Summary

1   At present there are two regimes. Where the shares of a company are to be listed on the Stock Exchange an issue must be accompanied by Listing Particulars, and the contents and liabilities for omissions and misstatements are governed by the Stock Exchange Regulations and the Financial Services Act.

2 Where the shares are not to be listed, an issue must be accompanied by a prospectus. This is governed by very similar rules contained in the Public Offer of Securities Regulations 1995, which implement the EC Prospectus Directive.

3 The remedy for defective Listing Particulars contained in the Financial Services Act and the similar remedy for defective prospectuses in the POSR are wide and comprehensive. It is unlikely that a plaintiff would contemplate using the other remedies that are theoretically available to them unless they can benefit from an enhanced measure of damages following the House of Lords decision in *Smith* v. *New Court Securities Ltd* where it held that an intentional wrongdoer in an action for fraudulent misrepresentation would be liable for all damage done by the representation regardless of forseeability issues.

Exercises

1 Consider the range of remedies available to a person who suffers loss as a result of misstatements in Listing Particulars/Prospectuses.

2 Find a prospectus in one of the broadsheet newspapers. Does the quantity of information that needs to be disclosed make them unreadable?

8 The Regulation of Investment Business

There is now an enormous amount of regulation which affects the way that 'investment business' is carried on. As investment business includes dealing in shares and debentures the regulatory framework has an effect not only on companies or firms which are involved in investment businesses but also companies whose shares are being dealt with. The Financial Services Act 1986 provided a framework within which there was originally to be a degree of self-regulation. However, the rules drafted by the various bodies involved are so detailed that little room for manoeuvre has been left and the system is hugely expensive. Although the system is in a constant state of change, there is little sign of the amount of regulatory burden being eased. It is questionable whether the aim of 'self-regulation' is being met at all. The decisions of the SIB are subject to judicial review and a body of case-law has been building up setting the limits of its powers (see *R* v. *SIB* [1995] 2 BCLC 76 and *R* v. *SIB* [1996] 2 BCLC 342) but in *Melton Medes* v. *SIB* (1994) *Times*, 27 July, the Chancery Court held that no action for breach of statutory duty would lie against a regulatory body. The whole structure of regulation is now under review and new legislation in the form of a Financial Services Act 1999 is expected.

8.1 The Bodies Involved

The chief body involved in the regulatory framework is the Securities and Investment Board (SIB). This is a company limited by guarantee and was given the original task of recognising a number of 'self regulating organisations' (SROs). After they have been recognised the SIB has the continuing task of supervising the SROs. All firms engaged in 'investment business' (which is very widely defined) must obtain an authorisation from an SRO or from the SIB itself. Direct authorisation by the SIB was not encouraged and only a small number of businesses are operating under direct authorisation by the SIB. A problem has been caused by the detailed nature of the rules laid down both by the SIB and the SROs. Each SRO deals with 'clients' from a particular field of investment business. A large operation may therefore need to belong to more than one SRO if its business is spread over a wide field. This means compliance with several sets of rules, some of which may not be compatible with each other.

8.2 The Important Provisions

Section 3 of the Financial Services Act 1986 (FSA) contains the provision upon which the whole structure turns. It provides:

'No person shall carry on, or purport to carry on, investment business in the United Kingdom unless he is an authorised person under Chapter III or an exempted person under Chapter IV of this Part of this Act.'

Before considering in more detail the way a person becomes an 'authorised' or 'exempted' person it is useful to know what is meant by 'investment business'. This is defined by s. 1 of the FSA and Parts I, II, and III of Schedule 1. The approach adopted by the Act was to include an enormous range of activities within the scope of the restriction in s. 3 and then try to exempt from the Act operations which could be seen as 'commercial' rather than 'investment' transactions. Obviously there is a very fine line between the two and considerable difficulty has been experienced in drawing the line. An example of this can be seen in the treatment of 'futures' contracts. Essentially these are contracts to buy a commodity at some time in the future. At one end of the scale these contracts are clearly investment contracts. This is when there is never any intention for one of the parties to the contract to deliver to the other any of the actual commodity involved, while at the same time it is clear that the right to the quantity of the commodity acquired will be sold on to another buyer quickly, perhaps even before the commodity exists or has been extracted from the ground (for example, wheat before it has grown, oil before extraction). At the other end of the scale, the FSA was never meant to regulate a contract between two parties to buy and sell a quantity of a commodity. There are many shades in between. If a cargo of oil is purchased with the buyer intending to take delivery, but the buyer's circumstances change and he resells that cargo, has this become an investment rather than a commercial contract? The treatment of futures in the statute is important, not because it will be of wide importance in company law, but because it is indicative of the whole approach of the statute which embraces all and then seeks to exclude.

8.3 Futures Contracts – An Example of How the FSA Works

Thus Schedule 1 paragraph 8 includes within the scope of the Act: 'Rights under a contract for the sale of a commodity or property of any other description under which delivery is to be made at a future date and at a price agreed upon when the contract is made.'

There follow seven notes. The first note disapplies paragraph 8 if 'the contract is made for commercial and not investment purposes'. The remaining six notes try to give an indication of how to differentiate between the two. Thus notes 2 and 3 read:

'(2) A contract shall be regarded as made for investment purposes if it is made or traded on a recognised investment exchange or made otherwise than on a recognised investment exchange but expressed to be traded on such an exchange or on the same terms as those on which an equivalent contract would be made on such an exchange.

(3) A contract not falling within note (2) above shall be regarded as made for commercial purposes if under the terms of the contract delivery is to be made within seven days.'

Following these concrete rules come more indeterminate ones. Notes (4), (5) and (6) give 'indications' of when a contract in this category shall be regarded as one for futures and when it shall be regarded as a commercial contract. Thus note (4) reads:

(4) The following are indications that any other contract [that is, a contract not within notes (2) and (3)] is made for a commercial purpose and the absence of any of them is an indication that it is made for investment purposes–
(a) either or each of the parties is a producer of the commodity or other property or uses it in his business;
(b) the seller delivers or intends to deliver the property or the purchaser takes or intends to take delivery of it.

Notes (5) and (6) give more 'indications' of where the line should be drawn, and note (7) sets out rules about when a price is taken to be agreed at the time of a contract even though that might not appear to be the case at first sight.

Something of the immense complexity of the system should be apparent from the foregoing discussion. The matters of most immediate concern to all companies are Schedule 1 Part 1 paragraph 1; which includes within the operation of the Act 'Shares and stock in the share capital of a company', and paragraph 2 which includes debentures (see Chapter 15 for a discussion of 'debentures'). The exceptions to the latter inclusion include cheques, letters of credit, banknotes and statements showing the balance in a current, savings or deposit account. That these should need to be specifically excepted from a scheme for investor protection shows how widely the provisions are drafted, catching many things which then need to be excluded.

Further elaboration is contained in the Act, for so far only the definition of 'investment' has been examined. What s. 3 prohibits is the carrying on of investment business. This is defined by s. 1(2) and Schedule 1, Part II of the FSA. It is defined in terms of certain activities carried on in relation to 'investments' as already defined. The activities are:

(1) dealing in investments.
(2) arranging deals in investments.
(3) managing investments.
(4) advising on investments.

Of course the boundaries of each of these activities is uncertain, and further difficulty is added by Part III of Schedule 1 which contains a list of 'excluded activities'. Perhaps most important of these are:

(i)   The act is only to apply to a person buying shares for himself or otherwise dealing in investments if it is done by way of a regular business. This excludes people buying shares from time to time as personal investments rather than to further a career. The difficulty of distinguishing between these two types of activity shows what fine lines have to be drawn.

(ii)   There is an exemption for dealing in investments which takes place amongst members of a group of companies or joint enterprises.

(iii) There is a general exemption where the true nature of the contract is the supply of goods or services or the sale of goods.

There are also exemptions for employees' share schemes, where shares in private companies are sold, where a trustee is making investments on behalf of a beneficiary, where advice is given in the course of exercising a profession or non-investment business and where advice is given in a newspaper or other publication 'if the principal purpose of the publication, taken as a whole and including any advertisements contained in it, is not to lead persons to invest in any particular investment.'

8.4 'In the United Kingdom'

Section 1(3) defines 'in the United Kingdom' in two ways. Not surprisingly it includes those who carry on investment business from a permanent place of business in the United Kingdom; but more widely it includes those who engage in the activities listed in the schedules which are caught by the Act and 'his doing so constitutes the carrying on by him of a business in the United Kingdom'. The ambit of this sub-section is not clear. Carrying on a business would presumably include making transactions via agents in the United Kingdom. It also probably includes communications sent by post, telex, telephone or fax. This would seem to be the case since Part IV of Schedule I contains exemptions for persons without a permanent residence in the United Kingdom whose services have been requested by a United Kingdom resident. In other words, if the first approach has come from the potential UK investor, the overseas investment firm will not be covered by the restrictions in the Act. If the first approach is made by the overseas firm to the UK investor, the firm will be governed by the provisions of the FSA.

8.5 Authorisation and Exemption, SROs and RPBs

Although authorisation can in theory be directly from SIB, the most common way of becoming authorised is to become a member of a self regulating organisation. Because the work of various professions is caught by the wide drafting of the provisions of the statute, there is provision for authorisation via a number of the organisations which oversee the workings of the professions. These bodies are known as 'recognised professional bodies' (RPBs). Both SROs and RPBs must be recognised by the SIB. The detailed rules for recognition of SROs and RPBs are set out in Schedules 2 and 3 of the FSA. So far as an SRO is concerned, the major requirement is that it must have rules 'such as to secure that its members are fit and proper persons to carry on investment business of the kind with which the organisation is concerned'. To this end the SRO must have adequate arrangements and resources for effective monitoring and enforcement of compliance with its rules (Schedule 2, para. 4). Schedule 2 para. 2 provides that the rules and practice relating to admission and expulsion of members and disciplinary rules must be fair and reasonable and include adequate provision for appeals. Similar provisions with regard to RPBs are contained in Schedule 3.

8.6 Exempted Persons

Chapter IV, Part I of the FSA provides that a number of institutions shall be 'exempted persons', that is, exempt from the controls in the statute. Section 35 of the FSA provides that the Bank of England is an exempted person. Others are recognised investment exchanges (such as the Stock Exchange and the Unlisted Securities Market), Lloyd's insurance market (s. 42) and 'listed money market institutions'. The list of money market institutions is issued by the Bank of England after approval by the Treasury (s. 43).

8.7 Unauthorised Investment Business

Where someone breaches the basic rule that unauthorised or non-exempt persons must not carry on investment business (s. 3) they commit a criminal offence (s. 4); the maximum penalty is two years imprisonment plus a fine. Section 5 makes agreements made by or through unauthorised persons unenforceable unless the court exercises a discretion given by s. 5(3). Under that sub-section the court may allow such an agreement to be enforced provided that it finds that the unauthorised person reasonably believed that the entry into the agreement was not in contravention of the Act and that it is just and equitable for the agreement to be enforced. The SIB may obtain an injunction if there is a reasonable likelihood of a person acting in breach of s. 3.

8.8 Conduct of Investment Business

Chapter v. of the FSA contains the framework within which the SIB and the SROs have made their rules. Section 47 makes it a criminal offence (maximum penalty seven years and a fine) to make misleading statements:

'(1) Any person who–
  (a) makes a statement, promise or forecast which is misleading, false or deceptive or dishonestly conceals any material facts; or
  (b) recklessly makes (dishonestly or otherwise) a statement, promise or forecast which is misleading, false or deceptive, is guilty of an offence if he makes the statement, promise or forecast or conceals the facts for the purpose of inducing, or is reckless as to whether it may induce, another person (whether or not the person to whom the statement, promise or forecast is made or from whom the facts are concealed) to enter or offer to enter into, an investment agreement or to exercise, or refrain from exercising, any rights conferred by an investment.'

This offence is very wide-ranging, particularly because of the broad definition of 'reckless' which has been adopted in the criminal law. 'Reckless' in this context means that the defendant either realised that there was a risk of inducing the other party to enter or offer to enter into an investment agreement or that he gave no thought to that risk where a reasonable person would have done so. Those accustomed to 'loud talk' in public houses beware! The width of the offence is an earnest of the government's intention to protect investors. However, it will only be fully effective if enforcement proceedings (prosecutions) are in fact brought.

Most of the rest of Chapter v. contains sections which give the regulatory organisations power to make rules regulating investment business. Two main categories of rules are envisaged: those which attempt to ensure fair dealing by investment firms; and those which seek to ensure that the firms involved in investment business are likely to remain solvent. There is also provision for a compensation fund.

8.9 Sanctions

Apart from the general criminal offence set out in s. 47 of the FSA and the prohibition on non-authorised or non-exempt persons being involved in investment business (see above), the Act contains a power to prevent the employment in investment business of any individual if it appears that he is 'not a fit and proper person to be employed in connection with investment business'. This power is exercised by the SIB. Written notice must be given if the SIB propose to exercise this power, and there is a right to have the case referred to the Financial Services Tribunal which is established by Chapter IX of Part I of FSA. Section 60 provides that the SIB may publish a statement as to misconduct by a person who is or was an authorised person. Section 61 confers a general power now invested in the SIB to prevent contraventions of investment rules or remedy existing contraventions. These powers are not available if the allegation is that the rules of an SRO or RPB have been contravened unless it appears that the relevant organisation is unable or unwilling to take appropriate measures itself. Section 62 and s. 62A provides an action available to 'a private investor who suffers loss' as a result of breach of rules or regulations made under the powers conferred by Chapter v. and certain other sections of the Act and breach of the rules of SROs and RPBs by their members.

There is no doubt that the powers of enforcement are very wide. The rules that were originally drawn up by the SIB and the SROs suffered from too much detail and, in the case of the SROs, too little co-ordination, so that firms were being subjected to the burden of complying with several very detailed and different systems of regulation. A reform of the rules was considered throughout 1989 and new rules have now come into force. Similarly, the number of SROs has fallen and will fall still further with the establishment of the Personal Investment Authority in summer 1994. There is no sign of any lessening of the burden of regulation, however.

8.10 **The New Approach to SIB and SRO Rules**

Instead of simply having one body of rules which are enforceable by SIB or SRO action under s. 61 and also by action by ordinary investors who have suffered loss under s. 62 the new approach seeks to simplify the system by taking out a great deal of the detail and having several 'tiers' of rules. Statements of general principles in broad terms are backed up by rules containing more detail. What seems to have happened, however, is that taken together with the rules of the SROs and RPBs, three tiers of regulation have come to exist, thus defeating the original plan to simplify the scheme.

8.11 **The Investment Services Directive**

The Investment Services Directive has now been implemented in the United Kingdom by the Investment Services Regulations 1995, the Financial Services Act 1986 (Investment Services) (Extension of Scope) Order 1995 and the Financial Services Act 1986 (EEA Regulated Market) (Exemption) Order 1995, which came into effect on 1 January 1996. This makes it easier for UK firms to offer investment services abroad and eases the entry into the UK market of firms from other EU member states.

Introduction

The Investment Services Directive was adopted in July 1993. The idea is that 'investment firms' should gain authorisation from their 'home' state. This authorisation would then act as a 'passport' to enable them to carry on that investment business in other member states (Articles 1 and 4). The service in question could be provided on a cross-border basis within the Community or the investment firm in question will be permitted to set up branches in the other Member States without needing to be authorised again. The explanatory memorandum issued by the Commission emphasises the numerous parallels between this Directive and the Second Banking Directive which seeks to provide a similar system for credit institutions. As will be seen, however, discrepancies between these two Directives are likely to cause problems. The idea, as expressed in the explanatory memorandum, is that where a credit institution is authorised under the Second Banking Directive to carry on investment activities, it will not require further authorisation under the Investment Services Directive. However, differences in the wording of the Directives may cause problems, particularly where the scope of an authorisation under the Second Banking Directive is an issue. The enforcement provisions may also overlap and cause difficulties.

The Directive provides for the monitoring of the financial soundness of the investment firm and its compliance with major conduct of business rules. Both these matters are to be within the exclusive competence of the home Member State (the state of registration or central management or control or residence). Other conduct of business rules are to be left to the Host State (the State where the relevant business is being carried on) to administer. In Article 9 the Directive seeks to identify those rules which are to be under the control of the home State. The explanatory memorandum hints that other rules will follow when there has been a greater degree of harmonisation.

Another issue which awaits a greater degree of harmonisation is the amount of capital which should be set aside by investment firms in respect of market risk arising from activities covered by the Directive. The Commission intends to deal with this issue in a separate Directive. It is hoped that this Directive will be brought into force at the same time as the Investment Services Directive.

One curious feature of the Directive as presently drafted is the compensation scheme. The Directive requires all Member States to establish a compensation fund to protect investors against default or bankruptcy by an investment business. Pending further harmonisation, however, the Host Country compensation rules would apply to branches of investment businesses authorised in other Member States. The home-country compensation schemes would apply to business done on a services basis.

The Directive can most easily be analysed under the following heads:

(i)   The scope of the Directive.
(ii)   The procedure of authorisation and minimum requirements.
(iii) The scope of the 'passport'; and
(iv)   The conduct of business rules and enforcement.

The scope of the Directive

This is determined by the definitions contained in Article 1 and by the annex to which reference is made in that Article.

Two definitions are of particular importance:

'Home member state' of a natural person is defined in terms of residence and of a legal person in terms of registered or (where there is none) head

office. The registered or head office test is clear but the residence test is likely to give rise to considerable uncertainty. The reference is not even to a principal place of business so that it is quite likely that some individuals may be regarded as resident in more than one Member State. The problem is likely to be even worse where partnerships are involved.

'*Investment firm*' is any natural or legal person whose business it is to engage in one or more of the activities set out in the Annex to the Directive. The Annex is divided into two sections: activities and instruments. The activities in section A are:

'1. Brokerage, i.e, the acceptance of investors' orders relating to any or all of the instruments referred to in Section B below and/or the execution of such orders on an exchange or market on an agency basis against payment of commission.
2. Dealing as principal, i.e., the purchase and sale of any or all of the instruments referred to in Section B below for own account and at own risk with a view to profiting from the margin between bid and offer prices.
3. Market making, i.e., maintenance of a market in any or all of the instruments referred to in Section B below by dealing in such instruments.
4. Portfolio management, i.e., the management against payment of portfolios composed of any or all of the instruments referred to in Section B below undertaken for investors otherwise than on a collective basis.
5. Arranging or offering underwriting services in respect of issues of the instruments referred to in point 1 of Section B below and distribution of such issues to the public.
6. Professional investment advice given to investors on an individual basis or on the basis of private subscription in connection with any or all of the instruments referred to in Section B below.
7. Safekeeping and administration of any of the instruments referred to in Section B below otherwise than in connection with the management of a clearing system.'

The instruments in Section B are:

1. Transferable securities including units in undertakings for collective investment in transferable securities;
2. Money market instruments (including certificates of deposit and Eurocommercial paper);
3. Financial futures and options; and
4. Exchange rate and interest rate instruments.

In principle, the approach adopted by the Annex is probably the right one in that it attempts to define the investment services coming within the scope of the Directive by specific categories of activities and in, for the most part, specific terms. This approach may help to avoid some of the problems caused by the different and blanket approach adopted in the

Financial Services Act which attempts (with varying degrees of success) to deal with certain problem areas by way of very specific exceptions.

The drafting of the Annex is an improvement on earlier versions in particular because it has eliminated 'ancillary activities' from the Annex and placed it in the main text. This removes the difficulty experienced in the interpretation of previous drafts where uncertainty existed because 'ancillary activities' appeared to be an activity standing alone. It has also adopted an approach which has split activities and instruments. This has increased the clarity of the scope of the Annex.

Two areas of uncertainty remain a problem in the Annex. The definitions of both 'management' and 'professional investment advice' have caused great difficulties under the Financial Services Act. At present 'management' might well include such people as trustees and personal representatives. Specific exceptions would be necessary if the intention was to exclude them. Such exceptions might well be difficult to draft and thus, in the final analysis, ineffective. 'Professional investment advice' is also uncertain of ambit. Is it envisaged, for example, that lawyers throughout the community who act for clients purchasing companies will require authorisation? If not, the wording needs alteration. As presently drafted it would appear to catch many professionals who provide investment advice as an ancillary part of some quite separate activity.

A further problem could be caused because the expression 'safekeeping and administration' is still very wide. It would, for example, catch the solicitor, who as part of services to a family trust, keeps the share certificates and pays out dividends to the beneficiaries even though he exercises no control over the management of the trust.

It is also noteworthy that commodities futures are not included. This exclusion may be sensible in view of the difficulty of fitting industries such as the oil industry into a regulatory regime. Several different approaches to the regulation of the oil industry have followed the inclusion of such contracts as the 15-day Brent contract within the scope of the Financial Services Act regulators. However, if the Directive is seen as a facilitating measure rather than a regulatory one, this exclusion may be opposed by participants in the commodities futures markets.

The procedure of authorisation and minimum requirements

The scheme of the Directive is that a firm obtains authorisation from a 'competent authority' in its home state. The authorisation will be valid for a particular activity (Article 4). That activity can then be carried on in any other Member State without the need to obtain further authorisation. The firm will also be authorised to carry out any activities ancillary to the one named in the 'passport'. Articles 4 and 8 contain the conditions for authorisation These are:

  (a) That the firm has sufficient initial financial resources having regard to the nature of the activity in question. It is intended to bring into force a Directive on capital adequacy to coincide with the coming into force of the Investment Services Directive.

(b) The persons who effectively direct the business of the firm are of sufficiently good repute and experience.

(c) That holders of qualified participations in the firm are suitable persons.

(d) That the firm has made sufficient provision against market risk 'in accordance with rules to be prescribed in a further co-ordinating Directive'.

Applications for authorisation are to be made to a 'competent authority' and accompanied by a programme of operations setting out the types of business envisaged and the structural organisation of the investment firm.

Applicants are to be notified of the fate of their application within three months (Article 4.4) and reasons for refusal must be given. If no notification has been given within six months this is deemed to be a refusal. Presumably reasons must be given in this instance also.

Authorisation may be withdrawn where the firm does not make use of it or renounces the authorisation; has obtained the authorisation by fraud; no longer fulfils the conditions under which authorisation was granted, particularly that it no longer possesses sufficient financial resources, or can no longer be relied on to fulfil its obligations towards its creditors; and in particular no longer provides security for the assets entrusted to it. There is a saving provision permitting the withdrawal of authorisation in other cases where national law provides for withdrawal.

A major problem could be caused by Article 4.2 as currently drafted. Shareholders who control 10 per cent or more of the voting rights or have more than 10 per cent of the capital, or anyone else who exercises significant influence over the firm, must be fit and proper. Enforcement problems under this provision would be immense. The Directive on acquisitions of major shareholdings will, when implemented, facilitate disclosure of shareholdings of 10 per cent and over but that proposal applies only to listed companies. Moreover, the major problem lies in determining which interests should be disregarded: for example, shares held by a market maker or shares held as security by a bank. Application of the concept of significant influence to partnerships, unincorporated associations or individuals increases the difficulty of determining whether the test is satisfied.

The scope of the 'passport'

Once an authorisation has been granted for a particular activity, an investment firm wishing to supply investment services in a Member State other than the home state must notify the competent authority of the relevant State of the activities it intends to undertake (Article 12). The firm may provide services into that State one month after notification. If a firm wishes to establish a branch in another Member State it must follow the procedure laid down in Article 11.

Article 4.1 makes it clear that following authorisation the investment firm concerned may engage in the 'activity' authorised, together with any ancillary activities. This drafting clears up uncertainty which existed in previous drafts. It was previously unclear whether the 'passport' was to be a general one or whether it did indeed relate to particular activities.

One major difficulty with this provision lies in its relationship with the Second Banking Directive. It is clear that the 'passport' for investment firms will be for a particular authorised activity and ancillary activities. This may cause difficulty where a credit institution seeks exemption under 4.5 on the grounds that it is authorised under the Second Banking Directive. The difficulty may arise because it is by no means clear that under the Second Banking Directive (Article 6 and Annex) the authorisation will be for a particular activity or whether it will be more general.

The conduct of business rules and enforcement (Article 7)

In addition to the above obligations, the Directive requires Member States to draw up 'prudential rules' which are to be observed by all investment firms whether or not they have the intention of operating in any other state (Article 9). The rules must require that the firm has sound administrative and accounting procedures, arranges for securities belonging to investors to be kept separately from its own securities and for money belonging to investors to be placed in an account or in accounts which are separate and distinct from the firm's own account. In addition, each firm must be a member of a compensation scheme in force in the home state of the firm. The firms will also be under obligations to supply sufficient information to the home state's authorities to enable them to assess its financial soundness. Each firm must keep adequate records and be subject to rules governing conflicts of interest.

The role of the 'host' state where the activities of the firm are carried on are unspecified save in the 'enforcement' provisions (Article 13). If the host state ascertains that a firm is not complying with the 'legal provisions in force in that Member State which are justified on the grounds of the public good' then the host authority requests the firm to put an end to the situation. If the firm fails to comply, the home state will be informed and is obliged to take the necessary measures to ensure compliance. In the event of these measures failing, the host state may take further action. It seems that all regulatory rules will henceforth be enforceable if they 'are justified on the grounds of the public good'. In a diverse Community it is difficult to see what extent of regulation will be accepted as 'in the public good'. The cumbersome nature of the enforcement procedure may be overcome partly by a provision that 'in exceptional circumstances' a host member state may take measures 'necessary to protect the interests of investors' (Article 13.5). However, this ability is subject to a power in the Commission to decide, after consultation, that the Member State must amend or abolish the emergency powers it has used.

Summary

1 No investment business may be carried on in the UK unless the person conducting the business is an exempt or authorised person under the Financial Services Act 1986.
2 Authorisation is usually obtained through membership of a self-regulatory organisation or a recognised professional body which have the task of overseeing the activities of their members. The SROs and RPBs are in turn overseen by the Securities and Investment Board.
3 The EC Investment Services Directive which seeks to provide firms with a 'passport' permitting them to operate throughout the Community has been implemented in the UK and will assist the establishment of a free market in financial services across Europe.

Exercises

1 The original idea of the structure to regulate the Financial Services market was that there should be self-regulation. Do you think this aim has been achieved?
2 What are the respective responsibilities of the home and host States under the Investment Services Directive?

9   Maintenance of Capital

The principal concern of the law in this area is that the company should get full value for the shares it issues and that having received the money, that money should be kept within the company. Because the members of a company are in control of it, they could make the company transfer all its assets to them. In particular, therefore, money should not be returned to the members of the company, leaving the creditors with an empty shell to rely on when their bills are due to be paid. In this area the original common law rules have, to a considerable extent, been overtaken by statutory rules, many of them introduced by the Companies Acts 1980 and 1981 as a direct result of the European Community's company law harmonisation programme. These rules are now part of the Companies Act 1985 which consolidated a number of previous Companies Acts.

9.1 **Fundamental Rule**

The basic common law rule was that it was illegal for a company to acquire its own shares. The reasoning was that the capital of a company could be discovered by adding up the amounts paid for the shares it had issued. If those shares had been purchased by the company itself, no money in respect of those shares had flowed into the company's coffers. Thus, a creditor would be relying on illusory prosperity if he relied on the value of shares issued when giving credit to the company. The rule was established in the case of *Trevor* v. *Whitworth* (1887) 12 App Cas 409 and is therefore often referred to as the rule in *Trevor* v. *Whitworth*. In that case Lord Watson said: 'It is inconsistent with the essential nature of a company that it should become a member of itself. It cannot be registered as a shareholder to the effect of becoming a debtor to itself for calls. . .'

This passage emphasises the difficulties that would arise if a company were able to buy its own shares. If they were not fully paid for, the company itself would be liable to pay itself money when the 'call' to pay the outstanding amount was made.

However, this 'blanket' prohibition was felt to be too restrictive. Resultant attempts to modify the rules and to define when it is permissible to pay money out to the shareholders have led to a very complex system of rules. We will deal first with the basis on which payment of money to members is permitted, since understanding this will help to make sense of the rules governing prohibited payments.

9.2 **Payment of Money to Members**

One of the difficulties of understanding these rules is that the law tends to treat the capital of a company as a fixed amount kept in a piggy bank. The reality is quite different – the money contributed by the shareholders is used in the business and used to buy a continually changing set of assets. These will go up or down in value. It is unlikely that their value will remain static. Consequently the rules designed to draw a sharp distinction between the capital of a company and profits available for distribution to members is based on a false view of the way companies work. The distinction is particularly false where the company is a small private company and the members are all directors or employees. Payment of such people is not governed by the rules on 'distributions' to members and count as ordinary trading debts. If not otherwise controlled it would be open to the members of such companies to pay the assets of the company to themselves by way of remuneration. If the company has resolved to pay such salaries the court will not usually enquire as to whether such a payment was reasonable, that is, the size of the payment will not normally invalidate it in civil proceedings (see *Re Halt Garage (1964) Ltd* [1982] 3 All ER 1016). However, it has been held that unreasonable payments of this nature can amount to theft of the company's property even when the alleged thieves are the sole owners and directors of the company, see the House of Lords decision in *R.* v. *Gomez* [1992] 3 WLR 1067.

Other controls on such practices are contained in the Insolvency Act 1986. Section 238 of that Act gives a liquidator of a company a power to apply to the court for an order cancelling the effect of a gift of the company's property made in the two years preceding commencement of the winding up, if the company was insolvent (see Chapter 17 for the definition of 'insolvent') at the time of the gift or if the gift made the company insolvent. The provision also applies to a transaction with a person in which the consideration given by the person was significantly less valuable than the consideration provided by the company.

As well as this, large payments to member-directors while the company is struggling have been considered as one reason, with others, for issuing a disqualification order against a director, preventing him from acting as a director. This power is given to the court by the Company Directors Disqualification Act 1986 (see Chapter 11).

9.3 **Distributions**

By far the majority of companies exist to make profits for their shareholders. There must therefore be a system by which those profits can be distributed to the shareholders. As explained above, the law seeks to permit distribution of profits alone, leaving intact a quantity of assets, known as 'capital', which is to be kept in the company as a source to which creditors can look for payment of their bills and, at the end of the company's life, as the fund out of which the shareholders will be repaid the amount they put into the company when they bought their shares. Thus, although the power to distribute money to the shareholders is implied, there need not be a specific clause in the articles permitting a distribution.

The rule is that the distributions of a company should not exceed its realised profits. Capital, which includes amounts held in the share premium and capital redemption reserve must remain intact.

9.4 Rules Governing Distributions

By S. 263(2) of the Companies Act 1985 the statutory rules governing distributions apply to 'every description of distribution of a company's assets to its members, whether in cash or otherwise' with the following exceptions:

(i)   return of capital or distribution of surplus assets on winding up;
(ii) return of capital to members in a properly authorised reduction of capital (including the cancellation or reduction of liability on partly-paid shares);
(iii) the issue of fully or partly-paid bonus shares;
(iv) the purchase or redemption of the company's own shares.

The exceptions will be examined in more detail later. The next step is to examine the rules surrounding the most common method of distribution of profits to the members of a company, which is by paying a dividend to members.

9.5 Dividends

Profits available for the purpose

The company's profits available for this purpose are set out in s. 263(3): 'its accumulated, realised profits, so far as not previously utilised by distribution or capitalisation, less its accumulated, realised losses, so far as not previously written off in a reduction or reorganisation of capital duly made'.

Realised and unrealised profits

The notion of restricting the amount available for distributions to realised profits was introduced into UK law by the Companies Act 1980 in accordance with the provisions of the Fourth Directive. It means that companies must examine their accounts and separate out any amounts that appear which are due to the revaluation of assets. Before this provision came to be in the law it was considered permissible to pay a dividend where assets had increased in value even when that asset had not been sold so that the value had been 'realised'. Realisation means turning an asset into cash. The realised profits of a company for a financial year is the profit on its sales of assets – that is, the amount by which income from the sale of its assets exceed associated expenses. An unrealised profit will occur when assets have risen in value: when, for example, the buildings owned by the company have increased in value, but those buildings have not been sold. Similarly a realised loss occurs when expenses associated with sales for a particular year exceed revenue derived from those sales, while an unrealised loss will occur where assets fall in value but they have not yet been sold at a loss. As a general rule expenses must be recorded in accounts when they are incurred, not when they are actually paid for. Similarly, income from sales of goods or supply of services must generally be recorded at the time of sale or supply rather than when the money is actually received, provided that there is an amount fixed at that time and provided also that there is a reasonable possibility of eventual collection of the debt (Companies Act 1985 Schedule 4, para. 13).

At the end of the year some money appearing in the income side of the accounts will not have been received by the company. These bad debts must be reflected in the accounts. This is done by calculating the percentage of the total trade debts which the company's past experience shows will not be paid. In a new concern, the pattern of business in the industry would provide first estimates. By s. 275(1) this provision for bad debts is deemed to be a realised loss.

Realised and unrealised losses

If a company is about to incur a future liability which cannot be precisely quantified it can set aside a fund called a 'provision' (Companies Act 1985 Schedule 4, para. 89), which will contain an amount estimated to be sufficient to cover the future liability. This liability has not yet been incurred so that it is not a 'realised' loss. However, s. 275(1) requires such a fund to be treated as a realised loss, thus preventing the company from counting the assets in the fund from being available for a distribution to the members.

Accumulation

There is now a rule that the losses of previous years must be made good before assets can be considered as available for distribution. This reverses the common law rule whereby losses in previous years could be ignored (s. 263(3) Companies Act 1985).

9.6 Public Companies

As well as the restrictions discussed above, public companies are subject to the further restrictions contained in s. 264 of the Companies Act 1985. By that section a distribution may not exceed the amount arrived at by the application of the formula: 'net assets less (the called up share capital plus the undistributable reserves)'. The undistributable reserves are:

(a) the share premium account: this contains any amount paid for a
     share over and above its par or face value;

(b)   the capital redemption reserve: this contains an amount equivalent to the value of shares legally redeemed (see below);
(c)   accumulated unrealised profits less accumulated unrealised losses; and
(d)   any other reserve which the company is forbidden to distribute under its memorandum and articles.

One of the important differences between public and private companies is contained in this formula, in that a public company must write off its unrealised losses against realised and unrealised profits before it can make a distribution out of the balance of its realised profits. A private company need not do this.

9.7 Members' Liability

Section 277(1) makes a member liable to repay a distribution he has received if, at the time of the distribution, he knew or had reasonable grounds for knowing, that it was being paid in contravention of the Act.

9.8 Other Permitted Payments to Members

We saw earlier that the rules concerning distributions do not apply to certain other payments to members. These are (s. 263(2) Companies Act 1985):

(a)   return of capital or distribution of surplus assets on winding up;
(b)   return of capital to members in a properly authorised reduction of capital (including the cancellation or reduction of liability on partly-paid shares);
(c)   issue of fully or partly-paid bonus shares;
(d)   purchase or redemption of the company's own shares.

The return of capital and assets on a winding up are covered by rules explained in Chapter 17. The rules relating to the other types of payment out are discussed below.

9.9 Reductions of Capital

The provisions regarding the reduction of capital are set out in ss. 135–141 of the Companies Act 1985. The reduction of a company's capital was traditionally regarded as a matter to be strictly controlled since it reduced the fund available for creditors.

Reduction by special resolution and confirmation by the court

Section 135 of the Companies Act 1985 provides that a company may reduce its share capital 'in any way' provided:

(a)   authorisation for the reduction is contained in the articles;
(b)   the company passes a special resolution to reduce its capital;
(c)   the court confirms the reduction.

Section 135(2) sets out particular situations where the power may be used. They are: to reduce members' liability to pay uncalled capital or to reflect a diminution of the company's assets. In a private company, a reduction of capital and the return of capital to a member or members may be necessary when a company changes hands on the death or retirement of a person who was chiefly concerned in the running of the business. Until 1981 this could only be done by special resolution and confirmation by the court. Now private companies in particular have other choices (see pp. 116–17). In *Carruth* v. *Imperial Chemical Industries Ltd* [1937] AC 707 it was held that it was proper to reduce the nominal value of one class of the company's shares so as to reflect the low price at which they were traded on the Stock Exchange.

Confirmation by the court

The court has refused to determine whether a reduction of capital is commercially sensible. However, the court will attempt to ensure that the reduction is not unfair. In *British and American Trustee and Finance Corporation Ltd* v. *Couper* [1894] AC 229, Lord Herschell LC said: 'There can be no doubt that any scheme which does not provide for uniform treatment of shareholders whose rights are similar, would be most narrowly scrutinised by the Court, and that no such scheme ought to be confirmed unless the Court be satisfied that it will not work unjustly or inequitably'.

In that case, the court had already ascertained that no interests of creditors would be affected by the reduction. It is clear, then, that two important considerations which will influence the court when deciding whether to sanction a reduction are:

(i)   whether and to what extent the interests of creditors will be affected, and;
(ii)   whether the reduction deals with different classes of shareholders fairly and equitably.

A third consideration referred to by the House of Lords judges in *Ex Parte Westburn Sugar Refiners Ltd* [1951] AC 625 was 'the public interest'. This was not very clearly defined but the concern seems to have been to ensure that sufficient capital was retained in the company to safeguard the interests of those 'who may in future form connections with the company as creditors or shareholders'. Political considerations such as whether the reduction was in response to and likely to defeat the purpose behind nationalisation of an industry were held to be irrelevant. It seems, then, that in this case a vague third requirement applied:

(iii) that the reduction should not be contrary to the public interest.

The validity of this consideration was doubted by Harman J, in *Re Jupiter House Investments (Cambridge) Ltd* [1985] BCLC 222, who considered it of more importance that:

(iv) the causes of the reduction should have been properly put to shareholders so that they were able to exercise an informed choice and that the reason for the reduction is supported by evidence before the court.

Despite these requirements it has been held that it is permissible to carry out a reduction of capital by extinguishing entirely a class of members. This was done in *British and American Trustee & Finance Corporation Ltd & reduced* v. *Couper* [1894] AC 229 and in *Re Saltdean Estate Co. Ltd* [1968] 1 WLR 1844. In *Re Saltdean Estate Co. Ltd* the company's preference shareholders were eliminated by returning the capital paid by them plus a premium of 50 per cent. It was further held in that case that the expulsion of the preference shareholders did not amount to a variation of their rights. In these circumstances 'variation' of rights is a very technical concept (explained in Chapter 14). Where a reduction of capital *does* involve a variation of the rights of one or more classes of shareholders, the special procedures explained in Chapter 14 must be followed as well as the s. 135 approval by the court of the reduction of capital.

9.10 **Interests of Creditors**

The Companies Act 1985 provides a special procedure where the interests of creditors are likely to be adversely affected by a reduction of capital. If the reduction involves either a diminution of a member's liability to pay future calls on shares or repayment of capital to members the special procedure comes into operation, subject to a discretion which the court has to dispense with it (s. 136(2) and s. 137(1), discretion s. 136(6)). By s. 136(2) the court may direct that this special procedure should be adopted in the case of any other type of reduction, but it was held in *Re Meux's Brewery Co. Ltd* [1919] 1 Ch 28 that where a company is not parting with a means of paying its creditors, the creditors must show a very strong reason why they should be heard in objection to the company's petition seeking approval for the reduction.

The special procedure involves drawing up a list of the creditors of the company. Section 141 makes it an offence to conceal the company's creditors or misrepresent their claims. The creditors that must be included are those who could prove for their claims if the company went into liquidation as at a date fixed by the court. The court may make an order confirming the reduction only when it is satisfied that every creditor on the list has either been paid in full or has positively consented to the reduction (s. 137(1)). The court may dispense with the consent of a creditor if it is satisfied that the company has made provision for paying him. In the case of a disputed claim the court must be satisfied that adequate provision has been made (s. 136(5)). Any creditor on the list is entitled to be heard by the court in opposition to the proposed reduction.

9.11 **Procedure**

If the court sanctions the reduction, the order approving the reduction must be registered with the Registrar. The reduction does not take effect until the registration has been carried out. The Registrar then certifies the registration and his certificate is conclusive evidence that all the requirements of the Act have been complied with (s. 138(4)).

9.12 **Bonus Shares**

These are shares which are issued with the value paid out of the profits of the company. Because they are wholly paid for by the company (ss.130(2) and 170(4) Companies Act 1985) rather than the member, and yet they confer a right on the member to participate in a shareout of capital in the event of the liquidation of the company, they represent a transfer of capital from the company to the member. This transfer would be prohibited by the rule against return of capital to members were it not permitted by the Companies Act 1985. Bonus shares are allotted to existing members of a company. Unless the articles of association of the particular company exclude the relevant provisions of Table A, Article 110 of Table A will govern a bonus share issue. This Article provides that the number of bonus shares to be allotted to a particular member is to be determined in the same way as his entitlement to dividend, that is, the number of bonus shares received by each member should be in proportion to the number of shares he holds, for example one bonus share for every ten shares held. A decision to issue bonus shares paid for by capital (a capitalisation issue) is to be taken by the directors on the authority of an ordinary resolution of its members.

9.13 **Redeemable Shares and Forfeiture of Shares**

The final permitted methods of the transfer of capital from the company to its members are by way of redeemable shares and the forfeiture of shares.

Redeemable shares

By s. 159 of the Companies Act 1985 a company may issue shares which are redeemable. (This power will be subject to further restrictions if and when s. 133 CA 1989 is brought into force; it will introduce new s. 159A into CA 1985.) This is permitted if authorisation for such a class of shares is contained in the articles. The company's articles must specify the date on or by which the shares are to be redeemed or may provide that the timing is to be determined by the directors, in which case it must be fixed by the directors before the redeemable shares are issued (s. 159A(2) CA 1985). The terms of redemption must provide for payment on redemption (s. 159(3)). The articles must specify the amount payable on redemption or provide a method of determining that amount. The method must not make reference to any person's discretion or opinion. When the temporary membership of the company conferred as a result of issue of these shares comes to an end the shares are cancelled and the nominal value of the shares is repaid to the member. Sometimes a redemption bonus will be paid as well as the nominal value of the shares.

Implications for the capital of the company

Normally the company is obliged to maintain a fund which must not be diminished by the repayment of redeemable shares. The repayment to a member on the redemption of a redeemable share will not represent a reduction of this core capital fund. This is always the case for a public company which can only redeem redeemable shares out of profits or the proceeds of a further issue of shares. However, a private company can, by adopting the procedure set out in the Act, redeem shares out of existing capital. The members of a private company may adopt a special resolution to enable its shares to be redeemed without the capital accounts being increased in exact proportion to the payments out. This could be of great value to a private company, particularly where the head of a small company was hoping to take his capital out of the company and retire. However, the legislature has hedged about the ability to reduce capital in this way with so many restrictions that the procedure is not as valuable as it otherwise could be.

Only a fully paid up share may be redeemed (s. 159(3) Companies Act 1985). When a redeemable share is redeemed it must be cancelled. The nominal value of the share is deducted from the share capital account. In a public company this reduction would be compensated by the transfer from the profit and loss account of an amount equivalent to the amount written off the share capital account. An alternative would be to issue new shares. However, the members of a *private* company may use the redemption of shares to reduce capital by adopting a resolution not to make up the amount in this way. There is a limit set to the extent to which a reduction in this way may be made. The amount set is called the 'permissible capital payment' (s. 171(3) Companies Act 1985). This is calculated so that a company must transfer the proceeds of new issues of shares and all distributable profits to the capital account which is to be reduced.

A resolution to redeem shares by a payment out of capital must be adopted between five and seven weeks before the payment is to be made (s. 174(1)). The persons holding the shares proposed for redemption may not vote in favour of the resolution to redeem the shares. Not more than a week before a resolution to make a payment out of capital is adopted by a company, the directors must make a statutory declaration of the size of the permissible capital payment (s. 173 Companies Act 1985). The directors' declaration must state:

(a)   that the company will be able to pay its other debts immediately after the redemption is made; and
(b)   the company will continue in business for the whole of the year following the redemption and for the whole of that year will be able to pay its debts.

A director who makes such a declaration without reasonable grounds for the opinion expressed in the declaration will be liable to a criminal penalty (s. 173(6) Companies Act 1985). If the company goes into insolvent liquidation within a year of making a redemption out of capital, the member whose shares were redeemed and the directors who made the declaration are liable to repay the amount paid out of capital in so far as this is necessary to pay the company's debts. There are extensive provisions requiring an auditor's report and requiring publicity of the redemption. Indeed these are so extensive that it prompted Dr Sealy to call for the replacement of the twenty sections involved with the single section used to achieve the same result in Canada (see L. S. Sealy, *Company Law and Commercial Reality* (Sweet and Maxwell, 1986)).

9.14 Purchase of Own Shares

Having seen at the outset of this chapter that there was a general rule which prohibits the purchase by a company of its own shares we now have to look at the exceptions which statutes have made to this rule. These exceptions are now so wide that it could be said that there is a general rule that a company *may* purchase its own shares, it is in the exceptional case that this manoeuvre is forbidden. However, although there are many situations in which it is permissible to purchase own shares, the correct procedure must be followed otherwise the purchase will be illegal. The strictness of the rules, and the prohibition of using this method to reduce the capital of a *public* company supports the traditional view that the general prohibition still stands, it is in exceptional cases that such a purchase is permitted.

The general scheme is much like the redeemable shares option. The articles of association of a company may contain a provision permitting the company to purchase its own shares (s. 162(1) Companies Act 1985). A standard authorisation appears at article 35 of Table A. The terms of each purchase must be approved by members. Authorisation given to a *public* company will not be valid for more than eighteen months. At the end of this time it must be renewed (s. 164(4) and s. 166(4) Companies Act 1985).

Shares must not be purchased unless they are fully paid for. This means that a company cannot buy its own shares when they are first issued. There are different detailed procedures for authorising the purchase depending on whether the shares are to be bought through the Stock Exchange or be private deals with known sellers (ss.164 and 166 Companies Act 1985). After the purchase has been made the reduction in the capital account must be made good (as for redeemable shares) by transfer of amounts from distributable profits or from capital raised by a new issue of shares.

9.15 Permitted Reductions of Capital

So far, this chapter has dealt with the circumstances in which a company can reduce its capital by redemption or purchase of shares, by the issue of bonus shares or by a reduction sanctioned by the court. It is notable that all these options are subject to strict control and that a *public* company cannot use purchase of its own shares or redemption of shares in order to reduce its capital – any capital lost that way must be made up by transfer of money to the capital account from distributable profits.

Other occasions on which a company can acquire its own shares are:

(a)   In pursuit of an employee share scheme (see Chapter 1) and
(b)   Where shares are surrendered or forfeited.
(c)   By gift.

The forfeiture or surrender of shares can be part of a reduction of capital scheme which is carried out under s. 135 and confirmed by the court. Without such confirmation shares may be forfeited only for non-payment of calls provided. The forfeiture must be done in accordance with an express power in the articles (*Lane's Case* (1862) 1 De GJ & Sm 504). In cases where a forfeiture could occur the shares may be validly surrendered (*Trevor* v. *Whitworth* (1887) 12 App Cas 409 at 417).

9.16 Reissue

If the company has power in its articles to reissue forfeited shares (standard clause Table A, Article 20) it may do so and may treat the share as partly paid up to the extent of the capital the company has received already in respect of the shares.

9.17 Public Companies

Shares in public companies that have been the subject of forfeiture or surrender must be disposed of within three years or cancelled (s. 146 Companies Act 1985).

9.18 **Illegal Transactions**

The procedures discussed in this chapter so far are the legal methods by which a company can come to own its own shares. We now have to consider transactions which fall on the other side of the line and are prohibited.

Financial assistance for the purchase of shares

Section 143 Companies Act 1985 prohibits a company from acquiring its own shares for a valuable consideration. This general rule applies to all circumstances other than those discussed above. This puts into statutory form the rule in *Trevor* v. *Whitworth* discussed at the beginning of this chapter. Any acquisition of shares in contravention of this rule is void, that is, it is taken as having never happened. A company which acquires its own shares is liable for an unlimited fine. Any officer of the company who knowingly and wilfully authorised or permitted the acquisition commits a criminal offence.

This rule is straightforward, although it must be remembered that acquisitions which are attempted incorrectly under one of the complicated provisions discussed above will fall into this category of prohibited transactions. Complications are rife when the logical extension of the rule is examined. This prohibits a company from providing financial assistance for the purchase of shares. Section 151 forbids two categories of behaviour:

(i)   Where a person is acquiring or proposing to acquire any shares in a company, it is unlawful for the company or any of its subsidiaries to give financial assistance directly or indirectly for the purpose of that acquisition, before or at the same time as the acquisition of the shares take place.

(ii) Where a person has acquired any shares in a company and has put himself or any other person in any way in debt in respect of that acquisition, it is unlawful for the company or any of its subsidiaries to give any financial assistance directly or indirectly for the purpose of reducing or discharging the liability incurred.

In an attempt to spread the net as widely as possible the reference to a person incurring any financial liability is further defined in s. 152(3)(a). It includes the case of a person changing his financial position by making any agreement or arrangement (whether enforceable or unenforceable and whether made on his own account or with any other person) or by any other means. This is an attempt to prevent evasion of the prohibition in s. 151 by means of informal arrangements. The problem with this approach is that such arrangements are difficult to prove. Proof that they existed to evade s. 151 is likely to depend on circumstantial evidence and the arrangements involved can be very complex. Financial assistance is defined by s. 152(1) and includes the widest imaginable range of transactions.

One problem that the courts have encountered concerns the involvement of the company in the illegal transaction. It is a general principle of English law that a plaintiff must not base a claim for compensation on an illegal act in which he was involved. 'No person should profit from his own wrong'. In the case of illegal payments being made out of company funds for the purchase of shares in that company, the company, as a separate legal person, is in law involved. The rules could therefore lead to the conclusion that the company (which in fact was the victim of this transaction) could not recover compensation because in law it was a party to the wrongful transaction. This difficulty was solved in the case of *Selangor United Rubber Estates* v. *Craddock* [1968] 1 WLR 1555. In that case, Craddock made a bid for the shares of the plaintiff company. The bid was made through an agent. Craddock got the money from a bank. Money from the plaintiff company was then transferred to the bank and lent to Craddock, who used it to repay the bank. The company claimed to recover the money from Craddock, claiming that because he had wrongfully been in possession of money which in fact belonged to the company, he held that money on trust for the company. Between themselves, that would make Craddock a trustee and the company the person entitled to benefit, 'the beneficiary', who could call for payment of the money in trust at any time. Ungoed Thomas J said:

'I appreciate that, in the ordinary case of a claim by a beneficiary against a trustee for an illegal breach of trust, the beneficiary is not a party to the illegality; but that, when directors act for a company in an illegal act with a stranger [in this case Craddock], the company is itself a party to the transaction and therefore the illegality. The company, therefore, could not rely on the transaction as "the source of civil rights" and, therefore, for example, it could not successfully sue the stranger with regard to rights which it was claimed the transaction conferred. . . The plaintiff's claim, however, for breach of trust is not made by it as a party to that transaction, or in reliance on any right which that transaction is alleged to confer, but against the directors and constructive trustees for perpetrating that transaction and making the plaintiff company party to it in breach of trust owing to the plaintiff company.'

The essence of the passage is that the company, being more sinned against than sinning, can recover the money. The wrong has been done to the company by its directors and their cronies and not by the company, even though it was perforce a party to the illegal transaction.

The major difficulty in this area is not so much the legal problems involved as the immense complexity of the arrangements that must be unravelled to discover if they contravene the section. In *Belmont Finance Corporation* v. *Williams Furniture Ltd (No. 2)* [1980] 1 All ER 393, the Court of Appeal accepted previous authority to the effect that a purchase of property at an inflated price in order to put the seller in funds to buy shares would contravene the predecessor section to s. 151. In the *Belmont* case itself, the judgments went further. Buckley LJ accepted that both parties to the transaction in question had honestly believed that they were entering into commercial transactions in which they were getting value for money. However, he went on to say:

'but it was certainly not a transaction in the ordinary course of Belmont's business or for the purposes of that business as it subsisted at the date of the agreement. It was an exceptional and artificial transaction and not in any sense an ordinary commercial transaction entered into for its own sake in the commercial interests of Belmont. It was part of a comparatively complex scheme for enabling Mr Grosscurth and his associates to acquire Belmont at no cash cost to themselves.'

The transaction was therefore caught by the prohibition against providing assistance even though both parties believed that it was a transaction for full value. It was significant to Buckley LJ that: 'It was not a transaction whereby Belmont acquired anything which Belmont genuinely needed or wanted for its own purposes.'

This decision was difficult to apply to complex transactions since the legality of those transactions depended wholly on whether the property which one party believed was being bought or sold was in the judgment of the court something which the company would have found of equal value if the share deal had not been related.

The section of the 1948 Companies Act (s. 54) under which the above cases were decided was repealed by the Companies Act 1981 and replaced by the present s. 151 of the Companies Act 1985. Section 153 of the Companies Act 1985 seeks to exempt transactions such as that in *Belmont* from the ambit of the section. Section 153(1) exempts from the ambit of the prohibition in s. 151 transactions which in fact give assistance if:

(a) the company's principal purpose in giving that assistance is not to give it for the purpose of any such acquisition, or the giving of the assistance for that purpose is but an incidental part of some larger purpose of the company, and

(b) the assistance is given in good faith in the interests of the company.

This provision was discussed at length in *Brady* v. *Brady* [1988] 2 All ER 617. That case arose from a complicated scheme to divide a business between two brothers who were unable to agree to work together amicably. Because the businesses had assets of unequal value, some complicated moves were made in order to achieve a fair distribution between the two brothers of the assets of what had been a family firm. In the course of this a transaction occurred which undoubtedly resulted in the original company (Brady) giving assistance to one of the new companies, Motoreal Ltd. in the acquisition by Motoreal of the shares in Brady. It was admitted that the assistance had been given but it was argued that the transaction was saved by the exceptions set out in s. 153.

Lord Oliver found that the first part of s. 153 could not apply. In this case the sole purpose and therefore the principal purpose of the assistance had been to enable the acquisition of shares. Consequently the company could not come within the 'principal purpose' exception. The company could only escape if it could show that the assistance was part of 'some larger purpose' of the company and that it had been given in good faith and in the interests of the company. Lord Oliver confessed that he found the concept of 'larger purpose' difficult to grasp but was anxious not to give it too wide a meaning as this would enable wholesale evasion of the rule in s. 151. He went on to say:

> 'there has always to be borne in mind the mischief against which s. 151 is aimed. In particular, if the section is not, effectively, to be deprived of any useful application, it is important to distinguish between a purpose and the reason why a purpose is formed. The ultimate reason for forming the purpose of financing an acquisition may, and in most cases probably will, be more important to those making the decision than the immediate transaction itself. But "larger" is not the same thing as "more important" nor is "reason" the same as "purpose". If one postulates the case of a bidder for control of a public company financing his bid from the company's own funds – the obvious mischief at which the section is aimed – the immediate purpose which it is sought to achieve is that of completing the purchase and vesting control of the company in the bidder. The reasons why that course is considered desirable may be many and varied. The company may have fallen on hard times so that a change of management is considered necessary to avert disaster. It may merely be thought, and no doubt would be thought by the purchaser and the directors whom he nominates once he has control, that the business of the company will be more profitable under his management than it was heretofore. These may be excellent reasons but they cannot, in my judgment, constitute a "larger purpose" of which the provision of assistance is merely an incident. The purpose and the only purpose of the financial assistance is and remains that of enabling the shares to be acquired and the financial or commercial advantages flowing from the acquisition, whilst they may form the reason for forming the purpose of providing the assistance are a by-product of it rather than an independent purpose of which the assistance can properly be considered to be an incident.'

The problem with this approach is that in seeking to avoid a construction which would permit wholesale evasion of the prohibition in s. 151, such a narrow view of the exception has been taken that it is difficult to envisage a deliberate scheme which would escape prohibition. If the financial assistance were provided by accident it might perhaps escape, but that seems an unlikely scenario. So long as the provision of assistance is deliberately with a view to the purchase of shares it will have been given for that 'purpose' according to Lord Oliver's formulation. The reason driving the whole arrangement would not be regarded as a larger purpose.

In *Brady* the scheme was held to have contravened s. 151 but was saved by virtue of the fact that it could be validly carried out under ss. 155, 156 and 158. A fairly liberal approach to construction seems to have been adopted in *Acatos* v. *Hutcheson plc* v. *Watson* [1994]1 BCLC 218 where the court held that the purchase of another company whose sole asset was a substantial holding of shares in the first company was not precluded by the rules against a company acquiring its own shares.

Exceptions

In this chapter we have already examined some of the exceptions to the rule in some detail. A complete list may, however, be of value. Section 153(3) Companies Act 1985 contains a list of transactions wholly outside the operation of s. 151. They are:

(a) A distribution of a company's assets by way of a dividend lawfully made including a distribution made in the course of winding up the company.

(b) The allotment of bonus shares.

(c) Any reduction of capital made under s. 135 and confirmed under s. 137 by the court.

(d) A redemption or purchase of any shares made in accordance with the relevant sections of the Act.

(e) Anything done by way of a court-approved reconstruction under s. 425 (see Chapter 16).

(f) Anything done under an arrangement made in pursuance of s. 110 of the Insolvency Act 1986, that is a reconstruction linked to a voluntary winding up (see Chapter 17).

(g) Anything done under an arrangement made between a company and its creditors which is binding on the creditors by virtue of Part I of the Insolvency Act 1986 (see Chapter 17).

More exceptions appear in s. 153(4) but a public company is only permitted to take advantage of these if the transaction does not reduce the company's net assets, or if it does so, then the assistance is provided out of distributable profits.

Three exceptions concern employee share schemes (see Chapter 1). The other exempts the lending of money in the ordinary course of its business by a company whose ordinary business includes moneylending.

Exemptions from s. 151 for private companies

There are further exceptions to the rule available only to private companies.

Private companies are permitted to provide financial assistance for their shares provided that they comply with the conditions in ss. 155–158

Companies Act 1985. These sections require that either the net assets of the company will not be reduced by the giving of the assistance (see *Parlett* v. *Guppys* (*Bridport Ltd and others* [1993] 1 BCLC 35), or that the assistance is provided out of distributable profits. There must be a special resolution of the company and the directors must make a statutory declaration that the company will, in their opinion, be able to pay its debts immediately after the assistance is given and that either (i) it will be able to pay its debts as they fall due during the year immediately following the giving of the assistance, or (ii) if it is intended to commence the winding up of the company within a year from the giving of the assistance, that the company will be able to pay its debts in full within a year of the commencement of the winding up.

Penalties
A criminal penalty attaches to contraventions of s. 151. In addition to the fine which may be levied on a company, if convicted, an officer of the company will be liable to a maximum of two years in prison (see s. 151(3) and Schedule 24).

Membership of holding companies

Section 23 Companies Act 1985 reinforces the rule that a company may not purchase its own shares. This section provides that a company may not be a member (or have its nominee as a member) of its holding company. It also makes void any allotment or transfer of shares in a company to its subsidiary (or nominee). This prevents ownership in cases where a true holding/subsidiary relationship exists (see Chapter 1).

9.19 **Serious Loss of Capital by a Public Company**

Section 142 Companies Act contains a measure first introduced into UK law as a supposed implementation of the EC Second Directive on company law. The Directive requires a meeting to be convened in the circumstances set out in s. 142 'to consider whether the company ought to be wound up or any other measures taken'. Curiously, the implementing provision has left out the reference to the main purpose of the meeting so that s. 142 requires that where the net assets of a public company are half or less than the amount of the company's called-up share capital, the directors of a company must convene an extraordinary meeting of the company to consider whether any, and if so, what, measures should be taken to deal with the situation. The meeting must be convened not less than twenty-eight days after the day on which a director learns that the company has lost capital to this extent. It must take place within fifty-six days of that date. The section is silent as to what happens if the meeting decides to do nothing. The section seems to have no other purpose than notifying the shareholders of the situation. Criminal sanctions attach to the failure of a director to call the meeting but no civil consequences flow from contravention of the section.

9.20 Accounts

The amount that a company has available for distribution must in principle be determined from its most recent accounts that have been laid before a general meeting. The directors must state in the balance sheet the total amount they recommend should be distributed as dividend (Companies Act 1985 Schedule 4, para. 51(3)). This will only happen after consideration of accounts drawn up according to strict rules.

9.21 Company Accounts

It is a fundamental principle of UK company law that annual accounts should be provided and circulated to members. The accounts are useful for members so that they can judge the state of the enterprise in which they have invested, and assess the performance of its directors. It may also be useful to creditors seeking reassurance that their debts will be paid.

Much legislative energy has been expended in attempting to compel companies to paint as accurate a picture as possible in their accounts. It is now a fundamental principle that, overall, the accounts must give a 'true and fair view' of the economic state of the company. A major difficulty is the valuation of the fixed assets of a company. If the value that is entered into the accounts is the value at the time of acquisition this could have been radically altered by inflation over a number of years. On the other hand, if a current valuation is entered, this will vary according to the method used in arriving at the valuation and also according to whether the asset is valued at the sum it would raise if sold, or valued as part of the company as a going concern.

9.22 FRSs and FREDs

The Accounting Standards Board is a body which issues documents called Financial Reporting Standards (FRSs) with the object of working towards a uniform approach to problems of providing a true and fair view of a company's financial state. The first consultation drafts are called Financial Reporting Exposure Drafts (FREDs). The final standards have a legal effect in that they may be considered by courts as providing a standard method of preparing accounts. Any departure from the standard will require explanation before the court will accept that the accounts in question have been properly drawn up.

Companies listed on the Stock Exchange must comply with FRS requirements (Admission of Securities to Listing (continuing obligations for companies) Ch. 5, para. 21(a)).

9.23 **The Obligation to Prepare Accounts**

The Companies Act 1989 Part I amended the law concerning company accounts. It inserted into the Companies Act 1985 new ss. 221–262, amended Schedule 4 and inserted new Schedule 4A.

New s. 221 provides:

'(1) Every company shall keep accounting records which are sufficient to show and explain the company's transactions and are such as to–
   (a) disclose with reasonable accuracy, at any time, the financial position of the company at that time, and
   (b) enable the directors to ensure that any balance sheet and profit and loss account prepared under this Part complies with the requirements of this Act.
(2) The accounting records shall in particular contain–
   (a) entries from day to day of all sums of money received and expended by the company, and the matters in respect of which the receipt and expenditure takes place
   (b) a record of the assets and liabilities of the company.'

The section also provides that a company dealing in goods must keep records of stock.

9.24 **Keeping the Records**

By new s. 222 the accounting records must be kept at a company's registered office or 'such other place as the directors think fit'. There are safeguards which require records to be available in the UK. The records must be open to inspection by the company's officers at all times. Private companies must keep their records for three years from the date at which they are made; public companies for six years.

9.25 **Accounting Reference Date**

By new s. 224(2) a company may, up to nine months after its incorporation, register an accounting reference date with the Registrar of Companies. If it does not do so the accounting reference dates will be

(i)   in the case of a company incorporated before the commencement of s. 3 Companies Act 1989, the 31st March;
(ii) in the case of a company incorporated after the commencement of that section, the last day of the month in which the anniversary of its incorporation falls.

The 'financial year' is calculated by reference to the accounting reference date, so that the annual accounts are prepared to cover the year before an accounting reference date.

9.26 **Duty to Prepare Individual Company Accounts**

Key sections in the statute are new ss. 226 and 227 Companies Act 1985. Section 226 requires the directors of every company to prepare for each financial year a balance sheet and profit and loss account. These 'annual accounts' are required 'to give a true and fair view of the state of affairs of the company as at the end of the financial year and a true and fair view of the profit or loss of the company for the financial year'. Individual company accounts must comply with Schedule 4 of Companies Act 1985 as amended by Schedule 1 of Companies Act 1989.

9.27 **Group Accounts**

Where companies are operating together, a fairer picture of the financial health of the enterprise as a whole will be given by 'consolidated' or 'group' accounts. Accordingly, new s. 227 Companies Act 1985 provides that if at the end of a financial year a company is a parent company, the directors have an additional duty to prepare group accounts, which must give a true and fair view of the state of affairs of the parent and its subsidiaries at the end of the year and also a true and fair view of the profit and loss of the undertakings included in the consolidation during that year. These accounts must comply with Schedule 4A which is inserted into CA 1985 by Companies Act 1989.

Considerable difficulty has been experienced in devising a law which adequately requires consolidation of accounts. The problem is partly one of devising a satisfactory definition of parent and subsidiary. The difficulties inherent in the old definition of the parent–subsidiary relationship were explained in Chapter 1. By new s. 258 Companies Act 1985 the following definition of the relationship applies for accounting purposes:

'(2) An undertaking is a parent undertaking in relation to another undertaking, a subsidiary undertaking, if–
(a) it holds a majority of the voting rights in the undertaking, or
(b) it is a member of the undertaking and has the right to appoint or remove a majority of the board of directors, or
(c) it has the right to exercise a dominant influence over the undertaking–
(i) by virtue of provisions contained in the undertaking's memorandum or articles, or
(ii) by virtue of a control contract, or
(d) it is a member of the undertaking and controls alone, pursuant to an agreement with other shareholders or members, a majority of the voting rights in the undertaking . . .

(4) An undertaking is also a parent undertaking in relation to another undertaking, a subsidiary undertaking, if it has a participating interest in the undertaking and–

(a) it actually exercises a dominant influence over it, or

(b) it and the subsidiary are managed on a unified basis.'

A 'participating interest' is defined by s. 260. It means an interest held on a long-term basis for the purposes of exercising influence or control, that is, other than for investment purposes. A holding of 20 per cent or more is presumed to be a participating influence unless the contrary is shown. This definition, particularly the references to 'dominant influence' are wider than the definition of the same relationship which is used for all other purposes (see Chapter 1 and s. 736 and s. 736A Companies Act 1985).

The company's auditors must have reported on the accounts (Companies Act 1985, s. 236) before a distribution can lawfully be made. By s. s 271(3) and (4), if the report of the auditors contains any qualification concerning the way in which profits, losses, assets, liabilities, provisions, share capital or reserves have been dealt with in the accounts they must state whether or not, in their opinion, the legality of the proposed distribution would be affected by the matters stated in the qualification. Their statement on this point must be presented to the members with the accounts.

An alternative justification for a distribution is on the basis of interim accounts more recent than the last annual accounts available. In the case of a private company no rules concerning the method of preparation of those accounts appear in the statute. So far as public companies are concerned, such interim accounts must be prepared as nearly as possible in the manner in which annual accounts are prepared. No auditor's report is required but such accounts must be filed with the Registrar (s. 272(4) Companies Act 1985). At the beginning of a company's life a distribution can be justified on the basis of initial accounts (s. 270(4) Companies Act 1985) to which the same conditions apply as for interim accounts save that in the case of a public company an auditor's report is required (s. 273 Companies Act 1985).

9.28 Conclusion

We have seen the immensely elaborate attempts that the law makes in order to try and preserve a fund in order to protect the interests of creditors. The necessity for such an elaborate scheme must be a matter of some doubt, particularly in view of the extent of director's duties which would also prohibit unreasonable use of capital. For a discussion of this area of law see M. J. Sterling 'Financial assistance by a company for the purchase of its shares' (1987) 8 CO law 99 and note that the reform of this area of the law is under active discussion. However, the United Kingdom has limited room for reform as it is obliged to conform with its obligations under the second EC Directive (see Chapter 18). These obligations include a duty to prohibit the purchase by a company of its own shares and the provision of financial assistance for such a purchase.

Summary

1 The law seeks to ensure that companies get full value for their shares and that a fund of money remains in the company so that creditors have something to rely on.

2 A basic rule is that a company cannot acquire its own shares. This is subject to a number of exceptions.

3 Money may be returned to members by way of an authorised distribution.

4 Dividends are paid out of profits available for the purpose.

5 If a company wishes to reduce its capital it must comply with strict controls.

6 In very restricted circumstances redeemable shares may be issued and a company permitted to purchase its own shares.

7 The rules about maintenance of capital are reinforced by the rule that a company may not provide financial assistance for the purchase of its own shares. This rule is also subject to exceptions.

Exercises

1 Are the above rules instrumental in ensuring a fund is available for creditors of the company?

2 Are the rules unnecessarily complicated?

3 Are there more exceptions than rules in this area?

10 The Balance of Power Inside the Company: Corporate Governance

A great deal has been written recently about 'corporate governance'. The debate ranges over many of the issues covered in the book because it concerns all issues about the best way to run a company. So people have been debating what is the best model of company to adopt (see Chapters 1 and 2), the best way to control directors, (see Chapter 11), whether or not EC dual board pattern should be adopted (see Chapter 18) and whether and to what extent the company owes 'social duties' to employees, the environment and the state generally. one of the issues is the proper balance of power between the factions within the company structure, and it is this issue which concerns us throughout this chapter. In it we examine some situations where the balance of power in a company is determined by the law and practice surrounding the procedures by which a company is managed. Many things may influence this balance, including matters not immediately governing the relationships between the various factions. For example, fears have been expressed that the new system of electronic transmission of shares operated by the Stock Exchange (CREST) will diminish the already small influence of the small investor by exacerbating the tendency to apathy. This is because most small investors will have to join with others and nominate someone to deal with the shares for them when asked to do so. A side-effect of this is that information from the company will only be sent directly to the investor if it is specifically requested. It is felt that this distancing can only decrease any sense of involvement by the small investor in the affairs of the company.

Theoretically, the general meeting of the body of shareholders has considerable power to make decisions which affect the management of the company by using the vote attached to their shares. This apparently independent power is subject to a number of practical qualifications. Others will appear throughout the chapter. First, a qualification of considerable importance is the right of shareholders to appoint a proxy.

10.1 Proxy Voting

Section 372(1) Companies Act 1985 confers a right on a shareholder to appoint a proxy to attend meetings and vote instead of him at those meetings. The proxy need not be a member. In the case of a private company the proxy has the same right to speak at the meeting as the member would have had. The articles of association will normally have regulations governing the form in which proxies may be made (see the sample form of proxy set out on p. 159).

Section 373 Companies Act 1985 provides that a proxy may both demand and vote on a poll.

10.2 Solicitation of Proxies

Two important elements which affect the balance of power between management and shareholders are (i) the management may themselves hold a considerable number of the shares, and (ii) the directors may employ the company's money in soliciting proxies on behalf of its policies. In *Peel* v. *London and North Western Rly Co* [1907] 1 Ch 5, the court held that the company was bound to explain its policy to shareholders, and was entitled to solicit votes in support of that policy at the company's expense. If an officer of the company issues invitations to appoint a proxy, those invitations must go to all members entitled to notice of the meeting or a criminal offence will be committed by him.

The ability of the directors to issue reasoned circulars accompanied by proxy forms mean that many issues affecting a company will be determined before the meeting is held and determined in favour of the management.

10.3 Formality of Procedure

It has been established for some time that agreement of all the members to a course of conduct was sufficient to bind the company, even when no formal meeting had been held. In *Cane* v. *Jones* [1980] 1 WLR 1451, this principle applied even in the case where the articles had in effect been altered. The informality principle now has statutory force as s. 113 Companies Act 1989. This inserts new sections 381A, 381B, and 382A into the Companies Act 1985.

New s. 381A provides that, in the case of a private company, anything which may be done by resolution of the company in general meeting or by resolution of a meeting of any class of members may be done by written resolution without a meeting and without any previous notice. This resolution in writing must be signed by or on behalf of all the members of the company who at the date of the resolution would be entitled to attend and vote at such a meeting.

There are two exceptions to this general power. Resolutions under s. 303 Companies Act 1985 to remove a director before the expiration of his term of office is one. The other is a resolution under s. 391 Companies Act 1985 to remove an auditor before the expiration of his term of office.

10.4 Elective Regime

Section 116 of the Companies Act 1989 (inserting new s. 379A Companies Act 1985) also introduced the 'elective regime' whereby the members of a private company may elect by resolution in general meeting to dispense with certain of the requirements of company law. The resolution must be agreed to by all the members entitled to attend and vote at the meeting. Such resolutions must be registered with the Registrar of Companies. Elective resolutions may:

(i)   make indefinite or extend for a fixed period of years the authority to allot shares (s. 80 Companies Act 1985 provides a maximum duration of 5 years).
(ii)   dispense with the laying of accounts and reports before general meetings.
(iii) dispense with the holding of annual general meetings.
(iv)   dispense with the requirement as to majorities required to authorise short notice of meetings (s. 369(4) provides for a majority of 95 per cent).
(v)   dispense with the annual appointment of auditors.

With these provisions in mind, the general rules applicable to meetings must now be examined. (The standard Table A articles relating to meetings are set out in the Casenotes at the end of this chapter.)

10.5 Meetings

Annual general meeting

Unless a company has opted out under the procedure explained above, it must hold an annual general meeting. This must be held in addition to any other meetings that are convened. Section 366 Companies Act 1985 also provides that so long as a company holds its first annual general meeting within eighteen months of incorporation, it need not hold it in the year of its incorporation or in the following year. Annual general meetings must not be more than fifteen months apart. If a meeting is not held in accordance with these rules s. 366(4) provides that the: 'company and every officer of it who is in default is liable to a fine'. Section 367 Companies Act 1985 provides that if a meeting is not held in accordance with the rules, the DTI may, on the application of any member, call a general meeting and make any consequential directions that are thought expedient. The Act does not specify in any detail the business to be transacted by the annual general meeting. This usually consists of:

(i)   the adoption of the annual accounts.
(ii)   the reading of the auditor's report and the appointment of auditors for the future.
(iii) the directors' report which will include the directors' recommendation of the dividend to be paid to shareholders. A resolution will be proposed that the amount recommended be paid by way of dividend.

(iv) appointment of directors where some are retiring.
(v) a resolution to pay the auditors.
(iv) a resolution to pay the directors.

Extraordinary general meeting

Article 37 of Table A provides that the directors may convene a meeting of members. They will do so if special business of importance requires a meeting of members. Section 368 gives to the holders of one-tenth of the voting power at a general meeting, the power to require the directors to convene such a meeting within twenty-one days. The meeting must be convened within that time limit, not necessarily held within it (see *Re Windward Islands (Enterprises) UK Ltd* [1983] BCLC 293). If the directors fail to convene a meeting within the twenty-one days, those requesting the meeting may do so. The expense will fall on the company. The directors must call a general meeting if the net assets of a public company become half or less of the amount of the company's called up capital (s. 142 Companies Act 1985). This rather strange provision does not specify in any way what the meeting is supposed to do about this situation. It merely makes the calling of a meeting mandatory.

By s. 371 Companies Act 1985, the court has a reserve power to call a meeting if 'for any reason it is impracticable' to call the meeting otherwise. An application to the court to order a meeting under this section can be made by any director or any member entitled to vote at the meeting. In *Re El Sombrero Ltd* [1958] Ch 900 the court held that to decide when the holding of a meeting was 'impracticable' the court must, in the words of Wynn-Parry J: 'examine the circumstances of the particular case and answer the question whether, as a practical matter, the desired meeting of the company can be conducted, there being no doubt, of course, that it can be convened and held.'

In that case the order was granted, the facts of the case being an illustration of the circumstances in which the power to order a meeting is very useful. In that case there were three shareholders, two of these being directors. A quorum of three was required for a meeting. The non-director shareholder, who held a majority of the shares, wished to convene a meeting to remove the directors. They refused to attend a meeting, thus preventing a quorum from being achieved. However, the Court of Appeal held that it would be wrong to use the power in s. 371 to call a meeting and determine its quorum if the effect of that would be to override class rights which were embedded in a shareholder agreement. In *Harman and another* v. *BML Group Ltd* [1994] 2 BCLC 674 the capital of the company was divided into A and B shares, the B shares being registered in the name of B. H and M held a majority of the A shares. Under an agreement signed by all the shareholders it was provided that a meeting of shareholders would not be quorate unless a B shareholder or proxy were present. H and M applied for an order under s. 371 Companies Act 1985 that a meeting of the company be summoned. The judge ordered that a meeting be summoned, ruling that any two members of the company would constitute a quorum. The Court of Appeal held that this was not a proper use of s. 371.

Section 376 confers a right to compel the inclusion of a resolution in the agenda of an annual general meeting on the holders of one-twentieth of the voting rights or to 100 members holding shares, the average paid up value of which is at least one hundred pounds.

Notice of meetings

Twenty-one days' notice of the holding of an annual general meeting must be given to the shareholders; fourteen days' notice of other meetings (s. 369 Companies Act 1985). Where the statute requires special notice to be given, the company must be notified twenty-eight days in advance of the meeting where the resolution is to be put, and must inform members of the resolution at the same time as notice of the meeting is given (s. 379 Companies Act 1985). An example of this situation is a resolution to remove a director under s. 303 Companies Act 1985.

The information disclosed in the notice of the meeting must be sufficient to enable the shareholder to exercise an informed judgement. The courts will require full disclosure of any benefits which directors will reap from proposed resolutions. In *Baillie* v. *Oriental Telephone and Electric Company Ltd* [1915] 1 Ch 503, the notice did not disclose the fact that the directors stood to gain substantially from the passing of certain resolutions. Lord Cozens-Hardy MR said:

'I feel no difficulty in saying that special resolutions obtained by means of a notice which did not substantially put the shareholders in the position to know what they were voting about cannot be supported, and in so far as these special resolutions were passed on the faith and footing of such a notice the defendants cannot act upon them.'

Class meetings

If there is a reason to convene a meeting of a particular class of shareholder, for example to consider the variation of share rights (see Chapter 14) only the holders of the shares of the particular class should be present. In *Carruth* v. *ICI* [1937] AC 707, Lord Russell of Killowen said:

'Prima facie a separate meeting of a class should be a meeting attended only by members of the class, in order that the discussion of the matters which the meeting has to consider may be carried on unhampered by the presence of others who are not interested to view those matters from the same angle as that of the class; and if the presence of outsiders was retained in spite of the ascertained wish of the constituents of the meeting for their exclusion, it would not, I think, be possible to say that a separate meeting of the class had been duly held.'

Quorum

The Act is silent as to the number of members who must be present before the proceedings at the meeting are to be regarded as valid. The articles will determine the relevant number. Article 40 of Table A provides: 'Two persons entitled to vote upon the business to be transacted, each being a member or a proxy for a member or a duly authorised representative of a corporation, shall be a quorum.'

If this article is excluded by the company's articles and not replaced by an article providing for a quorum, s. 370(4) will apply. This provides that 'two members personally present are a quorum'. The quorum of meetings may also be contained in shareholder's agreements (see *Harman and another* v. *BML Group Ltd* [1994] 2 BCLC 674 (above, p. 135).

Article 40 does not provide for proxy voting.

Except in the case of a single member company (see the end of this chapter), no single member can constitute a quorum, even if representing several shareholders (see *Re M.J. Shanley Contracting Ltd* (1979) 124 SJ 239). This rule is displaced when the meeting is called by the court or the DTI under the powers in ss. 371, 369 Companies Act 1985.

Resolutions

The decisions of a meeting are arrived at by voting on resolutions.

Ordinary resolutions
An ordinary resolution will be sufficient for any decision unless the legislation decrees that the particular decision can only be taken by extraordinary or special resolution. An ordinary resolution is one passed by a simple majority of members who vote on it.

Extraordinary resolutions
Section 378(1) provides:

> 'A resolution is an extraordinary resolution when it has been passed by a majority of not less than three fourths of such members as (being entitled to do so) vote in person or, where proxies are allowed, by proxy, at a general meeting of which notice specifying the intention to propose the resolution as an extraordinary resolution has been duly given.'

Such a resolution is sometimes required in order to vary class rights, to initiate or permit payment of a class of creditors in a voluntary winding up (see s. 125 Companies Act 1985; ss. 84, 165 Insolvency Act 1986).

Special resolutions
These are more often required. Alteration of articles by special resolution is dealt with in Chapter 4. Section 378(2) provides:

'A resolution is a special resolution when it has been passed by such a majority as is required for the passing of an extraordinary resolution and at a general meeting of which not less than 21 days' notice specifying the intention to propose the resolution as a special resolution, has been duly given.'

Thus, a three-quarters majority of the members validly casting votes at the meeting is required for a special resolution, but in addition twenty-one days' notice must be given.

Unanimous consent

As was discussed above (in s. 10.3), the members do not have to meet if they all agree to a particular course of conduct unless the course of conduct is illegal or there is a provision in the articles forbidding this method of proceeding. In the latter case it would seem that the unanimous consent of the shareholders can effect an alteration in the articles so that the effectiveness of such a prohibition must be in some doubt (see *Cane* v. *Jones*, [1981] 1 WLR 1451).

Voting

The voting rights of the shareholders will normally be set out in the articles. The usual method of voting is to take a show of hands. In this case, each member will have one vote. However, in some circumstances a member, dissatisfied with the outcome of a show of hands, may call for a 'poll'. The standard article appearing in Table A (Article 54) provides that on a poll 'every member shall have one vote for every share of which he is the holder'.

It can clearly be seen that the outcome of a vote on a poll may radically differ from that on a show of hands. The right to demand a poll is therefore of considerable importance. The circumstances in which a poll may be demanded may appear in the articles. However, the Companies Act provides a 'minimum standard' for the articles. It reads:

'(1) A provision contained in a company's articles is void in so far as it would have the effect either –
  (a) of excluding the right to demand a poll at a general meeting on any question other than the election of the chairman of the meeting or the adjournment of the meeting; or
  (b) of making ineffective a demand for a poll on any such question which is made either –
      (i) by not less than 5 members having the right to vote at the meeting; or(ii) by a member or members representing not less than one-tenth of the total voting rights of all the members having the right to vote at the meeting; or
      (iii) by a member or members holding shares in the company conferring a right to vote at the meeting, being shares on

which an aggregate sum has been paid up equal to not
less than one-tenth of the total sum paid up on all the
shares conferring that right.

(2) The instrument appointing a proxy to vote at a meeting of a
company shall be deemed also to confer authority to demand or
join in demanding a poll; and for the purposes of subsection (i)
a demand by a person as proxy for a member is the same as a
demand by the member.'

Exercise of voting rights

There is considerable weight of authority to support the proposition that a
shareholder may exercise his right to vote as he pleases and does not have
any duty to take into account the interests of others or of the company. In
Pender v. *Lushington* (1877) 6 Ch D 70, Jessel MR said:

'[A] man may be actuated in giving his vote by interests entirely adverse
to the interests of the company as a whole. He may think it more for his
particular interest that a certain course may be taken which may be in
the opinion of others very adverse to the interests of the company as a
whole, but he cannot be restrained from giving his vote in what way he
pleases because he is influenced by that motive.' (See also *North West
Transportation* v. *Beatty* (1887) 12 App Cas 589).

An inroad into this principle appeared to be made by the judgment in
the case of *Clemens* v. *Clemens Bros Ltd* [1976] 2 All ER 268. In that case a
challenge was made to a resolution to issue further shares to directors.
This would have had the effect of substantially reducing (from 45 per cent
to below 25 per cent) the voting power of the plaintiff. Foster J said:

'I think that one thing which emerges from the cases to which I have
referred is that in such a case as the present Miss Clemens is not entitled
to exercise her majority vote in whatever way she pleases. The difficulty
is in finding a principle, and obviously expressions such as "bona fide
for the benefit of the company as a whole", "fraud on a minority" and
"oppressive" do not assist in formulating such a principle'.

I have come to the conclusion that it would be unwise to try to
produce a principle, since the circumstances of each case are infinitely
varied. It would not, I think, assist to say more than that in my
judgement Miss Clemens is not entitled as of right to exercise her votes
as an ordinary shareholder in any way she pleases . . . I cannot escape
the conclusion that the resolutions have been framed so as to put into
the hands of Miss Clemens and her fellow directors complete control of
the company and to deprive the plaintiff of her existing rights as a
shareholder with more than 25% of the votes . . . They are specifically
and carefully designed to ensure not only that the plaintiff can never get
control of the company but to deprive her of what has been called her
negative control. Whether I say that these proposals are oppressive to

the plaintiff or that no one could honestly believe that they are for her benefit matters not. A court of equity will in my judgment regard these considerations as sufficient to prevent the consequences arising from Miss Clemens using her legal right to vote in the way she has and it would be right for a court of equity to prevent such consequences taking effect.'

This passage is clearly irreconcilable with the traditional view above. The right to vote as a shareholder pleases derives from the idea that the right to vote is a property right which should not be subject to equitable restraints. It is possible to reconcile the two cases by arguing that a shareholder has the right to vote to protect the value of shares in any way they wish, but the best interests of the company can override that right and a decision contrary to these best interests will not be upheld.

Adjournments

Article 45 of Table A provides that the chairman shall adjourn the meeting if so directed by the meeting. Article 51 provides that a poll demanded on the question of adjournment shall be taken forthwith. If the articles give the power of adjournment to the chairman, the majority cannot compel an adjournment (see *Salisbury Gold Mining Co.* v. *Hathorn* [1897] AC 268). An adjourned meeting is a continuation of the original meeting (see *Will* v. *Murray* (1850) 4 Ex 843). Section 381 Companies Act 1985 provides that where a resolution is passed at an adjourned meeting of a company the resolution shall for all purposes be treated as having been passed on the date on which it was in fact passed, and shall not be deemed to be passed on any earlier date.

Shareholder agreements

Shareholders are free to agree among themselves how they will vote on particular issues. These agreements may be enforced by mandatory injunction (*Puddephatt* v. *Leith* [1916] 1 Ch 200. Such agreements can substantially affect the balance of power among the various groups of shareholders and anyone seeking to understand how any particular company functions would need to know of the existence and content of such agreements. The agreements may supplement the articles of association and contain quite fundamental rights (see discussion of *Harman and another* v. *BML Group Ltd* [1994] 2 BCLC 674 (above, p. 135).

10.6 Management of the Company

We saw in Chapter 1 that one of the advantages of incorporation was to create a legal being separate from its members which could operate at a distance from those members. Used properlyThe this enables (though not obliges) companies to be run by specialists. The members may simply regard the company as an investment for their money. The persons actually concerned in the running of the company are known as the directors. Even if they have not been appointed officially, the law will in many instances treat them in the same way as directors because they will qualify as 'shadow directors' (this term is discussed more fully on p. 143). If they wish one person to be particularly concerned with the everyday running of the business, that person should be appointed as managing director. If the shareholders are not content to have their money managed on their behalf by the directors, but wish to have a say in the way that the company is run, the chances are quite high that they will come into conflict with the 'professional' management in the form of the directors. Berle and Means found (*The Modern Corporation and Private Property* (New York, 1932); see also P. S. Florence, *Ownership, Control and Success of Large Companies* (New York, 1961)), that where ownership of shares in large American corporations was widely dispersed, no individual or group was in a position to control the corporation; instead management was in control. Large institutional investors such as pension funds and insurance companies are in a position to exercise control over management. However, such control seems usually to be exercised in an informal way rather than through the formal mechanisms of meetings, which is where, according to the company's constitution, decisions will be taken. Most meetings of public companies are poorly attended. The UK government's policy of encouraging small shareholdings (in, for example, privatised industries) would seem likely to exacerbate this problem, as the difficulty and expense of attending a meeting when the shareholder has only a small sum at stake will not be undertaken. In large public companies the management are in control of business decisions and are out of control in the sense that they are not effectively accountable to other organs of the company. This perception may have fuelled the debate about the benefits of a two-tier structure of management, with a supervisory board of directors overseeing the directors involved in day-to-day business decisions. Such a system is an option that a company could adopt under the EC proposals for a Fifth Directive and for a European Company Statute (see Chapter 18). In any event, under those proposals there would be a 'supervisory' element to the board structure. It was also instrumental in starting the committee enquiry which eventually reported as the Cadbury Committee on the Financial Aspects of Corporate Governance. This produced a Code, which relied heavily on the appointment of non-executive directors. All companies whose shares are listed on the Stock Exchange must either comply with the Code or make an annual statement to say why it does not comply.

In the case of small companies, the system of agreement at formal meetings may also be unreal. Decisions may well be made by the few people who actually run the business, meeting informally day by day. If there are any other shareholders they may take no interest in the business at all.

Others are interested in the way that the company is run as well. Employees have a very considerable interest in the decisions that are made in the course of managing the business. Creditors are also concerned, particularly when the company has fallen upon hard times. Each of these groups has some claim to be consulted or at least have their interests considered when management decisions are made. In this chapter we shall examine the way that each of these interest groups can influence decisions about the way that the company is managed.

With the reservations expressed above in mind, we turn to examination of the rules governing the appointment and removal of officers of the company, managing directors and shadow directors, directors meetings, the general meeting, the relationship between managers and shareholders, and the influence of employees and creditors.

10.7 **Appointment of Directors**

Section 282 Companies Act 1985 provides that every company must have at least one director. The term director is not fully defined (but see s. 741 Companies Act 1985 and discussion of 'shadow directors' on p. 143, nor is there anywhere in the legislation much positive guidance as to how a director should act. There is a considerable body of both statute and case law which will show directors what they must not do, but except in general terms such as insisting that directors act 'bona fide', there is little guidance on how the company should be managed. Much of the structure of management will appear in the articles of association which will often adopt at least parts of Table A, although modifications may be made to accommodate peculiarities relating to the particular company.

The first directors of any company are the directors named in a statement signed by all the subscribers and delivered with the memorandum and articles of association of the company to the Registrar of Companies when the company is formed.

Until the subscribers to the memorandum have made appointments the company cannot act except by a decision of the general meeting (which is made by a majority at a meeting of subscribers or in writing by all the subscribers without a meeting. *John Morley Building Co* v. *Barras* [1891] 2 Ch 386, *Re Great Northern Salt and Chemical Works Co.* (1890) 44 Ch D 472). Articles 64–98 of Table A are relevant to all aspects of procedure relating to directors. These Articles of Table A appear in the Casenotes at the end of this chapter. A company need not adopt articles which follow these provisions, but in practice they often do so. Thus Article 70 provides that 'the business of the company shall be managed by the directors who may exercise all the powers of the company'. Article 84 permits the appointment of a managing director who is not subject to the practice, enshrined in these model articles, whereby the directors retire by rotation. All the first directors retire at the first annual general meeting, and at every subsequent meeting one-third of the directors retire (Article 73). These provisions may be excluded from the articles of a private company.

Number

Section 282 Companies Act 1985 requires public companies to have at least two directors. A private company must have at least one director. Article 64 of Table A requires there to be at least two directors unless the company determines otherwise by ordinary resolution.

Definition

Section 741 Companies Act 1985 has a partial definition of director and also defines 'shadow director'. The latter is a term used in the statute where there is a possibility that someone responsible for misfeasance could escape liability where he had not officially been appointed as a director, but was really in charge of the business. Section 741 reads:

(1) In this Act 'director' includes any person occupying the position of director, by whatever name called.

(2) In relation to a company, 'shadow director' means a person in accordance with whose directions or instructions the directors of the company are accustomed to act. However, a person is not deemed a shadow director by reason only that the directors act on advice given by him in a professional capacity.

This latter exception prevents a person who is only giving advice as, for example, a solicitor to the company, from being regarded as a shadow director and thus sharing some of the responsibilities of true directors, merely because the directors usually act on his advice. Shadow directors are creatures of statute and so will only be under a duty to the company where such a duty is specifically imposed by statute. This is done where responsibilities would easily be evaded by someone who was the real 'power behind the throne' but was not officially a director. Examples of the imposition of duties on shadow directors can be found in the chapter concerning the statutory liability of directors (Chapter 12) and the insolvency of a company (Chapter 17). The definition of shadow director has now been considered by the courts. In *Re Hydrodan (Corby) Ltd* [1994] BCC 161 Millett J made it clear that a shadow director is different from a *de facto* director, i.e. a person acting as a director without valid appointment. He said that there are four steps to establishing that someone was a shadow director. These are: (i) the identity of the appointed and acting directors must be established; (ii) it must be established that the alleged shadow director directed those directors as to their actions in relation to the company; (iii) it must be established that the directors followed those directions; (iv) it must be established that the directors were accustomed to follow directions from the alleged shadow director. Those factors were not established in *Re Unisoft Group Ltd*

(No. 2) [1994] BCC 766 where it was held that compliance by one of a number of directors with the directions of an outsider could not make that outsider a shadow director. Only if the whole board or a governing majority were accustomed to act on the directions of the outsider would he become a shadow director.

In order to prevent evasion of duties by the use of members of a director's family or a company controlled by a director, statute often extends a prohibition relating to a transaction to 'connected persons' or 'associated companies'. By Companies Act 1985, s. 346, the persons 'connected with' a director are:

(a) The director's spouse.
(b) The director's legitimate or illegitimate children and stepchildren under 18.
(c) Any company if the director and persons connected with him are interested in more than 20 per cent of its equity share capital (or control more than 20 per cent of its voting rights). This is an 'associated company'.
(d) A trustee of any trust under which any person mentioned in (a), (b) or (c) could benefit, apart from an employee's share scheme or a pension scheme.
(e) Any partner (in a business or profession) of the director or of any person mentioned in (a), (b) or (c).

Age

The only stipulation as to the age of directors appears in ss. 293 and 294 Companies Act 1985. These sections apply only to public companies, or private companies which are subsidiaries of public companies. Further, the effect of s. 293 may be excluded by the articles of association. If it is not, it prevents the appointment to a relevant company of a director who is aged seventy or over. It further requires a director reaching that age to retire at the annual general meeting following his seventieth birthday. However, the section is subject to one further qualification. Section 293(5) Companies Act 1985 reads:

'Nothing in [the preceding subsections] prevents the appointment of a director at any age, or requires a director to retire at any time, if his appointment is or was made or approved by the company in general meeting; but special notice is required of a resolution appointing or approving the appointment of a director for it to have effect under this subsection, and the notice of the resolution given to the company, and by the company to its members, must state, or have stated, the age of the person to whom it relates.'

Section 294 Companies Act applies to the same type of companies as are covered by s. 293. Section 294 requires the disclosure by a person appointed or about to be appointed to a directorship of a relevant company of his age if that is (i) seventy or over; or (ii) above the retiring age set out in the articles of association.

Remuneration

Directors are in a curious position, as their appointment to a directorship does not entitle them to be paid, even if they in fact do work for the company (See *Re George Newman and Co.* [1895] 1 Ch 674). However, the articles of association may provide for director's pay (as in Article 82 of Table A). This will not benefit the director unless he is in a position to enforce any provision in his favour in the articles by using s. 14 (see Chapter 5). Usually the right to be paid will arise from a contract of employment made with the company. Some of the terms of that contract may be discoverable by looking at the articles where, e.g. the amount that directors are to be paid may be specified. The situation which arises then is clearly set out in *Re New British Iron Co. ex Parte Beckwith* [1898] 1 Ch 324 where the articles of association contained the following provision:

'62: The remuneration of the board shall be an annual sum of £1,000 to be paid out of the funds of the company, which sum shall be divided in such manner as the board shall from time to time determine.'

Wright J said:

'Article 62 fixes the remuneration of the directors at the annual sum of £1,000. That article is not in itself a contract between the company and the directors; it is only part of the contract constituted by the articles of association between the members of the company *inter se*. But where on the footing of that article the directors are employed by the company and accept office the terms of article 62 are embodied in and form part of the contract between the company and the directors. Under the article as thus embodied the directors obtain a contractual right to an annual sum of £1,000 as remuneration.'

In *Re Richmond Gate Property* [1965] 1 WLR 335, the articles provided that the directors were to be paid such remuneration as the board of directors determined by resolution. The company was wound up before a resolution settling the amount to be paid had been passed. The directors were entitled to nothing under the employment contract. Plowman J said:

'a contract exists between [the applicant] and the company for payment to him of remuneration as managing director, and that remuneration depends on article 108 of Table A [equivalent article is Article 84 of Table A to Companies Act 1985], and is to be such amount "as the directors may determine"; in other words, the managing director is at the mercy of the board, he gets what they determine to pay him, and if they do not determine to pay him anything he does not get anything. That is his contract with the company, and those are the terms on which he accepts office.'

It was argued in that case that the directors should be entitled to be paid for work which they had actually done under a claim known as a '*quantum meruit*' claim. It was held, however, that because there was a contract of employment, such a claim was excluded.

Considerable public disquiet concerning large pay rises awarded to directors of public companies led the Confederation of British Industry to set up a committee chaired by Sir Richard Greenbury to consider the remuneration of directors. The committee drew up a Code of Best Practice (contained in its 1995 report). A company listed on the Stock Exchange must state in its annual report and accounts whether it has complied with the Code. The best-practice provisions require the directors of a listed company to set up a remuneration committee, consisting exclusively of non-executive directors, to determine the company's policy on executive director's pay and specific packages for each executive director. This attempt to inject some objectivity into the level of pay does not seem to have had a significant impact.

10.8 **Removal of a Director**

Section 303 Companies Act 1985 provides: '(1) A company may, by ordinary resolution remove a director before the expiration of his period of office, notwithstanding anything in its articles or in any agreement between it and him.'

This sweeping power apparently given to the general meeting to remove a director is, however, subject to two very significant qualifications. One appears in statutory form in s. 303(5) Companies Act which expressly preserves the right of a director dismissed in accordance with s. 303 to damages for any breach of contract of employment that has occurred. The rule is that the director may be dismissed, but because he has been dismissed by the company who is also the other party to his employment contract, he will be entitled to damages on the principle expressed in *Stirling* v. *Maitland* (1864) 5 B&S 840, where Cockburn LJ said: 'if a party enters into an arrangement which can only take effect by the continuance of a certain existing set of circumstances, there is an implied engagement on his part that he shall do nothing of his own motion to put an end to that state of circumstances under which alone the arrangement can be operative.'

Thus, a director's employment contract can only continue to operate when the company refrains from dismissing him by passing a resolution under s. 303. If such a resolution is passed, it is effective to dismiss him, but it is at the same time a breach of contract and damages for that breach must be paid. The same principle applies where the company is in breach of such a contract by alteration of its articles. See *Southern Foundries* v. *Shirlaw* [1940] AC 701; *Shindler* v. *Northern Raincoat Co. Ltd* [1960] 1 WLR 1038; *Nelson* v. *James Nelson & Sons Ltd* [1914] 2 KB 770; and *Read* v. *Astoria Garage (Streatham) Ltd* [1952] 2 All ER 292 (see Chapter 5). A provision which may in some cases alleviate this liability is to be found at s. 319 Companies Act 1985. This provides that a director may not be employed for a period exceeding five years unless there is prior approval of the contract by the general meeting. Any term included in a director's employment contract which contravenes this prohibition is void to the extent five years are exceeded. Unless the general meeting so approve, this will limit the damages payable to the amount payable to the director for what remains of the five-year period at the time of his dismissal. The director will also be under a duty to 'mitigate' the damage, that is, to take any reasonable steps available to him to limit the amount payable to him. The Cadbury Committee recommended that contracts should only be for three years. Whatever the length of the contract, it is common practice for directors to have 'rolling' contracts which renew themselves daily. Thus each day the contract stretches three or five years into the future.

However, if a director is appointed for more than five years without the approval of a general meeting of shareholders, his appointment does not take effect as one for five years but as an appointment which could be terminated by either party (the company or himself) on giving reasonable notice (s. 319(6)).

The second qualification to the power to remove a director by using s. 303 arises because of the strange decision in *Bushell* v. *Faith* [1970] AC 1099. In that case, the articles of a private company provided that 'in the event of a resolution being proposed at any general meeting for the removal from office of any director any shares held by that director shall on a poll in respect of such resolution carry the right of three votes per share'. Since only three persons were involved (a brother and two sisters), the situation was that if an ordinary resolution was passed under the predecessor section to s. 303, the sisters outvoted the brother by two to one, and he was removed as a director. If his special voting right was taken into account the same resolution was defeated by 3:2. This meant that the director in question was effectively irremovable. It was argued that such a 'weighted voting provision' was inconsistent with s. 303, since that section had been intended to prevent entrenchment of directors by inserting provisions in the articles. The relevant section (now s. 303) therefore contains the words 'notwithstanding anything in the articles'. Lord Upjohn said:

'My Lords, when construing an Act of Parliament it is a canon of construction that its provisions must be construed in the light of the mischief which the Act was designed to meet. In this case the mischief was well known; it was a common practice, especially in the case of private companies, to provide in the articles that a director should be irremovable or only removable by an extraordinary resolution; in the former case the articles would have to be altered by special resolution before the director could be removed and of course in either case a three-quarters majority would be required. In many cases this would be impossible, so the Act provided that notwithstanding anything in the articles an ordinary resolution would suffice to remove a director.'

Despite the identification of the 'mischief' at which the section was aimed, and the admission that the device used in the case made the director irremovable, the House of Lords came to the conclusion that it was permissible to have this type of weighted voting provision and that it was not in conflict with the predecessor to s. 303. This was said to be because no restriction had been placed on the company's right to specify the voting rights of particular shares. There is much to be said for the dissenting judgement of Lord Morris of Borth-y-Guest, who said:

'Some shares may, however, carry a greater voting power than others. On a resolution to remove a director shares will therefore carry the voting power that they possess. But this does not, in my view, warrant a device such as article 9 introduces. Its unconcealed effect is to make a director irremovable. If the question is posed whether the shares of the respondent possess any added voting weight the answer must be that they possess none whatever beyond, if valid, an *ad hoc* weight for the special purpose of circumventing [now s. 303]. If article 9 were writ large it would set out that a director is not to be removed against his will and that in order to achieve this and to thwart the express provision of [now s. 303] the voting power of any director threatened with removal is to be deemed to be greater than it actually is. The learned judge thought that to sanction this would be to make a mockery of the law. I think so too.'

Note that a similar effect to that of *Bushell* v. *Faith* can be achieved using shareholder agreements (discussed above at 10.3).

10.9 Disqualification

A person subject to a disqualification order made under the Company Directors Disqualification Act 1986 may not act as a director (see Chapter 12). The articles may contain other situations which will require a director to vacate office (see Table A, Article 81 (see Casenotes)).

10.10 Directors' Meetings

The rules governing directors' meetings are usually to be found in the articles of association (see Table A Articles 88–98 in Casenotes). A common provision (Table A, Article 94 in Casenotes) is that a director who is interested in a matter, including a contract or arrangement which is before the board, shall not vote on it or be counted in the quorum unless the matter comes within one of the exceptions stated in the articles, or the rule is suspended by the general meeting.

One clear rule is that notice must be given to all directors of a meeting (see *Re Portuguese Copper Mines* (1889) 42 Ch D 160) unless he is abroad and unable to be reached by notice (see *Halifax Sugar Refining Co.* v. *Franklyn* (1890) 59 LJ Ch 591).

Standard Article 88 of Table A provides that a chairman shall have a casting vote in case the board are equally divided on a question.

10.11 **Managing Director**

It is usual to include in the articles of association a power for the directors to appoint one or more of their number to be managing director or directors and permitting the delegation of such powers as are necessary for him or them to manage the business. It will be the business of such an appointee to be closely involved in the day-to-day running of the business. He will be an 'executive' director. Others on the board may consider themselves to be 'non-executive' directors and to be chiefly concerned with matters of policy rather than the nitty-gritty of the management of the company.

Article 84 of Table A (see Casenotes) allows the directors to appoint a managing director (and other executive directors) on such terms as they determine and, by Article 72, to delegate such of their powers as they consider desirable. This delegation may be altered or revoked. However, if the managing director is removed from office before his contract of employment expires, this will entitle him to damages for breach of contract (see *Nelson* v. *James Nelson & Sons* [1914] 2 KB 770) under the doctrine discussed above in relation to s. 303, that the one party to a contract must not do anything which prevents the other party from completing his side of the bargain. There is thus some difficulty between the rule often to be found in the articles that the delegation of powers by the board may be revoked, and the commission of a breach of contract by the company, who may, by such a revocation, be preventing the managing director from continuing to carry out his employment. A case in which the relationship between these two rules arose is *Harold Houldsworth & Co (Wakefield) Ltd* v. *Caddies* [1955] 1 WLR 352. The case is of limited use as a precedent for the future, as it is generally considered to have turned on the construction of the particular contract of employment in that case. Under that contract, Caddies had been appointed managing director of Houldsworth (the parent company). The contract provided that he should perform the duties and exercise the powers in relation to the business of the company and the business of its existing subsidiaries 'which may from time to time be assigned to or vested in him by the board of directors of the company'.

At first Caddies managed Houldsworth and a subsidiary. However, a dispute arose between Caddies and his fellow directors. The board of directors instructed Caddies to thereafter confine his attentions to the subsidiary alone. The House of Lords held that this was not a breach of the contract of employment. If the contract had not contained the clause giving such wide discretion to the board to define Caddies' job from time to time, the action would have been a breach of contract.

The powers of a managing director were considered in *Mitchell & Hobbs (UK)* v. *Mill* [1996] 2 BCLC 102 where it was held that the proper construction of Table A, regulation 70 (see the next section for a further discussion of this regulation) led to the result that a managing director did not have the power to commence legal proceedings on behalf of the company without reference to the other directors or shareholders. The regulation provided that the power to manage the company could be exercised by the board of directors, but not by a single director. The court also held that Table A, regulation 72 did not give any powers to a managing director over and above those held by the other directors unless such powers had been delegated by the board.

10.12 **Relationship Between the Board of Directors and the General Meeting**

For companies registered prior to 1 July 1985, the relationship between these two organs was usually governed by an article similar or identical to Article 80 of Table A annexed to the Companies Act 1948. This read:

> 'The business of the company shall be managed by the directors who may pay all expenses incurred in promoting and registering the company, and may exercise all such powers of the company as are not, by the Act, or by these regulations, required to be exercised by the company in general meeting, subject, nevertheless, to any of these regulations, to the provisions of the Act and to such regulations, being not inconsistent with the aforesaid regulations or provisions as may be prescribed by the company in general meeting; but no regulations made by the company in general meeting shall invalidate any prior act of the directors which would have been valid if that regulation had not been made.'

This appeared to reserve to the general meeting a power to make regulations to govern the conduct of directors. The scope of this power was most uncertain until the judges determined the balance of power issue firmly in favour of the directors to the detriment of the powers of the general meeting. Thus in *Automatic Self Cleansing Filter Syndicate Company Ltd* v. *Cunningham* [1906] 2 Ch 34, the Court of Appeal held that a resolution passed by a simple majority of shareholders (an ordinary resolution) was not effective. The resolution purported to order the directors to go ahead with an agreement to sell the whole of the assets of the company. The directors believed that this was an unwise course. Warrington J said:

> 'The effect of this resolution, if acted upon, would be to compel the directors to sell the whole of the assets of the company, not on such terms and conditions as they think fit, but upon such terms and conditions as a simple majority of the shareholders think fit. But it does not rest there. Article 96 [this was very similar to Article 80 of Table A to the 1948 Act above] provides that the management of the business

and control of the company are to be vested in the directors. Now that article, which is for the protection of a minority of the shareholders, can only be altered by a special resolution, that is to say, by a resolution passed by a three-fourths majority, at a meeting called for the purpose, and confirmed at a subsequent meeting. If that provision could be revoked by a resolution of the shareholders passed by a simple majority, I can see no reason for the provision which is to be found in Article 81 that the directors can only be removed by a special resolution. It seems to me that if a majority of shareholders can, on a matter which is vested in the directors, overrule the discretion of the directors, there might just as well be no provision at all in the articles as to the removal of directors by special resolution. Moreover, pressed to its logical conclusion, the result would be that when a majority of the shareholders disagree with the policy of the directors, though they cannot remove the directors except by special resolution, they might carry on the whole of the business of the company as they pleased, and thus, though not able to remove the directors, overrule every act which the board might otherwise do. It seems to me on the true construction of these articles that the management of the business and control of the company are vested in the directors, and consequently that the control of the company as to any particular matter, or the management of any particular transaction or any particular part of the business of the company, can only be removed from the board by an alteration of the articles, such alteration, of course, requiring a special resolution.'

This approach was recently adopted in *Breckland Group Holdings Ltd* v. *London and Suffolk Properties Ltd* [1989] BCLC 100, where the court held that since the company's articles of association adopted regulation 80 of Table A of Schedule 1 to the 1948 Companies Act, the conduct of the business of the company was vested in the board of directors, and the shareholders in general meeting could not intervene to adopt unauthorised proceedings.

It seems to have been the case that the general meeting could not interfere in management decisions by way of an ordinary resolution, even under the 1948 Companies Act. The 1985 equivalent is Article 70 of the Table A attached to the Companies Act 1985 (by SI 1985 No. 805). This reads:

'Subject to the provisions of the Act, the memorandum and the articles and to any directions given by special resolution, the business of the company shall be managed by the directors who may exercise all the powers of the company. No alteration of the memorandum or articles and no such direction shall invalidate any prior act of the directors which would have been valid if that alteration had not been made or that direction had not been given. The powers given by this regulation shall not be limited by any special power given to the directors by the articles and a meeting of directors at which a quorum is present may exercise all powers exercisable by the directors.'

The justification for the insistence that there should be no interference in director-control save by a special resolution was well expressed in *Gramophone and Typewriter Ltd* v. *Stanley* [1908] 2 KB 89. Buckley LJ said:

> 'The directors are not servants to obey directions given by the shareholders as individuals; they are agents appointed by and bound to serve the shareholders as their principals. They are persons who may by the regulations be entrusted with the control of the business, and if so entrusted they can be dispossessed from that control only by the statutory majority which can alter the articles.'

When coupled with the knowledge that a very few persons can hold a large number of the shares in a company, that directors can be entrenched by *Bushell* v. *Faith* clauses, and that shareholders with small stakes in a company rarely take an interest in meetings, it can be seen that 'shareholder democracy' is an extremely hollow concept and the directors will often have complete freedom from control in managing the business.

10.13 **Where the Board of Directors Ceases to Function**

The above analysis holds good for the situation where the board of directors is a functioning organ of the company. If for some reason the directors are unable or unwilling to exercise their powers of management, those powers revert to and are exercisable by the company in general meeting. In *Alexander Ward & Co Ltd* v. *Samyang Navigation Co. Ltd* [1975] 2 All ER 424, the House of Lords held that the company could act through its two shareholders to recover its debts. This was possible despite an article in the company's constitution which read as follows: 'The business of the Company shall be managed by the Directors, who . . . may exercise all such powers of the company as are not by the [Hong Kong] Ordinance or by these Articles required to be exercised by the Company in General Meeting.'

The company had no directors at the relevant time. Lord Hailsham said:

> 'In my opinion, at the relevant time the company was fully competent either to lay attestments or to raise proceedings in the Scottish courts. The company could have done so either by appointing directors, or, as I think, by authorising proceedings in general meeting, which in the absence of an effective board, has a residual authority to use the company's powers. it had not taken, and did not take the steps necessary to give authority to perform the necessary actions. But it was competent to have done so, and in my view it was therefore a competent principal . . . So far as regards the powers of general meeting, in *Gower Modern Company Law*, (3rd edn 1969), pp. 136–37 it is stated:
>
> > "It seems that if for some reason the board cannot or will not exercise the powers vested in them, the general meeting has been held effective

where there was a deadlock on the board, where an effective quorum could not be obtained, where the directors are disqualified from voting, or, more obviously, where the directors have purported to borrow in excess of the amount authorised by the articles."

Moreover, although the general meeting cannot restrain the directors from conducting actions in the name of the company, it still seems to be the law (as laid down in *Marshall's Valve Gear Co.* v. *Manning, Wardle & Co*) [1909] 1 Ch 267, that the general meeting can commence proceedings on behalf of the company if the directors fail to do so. In that case counsel attempted to draw a distinction between the cases supposed in this passage, where the directors were for some reason unable or unwilling to act, and the instant case where there were no directors. I see no difference in the distinction. . .'

10.14 Single Member Companies

As already discussed (see Chapter 1) the rules as to meetings, etc. do not apply where the company is a single member company.

10.15 The Secretary

Section 283 Companies Act 1985 provides that every company must have a secretary. A sole director of a company may not also be the company secretary. The increased importance of the company secretary was recognised by Lord Denning in *Panorama Developments Ltd* v. *Fidelis Furnishing Fabrics* (see Chapter 7). In that case, it was held that a company secretary had the power to make certain contracts on behalf of the company. Contracts to hire cars were held to be binding on the company, despite the fact that the company secretary in question had hired the cars ostensibly for the company, but in fact for his own use. The increased importance of company secretaries is also recognised by section 286 Companies Act 1985. This applies only to public companies and imposes a duty on the directors of such companies to 'take all reasonable steps to secure that the secretary (or each joint secretary) of the company is a person who appears to them to have the requisite knowledge and experience to discharge the functions of secretary of the company'. There follows a list of acceptable qualifications for the post which include membership of a number of accountants' professional organisations and legal qualifications. However, these qualifications are not exclusive, as s. 286(1)(c) provides that the secretary may be: 'a person who, by virtue of his holding or having held any other position or his being a member of any other body, appears to the directors to be capable of discharging those functions.'

The secretary is responsible for making sure that the documents that a company must send to the Registrar are accurate and are sent on time.

With the increasing complexity of requirements to make disclosure of company affairs in this way, the role has become considerably more complex and important.

10.16 Employees

By s. 309 Companies Act 1985:

'(1) The matters to which the directors of a company are to have regard in the performance of their functions include the interests of a company's employees in general, as well as the interests of its members.'

The duty thus imposed on directors has no effective enforcement mechanism. If there was an alleged failure to take account of employees' interests the failure would theoretically have to be enforced by the company voting in general meeting to bring an action against the directors. It seems unlikely that there would be enough employee shareholders or a sufficient number of altruistic shareholders in order to achieve the necessary majority. Even if it were possible, proof that employees' interests had not been considered might be extremely difficult.

The status of employees in company law is a matter of considerable concern to the EC legislators. All the Member States of the EC, with the exception of Ireland and the UK, have in place some form of compulsory system for ensuring worker participation in the running of companies. The basic source for the comparison which follows is a working document of the European Parliament dated 13/12/89, PE136.297, rapporteur: Christine Oddy. It must be understood that many countries adopt a 'two-tier' structure of boards of directors: an administrative board which usually consists of executive directors, and a 'supervisory board' on which sit non-executive directors.

10.17 Denmark

Depending on its size, the workforce of companies employing at least fifty persons, has the right to elect at least two members and up to one-third of the members of the administrative board (Law No. 370 of 13.6.73 as amended). The administrative board must furnish adequate ways and means to publish economic, social and commercial information about the company to its workforce. Outside the administrative board, the representatives of the workforce are generally the shop stewards elected to represent a trade union, and the convener for the company who is elected by the shop stewards.

10.18 France

The statutes of a limited liability company *may* provide for the election by the workforce of up to four members of the administrative board, being no more than a third of the total of the other members of the board (*Ordonnance* No. 86/1135 of 21.10.86).

All companies employing more than fifty persons must set up a work council; at any site where more than fifty are employed a specific work council for that site must be set up; in this latter event a central works council is established at company level (*Code de Travail* – Articles L62, L63, L321, L420, L431 *et seq.*).

10.19 Germany

In limited liability companies in the mining and iron and steel sectors employing more than 1000 persons and in other companies employing more than 2000 persons, the supervisory board is made up of an equal number of shareholders' and workers' representatives. Companies employing more than 500 persons must have a third of the members of the supervisory board representing the workforce. The worker representatives are both elected by the workforce and a lesser number nominated by the trade unions.

Under the Works Constitution Act 1972, works councils must be set up in all establishments employing at least five employees.

10.20 The Netherlands

The two-tier structure of management and supervisory boards is compulsory for all companies employing more than 100 persons. The first members of the supervisory board are nominated in the articles of incorporation and thereafter co-opt on to the board new members or replacement members from among candidates that may be recommended by the shareholders, the administrative board or the works council. Any appointment may be challenged by the shareholders or the works council before an economic and social committee, if the representative 'equilibrium' of the supervisory board would thereby be upset.

Works councils must be set up where an undertaking employs more than thirty-five persons. The law also requires joint employer–staff meetings in undertakings employing 10–34 persons in the event of planned redundancies or planned significant changes in working conditions.

10.21 Belgium

A works council must be set up in any undertaking defined as a 'technical operating unit' or legal entity employing more than 100 persons. A law of 27.11.73 details the information which must be transmitted to the works council, which must be consulted before implementation of management decisions. The employer must reply to the stated positions of the works council.

10.22 **Italy**

Under law No. 300 of 20.5.70 ('Statute of Worker's Rights'), workers in establishments or plants where more than fifteen persons are employed have the right to elect plant representatives. The scope of worker information and consultation is generally fixed by collective bargaining agreements. Works councils are widespread.

10.23 **Luxembourg**

In all plants or establishments employing more than fifteen persons there must be set up elected staff delegations, one representing the blue-collar workers, the other the office employees. Any undertaking employing more than 150 persons must establish a Mixed Committee (*Comite mixte*), of which half are nominated by the head of the company, half are elected by the staff delegations. The Mixed Committee has a power of decision in all matters relating to personnel policy, controls of worker efficiency and performance, health and safety measures, plant or workshop regulations and rewards for efficiency-inducing ideas, and has a right to be consulted (among other things) on investment and expansion plans, vocational training and productivity levels. (Law of 6.5.74.)

The same law requires limited liability companies employing more than 1,000 to have one-third of its administrative board elected by the staff delegations.

10.24 **Spain**

Works councils, directly elected by the workforce, must be established in limited liability companies employing more than fifty persons. In undertakings employing from 11 to 50 members, a staff delegation must be established with the same rights as the works council, which includes the right to information of an economic and social nature and the right to give an opinion on, among other things, investment and restructuring plans, and vocational training.

10.25 **Greece**

The workforce at a plant or establishment which employs at least fifty persons has the right to set up a works council to represent the workforce *vis-à-vis* management. Works councils adopt plant or workshop regulations including health and safety matters. They fix vocational training programmes and are informed and consulted on investment and restructuring plans, collective redundancies and any other decisions which will have a serious impact on working conditions.

10.26 **Portugal**

Enshrined in the Portuguese constitution is the right of workers to set up 'workers' commissions' within undertakings. These commissions are elected by the workforce and are entitled to receive all information to enable them to operate efficiently.

10.27 **Ireland**

Companies are not obliged to set up works councils or provide for worker representation on boards of directors. The Worker Participation (State Enterprise) Act 1977 provides that workers may elect a third of the board of a number of State undertakings. Safety committees are set up in undertakings employing more than twenty-one persons. These committees may make representations to the employer on health and safety matters.

10.28 **United Kingdom**

We have already discussed the toothless requirement for the directors to take account of employees' interests imposed by s. 309 Companies Act 1985.

British labour law, apart from the health and safety regulations, does not provide for the establishment of worker representative bodies within undertakings. Dealings between management and workforce are generally conducted at local level between the employer and a trade union recognised by the employer for the purpose of collective bargaining. It should be noted that collective agreements are not legally enforceable in courts or tribunals unless management and trade unions expressly agree in writing that the collective agreement should be legally enforceable.

There are, however, some statutory provisions giving certain information rights to recognised trade unions. Under s. 17 of the Employment Protection Act 1975, an employer is obliged to transmit, upon request, to the representatives of an independent trade union recognised for the purpose of collective bargaining, information 'without which the trade union representatives would be to a material extent impeded in carrying on with him such collective bargaining' and information 'which it would be in accordance with good industrial relations practice' to disclose. Among the exceptions to this general duty are included:

- information 'the disclosure of which would cause substantial injury to the employer'; and
- information whose 'compilation or assembly would involve an amount of work or expenditure out of reasonable proportion to the value of the information'.

Under the Employment Protection Act 1975 the Advisory, Conciliation and Arbitration Service (ACAS) has drawn up a Code of Practice

(Statutory Instrument 77/937) which lists information relevant to collective bargaining and attempts to define the concept of 'substantial injury' to the employer in disclosing certain information.

The 1982 Employment Act provides that the Board of Directors of Companies employing more than 250 employees must report annually to the shareholders on the supply of bargaining information to and the availability of consultation with the workforce (s. 235 and Part V of Schedule 7 Companies Act 1985). A report by Brown and Rycroft, published in 1989 by the British Institute of Management entitled *Involved in Europe* suggests that there is general agreement that the requirement to make a statement stimulates very little activity. Just before the requirement to report came into force on 1 January 1984, the employment minister said:

'I shall be watching developments closely and I shall be profoundly disappointed if it appears that even a minority of employers appear to be willing by inactivity to provide ammunition for those who agree that prescriptive legislation such as that which would be imposed by the draft "Vredling" and fifth company law directives is the only way of achieving progress.'

The 'Vredling' directive, which concerns itself with employees rights, has been dormant for some time. Although little recent progress has been made, however, the EC still has on the agenda the draft Fifth Directive and the European Company Statute as well as the European works council Directive (see Chapter 18). It seems in view of the situation existing throughout the Community, that the UK will come under increasing pressure to introduce laws requiring formal participation by employees in decisions made by companies.

10.29 **Creditors**

Creditors have a considerable interest in the running of a company. It seems, however, that their interests need only be expressly addressed when liquidation is a real possibility (see Chapter 17).

Summary

1   The voting power of shareholders may be more apparent than real. One limitation in practice is the power of management to solicit proxy votes.
2   Ordinary resolutions passed at meetings of shareholders require a simple majority. Special resolutions require a 75 per cent majority.
3   There are a number of technical rules concerning the conduct of meetings but it is doubtful if there is a general principle that a shareholder must use his vote otherwise than in his own selfish interest.
4   The power of shareholders over management is probably less than it would appear from the legal framework.
5   A company must have at least two directors.

6   Appointment as a director does not as such entitle the appointee to payment.

7   Section 303 CA 1985 provides for the removal of directors but this power does not prevent the director from gaining compensation for loss of office if he is dismissed in breach of contract.

8   A managing director may be appointed to manage the day-to-day affairs of the company.

9   The general meeting may not interfere in the general conduct of business by the directors unless the board of directors is unable or unwilling to exercise its usual functions.

10   The secretary of a company, particularly of a public company is to be regarded as 'more than a mere clerk' and as being capable of committing the company to binding contracts in his sphere of competence.

11   The directors must have regard to the interests of employees but there is no effective method of enforcing this obligation.

12   All the other Member States of the EC except Ireland have formal mechanisms for employee involvement.

Casenotes

SCHEDULE

TABLE A

REGULATIONS FOR MANAGEMENT OF A COMPANY LIMITED BY SHARES

INTERPRETATION

1. In these regulations—

'the Act' means the Companies Act 1985 including any statutory modifications or re-enactment for the time being in force.

'the article' means the articles of the company.

'clear days' in relation to the period of a notice means that period excluding the day when the notice is given or deemed to be given and the day for which it is given or on which it is to take effect.

'executed' includes any mode of execution.

'office' means the registered office of the company.

'the holder' in relation to shares means the member whose name is entered in the register of members as the holder of the shares.

'the seal' means the common seal of the company.

'secretary' means the secretary of the company or any other person appointed to perform the duties of the secretary of the company, including a joint, assistant or deputy secretary.

'the United Kingdom' means Great Britain and Northern Ireland.

Unless the context otherwise requires, words or expressions contained in these regulations bear the same meanings as in the Act but excluding any statutory modification thereof not in force when these regulations become binding on the company.

SHARE CAPITAL

2. Subject to the provisions of the Act and without prejudice to any rights attached to any existing shares, any share may be issued with such rights or restrictions as the company may by ordinary resolution determine.

3. Subject to the provision of the Act, shares may be issued which are to be redeemed or are to be liable to be redeemed at the option of the company or the holder on such terms and in such manner as may be provided by the articles.

4. The company may exercise the powers of paying commissions conferred by the Act. Subject to the [provisions] of the Act, any such commission may be satisfied by the payment of cash or by the allotment of fully or partly paid shares or partly in one way and partly in the other.

5. Except as required by law, no person shall be recognised by the company as holding any share upon any trust and (except as otherwise provided by the articles or by law) the company shall not be bound by or recognise any interest in any share except an absolute right to the entirety thereof in the holder.

NOTES

Reg 4: amended by substituting the 'provisions' for the word 'provision' by SI 1985 No. 1052, with effect from 1 August 1985.

SHARE CERTIFICATES

6. Every member, upon becoming the holder of any shares, shall be entitled without payment to one certificate for all the shares of each class held by him (and, upon transferring a part of his holding of shares of any class, to a certificate for the balance of such holding) or several certificates each one for one or more of his shares upon payment for every certificate after the first of such reasonable sum as the directors may determine. Every certificate shall be sealed with the seal and shall specify the number, class and distinguishing numbers (if any) of the shares to which it relates and the amount or respective amounts paid up thereon. The company shall not be bound to issue more than one certificate for shares held jointly by several persons and delivery of a certificate to one joint holder shall be a sufficient delivery to all of them.

7. If a share certificate is defaced, worn-out, lost or destroyed, it may be renewed on such terms (if any) as to evidence and indemnity and payment of the expenses reasonably incurred by the company in investigating evidence as the directors may determine but otherwise free of charge, and (in the case of defacement or wearing-out) on delivery up of the old certificate.

LIEN

8. The company shall have a first and paramount lien on every share (not being a fully paid share) for all moneys (whether presently payable or not) payable at a fixed time or called in respect of that share. The directors may at any time declare any share to be wholly or in part exempt from the provisions of this regulation. The company's lien on a share shall extend to any amount payable in respect of it.

9. The company may sell in such manner as the directors determine any shares on which the company has a lien if a sum in respect of which the lien exists is presently payable and is not paid within fourteen clear days after notice has been given to the holder of the share or to the person entitled to it in consequence of the death or bankruptcy of the holder, demanding payment and stating that if the notice is not complied with the shares may be sold.

10. To give effect to a sale the directors may authorise some person to execute an instrument of transfer of the shares sold to, or in accordance with the directions of, the purchaser. The title of the transferee to the share shall not be affected by any irregularity in or invalidity of the proceedings in reference to the sale.

11. The net proceeds of the sales, after payment of the costs, shall be applied in payment of so much of the sum for which the lien exists as is presently payable, and any residue shall (upon surrender to the company for cancellation of the certificate for the shares sold and subject to a like lien for any moneys not presently payable as existed upon the shares before the sale) be paid to the person entitled to the shares at the date of the sale.

CALLS ON SHARES AND FORFEITURE

12. Subject to the terms of allotment, the directors may make calls upon the members in respect of any moneys unpaid on the shares (whether in respect of nominal value or premium) and each member shall (subject to receiving at least fourteen clear day's notice specifying when and where payment is to be made) pay to the company as required by the notice the amount called on his shares. A call may be required to be paid by instalments. A call may, before receipt by the company of any sum due thereunder, be revoked in whole or part and payment of a call may be postponed in whole or in part. A person upon whom a call is made shall remain liable for calls made upon him notwithstanding the subsequent transfer of the shares in respect whereof the call was made.

13. A call shall be deemed to have been made at the time when the resolution of the directors authorising the call was passed.

14. The joint holders of a share shall be jointly and severally liable to pay all calls in respect thereof.

15. If a call remains unpaid after it has become due and payable the person from whom it is due and payable shall pay interest on the amount unpaid from the day it became due and payable until it is paid at the rate fixed by the terms of allotment of the share or in the notice of the call or, if no rate is fixed, at the appropriate rate (as defined by the Act) but the directors may waive payment of the interest wholly or in part.

16. An amount payable in respect of a share on allotment or at any fixed date, whether in respect of nominal value or premium or as an instalment of a call, shall be deemed to be a call and if it is not paid the provisions of the articles shall apply as if that amount had become due and payable by virtue of a call.

17. Subject to the terms of allotment, the directors may make arrangements on the issue of shares for a difference between the holders in the amounts and the times of payment of calls on their shares.

18. If a call remains unpaid after it has become due and payable the directors may give to the person from whom it is due not less than fourteen clear days' notice requiring payment of the amount unpaid together with any interest which may have accrued. The notice shall name the place where payment is to be made and shall state that if the notice is not complied with the shares in respect of which the call was made will be liable to be forfeited.

19. If the notice is not complied with any share in respect of which it was given may, before the payment required by the notice has been made, be forfeited by a resolution of the directors and the forfeiture shall include all dividends or other moneys payable in respect of the forfeited shares and not paid before the forfeiture.

20. Subject to the provisions of the Act, a forfeited share may be sold, re-allocated or otherwise disposed of on such terms and in such manner as the directors determine either to the person who was before the forfeiture the holder or to any other person and at any time the before sale, re-allotment or other disposition, the forfeiture may be cancelled on such terms as the directors think fit. Where for the purposes of its disposal a forfeited share is to be transferred to any person the directors may authorise some person to execute an instrument of transfer of the share to that person.

21. A person any of whose shares have been forfeited shall cease to be a member in respect of them and shall surrender to the company for cancellation the certificate for the shares forfeited but shall remain liable to the company for all moneys which at the date of forfeiture were presently payable by him to the company in respect of those shares with interest at the rate at which interest was payable on those moneys before the forfeiture or, if no interest was so payable, at the appropriate rate (as defined in the Act) from the date of forfeiture until payment but the directors may waive payment wholly or in part or enforce payment without any allowance for the value of the shares at the time of forfeiture or for any consideration received on their disposal.

22. A statutory declaration by a director or the secretary that a share has been forfeited on a specified date shall be conclusive evidence of the facts stated in it as against all persons claiming to be entitled to the share and the declaration shall (subject to the execution of an instrument of transfer if necessary) constitute a good title to the share and the person to whom the share is disposed of shall not be bound to see to the application of the consideration, if any, nor shall his title to the share be affected by any irregularity in or invalidity of the proceedings in reference to the forfeiture or disposal of the share.

TRANSFER OF SHARES

23. The instrument of transfer of a share may be in any usual form or in any other form which the directors may approve and shall be executed by or on behalf of the transferor and, unless the share is fully paid, by or on behalf of the transferee.

24. The directors may refuse to register the transfer of a share which is not fully paid to a person of whom they do not approve and they may refuse to register the transfer of a share on which the company has a lien. They may also refuse to register a transfer unless –
  (a) it is lodged at the office or at such other place as the directors may appoint and is accompanied by the certificate for the shares to which it relates and such other evidence as the directors may reasonably require to show the right of the transferor to make the transfer;
  (b) it is in respect of only one class of shares; and
  (c) it is in favour of not more than four transferees.

25. If the directors refuse to register a transfer of a share, they shall within two months after the date on which the transfer was lodged with the company send to the transferee notice of the refusal.

26. The registration of transfers of shares or of transfers of any class of shares may be suspended at such times and for such periods (not exceeding thirty days in any year) as the directors may determine.

27. No fee shall be charged for the registration of any instrument of transfer or other document relating to or affecting the title to any share.

28. The company shall be entitled to retain any instrument of transfer which is registered, but any instrument of transfer which the directors refuse to register shall be returned to the person lodging it when notice of the refusal is given.

TRANSMISSION OF SHARES

29. If a member dies the survivor or survivors where he was a joint holder, and his personal representatives where he was a sole holder or the only survivor of joint holders, shall be the only person recognised by the company as having any title to his interest; but nothing herein contained shall release the estate of a deceased member from any liability in respect of any share which had been jointly held by him.

30. A person becoming entitled to a share in consequence of the death or bankruptcy of a member may, upon such evidence being produced as the directors may properly require, elect either to become the holder of the share or to have some person nominated by him registered as the transferee. If he elects to become the holder he shall give notice to the company to that effect. If he elects to have another person registered he shall execute an instrument of transfer of the share to that person. All the articles relating to the transfer of shares shall apply to the notice or instrument of transfer as if it were an instrument of transfer executed by the member and the death or bankruptcy of the member had not occurred.

31. A person becoming entitled to a share in consequence of the death or bankruptcy of a member shall have the rights to which he would be entitled if he were the holder of the share, except that he shall not, before being registered as the holder of the share, be entitled in respect of it to attend or vote at any meeting of the company or at any separate meeting of the holders of any class of shares in the company.

ALTERATION OF SHARE CAPITAL

32. The company may by ordinary resolution –

(a) increase its share capital by new shares of such amount as the resolution prescribes;

(b) consolidate and divide all or any of its share capital into shares of larger amount than its existing shares;

(c) subject to the provisions of the Act, sub-divide its shares, or any of them, into shares of a smaller amount and the resolution may determine that, as between the shares resulting from the sub-division, any of them may have any preference or advantage as compared with the others; and

(d) cancel shares which, at the date of the passing of the resolution, have not been taken or agreed to be taken by any person and diminish the amount of its share capital by the amount of the shares so cancelled.

33. Whenever as a result of a consolidation of shares any members would become entitled to fractions of a share, the directors may, on behalf of those members, sell the shares representing the fractions for the best price reasonably obtainable to any person (including, subject to the provisions of the Act, the company) and distribute the net proceeds of sale in due proportion among those members, and the directors may authorise some person to execute an instrument of transfer of the shares to, or in accordance with the directions of, the purchaser. The transferee shall not be bound to see to the application of the purchase money nor shall his title to the shares be affected by any irregularity in or invalidity of the proceedings in reference to the sale.

34. Subject to the provisions of the Act, the company may by special resolution reduce its share capital, any capital redemption reserve and any share premium account in any way.

PURCHASE OF OWN SHARES

35. Subject to the provisions of the Act, the company may purchase its own shares (including any redeemable shares) and, if it is a private company, make a payment in respect of the redemption or purchase of its own shares otherwise than out of distributable profits of the company or the proceeds of a fresh issue of shares.

GENERAL MEETINGS

36. All general meetings other than annual general meetings shall be called extraordinary general meetings.

37. The directors may call general meetings and, on the requisition of members pursuant to the provisions of the Act, shall forthwith proceed to convene an extraordinary general meeting for a date not later than eight weeks after receipt of the requisition. If there are not within the United Kingdom sufficient directors to call a general meeting, any director or any member of the company may call a general meeting.

NOTICE OF GENERAL MEETINGS

38. An annual general meeting and an extraordinary general meeting called for the passing of a special resolution or a resolution appointing a person as a director shall be called by at least twenty-one clear days' notice. All other extraordinary general meetings shall be called by at least fourteen days' notice but a general meeting may be called by shorter notice if it is so agreed –

- (*a*) in the case of an annual general meeting, by all the members entitled to attend and vote thereat; and
- (*b*) in the case of any other meeting by a majority in number of the members having a right to attend and vote being a majority together holding not less than ninety-five per cent in nominal value of the shares giving that right.

The notice shall specify the time and place of the meeting and the general nature of the business to be transacted and, in the case of an annual general meeting, shall specify the meeting as such.

Subject to the provisions of the articles and to any restrictions imposed on any shares, the notice shall be given to all the members, to all persons entitled to a share in consequence of the death or bankruptcy of a member and to the directors and auditors.

39. The accidental omission to give notice of a meeting to, or the non-receipt of notice of a meeting by, any person entitled to receive notice shall not invalidate the proceedings at that meeting.

PROCEEDINGS AT GENERAL MEETINGS

40. No business shall be transacted at any meeting unless a quorum is present. Two persons entitled to vote upon the business to be transacted, each being a member or a proxy for a member or a duly authorised representative of a corporation, shall be a quorum.

41. If such a quorum is not present within half an hour from the time appointed for the meeting, or if during a meeting such a quorum ceases to be present, the meeting shall stand adjourned to the same day in the next week at the same time and place or [to] such time and place as the directors may determine.

42. The chairman, if any, of the board of directors or in his absence some other director nominated by the directors shall preside as chairman of the meeting, but if neither the chairman not such other director (if any) be present within fifteen minutes after the time appointed for holding the meeting and willing to act, the directors present shall elect one of their number to be chairman and, if there is only one director present and willing to act, he shall be chairman.

43. If no director is willing to act as chairman, or if no director is present within fifteen minutes after the time appointed for holding the meeting, the members present and entitled to vote shall choose one of their number to be chairman.

44. A director shall, notwithstanding that he is not a member, be entitled to attend and speak at any general meeting and at any separate meeting of the holders of any class of shares in the company.

45. The chairman may, with the consent of a meeting at which a quorum is present (and shall if so directed by the meeting), adjourn the meeting from time to time and from place to place, but no business shall be transacted at an adjourned meeting other than business which might properly have been transacted at the meeting had the adjournment not taken place. When a meeting is adjourned for fourteen days or more, at least seven clear days' notice shall be given specifying the time and place of the adjourned meeting and the general nature of the business to be transacted. Otherwise it shall not be necessary to give any such notice.

46. A resolution put to the vote of a meeting shall be decided on a show of hands unless before, or on the declaration of the result of, the show of hands a poll is duly demanded. Subject to the provisions of the Act, a poll may be demanded –

- (*a*) by the chairman; or
- (*b*) by at least two members having the right to vote at the meeting; or
- (*c*) by a member or members representing not less than one-tenth of the total voting rights of all members having the right to vote at the meeting; or
- (*d*) by a member or members holding shares conferring a right to vote at the meeting being shares on which an aggregate sum has been paid up equal to not less than one-tenth of the total sum paid up on all the shares conferring that right;

and a demand by a person as proxy for a member shall be the same as a demand by the member.

47. Unless a poll is duly demanded a declaration by the chairman that a resolution has been carried or carried unanimously, or by a particular majority, or lost, or not carried by a particular majority and an entry to that effect in the minutes of the meeting shall be conclusive evidence of the fact without proof of the number or proportion of the votes recorded in favour of or against the resolution.

48. The demand for a poll may, before the poll is taken, be withdrawn, but only with the consent of the chairman and a demand so withdrawn shall not be taken to have invalidated the result of a show of hands declared before the demand was made.

49. A poll shall be taken as the chairman directs and he may appoint scrutineers (who need not be members) and fix a time and place for declaring the result of the poll. The result of the poll shall be deemed to be the resolution of the meeting at which the poll was demanded.

50. In the case of an equality of votes, whether on a show of hands or on a poll, the chairman shall be entitled to a casting vote in addition to any other vote he may have.

51. A poll demanded on the election of a chairman or on a question of adjournment shall be taken forthwith. A poll demanded on any other question shall be taken either forthwith or at such time and place as the chairman directs not being more than thirty days after the poll is demanded. The demand for a poll shall not prevent the continuance of a meeting for the transaction of any business other than the question on which the poll was demanded. If a poll is demanded before the declaration of the result of a show of hands and the demand is duly withdrawn, the meeting shall continue as if the demand had not been made.
52. No notice need be given of a poll not taken forthwith if the time and place at which it is to be taken are announced at the meeting at which it is demanded. In any other case at least seven clear days' notice shall be given specifying the time and place at which the poll is to be taken.

53. A resolution in writing executed by or on behalf of each member who would have been entitled to vote upon it if it had been proposed at a general meeting at which he was present shall be as effectual as if it had been passed at a general meeting duly convened and held and may consist of several instruments in the like form each executed by or on behalf of one or more members.

NOTES

Reg 41: amended by inserting the word 'to' before 'time and place as the directors may determine' by SI 1985 No 1052.

VOTES OF MEMBERS

54. Subject to any rights or restrictions attached to any shares, on a show of hands every member who (being an individual) is present in person or (being a corporation) is present by a duly authorised representative, not being himself a member entitled to vote, shall have one vote and on a poll every member shall have one vote for every share of which he is the holder.

55. In the case of joint holders the vote of the senior tenders a vote, whether in person or by proxy, shall be accepted to the exclusion of the votes of the other joint holders; and seniority shall be determined by the order in which the names of the holders stand in the register of members.

56. A member in respect of whom an order had been made by any court having jurisdiction (whether in the United Kingdom or elsewhere) in matters concerning mental disorder may vote, whether on a show of hands or on a poll, by his receiver, curator bonis or other person authorised in that behalf appointed by that court, and any such receiver, curator bonis or other person may, on a poll, vote by proxy. Evidence to the satisfaction of the directors of the authority of the person claiming to exercise the right to vote shall be deposited at the office, or at such other place as is specified in accordance with the articles for the deposit of instruments of proxy, not less than 48 hours before the time appointed for holding the meeting or adjourned meeting at which the right to vote is to be exercised and in default the right to vote shall not be exercisable

57. No member shall vote at any general meeting or at any separate meeting of the holders of any class of shares in the company, either in person or by proxy, in respect of any share held by him unless all moneys presently payable by him in respect of that share have been paid.

58. No objection shall be raised to the qualification of any voter except at the meeting or adjourned meeting at which the vote objected to is tendered, and every vote not disallowed at the meeting shall be valid. Any objection made in due time shall be referred to the chairman whose decision shall be final and conclusive.

59. On a poll votes may be given either personally or by proxy. A member may appoint more than one proxy to attend of the same occasion.

60. An instrument appointing a proxy shall be in writing, executed by or on behalf of the appointor and shall be in the following form (or in a form as near thereto as circumstances allow or in any other form which is usual or which the directors may approve) —

    "   PLC/Limited
                I/We,   , of
                                            , being a
member/members of the above-named company, hereby appoint
                                    of
                                , or failing him,
  of   , as my/our proxy to vote in my/our name[s] and on my/our
behalf at the annual/extraordinary general meeting of the company to be held on
      19   , and at any adjournment thereof.
Signed on   19   ."

61. Where it is desired to afford members an opportunity of instructing the proxy how he shall act the instrument appointing a proxy shall be in the following form (or in a form as near thereto as circumstances allow or in any other form which is usual or which the directors may approve) —

''
                              PLC/Limited
                    I/We,   , of
                                                                      , being a
member/members of the above-named company, hereby appoint
                                             of
                                         , or failing him,
        of   , as my/our proxy to vote in my/our name[s] and on my/our
behalf at the annual/extraordinary general meeting of the company to be held on
            19   , and at any adjournment thereof. This form is to be used in respect
the resolutions mentioned below as follows:
        Resolution No 1 *for *against.
        Resolution No 2 *for *against.
    *Strike out whichever is not desired.
    Unless otherwise instructed, the proxy may vote as he thinks fit or abstain from
voting.
    Signed this   day of   19   ''

62. The instrument appointing a proxy and any authority under which it is
executed or a copy of such authority certified notarially or in some other way
approved by the directors may –

(a) be deposited at the office or at such other place within the United
    Kingdom as is specified in the notice convening the meeting or in any
    instrument of proxy sent out by the company in relation to the meeting not
    less than 48 hours before the time for holding the meeting or adjourned
    meeting at which the person named in the instrument proposes to vote; or
(b) in the case of a poll taken more than 48 hours after it is demanded, be
    deposited as aforesaid after the poll has been demanded and not less than
    24 hours before the time appointed for the taking of the poll; or
(c) where the poll is not taken forthwith but is taken not more than 48 hours
    after it was demanded, be delivered at the next meeting at which the poll
    was demanded to the chairman or to the secretary or to any director;

and an instrument of proxy which is not deposited or delivered in a manner so
permitted shall be invalid.

63. A vote given or poll demanded by proxy or by the duly authorised
representative of a corporation shall be valid notwithstanding the previous
determination of the authority of the person voting or demanding a poll unless
notice of the determination was received by the company at the office or at such
other place at which the instrument of proxy was duly deposited before the
commencement of the meeting or adjourned meeting at which the vote is given or
the poll demanded or (in the case of a poll taken otherwise than on the same day as
the meeting or adjourned meeting) the time appointed for taking the poll.

NUMBER OF DIRECTORS

64. Unless otherwise determined by ordinary resolution, the number of directors
(other than alternate directors) shall not be subject to any maximum but shall be not
less than two.

ALTERNATE DIRECTORS

65. Any director (other than an alternate director) may appoint any other director, or any other person approved by resolution of the directors and willing to act, to be an alternate director and may remove from office an alternate director so appointed by him.

66. An alternate director shall be entitled to receive notice of all meetings of directors and of all meetings of committees of directors of which his appointor is a member, to attend and vote at any such meeting at which the director appointing him is not personally present, and generally to perform all the functions of his appointor as a director in his absence but shall not be entitled to receive any remuneration from the company for his services as an alternate director. But it shall not be necessary to give notice of such a meeting to an alternate director who is absent from the United Kingdom.

67. An alternate director shall cease to be an alternate director if his appointor ceases to be a director; but, if a director retires by rotation or otherwise but is reappointed or deemed to have been reappointed at the meeting at which he retires, any appointment of an alternate director made by him which was in force immediately prior to his retirement shall continue after his reappointment.

68. Any appointment or removal of an alternate director shall be by notice to the company signed by the director making or revoking the appointment or in any other manner approved by the directors.

69. Save as otherwise provided in the articles, an alternate director shall be deemed for all purposes to be a director and shall alone be responsible for his own acts and defaults and he shall not be deemed to be the agent of the director appointing him.

POWERS OF DIRECTORS

70. Subject to the provisions of the Act, the memorandum and the articles and to any directions given by special resolution, the business of the company shall be managed by the directors who may exercise all the powers of the company. No alteration of the memorandum or articles and no such direction shall invalidate any prior act of the directors which would have been valid if that alteration had not been made or that direction had not been given. The powers given by this regulation shall not be limited by any special power given to the directors by the articles and a meeting of directors at which a quorum is present may exercise all powers exercisable by the directors.

71. The directors may, by power of attorney or otherwise, appoint any person to be the agent of the company for such purposes and on such conditions as they determine, including authority for the agent to delegate all or any of his powers.

DELEGATION OF DIRECTORS' POWERS

72. The directors may delegate any of their powers to any committee consisting of one or more directors. They may also delegate to any managing director or any director holding any other executive office such of their powers as they consider desirable to be exercised by him. Any such delegation may be made subject to any conditions the directors may impose, and either collaterally with or to the exclusion of their own powers and may be revoked or altered. Subject to any such conditions, the proceedings of a committee with two or more members shall be governed by the articles regulating the proceedings of directors so far as they are capable of applying.

APPOINTMENT AND RETIREMENT OF DIRECTORS

73. At the first annual general meeting all the directors shall retire from office, and at every subsequent annual general meeting one-third of the directors who are subject to retirement by rotation or, if their number is not three or a multiple of three, the number nearest to one-third shall retire from office; but, if there is only on director who is subject to retirement by rotation, he shall retire.

74. Subject to the provisions of the Act, the directors to retire by rotation shall be those who have been longest in office since their last appointment or reappointment, but as between persons who became or were last reappointed directors on the same day those to retire shall (unless they otherwise agree among themselves) be determined by lot.

75. If the company, at the meeting at which a director retires by rotation, does not fill the vacancy the retiring director shall, if willing to act, be deemed to have been reappointed unless at the meeting it is resolved not to fill the vacancy or unless a resolution for the reappointment of the director is put to the meeting and lost.

76. No person other than a director retiring by rotation shall be appointed or reappointed a director at any general meeting unless –

    (*a*) he is recommended by the directors;

or

    (*b*) not less than fourteen nor more than thirty-five clear days before the date appointed for the meeting, notice executed by a member qualified to vote at the meeting has been given to the company of the intention to propose that person for appointment or reappointment stating the particulars which would, if he were so appointed or reappointed, be required to be included in the company's register of directors together with notice executed by that person of his willingness to be appointed or reappointed.

77. Not less than seven nor more than twenty-eight clear days before the date appointed for holding a general meeting notice shall be given to all who are entitled to receive notice of the meeting of any person (other than a director retiring by rotation at the meeting) who is recommended by the directors for appointment or reappointment as a director at the meeting or in respect of whom notice has been duly given to the company of the intention to propose him at the meeting for appointment or reappointment as a director. The notice shall give the particulars of that person which would, if he were so appointed or reappointed, be required to be included in the company's register of directors.

78. Subject as aforesaid, the company may by ordinary resolution appoint a person who is willing to act to be a director either to fill a vacancy or as an additional director and may also determine the rotation in which any additional directors are to retire.

79. The directors may appoint a person who is willing to act to be a director, either to fill a vacancy or as an additional director, provided that the appointment does not cause the number of directors to exceed any number fixed by or in accordance with the articles as the maximum number of directors. A director so appointed shall hold office only until the next following annual general meeting and shall not be taken into account in determining the directors who are to retire by rotation at the meeting. If not reappointed at such annual general meeting, he shall vacate office at the conclusion thereof.

80. Subject as aforesaid, a director who retires at an annual general meeting may, if willing to act, be reappointed. If he is not reappointed, he shall retain office until the meeting appoints someone in his place, or if it does not do so, until the end of the meeting.

DISQUALIFICATION AND REMOVAL OF DIRECTORS

81. The office of a director shall be vacated if –

(a) he ceases to be a director by virtue of any provision of the Act or he becomes prohibited by law from being a director; or

(b) he becomes bankrupt or makes any arrangement or composition with his creditors generally; or

(c) he is, or may be, suffering from mental disorder and either –

(i) he is admitted to hospital in pursuance of an application for admission for treatment under the Mental Health Act 1983 or, in Scotland, an application for admission under the Mental Health (Scotland) Act 1960, or

(ii) an order is made by a court having jurisdiction (whether in the United Kingdom or elsewhere) in matters concerning mental disorder for his detention or for the appointment of a receiver, curator bonis or other person to exercise powers with respect to his property or affairs; or

(d) he resigns his office by notice to the company; or

(e) he shall for more than six consecutive months have been absent without permission of the directors from meetings of directors held during that period and the directors resolve that his office be vacated.

REMUNERATION OF DIRECTORS

82. The directors shall be entitled to such remuneration as the company may by ordinary resolution determine and, unless the resolution provides otherwise, the remuneration shall be deemed to accrue from day to day.

DIRECTORS' EXPENSES

83. The directors may be paid all travelling, hotel and other expenses properly incurred by them in connection with their attendance at meetings of directors or committees of directors or general meetings or separate meetings of the holders of any class of shares or of debentures of the company or otherwise in connection with the discharge of their duties.

DIRECTORS' APPOINTMENTS AND INTERESTS

84. Subject to the provisions of the Act, the directors may appoint one or more of their number to the office of managing director or to any other executive office under the company and may enter into an agreement or arrangement with any director for his employment by the company or for the provision by him of any services outside the scope of the ordinary duties of a director. Any such appointment, agreement or arrangement may be made upon such terms as the directors determine and they may remunerate any such director for his services as they think fit. Any appointment of a director to an executive office shall terminate if he ceases to be a director but without prejudice to any claim to damages for breach of the contract of service between the director and the company. A managing director and a director holding any other executive office shall not be subject to retirement by rotation.

85. Subject to the provisions of the Act, and provided that he has disclosed to the directors the nature and extent of any material interest of his, a director notwithstanding his office –

- (*a*) may be a party to, or otherwise interested in, any transaction or arrangement with the company or in which the company is otherwise interested;
- (*b*) may be a director or other officer of, or employed by, or a party to any transaction or arrangement with, or otherwise interested in, any body corporate promoted by the company or in which the company is otherwise interest; and
- (*c*) shall not, by reason of his office, be accountable to the company for any benefit which he derives from any such office or employment or from any such transaction or arrangement or from any interest in any such body corporate and no such transaction or arrangement shall be liable to be avoided on the ground of any such interest or benefit.

86. For the purposes of regulation 85 –

- (*a*) a general notice given to the directors that a director is to be regarded as having an interest of the nature and extent specified in the notice in any transaction or arrangement in which a specified person or class of persons is interested shall be deemed to be a disclosure that the director has an interest in any such transaction of the nature and extent so specified; and
- (*b*) an interest of which the director has no knowledge and of which it is unreasonable to expect him to have knowledge shall not be treated as an interest of his.

DIRECTORS' GRATUITIES AND PENSIONS

87. The directors may provide benefits, whether by the payment of gratuities or pensions or by insurance or otherwise, for any director who has held but no longer holds any executive office or employment with the company or with any body corporate which is or has been a subsidiary of the company or a predecessor in business of the company or of any such subsidiary, and for any member of his family (including a spouse and a former spouse) or any person who is or was dependent on him, and may (as well before as after he ceases to hold such office or employment) contribute to any fund and pay premiums for the purchase or provision of any such benefit.

PROCEEDINGS OF DIRECTORS

88. Subject to the provisions of the articles, the directors may regulate their proceedings as they think fit. A director may, and the secretary at the request of a director shall, call a meeting of the directors. It shall not be necessary to give notice of a meeting to a director who is absent from the United Kingdom. Questions arising at a meeting shall be decided by a majority of votes. In the case of an equality of votes, the chairman shall have a second or casting vote. A director who is also an alternate director shall be entitled in the absence of his appointor to a separate vote on behalf of his appointor in addition to his own vote.

89. The quorum for the transaction of the business of the directors may be fixed by the directors and unless so fixed at any other number shall be two. A person who holds office only as an alternate director shall, if his appointor is not present, be counted in the quorum.

90. The continuing directors or a sole continuing director may act notwithstanding any vacancies in their number, but, if the number of directors is less than the number fixed as the quorum, the continuing directors or director may act only for the purpose of filling vacancies or of calling a general meeting.

91. The directors may appoint one of their number to be the chairman of the board of directors and may at any time remove him from that office. Unless he is unwilling to do so, the director so appointed shall preside at every meeting of directors at which he is present. But if there is no director holding that office, or if the director holding it is unwilling to preside or is not present within five minutes after the time appointed for the meeting, the directors present may appoint one of their number to be chairman of the meeting.

92. All acts done by a meeting of directors, or of a committee of directors, or by a person acting as a director shall, notwithstanding that it be afterwards discovered that there was a defect in the appointment of any director or that any of them were disqualified from holding office, or had vacated office, or were not entitled to vote, be as valid as if every such person had been duly appointed and was qualified and had continued to be a director and had been entitled to vote.

93. A resolution in writing signed by all the directors entitled to receive notice of a meeting of directors or of a committee of directors shall be as valid and effectual as if it had been passed at a meeting of directors or (as the case may be) a committee of directors duly convened and held and may consist of several documents in the like form each signed by one or more directors; but a resolution signed by an alternate director need not also be signed by his appointor and, if it is signed by a director who has appointed an alternate director, it need not be signed by the alternate director in that capacity.

94. Save as otherwise provided by the articles, a director shall not vote at a meeting of directors or of a committee of directors on any resolution concerning a matter in which he has, directly or indirectly, an interest or duty which is material and which conflicts or may conflict with the interests of the company unless his interest or duty arises only because the case falls within one or more of the following paragraphs –

(*a*) the resolution relates to the giving to him of a guarantee, security, or indemnity in respect of money lent to, or an obligation incurred by him for the benefit of, the company or any of its subsidiaries;

(*b*) the resolution relates to the giving to a third party of a guarantee, security, or indemnity in respect of an obligation of the company or any of its subsidiaries for which the director has assumed responsibility in whole or part and whether alone or jointly with others under a guarantee or indemnity or by the giving of security;

(*c*) his interest arises by virtue of his subscribing or agreeing to subscribe for any shares, debentures or other securities of the company or any of its subsidiaries or by virtue of his being, or intending to become, a participant in the underwriting or sub-underwriting of an offer of any such shares, debentures, or other securities by the company or any of its subsidiaries for subscription, purchase or exchange;

(*d*) the resolution relates in any way to a retirement benefits scheme which has been approved, or is conditional upon approval, by the Board of Inland Revenue for taxation purposes.

For the purposes of this regulation, an interest of a person who is, for any purpose of the Act (excluding any statutory modification thereof not in force when this regulation becomes binding on the company), connected with a director shall be treated as an interest of the director and, in relation to an alternate director, an interest of his appointor shall be treated as an interest of the alternate director without prejudice to any interest which the alternate director has otherwise.

95. A director shall not be counted in the quorum present at a meeting in relation to a resolution on which he is not entitled to vote.

96. The company may by ordinary resolution suspend or relax to any extent, either generally or in respect of any particular matter, any provision of the articles prohibiting a director from voting at a meeting of directors or of a committee of directors.

97. Where proposals are under consideration concerning the appointment of two or more directors to offices or employments with the company or any body corporate in which the company is interested the proposals may be divided and considered in relation to each director separately and (provided he is not for another reason precluded from voting) each of the directors concerned shall be entitled to vote and be counted in the quorum in respect of each resolution except that concerning his own appointment.

98. If a question arises at a meeting of directors or of a committee of directors as to the right of a director to vote, the question may, before the conclusion of the meeting, be referred to the chairman of the meeting and his ruling in relation to any director other than himself shall be final and conclusive.

SECRETARY

99. Subject to the provisions of the Act, the secretary shall be appointed by the directors for such a term, at such remuneration and upon such conditions as they may think fit; and any secretary so appointed may be removed by them.

MINUTES

100. The directors shall cause minutes to be made in books kept for the purpose –

  (*a*) of all appointments of officers made by the directors; and
  (*b*) of all proceedings at meetings of the company, of the holders of any class of shares in the company, and of the directors, and of committees of directors, including the names of the directors present at each such meeting.

THE SEAL

101. The seal shall only be used by the authority of the directors or of a committee of directors authorised by the directors. The directors may determine who shall sign any instrument to which the seal is affixed and unless otherwise so determined it shall be signed by a director and by the secretary or by a second director.

DIVIDENDS

102. Subject to the provisions of the Act, the company may by ordinary resolution declare dividends in accordance with the respective rights of the members, but no dividend shall exceed the amount recommended by the directors.

103. Subject to the provisions of the Act, the directors may pay interim dividends if it appears to them that they are justified by the profits of the company available for distribution. If the share capital is divided into different classes, the directors may pay interim dividends on shares which confer deferred or non-preferred rights with regard to dividend as well as on shares which confer preferential rights with regard to dividend, but no interim dividend shall be paid on shares carrying deferred or non-preferred rights if, at the time of payment, any preferential dividend is in arrear. The directors may also pay at intervals settled by them any dividend payable at a fixed rate if it appears to them that the profits available for distribution justify the payment. Provided the directors act in good faith they shall not incur any liability to the holders of shares conferring preferred rights for any loss they may suffer by the lawful payment of an interim dividend on any shares having deferred or non-preferred rights.

104. Except as otherwise provided by the rights attached to shares, all dividends shall be declared and paid according to the amounts paid up on the shares on which the dividend is paid. All dividends shall be apportioned and paid proportionately to the amounts paid up on the shares during any portion or portions of the period in respect of which the dividend is paid; but, if any share is issued on terms providing that it shall rank for dividend as from a particular date, that share shall rank for dividend accordingly.

105. A general meeting declaring a dividend may, upon the recommendation of the directors, direct that it shall be satisfied wholly or partly by the distribution of assets and, where any difficulty arises in regard to the distribution, the directors may settle the same and in particular may issue fractional certificates and fix the value for distribution of any assets and may determine that cash shall be paid to any member upon the footing of the value so fixed in order to adjust the rights of members and may vest any assets in trustees.

106. Any dividend or other moneys payable in respect of a share may be paid by cheque sent by post to the registered address of the person entitled or, if two or more persons are the holders of the share or are jointly entitled to it by reason of the death or bankruptcy of the holder, to the registered address of that one of those persons who is first named in the register of members or to such person and to such address as the person or persons entitled may in writing direct. Every cheque shall be made payable to the order of the person or persons entitled or to such other person as the person or persons entitled may in writing direct and payment of the cheque shall be a good discharge to the company. Any joint holder or other person jointly entitled to a share as aforesaid may give receipts for any dividend or other moneys payable in respect of the share.

107. No dividend or other moneys payable in respect of a share shall bear interest against the company unless otherwise provided by the rights attached to the share.

108. Any dividend which has remained unclaimed for twelve years from the date when it became due for payment shall, if the directors so resolve, be forfeited and cease to remain owing by the company.

ACCOUNTS

109. No member shall (as such) have any right of inspecting any accounting records or other book or document of the company except as conferred by statute or authorised by the directors or by ordinary resolution of the company.

CAPITALISATION OF PROFITS

110. The directors may with the authority of an ordinary resolution of the company –

(a) subject as hereinafter provided, resolve to capitalise any undivided profits of the company not required for paying any preferential dividend (whether or not they are available for distribution) or any sum standing to the credit of the company's share premium account or capital redemption reserve;

(b) appropriate the sum resolved to be capitalised to the members who would have been entitled to it if it were distributed by way of dividend and in the same proportions and apply such sum on their behalf either in or towards paying up the amounts, if any, for the time being unpaid on any shares held by them respectively, or in paying up in full unissued shares or debentures of the company of a nominal amount equal to that sum, and allot the shares or debentures credited as fully paid to those members, or as they may direct, in those proportions, or partly in one way and partly in the other: but the share premium account, the capital redemption reserve, and any profits which are not available for distribution may, for the purposes of this regulation, only be applied in paying up unissued shares to be allotted to members credited as fully paid;

(c) make such provision by the issue of fractional certificates or by payment in cash or otherwise as they determine in the case of shares or debentures becoming distributable under this regulation in fractions; and

(d) authorise any person to enter on behalf of all the members concerned into an agreement with the company providing for the allotment to them respectively, credited as fully paid, of any shares or debentures to which they are entitled upon such capitalisation, any agreement made under such authority being binding on all such members.

NOTICES

111. Any notice to be given to or by any person pursuant to the articles shall be in writing except that a notice calling a meeting of the directors need not be in writing.

112. The company may give any notice to a member either personally or by sending it by post in a prepaid envelope addressed to the member at his registered address or by leaving it at that address. In the case of joint holders of a share, all notices shall be given to the joint holder whose name stands first in the register of members in respect of the joint holding and notice so given shall be sufficient notice to all the joint holders. A member whose registered address is not within the United Kingdom and who gives to the company an address within the United Kingdom at which notices may be given to him shall be entitled to have notices given to him at that address, but otherwise no such member shall be entitled to receive any notice from the company.

113. A member present, either in person or by proxy, at any meeting of the company or of the holders of any class of shares in the company shall be deemed to have received notice of the meeting and, where requisite, of the purposes for which it was called.

114. Every person who becomes entitled to a share shall be bound by any notice in respect of that share which, before his name is entered in the register of members, has been duly given to a person from whom he derives his title.

115. Proof that an envelope containing a notice was properly addressed, prepaid and posted shall be conclusive evidence that the notice was given. A notice shall, ... be deemed to be given at the expiration of 48 hours after the envelope containing it was posted.

NOTES

Reg. 115: amended by deleting the words 'unless the contrary is proved' by SI 1985 No. 1052.

---

116. A notice may be given by the company to the persons entitled to a share in consequence of the death or bankruptcy of a member by sending or delivering it, in any manner authorised by the articles for the giving of notice to a member, addressed to them by name, or by the title of representatives of the deceased, or trustee of the bankrupt or by any like description at the address, if any, within the United Kingdom supplied for that purpose by the persons claiming to be so entitled. Until such an address has been supplied, a notice may be given in any manner in which it might have been given if the death or bankruptcy had not occurred.

WINDING UP

117. If the company is wound up, the liquidator may, with the sanction of an extraordinary resolution of the company and any other sanction required by the Act, divide among the members in specie the whole or any part of the assets of the company and may, for that purpose, value any assets and determine how the division shall be carried out as between the members or different classes of members. The liquidator may, with the like sanction, vest the whole or any part of the assets in trustees upon such trusts for the benefit of the members as he with the like sanction determines, but no member shall be compelled to accept any assets upon which there is a liability.

INDEMNITY

118. Subject to the provisions of the Act but without prejudice to any indemnity to which a director may otherwise be entitled, every director or other officer or auditor of the company shall be indemnified out of the assets of the company against any liability incurred by him in defending any proceedings, whether civil or criminal, in which judgment is given in his favour or in which he is acquitted or in connection with any application in which relief is granted to him by the court from liability for negligence, default, breach of duty or breach of trust in relation to the affairs of the company.

Exercises

1 Which legal provisions assist shareholders to gain control over the management and which militate against this?
2 Should employees have a say in the running of a company?

11 Directors' Duties

A director of a company will often be dealing with other people's property, not only in the legal sense in that he will be in charge of the property of the company, but also the company may have shareholders who have put money into the company by buying shares but have little or no control over what the directors do. Their investment will be lost if the company becomes insolvent. Also, if goods or services are supplied to a company on credit, the directors will be dealing with money to which the creditors have a claim until they are paid in full. It is obviously necessary to control the behaviour of someone in such a position of power and to impose upon him a standard of conduct which will protect people who stand to lose if the director is either incompetent or dishonest. There are three major difficulties in imposing such a standard:

1. Directors vary very considerably in the extent of their involvement with a company. It is now becoming recognised practice to separate the members of a board of directors into 'executive' and 'non-executive' members. The executive directors will be very closely involved with the day-to-day affairs of the company and the amount of knowledge that they might be expected to have about the internal affairs of the company will far exceed that of the non-executive members, whose job is to take an overall view of the running of the company, lend what expertise they have to the making of policy decisions, and sound warning bells if anything suspicious comes to their notice. This separation was not common practice in the past and is by no means universal now. The law has sought, therefore, to impose a standard of conduct on all directors regardless of their degree of involvement with the company. To formulate a standard of conduct which would be fair to all types of director has proved difficult.

2. Not only are there different types of director, there are also different types of company. Companies vary from huge multinational giants such as ICI to small family businesses run by one person (though they must have two shareholders unless they are a designated 'single member company', see Chapter 1) which have decided that the business could be best managed in corporate form. This huge difference in the size and complexity of companies has also caused difficulty in formulating a standard by which the performance of all company directors can be judged. There has been considerable reluctance, until recent legislation, (much of it EC Directive-driven) to attempt to impose different director's duties depending on the type of his company. Now, in statutes, the distinction is often drawn between directors of public companies and directors of private companies. This distinction is sometimes criticised because there can be large and complex private companies as well as small and relatively simple public companies. Nevertheless, if a distinction is to

be made, no distinction would ever be wholly satisfactory and the public/ private distinction seems to work as well as any would.

The case law in this area is still very important. In the case law on directors' duties no formal distinction is normally made between different types of companies. Rather, the cases impose a sliding scale of responsibility which depends on what can reasonably be expected of someone in that position. A complex body of both case and statute law has grown up. Not all of it is satisfactory, as we will see.

3. The third difficulty in formulating a standard of behaviour for directors is to be found in the nature of the decisions that they make. Most of these decisions will be business decisions about which contracts it would be best for the company to enter into. It is very difficult for a court of law looking at events with hindsight to judge whether that decision was commercially foolish at the time it was made. It may have turned out badly for the company but that may be because of factors which could not be foreseen by the directors when the decision was made. The courts do not wish to encourage directors to become too cautious by imposing too high a duty of care. They must therefore respect decisions which they believe were made in good faith even though they may have been commercially disastrous for the company as things turned out. The difference in the sizes and complexity of companies and the differences in the degree of involvement of the directors in question, coupled with the unique economic circumstances surrounding each decision, make it difficult for the court to build up a body of precedents. This is unlike judging the performance of other professions where often similarly qualified persons have had similar decisions to make.

11.1 The Cadbury Report

In response to a number of financial scandals a committee chaired by Sir Adrian Cadbury was set up in May 1991. Its function was to make recommendations aimed at tightening corporate control mechanisms. The Committee focused on financial control mechanisms, particularly the Board of Directors, auditing and shareholder responsibility.The Committee published its final report in December 1992. The Committee's central recommendation was that the Boards of all listed companies registered in the UK should comply with a Code of Best Practice. Smaller listed companies, who could not comply with the Code immediately would have to give their reasons for non-compliance as an alternative (p. 19, para. 3.15).

The Committee were of the opinion that compliance with the Code as a listing requirement would ensure an open approach to the disclosure of information, contribute to the efficient working of the market economy, prompt boards to take effective action and allow shareholders to scrutinise companies more thoroughly (p. 19, para. 3.15). The Stock Exchange has acted to require compliance in the way suggested by the Cadbury

Committee and a number of bodies not affected by listing requirements have issued guidance along 'Cadbury' lines. Examples are the Building Societies Commission and the Friendly Societies Commission. The report has undoubtedly caused considerable thought to be given to the issue of corporate governance and it is to be hoped that the debate will be continued. The make-up and function of the Board was by far the most controversial area. The Committee emphasised that tests of a Board's effectiveness included the way in which members as a whole work together (p. 20, para. 4.2). They also felt that executive and non-executive directors were likely to contribute in different and complementary ways. Non-executive directors could make two particularly important contributions which would not conflict with the unitary nature of the board (p. 20, para. 4.5). These were the role of 'reviewing' the performance of the board and executive (p. 20, para. 4.5) and taking the lead 'where potential conflicts of interest arise (p. 21, para. 4.6).

The Committee emphasised the need for the Financial audit of companies to be tighter but made no very radical recommendations as to how this should be achieved. The proper scope of auditor liability is clearly a nettle which the Cadbury Committee failed to grasp and should continue to be the subject of lively debate.

The Committee had very little to say about private individual shareholders and focused on the perceived power of institutional shareholders to ensure that the company complied with the Code. In response to the draft report issued by the Cadbury Committee for comment the Institutional Shareholders Committee submitted a paper addressing 'The Responsibilities of Institutional Shareholders'. This was not a specific response to the Cadbury proposals but dealt with some of the issues raised in the draft report. The Institutional Shareholder Committee acknowledge that 'Because of the size of their shareholdings, institutional investors, as part proprietors of a company, are under a strong obligation to exercise their influence in a responsible manner'. The paper (published in December 1991) examines ways in which this responsibility should be fulfilled including 'regular, systematic contact at senior executive level to exchange views and information on strategy, performance, Board Membership and quality of management'. They also felt that institutional investors 'should support Boards by a positive use of voting rights, unless they have good reason for doing otherwise' and 'should take a positive interest in the composition of Boards of Directors with particular reference to:

(i) Concentrations of decision-making power not formally constrained by checks and balances appropriate to the particular company
(ii) The appointment of a core of non-executives of appropriate calibre, experience and independence.'

The Cadbury Committee clearly accepted these views and placed heavy reliance on the power of institutional shareholders within a company.

The Cadbury Committee's recommendations have drawn considerable criticism. The voluntary nature of the Code has been attacked, but so too has the Stock Exchange's attempt to give the Code some teeth. The major criticism that has surfaced is that the reliance on non-executive directors leads to a type of two-tier board with different directors fulfilling different functions. This criticism must be viewed in the light of a proper understanding of the two-tier board system as it operates elsewhere in Europe. It often includes provision for a supervisory board which has the power to dismiss the executive board. The Cadbury proposals do not go very far towards that system, there is no suggestion that appointment and dismissal of all directors should be removed from shareholder control.

A new committee, the Hampel Committee, has been convened to consider further some of the issues examined by the Cadbury committee and to make other recomendations on corporate governance issues. It is expected to produce a report shortly.

11.2 **Duty Owed to the Company**

It is important to remember that directors owe their duties to that legal person 'the company' rather than to shareholders or potential share-holders. This is particularly significant where the enforcement of those duties is in question, because the general rule is that directors' duties can only be enforced by the company suing directors (see further discussion on the effect of this rule in Chapter 13). The principle can be illustrated by the facts of *Percival* v. *Wright* [1902] 2 Ch 421. In that case, shareholders wrote to the secretary of a company asking if he knew anyone likely to buy their shares. The chairman and two other directors purchased the shares at £2.10s. per share. The shareholders subsequently discovered that prior to the negotiations for the sale of the shares the chairman and directors had been approached by a third party. The third party wished to purchase the company and was offering a price which would mean that each share would be valued at well over £2.10s. The shareholders asked for the sale of the shares to be set aside by the court on the grounds that the chairman and directors had been in breach of a duty to the shareholders. Swinfen-Eady J refused to set aside the sale and firmly rejected the idea that there was any duty owed by the chairman and directors to the shareholders. Their duties were owed to the company. This situation may well now be caught by the s. 459 remedy (see Chapter 13). However, the fundamental principle that directors owe their duty to the company is unchanged. This principle may cause difficulties where there are several companies acting as a group. Normally one company is seen as the 'parent' company and will hold a majority of the shares in its subsidiary companies. The exact relationship between parent and subsidiary is discussed elsewhere (see Chapters 1 and 10). In these circumstances directors may be appointed to the board of the subsidiary by the parent company. It is very tempting for them to look after the interests of the parent company and ignore the interests of the subsidiary. That they must not do so is clearly illustrated by the case *Scottish Co-operative Society* v. *Meyer* [1959] AC 324 where Lord Denning emphasised that the duty of directors was owed to the particular company which had appointed them (see Casenotes). This is another area of law where reform is being actively considered. Many companies do act with group interests in mind and it seems sensible to bring the law more into accord with commercial practice.

11.3 What is the Company?

In Chapter 3 various different models of companies were described. The model chosen makes a difference to the way in which directors exercise their duties to the company, because the interests which are seen as making up the company vary with the model chosen. To say that the directors owe a duty to the company is clear, but it makes no sense if the company is regarded as a legal personality or piece of paper alone. The directors must take note of the interests of the human beings who are actively involved in the company's affairs. Which persons are entitled to have their interests regarded?

1. Members
Clearly the member's interests are of very considerable importance although that also raises the problem of whether a dissenting minority of members have a right to have their interests considered. This question is considered in more detail in the chapter concerning shareholders' rights (Chapter 13) and in the chapter where alteration of the articles of association and the '*bona fides*' test is considered (Chapter 5).

2. Employees
By s. 309 of the Companies Act 1985 company directors are 'to have regard' to the interests of employees as well as the interests of members. However, this duty to have regard to employees interests is expressed to be part of the general duty owed by directors to the company. It can only therefore be enforced by the company. The employees would have no standing to complain to the court that their interests had not been considered. This duty has no enforcing teeth and can be seen as mere 'window dressing'.

3. Creditors
Creditors also have their money tied up in the company. It is logical to expect their interests to be important to the directors in making a decision. In *Lonrho* v. *Shell Petroleum* [1980] 1 WLR 627 this factor was acknowledged by Lord Diplock, who said: 'it is the duty of the board to consider . . . the best interests of the company. These are not exclusively those of its shareholders but may include those of its creditors' (p. 634).
   The Court of Appeal confirmed this view in *The Liquidator of the Property of West Mercia Safetywear Ltd* v. *Dodd and Another* [1988]

BCLC 250. However, in that case the interests of the company were said to include the interests of creditors because the company was insolvent at the relevant time. In *Lonrho* insolvency was not an issue. Nor was insolvency an issue in *Winkworth* v. *Edward Baron* [1987] BCLC 193 where Lord Templeman referred to a duty owed directly to creditors. In *Brady* v. *Brady* [1988] BCLC 20, Nourse LJ regarded the interests of the company as synonymous with the interests of the creditors where the company was insolvent or 'doubtfully solvent'. It seems clear:

(i)   Where the company is insolvent the interests of creditors and the interests of the company coincide to a considerable degree see *Standard Charted Bank* v. *Walker* [1992] 1 WLR 561.

(ii) Where a company is approaching insolvency the interests of the creditors are important where an assessment is made of whether the directors acted in the interests of the company. (What is not clear is precisely at what stage in the slide into insolvency the creditors' interests become paramount or what test is to be applied to determine the directors' appreciation of the insolvency. If they ought to have known of the insolvency but did not are they still liable? The cases provide no clear answer. See further on this Vanessa Finch, *Company Lawyer*, vol. 10, no. 1, p. 23.)

(iii) In the case of a solvent company the interests of creditors should still be considered but it is unclear what weight the directors should give to consideration of those interests.

In the following text the duties of directors are dealt with under two headings:
(1) Duties of care and skill; and
(2) Fiduciary (trustee-like) duties.

The statutory duties of directors are covered in the next chapter.

11.4 Duties of Care and Skill

The difference in the degree of involvement of directors can be well illustrated by the facts of the old case known as *The Marquis of Bute's Case* [1892] 2 Ch 100.

The Marquis of Bute became president of the Cardiff Savings Bank when he was six months old, having inherited the office from his father. He attended only one board meeting of the bank in thirty-eight years. However, he was held not liable for irregularities which occurred in the lending operations of the bank. The judge held that he could not be considered liable as he knew nothing about what was going on. There was no hint that he ought to have kept himself informed. Similarly, in *Dovey* v. *Cory* [1901] AC 477 the director was able to escape liability for malpractice which had occurred, on the grounds that he had relied on information given to him by the chairman and general manager of the company. The standard applied here seems to be somewhat stricter than that in the *Marquis of Bute's Case* since the court held that the reliance on the chairman and general manager was *reasonable* and that the director had not been *negligent*. The standard in this case was one of negligence, that is, the director must have acted as a reasonable man. If a reasonable man would have been suspicious of the information that was given and would have investigated further, a director who failed to do so could well have been liable for the loss caused by the irregularity. This may well be a higher standard than that imposed in the previous case where there seems to be no suggestion that a 'reasonable man' test should be used to judge the Marquis's inaction.

A case in which these issues were fully explored is *Re City Equitable Fire Insurance* [1925] Ch 407. That case is still generally regarded as the most important in this area and the standards laid down in it have not been challenged directly in any subsequent case, although as we shall see, the standard laid down there may have been altered in an oblique way by the cases decided under the Company Directors Disqualification Act 1986 and its predecessor sections of the Companies Act 1985.

In *Re City Equitable Fire Insurance* the judge set out three important rules:

1. A director need not exhibit in the performance of his duties a greater degree of skill than may reasonably be expected from a person of his knowledge and experience.

2. A director is not bound to give continuous attention to the affairs of his company. His duties are of an intermittent nature to be performed at periodical board meetings and at meetings of any committee of the board on which he happens to be placed. He is not, however, bound to attend all such meetings, though he ought to attend whenever in the circumstances he is reasonably able to do so.

3. In respect of all duties that, having regard to the exigencies of business and the articles of association, may properly be left to some other official, a director is, in the absence of grounds for suspicion, justified in trusting that official to perform such duties honestly.

These rules have been affirmed recently in *Dorchester Finance Co. Ltd* v. *Stebbing* [1989] BCLC 498 where it was also held that there was no difference in the duties owed by executive and non-executive directors.

Notable aspects of these rules are:

Rule 1
The standard is not a 'reasonable professional director' standard but refers to the reasonable man with the skill and experience actually possessed by the particular director in question. This has two effects. If someone like the baby Marquis of Bute is appointed to the board of a company he will presumably be held not liable for irregularities, as a small baby has extremely limited skill and experience. This may be fair from the baby's point of view but the standard does little to protect the public. However,

leaving such extreme examples aside, the standard is capable of working quite well and of having sufficient flexibility to be valuable in different types of companies for judging the behaviour of different types of directors. Larger and more complex businesses are more likely to employ highly qualified and experienced directors to run affairs. Under the test in Rule 1 such people will have a higher standard of skill expected of them. Thus the more complex the operation, the more the interests of those with money at stake will be protected. The test is therefore only seriously inadequate where a very inappropriate appointment has been made, whether the operation is large or small.

Rule 2
Similar considerations apply to Rule 2, since the duty is to attend meetings and give attention to company affairs 'whenever in the circumstances [the director] is reasonably able to do so'. In the case of a full-time salaried director of a large company it is obviously reasonable to expect his working life to be devoted to the affairs of the company. The standard will vary to take into account different types of director so that a non-executive director will not be bound to give the affairs of the company so much of his time as would an executive director.

Rule 3
At first sight this seems to benefit a director who absents himself or who fails to keep himself informed on company matters so that he will not be aware of any 'grounds for suspicion' and so can safely leave the running of the company to others. However, if this rule is taken in conjunction with the other two rules, it will be seen that the director is obliged (by Rules 1 and 2) to take proper part in the affairs of the company so that unless his appointment has been manifestly foolish (as in the case of the baby Marquis) the rules will work together to provide a sliding scale of responsibility which will weigh heaviest on those most able to do the job, and whose expectations of reward from the job are probably highest.

In extreme cases, however, the rules will not protect those with money at stake. There has long been a call for an objective standard of competence to be imposed so that directors could not do the job if they were dishonest or foolish (or six months old). Parliament has not directly introduced such a standard. However, the courts may well be moving in that direction. In *Re D'Jan of London Ltd* [1993] BCC 646 Hoffman LJ stated that the common law duty of care owed by directors was accurately stated in s. 214 Insolvency Act 1986. This requires a director to conduct himself as 'a reasonably diligent person having both –

(a) the general knowledge, skill and experience that may reasonably be expected of a person carrying out by that director in relation to the company, and

(b) the general knowledge, skill and experience that that director has.'

The statement by Hoffman LJ was made in relation to an application under s. 212 Insolvency Act which gives a remedy against directors who have been guilty of 'any misfeasance or breach of fiduciary or other duty in relation to the company'. The Company Directors Disqualification Act 1986 (dealt with in more detail in the next chapter) may also be influencing the courts and may lead to the introduction of an objective description of directors' duties. The courts must, under s. 6, disqualify a director from managing a company if he has been a director of a company which has become insolvent (either while he was acting for it or later) and the court finds that his conduct 'makes him unfit to be concerned in the management of a company'. By s. 6(4) the minimum period of disqualification is two years and the maximum fifteen years. Although this legislation raises many questions (see the next chapter), the major issue relevant here is what is meant by 'unfitness'. If the courts are expecting directors to live up to a high standard in order to escape being called 'unfit' it is possible that this legislation will have the effect of raising the standards expected of directors generally. This will only be by a type of 'knock-on' effect if it happens at all because the legislation has no direct effect on the standards set out in *Re City Equitable Fire*. However, it may seem strange to the courts if a position is reached where a director has been found unfit and disqualified and yet is not liable to account for irregularities under the rule in that case. There may well be a tendency to adopt a similar standard to judge directors by. For a further discussion of this issue see Chapter 12.

Another possible influence on the standard by which directors are judged is the Fifth Directive of the EC. This is currently being considered by the Council, but has made very slow progress because it has aroused considerable opposition, not least from the United Kingdom.

Article 14 of the Fifth Directive provides for the liability of directors. They are to be liable (as a minimum) for all 'damage sustained by the company as a result of breaches of duty by the members of [the board or boards of directors] in carrying out their functions'. Liability is without limit but individual members may escape liability if they prove that no fault is personally attributable to them. Proof that the act in question falls outside the special field of the member will not of itself be sufficient to escape liability. Where there are two boards of directors the authorisation of the 'supervisory' board for the act in question will not exempt the members of the management board from liability. Similarly the authorisation of the general meeting will not prevent directors from being liable. Waiver of liability can only be by an express resolution which may be blocked by the holders of 10 per cent of the shares (Article 17). There is to be a minimum limitation period of three years for Article 14 liability (Article 21).

These provisions create serious problems. One difficulty is the lack of definition of the concept of breach of duty. Because this Directive will have to become law in each Member State by each State passing its own national legislation interpreting its provisions, there is room for much variation in the standard that will be imposed. It could leave national laws unchanged and differing from each other. This would happen if the

Member States interpreted 'breach of duty' to mean 'breaches of duty according to our own national laws as they stand at the moment'. If, on the other hand, the imposition of unlimited liability for negligence in the management of the company is envisaged, the provisions as to the potential liability of directors are radical and could cause the same problems as have been experienced in the United States, where the imposition of huge liabilities on the board of directors for negligence (see *Smith* v. *Van Gorkom* 488 A.2d 858 (Supreme Court of Delaware 1985) (see Casenotes) has led to the adoption by a number of States of legislation permitting the elimination of the liability of directors for various breaches of duty. The imposition of liability for negligence proved too strict in view of the huge sums of money involved and led to a distinct reluctance to join boards as non-executive (outside) directors.

An example of such a law is Delaware Corporation Law s. 102 (b) (7) which was adopted on 1 July 1986 and reads:

> 'the certificate of incorporation may also contain any or all of the following matters:
> (7) A provision eliminating or limiting the personal liability of a director to the corporation or its stockholders for monetary damages for breach of fiduciary duty as director, provided that such provision shall not eliminate or limit the liability of a director, (i) For any breach of the directors duty of loyalty to the corporation or its stockholders; (ii) for acts or omissions not in good faith or which involve intentional misconduct or knowing violation of the law; (iii) under s. 174 of this title [relating to limitations on distributions to stockholders]; or (iv) for any transaction from which the directors derived an improper personal benefit. No such provision shall eliminate or limit the liability of a director for any act or omission occurring prior to the date when such provision became effective . . . '

This rule of Delaware law is in stark contrast to the rule contained in s. 310 of the Companies Act 1985 which makes void any provision which seeks to exempt any officer or auditor from 'any liability which by virtue of any rule of law would otherwise attach to him in respect of any negligence, breach of duty or breach of trust of which he may be guilty in relation to the company'.

It is too early yet to predict whether the Company Directors Disqualification Act 1986 or the EC Fifth Directive will have the effect of encouraging the adoption of the approach suggested by Hoffman LJ in D'Jan. All indications are that the courts are moving in the direction of requiring directors to perform according to an objective standard. The excuse of incompetence may well be on the way out.

One aspect of company law that always influences the standard imposed on directors in practice is the means of enforcing the duties that are owed. More will be said on this matter in Chapter 13, but it should always be borne in mind that there is no point in imposing a duty on someone if there are no effective means of enforcing that duty.

11.5 **Fiduciary Duties**

It is traditional to give a list of the breaches of fiduciary duties of directors under headings such as: misappropriation of company property; exercise of powers for an improper purpose; fettering discretion; and not permitting interest and duty to conflict. While no one would dispute that these are all areas where directors have been found to be in breach of duty, the listing of the duties in this way tends to obscure the fundamental point that a director is under one overriding duty and that is to act *bona fide* in the interests of the company. The list of duties that has grown out of the case law is in fact a list of situations where a director is most likely to be in breach of his fundamental duty. Thus, for example, if a director finds himself in a position where he has a conflict of interests he is in dire peril of being found to be in breach of his overriding duty to act *bona fide* for the benefit of the company. A tendency to use the list of situations as a statement of the duties themselves can have two effects; one is to create a straitjacket into which to force behaviour, that is, if the behaviour does not come under one of these headings it cannot be a breach of duty despite the fact that it is not in the company's interests; secondly, to obscure the debate about the possibility that behaviour that does come under one of these headings can be excused by the company voting to that effect in general meeting. It is difficult to accept the ratification (excusing) of something which is the breach of a fundamental duty. It is easier to see how, if a director places himself in one of the perilous situations, but his behaviour has not breached the fundamental duty of *bona fides*, such behaviour may be regarded as acceptable by the company. Behaviour which is not *bona fide* for the benefit of the company cannot be condoned unless 'the company' (in the wide sense explained above – members, creditors and ?employees) agree. Thus, where sole shareholders and directors took money from a company this was nevertheless held to be theft despite the fact that they clearly had the agreement of all the members (themselves) to do so (*Re Attorney General's Reference* No. 2, 1982 and *R. v. Phillipou* [1989] Crim LR 559 and 585. These cases were affirmed by the House of Lords in *R. v. Gomez* [1993] 3 WLR 1067. The distinction between the overriding duty of good faith and the effect of putting oneself in one of the perilous situations varies with the seriousness with which the particular behaviour is viewed. Thus, it will be a most unusual situation where there has been a 'misappropriation of company property' but the directors can nevertheless be held to have acted *bona fide* for the benefit of the company and therefore can be excused by a majority of shareholders against the wishes of the minority. As we have seen, where dishonesty is proved, not even the unanimous consent of the shareholders will suffice to excuse the behaviour. However, where there is much more equivocal behaviour, such as using powers given for one purpose to achieve a different object, it is much easier for the court to accept that the directors are acting *bona fide* and thus may be excused by the company.

11.6 **Are the Prohibitions Absolute?**

We have seen already that the answer to this question is no. The behaviour may be forgiven by the company with a varying degree of ease depending on how serious a view the court takes of the behaviour. Thus, use of powers for an improper purpose is regarded as unlikely to breach the *bona fide* rule and may normally be condoned by a majority of the general meeting. At the other end of the scale, theft or fraud may not be condoned unless all those affected agree to the behaviour.

A further point to note under this head is that the prohibitions may themselves be redefined by the company in advance. This clearly points to the difference between the fundamental duty and the prohibitions or disabilities as they were called on one case (*Movitex* v. *Bulfield* [1988] BCLC 104). It would be unthinkable for the court to permit an insertion in the articles of a clause allowing the directors to act in bad faith against the interests of the company. The legislature accepted that such a clause would be wrong. Section 310 of the Companies Act 1985 reads:

> '(1) This section applies to any provision, whether contained in a company's articles or in any contract with the company or otherwise, for exempting any officer of the company or any person (whether an officer or not) employed by the company as auditor from, or indemnifying him against, any liability which by virtue of any rule of law would otherwise attach to him in respect of any negligence, default, breach of duty or breach of trust of which he may be guilty in relation to the company.
> (2) Except as provided by the following subsection, any such provision is void.'

The courts have, however, permitted the articles of association to remove or redefine what would otherwise be disabilities or prohibitions.

An example of the way the system works is to be found in *Movitex* v. *Bulfield and others* [1988] BCLC 104. There it was held that the true explanation of what was urged by counsel for the company to be the 'self-dealing' duty, or in other words the duty not to allow oneself to be in a position where duty and interest conflict, was that a director was, because of his position, unable (under a disability) to act in certain ways, because it was likely that his behaviour would be seen as a breach of his fundamental duty of good faith. The company could agree in advance that certain types of behaviour would not automatically be regarded as breach of the fundamental duty. Thus the articles (which allowed self-dealing transactions in certain circumstances) had not exempted the directors from a duty contrary to the provisions of s. 310, they had relieved the director from a prohibition or disability he would normally be under.

11.7 **The Categories of Prohibitions or Disabilities**

The categories of behaviour that have been identified from the cases as most likely to cause the director to be in breach of a fundamental duty are:

1. misappropriation of company property;
2. putting oneself in a situation where duty and interest conflict; and
3. exercising powers given for one purpose in order to achieve another.
4. causing the company to act *ultra vires* (see Chapter 4).

Misappropriation of company property

This may happen in a more sophisticated way than merely taking money from the company. An example is *Menier* v. *Hooper's Telegraph Works* [1874] LR 9 Ch 350. In that case, Hooper's company was a substantial shareholder in the European Telegraph company and had contracted with it to make and lay a cable to South America under certain concessions granted to the European company by the foreign governments concerned. Menier, a minority shareholder in the European company, claimed that Hooper's company had used its votes to procure the diversion of this business to a third company, to cause the abandonment of proceedings brought by the European company to assert its right to the concessions, and to have the European company wound up. James LJ said:

> 'Hooper's company have obtained certain advantages by dealing with something which was the property of the whole company. The minority of the shareholders say in effect that the majority has divided the assets of the company, more or less, between themselves, to the exclusion of the minority. I think it would be a shocking thing if that could be done, because if so the majority might divide the whole assets of the company, and pass a resolution that everything must be given to them, and that the minority should have nothing to do with it.'

The court upheld Menier's claim (p. 353).

Similarly, in *Cook* v. *Deeks* [1916] 1 AC 554 the directors of a company were involved in negotiating a series of construction contracts with the Canadian Pacific Railway. The last of the series of contracts was negotiated in the same way as the others, but when the negotiations were complete, the directors took the contracts in their own names. It was held that, because the directors were acting for the company at the time of the negotiations, the benefit of the contracts belonged to the company. The directors could not therefore take the benefit of those contracts for themselves.

Conflict of duty and interest

If a director puts himself into a position where his duty to the company is in conflict with his other interests he is in peril of being held to be in breach of his duty of good faith to the company. The more serious the courts judge the conflict to be, the less likely are they to permit a majority of the company to ratify the actions of the directors, particularly where there is a dissenting minority.

An example of a situation in which duty and interest can be in conflict is *Scottish Co-operative Society* v. *Meyer* [1959] AC 324 (see Casenotes) where three directors were both directors of a parent company and directors of a subsidiary of that parent. As soon as the interests of these two companies conflicted, the directors were unable to fulfil their duty to both companies.

Another situation which can easily bring a director's duty into conflict with his interests is where a director contracts with his company. There are now extensive statutory rules covering this area (see the next chapter), but the general rule is that a director is in peril of being in breach of his overriding duty if he makes a contract in which he has a personal interest with his company. In *Aberdeen Railway Co.* v. *Blaikie Bros* (1854) 1 Macq 461. (HL) Lord Cranworth said:

'it is a rule of universal application that no one, having [fiduciary] duties to discharge, shall be allowed to enter into engagements in which he has or can have a personal interest conflicting or which possibly may conflict with the interests of those whom he is bound to protect.'

This rule has been referred to as the self-dealing rule (see *Movitex Ltd.* v. *Bulfield* on page 190. It is by no means absolute and this is an area where the company will readily be able to ratify acts done in breach of the general rule provided there has been sufficient disclosure and the directors are apparently acting honestly. This is also an area where the duty itself can be modified in advance of any action by directors. This can be done by redefining the duties in the articles of association (see *Movitex*, above) The statutory provisions are examined in more detail in Chapter 12.

The most difficult area where interest and duty often conflict is where a director is alleged to have profited personally from an opportunity or information which came to him in his capacity as director. A famous case where this type of situation was in issue was *Regal (Hastings) Ltd* v. *Gulliver* [1942] 1 All ER 378.

In that case the directors of the appellant company, which owned a cinema, were anxious to acquire two other cinemas. A subsidiary company was formed for the purpose of acquiring the additional cinemas. Its capital was 5000 shares with a par value of £1. A lease of two cinemas was offered provided that the subsidiary company's capital was paid up. It was the directors' intention that the appellant company should own all the shares in the subsidiary company. However, the appellant company could only afford to invest £2000. Accordingly, the directors and the company solicitor each took 500 shares, and three investors found by the chairman also took 500 shares each. Subsequently the shares in the company and the subsidiary were sold, and the new shareholders of the company sought to make the directors, the solicitor and the chairman liable to account to the company for the profit made in respect of the subsidiary company's shares. The House of Lords held that the directors were liable to account to the company for their profit.

It is notable that this is a case where the company was unable to make use of the opportunity, which was then taken advantage of by the directors.

A case in which the principle in *Regal Hastings* was applied is *Industrial Developments* v. *Cooley* [1972] 1 WLR 443. In that case the defendant was managing director of the plaintiff company. While serving in that capacity he became aware of information that would have been valuable to the company, but instead of passing it on to the company he kept it to himself. He also obtained his release from the company by dishonest representations and for the purpose of obtaining a lucrative contract for himself. The plaintiff company could not have obtained the contract because the other party to the contract was opposed to the 'set-up' of the plaintiff company and the group of which it was a part. Despite this, and despite the fact that the defendant had made it clear to the other party to the contract that he was dealing with him on a personal basis and not in the capacity of managing director of the plaintiffs, the court held that the defendant must account to the plaintiff company for the profits that had been made from the contract.

A contrasting case is *Island Export Finance Ltd* v. *Umunna and Another* [1986] BCLC 460. In that case the defendant was managing director of the plaintiff company. He secured for the company a contract for postal caller boxes in the Cameroons. He subsequently resigned from the company solely due to dissatisfaction with it. At the time of his resignation the company was not seeking any further contracts for postal caller boxes. The defendant then procured two such contracts for his own company. The court held that there had been no breach of duty. It accepted that a duty could continue after resignation but the facts in this case pointed to there having been no breach. The facts singled out as particularly important in coming to this conclusion were:

(i)   The company had only a vague hope of further contracts rather than an expectation and were not actively seeking new contracts at the time of the defendant's resignation.
(ii) The resignation was not prompted or influenced by the desire to obtain the contracts for himself.
(iii) The information about the contracts was not confidential information, since it merely amounted to knowledge of the existence of a particular market. To prevent directors using such information would conflict with public policy on the restraint of trade.

Another case which failed was *Framlington Group Plc and another* v. *Anderson and others* [1995] 1 BCLC 475. In that case the defendants were directors of and employees of the plaintiffs. The defendants were free, if they left the employment of the plaintiffs, to set up or join a competing business and take with them the plaintiff's clients. They were all private client fund managers. R plc offered all three defendants jobs. At the same time R plc negotiated a transfer of funds from the plaintiff company. This negotiation was carried out by other members of the plaintiff company and the defendants were told not to get involved. The defendants did not inform the plaintiff company of the employment packages they negotiated. The plaintiffs claimed that the benefits received by the defendants from R plc were secret profits and should be paid to the company. The court held in favour of the defendants. The fact of the negotiations on employment had been known to the plaintiff company, which had taken deliberate steps to keep the two negotiations separate and had told the defendants that they were not concerned with the detail of the employment package which was being negotiated.

In *Thomas Marshall (Exports) Ltd* v. *Guinle* [1979] Ch 227, Megarry VC sought to identify the type of information which would be protected by the courts in that they would prevent the disclosure of it or prevent anyone owing a duty to the company which was entitled to the benefit of the information from profiting from it. He said:

'First, I think that the information must be information the release of which the owner believes would be injurious to him or of advantage to his rivals or others. Second, I think the owner must believe that the information is confidential or secret, i.e., that it is not already in the public domain. It may be that some or all of his rivals already have the information: but as long as the owner believes it to be confidential I think he is entitled to try and protect it. Third, I think that the owner's belief under the two previous heads must be reasonable. Fourth, I think that the information must be judged in the light of the usage and practices of the particular industry or trade concerned. It may be the information which does not satisfy all these requirements may be entitled to protection as confidential information or trade secrets: but I think that any information which does satisfy them must be of a type which is entitled to protection.' (p. 248)

From these cases the following principles emerge:
1. A director is in danger of being in breach of his fundamental duty to the company if he places himself in a position where one of his private interests comes into conflict with the company's interests.
2. This duty can continue after resignation.
3. Use of information or opportunity which comes to the director because of his position in the company will be very likely to be a breach of his duty to the company even if he tries to disassociate himself from the company by: (a) saying he is acting in a private capacity on this occasion; or (b) resigning for the purpose of exploiting the information or opportunity.
4. Confidential information includes those categories described by Megarry VC in *Thomas Marshall*, but that definition was not exclusive, so other information may be included.

As in other areas of 'duty' it must be remembered that breaches may be excused by the majority on the same principles as described briefly above and examined in more detail in Chapter 13.

Fettering discretion

Sometimes it is said that there is another heading of prohibition which is that directors may not fetter their discretion. In fact this is probably merely another way in which directors have an interest in conflict with their duty to the company. If they bind themselves by agreement to act in a particular way they have a personal interest in fulfilling that engagement. This is in conflict with their duty to be able to act always in the best interests of the company. The issue was discussed in *Fulham Football Club and others* v. *Cabra Estates Plc* [1994] 1 BCLC 363. In that case the directors of Fulham Football Club (the company) agreed with the respondents to support planning applications for the development of land leased by the company and oppose different plans proposed by the local council. Large sums of money were paid to the company as a result of that agreement. A number of planning applications failed and enquiries were held and the issue in the case was whether the undertakings by the directors applied to new planning applications by the respondents and others, whether the undertakings had been improper in fettering the discretion of the directors and whether the agreement was subject to an implied term that the directors would not be required to do anything contrary to their fiduciary duties. The Court of Appeal held that the agreement was valid, was not an improper fettering of discretion and was not subject to the suggested implied term. The company had gained substantially from the agreement. The test to be applied was 'was the contract as a whole *bona fide* for the benefit of the company?'. If it was then the directors were entitled to bind themselves to do anything necessary to carry it out.

Use of powers for an improper purpose

The courts have decided that certain of the powers of directors have been given to them for a particular purpose. If the directors use them to achieve a different object the court will intervene to prevent this, if they are requested to do so. This is one area, however, where the courts are very often happy to permit the majority to excuse the action of the directors, so that this is perhaps an area where a director is in the least danger of being found to be in breach of his fundamental duty. A good example is the power to issue shares. The courts have determined that where directors have this power the purpose for which it was bestowed was to raise capital. It is a power which can easily be used to fend off a takeover or to prevent themselves from being removed from office. This can be done by diluting the voting capacity of a hostile element of shareholders by the issue of new shares. *Punt* v. *Symonds & Co* [1903] 2 Ch 506 and *Piercy* v. *S. Mills & Co. Ltd* [1920] 1 Ch 77 (see Casenotes) are good examples of this type of manoeuvring. A slightly more complicated problem arose in the case of *Howard Smith* v. *Ampol Petroleum Ltd* [1974] AC 821. In that case a company was threatened with a take-over by two associates who between them held 55 per cent of the company's shares. The company needed more capital but proposed to obtain it by issuing over four million shares to members other than the take-over bidders. This allotment would have reduced the take-over bidders to a minority in the company and was held to be a misuse of the directors' powers. The case was complicated by the fact that the issue had been made for two purposes; to raise capital (the proper purpose) and to defeat the take-over (an improper purpose). The court reached the conclusion that directors would be acting within their powers if the dominant or substantial purpose of the exercise of those powers was proper. Lord Wilberforce, giving the advice of the Privy Council, said:

'In their Lordship's opinion it is necessary to start with a consideration of the powers whose exercise is in question . . . Having ascertained, on a fair view, the nature of this power, and having defined as can best be done in the light of modern conditions the, or some, limits within which it may be exercised, it is then necessary for the court, if a particular exercise of it is challenged, to examine the substantial purpose for which it was exercised, and to reach a conclusion whether that purpose was proper or not. In doing so it will be necessary to give credit to the *bona fide* opinion of the directors, if such is found to exist, and will respect their judgment as to matters of management; having done this, the ultimate conclusion has to be as to the side of a fairly broad line on which the case falls' (p. 835).

Lord Wilberforce also emphasised that the court would not simply accept a statement by directors that they acted for a particular purpose. He said:

'[When] a dispute arises whether directors of a company made a particular decision for one purpose or another, or whether, there being more than one purpose, one or another purpose was the substantial or primary purpose, the court, in their Lordships' opinion, is entitled to look at the situation objectively in order to estimate how critical or pressing, or substantial or, *per contra*, insubstantial an alleged requirement may have been. If it finds that a particular requirement, though real, was not urgent, or critical, at the relevant time, it may have reason to doubt, or discount, the assertions of individuals that they acted solely in order to deal with it, particularly when the action they took was unusual or even extreme' (p. 832).

In *Re Looe Fish Ltd* [1993] BCC 368 the failure by a director to exercise the power of allotment of shares for the purpose for which it was conferred led to disqualification under s. 8 Company Directors Disqualification Act 1986. See also *Bishopgate Investment Management (in liquidation)* v. *Maxwell* [1993] BCC 120.

11.8 **Consequences of a Breach**

A director may be prevented from doing an action in breach of his duties by an injunction and if he has profited from the breach he will be obliged to pay the company any money that he has made because of the breach. A director may become a constructive trustee of money which has been mishandled. As well as these remedies, breach of directors duties may be the foundation of actions open to shareholders or the company (see further, Chapter 13).

11.9 **Relief from Liability**

The company may relieve the directors from liability except where the breach is fundamental and unforgivable (as in *Attorney General's Reference No. 2 of 1982* see page 189 in 2nd ed. Another way that this is often put is that it is a 'fraud on the minority'. However, in the Attorney General's Reference there was no minority so that the better way to express the principle is that the breach was fundamental, unforgivable, or in other words, a fraud on the company. The relieving of directors from liability by a majority vote is further discussed in Chapter 13.

A company must not seek to relieve directors from liability for breaches of duty in advance because of s. 310 of the Companies Act 1985. This is set out and discussed above. Section 310(3) reads:

'This section does not prevent a company –
(a) from purchasing and maintaining for any such officer or auditor insurance against such liability, or
(b) from indemnifying any such officer or auditor against any liability incurred by him –
   (i) in defending any proceedings (whether civil or criminal) in which judgment is given in his favour or he is acquitted, or
   (ii) in connection with any application under s. 144(3) or (4) [acquisition of shares by innocent nominee] or s. 727 [general power to grant relief in case of honest and reasonable conduct] in which relief is granted to him by the court.'

11.10 **Relief by the Court**

By s. 727 of the Companies Act 1987 (see Casenotes) the court has power to relieve a director of liability where he has been in breach of duty but nevertheless the court finds that he has acted honestly and reasonably and in all the circumstances of the case he ought fairly to be excused.

This section was considered by the Court of Appeal in *Customs and Excise Commissioners* v. *Hedon Alpha Ltd* [1981] 2 All ER 697. The court held that the relief could only be claimed and granted in proceedings brought to enforce directors' duties under the common law or the Companies Acts. It did not apply to any other proceedings brought by third parties against the director in his capacity as an officer of the company.

A company may, however, indemnify a director against the expense of defending any such proceedings, provided the court finds in his favour or (under s. 727) relief is granted by the court.

Summary

1 Directors' duties under the common law can be divided into a duty to act carefully and with a certain degree of skill.
2 The duty of care and skill is contained in the *City Equitable Fire* case. There is a sliding scale which sets a higher standard for directors who are most closely involved with the running of the company.
3 There have been calls for and there may be a move towards an objective standard. In the future the duty of care will be affected by the cases on disqualification of directors and may be affected by the EC Fifth Directive.
4 Directors are under an equitable duty to act *bona fide* for the benefit of the company. This duty is owed to the company and not to the members. If they put themselves into certain positions they are in danger of breaching this duty.
5 Those positions are: where they appropriate company property; where they put themselves in a position where their interests and duty conflict; and where they use powers given for one purpose to effect another purpose.
6 The courts may permit the company, acting by a majority in general meeting, to forgive directors who have acted in any of the ways described in (5). The ease with which this will be allowed depends on the view taken by the court of the seriousness of the behaviour. This topic is covered in more detail in Chapter 13.
7 The company may define in advance behaviour which will not be regarded as a breach of duty but a company must not exempt directors from the consequences which follow when a duty has been broken (s. 310 CA 1985).
8 The court has a power to release a director from the consequences of a breach of duty where he has acted honestly and reasonably and ought, in all the circumstances of the case, to be excused (s. 727 CA 1985).

Casenotes

1 *Scottish Co-operative Wholesale Society Ltd* v. *Meyer* [1959] AC 324
The appellant company formed a subsidiary company to manufacture rayon cloth at a time when manufacture of rayon was subject to a system of licensing. The appellant company was entitled to nominate three directors of the board of the subsidiary. It nominated three of its own directors with the result that three directors held office as directors of both the parent (appellant company) and the subsidiary company. When licensing of rayon ceased, the appellant company was able, because of the votes of those three directors, to transfer the rayon business to another part of its operation. This had the effect of causing the subsidiary's affairs to come to a standstill. It made no profits and the value of its shares fell greatly. The action was brought by shareholders who claimed the company's affairs had been

conducted in an 'oppressive' manner. This was the language of s. 210 of the Companies Act 1948, the predecessor to ss. 459–461 Companies Act 1985 (see Chapter 13). The House of Lords found that the affairs of the subsidiary had been conducted in an oppressive manner, in particular because of the breach of duty of the directors nominated by the appellant company. Lord Denning said:

'What, then, is the position of the nominee directors here? Under the articles of association of the textile company the co-operative society was entitled to nominate three out of the five directors, and it did so. It nominated three of its own directors and they held office, as the articles said, 'as nominees' of the co-operative society. These three were therefore at one and the same time directors of the co-operative society – being three out of twelve of that company – and also directors of the textile company – three out of five there. So long as the interests of all concerned were in harmony, there was no difficulty. The nominee directors could do their duty by both companies without embarrassment. But, so soon as the interests of the two companies were in conflict, the nominee directors were placed in an impossible position . . . It is plain that, in the circumstances, these three gentlemen could not do their duty by both companies, and they did not do so. They put their duty to the co-operative society above their duty to the textile company in the sense, at least, that they did nothing to defend the interests of the textile company against the conduct of the co-operative society. They probably thought that 'as nominees' of the co-operative society their first duty was to the co-operative society. In this they were wrong. By subordinating the interests of the textile company to those of the co-operative society, they conducted the affairs of the textile company in a manner oppressive to the other shareholders (pp. 366–7).'

2 *Re Dawson Print Group* [1987] BCLC 601

The defendant director was a director of two companies, both of which were wound up in April and May 1983. The first company (DPG) had assets of approximately £3850 and debts of approximately £111,000, of which £40,000 was represented by unpaid VAT, PAYE and National Insurance Charges (NIC). The second company (Princo) had assets of approximately £3450 and debts of approximately £21,000, of which £5500 was for VAT, PAYE and NIC. A disqualification order was sought under s. 300 of the Companies Act 1985 which was the predecessor to s. 6 of the Company Directors Disqualification Act 1986. The Companies Act section differs from its replacement in that disqualification is discretionary. From subsequent cases it appears that this difference has little effect on the courts' view of the behaviour of the directors in question and the courts' judgment of whether they are 'unfit' to be directors.

Hoffman J refused to disqualify the director. He took into account:

(i)   the fact of large debts owed to the Crown; he did not consider this of great significance;
(ii) the young age of the director (first appointed at twenty);
(iii) the fact that there had been no 'breach of commercial morality' or 'really gross negligence';
(iv) the fact that this director was now running a successful company; and
(v)   some of the losses could be accounted for by unforeseeable bad luck and the behaviour of other people.

3 *Re Stanford Services* [1987] BCLC 607

This was also an application to disqualify a director under s. 300 of the Companies Act 1985. The two companies in which the director was principally involved were insolvent. The approximate sums involved were: first company: assets £46,200; liabilities: £253,880, including £12,400 PAYE, £13,100 NIC, £14,900 VAT. Second company: assets £451,800; liabilities: £779,600, including £29,400 PAYE, £27,700 NIC and £33,800 VAT.

Vinelott J imposed a disqualification order for two years. Important factors were:

1. the debts to the Crown were large and the companies had only continued to trade by not paying them;
2. there had been a failure to keep and file proper accounts;
3. there was evidence of recklessness in acquiring or commencing the companies; and
4. there was evidence of negligence in carrying on the businesses when a reasonable person would have known them to be insolvent, and in paying himself large sums at such a time.

4 *Smith* v. *Van Gorkom* [1985] 488 A.2d

Van Gorkom was the chief executive officer and chairman of the board of directors of Trans Union Corporation, a publicly-held corporation principally involved in the leasing of rail cars. He was nearly sixty-five years old and approaching retirement. Trans Union had a substantial cash flow but its taxable income was insufficient to permit it to take full advantage of tax benefits it was entitled to under the Internal Revenue Code. For several years, Trans Union had therefore tried to purchase income-producing businesses, apparently without great success. During discussions about strategy, the possibility of selling Trans Union to a larger corporation was raised, as was the possibility of a buy-out by management of the interests of the public shareholders. Studies showed that the cash flow would cover a management buy-out at $50 but $60 would be difficult to do. At a meeting, Van Gorkom vetoed the idea of a buy-out but stated that he would accept $55 for the 75,000 shares that he owned. (The price of the stock of Trans Union at this time was about $38 per share.) Following these discussions, Van Gorkom on his own decided to approach Jay Pritzker, a well-known takeover specialist, with a proposal that Pritzker should purchase the company at $55 per share. Pritzker was a personal acquaintance of Van Gorkom. Pritzker and Van Gorkom quickly worked out a proposed deal (though after some negotiation) under which (1) Pritzker would be entitled to buy one million shares of Trans Union at $38 per share; (2) Pritzker's wholly-owned corporation would agree to enter into a statutory merger with Trans Union pursuant to which each shareholder of Trans Union would receive $55 per share; and (3) the merger was subject to cancellation if a higher price was forthcoming from another bidder within ninety days. Approval of this deal required the approval of the Trans Union's board of directors and a majority of its shareholders. The board of directors of Trans Union consisted of five executive and five non-executive directors. The nine directors present at the meeting unanimously approved the deal despite the fact that there had been no independent valuation of the shares of Trans Union. Seventy per cent of the shareholders of Trans Union approved the deal. A suit was filed by a minority of Trans Union's shareholders alleging that the directors had failed to exercise due care in reviewing and recommending approval of the transaction. The Delaware Supreme Court rejected defences put forward by the defendant directors and the case was adjourned for determination of damages. It was then settled, by the plaintiff's accepting a payment of $23.5 million.

The massive liability incurred by the defendants was based on lack of due care, not fraud or breach of fiduciary duties. It led to a severe (but temporary) shortage of well-qualified persons willing to act as directors (see further, *Hamilton* [1988] 4 JIBL 152).

5 *Punt* v. *Symonds* [1903] 2 Ch 506
This was a case where friction had arisen between two factions of shareholders. The directors issued new shares. Byrne J said:

'It is argued on the evidence that but for the issue by the directors of the shares under their powers as directors, and, therefore, in their fiduciary character under the general power to issue shares, it would have been impossible to pass the resolution proposed; and that the shares were not issued *bona fide*, but with the sole object and intention of creating voting power to carry out the proposed alteration in the articles. On the evidence I am quite clear that these shares were not issued *bona fide* for the general advantage of the company, but that they were issued with the immediate object of controlling the holders of the greater number of shares in the company, and of obtaining the necessary statutory majority for passing a special resolution while, at the same time, not conferring upon the minority the power to demand a poll. I need not go through the affidavits. I am quite satisfied that the meaning, object, and intention of the issue of these shares was to enable the shareholders holding the smaller amount of shares to control the holders of a very considerable majority. A power of the kind exercised by the directors in this case, is one which must be exercised for the benefit of the company: primarily it is given them for the purpose of enabling them to raise capital when required for the purposes of the company. There may be occasions when the directors may fairly and properly issue shares in the case of a company constituted like the present for other reasons. For instance, it would not be at all an unreasonable thing to create a sufficient number of shareholders to enable statutory powers to be exercised; but when I find a limited issue of shares to persons who are obviously meant and intended to secure the necessary statutory majority in a particular interest, I do not think that is a fair and *bona fide* exercise of the power (pp. 515–16).'

6 *Piercy* v. *S. Mills & Company Ltd* [1920] 1 Ch 77
This also concerned a dispute between controllers of a company. Peterson J said:

'With the merits of the dispute as between the directors and the plaintiff I have no concern whatever. The plaintiff and his friends held a majority of shares in the company, and they were entitled, so long as that majority remained, to have their views prevail in accordance with the regulations of the company; and it was not, in my opinion, open to the directors, for the sole purpose of converting a minority into a majority, and solely for the purpose of defeating the wishes of the existing majority, to issue the shares which are in dispute in the present action (pp. 84–5).'

7 *Section 727 Companies Act 1987*
(1) If in any proceedings for negligence, default, breach of duty or breach of trust against any officer of a company or a person employed by a company as auditor (whether he is or is not an officer of the company) it appears to the court hearing the

case that that officer or person is or may be liable in respect of the negligence, default, breach of duty or breach of trust, but that he has acted honestly and reasonably, and that having regard to all the circumstances of the case (including those connected with his appointment) he ought fairly to be excused for the negligence, default, breach of duty or breach of trust, that court may relieve him, either wholly or partly from his liability on such terms as it thinks fit.

(2) If any such officer or person as above-mentioned has reason to apprehend that any claim will or might be made against him in respect of any negligence, breach of duty or breach of trust, he may apply to the court for relief; and the court on the application has the same power to relieve him as under this section it would have had if it had been a court before which proceedings against that person for negligence, default, breach of duty or breach of trust had been brought.

(3) Where a case to which sub-section (1) applies is being tried by a judge with a jury, the judge, after hearing the evidence, may, if he is satisfied that the defendant or defender ought in pursuance of that sub-section to be relieved either in whole or in part from the liability sought to be enforced against him, withdraw the case in whole or in part from the jury and forthwith direct judgment to be entered for the defendant or defender on such terms as to costs or otherwise as the judge may think proper.

Exercises

1 To whom does a director owe his duties?

2 What factors make it difficult to impose one standard on all directors?

3 Explain the effect of the ruling in *Re City Equitable Fire* on an executive director of a large company.

4 John and Mary are directors of Wash Ltd. They become suspicious of the behaviour of Joe, the third director of the company. He has recently bought a Porsche and has taken several foreign holidays. John and Mary know that his salary as director would not be sufficient to pay for these luxuries. John discovers that Joe has been buying raw materials for Wash Ltd from a company in which he, Joe, owns all but one of the shares. The price of these materials appears to be excessive. John tells Mary that she is better off knowing nothing about what is going on. She agrees. John then uses his powers under the articles to issue enough shares to friends to ensure that Joe is voted out of office. The company becomes insolvent. It has paid no VAT, PAYE or NIC for many months. What breaches of duty have been committed? Is it likely that any of the directors will be disqualified?

12 Statutory Duties of Directors

The general duties of directors (see Chapter 11) are in some cases reinforced by specific statutory duties spelt out in what are usually very complicated provisions. A general overview of some of the more important sections is given here. The detail of some of the provisions appear in the Casenotes. Many of these duties were introduced as a result of financial scandals. The government of the day wished to be seen to be 'doing something' to remedy the situation. Very few of the provisions in Part X of the Companies Act 1985 are enforced and abolition of this part of the Companies Act is under active consideration. The Companies Act 1985, s. 320–330 prohibits companies from entering into contracts for the buying and selling of property, making loans and similar transactions to or in favour of directors and, in some cases, persons connected with them. 'Director', for the purpose of these sections, includes 'shadow' director.

Four classes of person are connected with a director for the purposes of s. 330:

(i) the director's spouse, or his infant child or step-child (Companies Act 1985, s. 346);
(ii) a company with which the director is associated. A director is associated with a company if he and the persons connected with him (a) are interested in at least one-fifth of the nominal value of the equity share capital, or (b) are entitled to exercise or control more than one-fifth of the voting power at a company's general meeting (s. 364);
(iii) a trustee of any fixed or discretionary trust whose beneficiaries include the director, his spouse, any of his children or step-children, or a company with which he is associated;
(iv) a partner of the director or of any person connected with the director by reason of the fact that he falls within categories (i) – (iii) above.

12.1 Prohibited Transactions

Sections 320–322 deal with contracts by which a company sells to or buys from a director or connected person property of any sort and provides that the company may not enter into such an arrangement unless there is prior approval by the general meeting (s. 320(1)). Section 330 *et seq.* contain comprehensive provisions on companies making loans to and entering into equivalent transactions with directors and connected persons. By s. 330(2), no company may lend money to any of its directors or to a director of its holding company, nor may it guarantee or provide security in connection with a loan made by a third person to such a director.

12.2 **Public Companies**

The prohibitions applying to public companies extend to dealings with connected persons and also extend to 'quasi-loans'.

By s. 331(4) a 'quasi-loan' is a transaction under which a creditor pays, whether by agreement or otherwise, a sum from a borrower, or reimburses expenditure incurred by a third party for the borrower, on the terms that the borrower or someone on his behalf will reimburse the creditor, or in circumstances giving rise to a liability on the borrower to reimburse the creditor.

12.3 **General Exceptions**

There are a number of general exceptions to the prohibitions in s. 330:

(i)   Section 334 exempts loans made to a director of the company or of its holding company if the aggregate of such loans outstanding does not exceed £5000.
(ii) Section 336 disapplies the prohibitions where the deal is with or in favour of a company's holding company.
(iii) Section 337 permits companies to provide its directors with funds (but only up to £10,000 so far as public companies are concerned) to enable them to perform their duties or meet expenditure incurred or to be incurred in the performance of their duties. This power is subject to disclosure to and approval of the general meeting, or repayment of the sum within six months of the meeting.
(iv) Companies which lend money in the ordinary course of business are permitted to make loans to directors if they are made on ordinary commercial terms. The limit is £100,000 in the case of public companies which are not authorised banks (ss. 338, 339).

12.4 **Civil Remedies and Criminal Penalties**

An arrangement entered into in contravention of the section may normally be avoided by the company and a director authorising the arrangement is liable to account to the company for any gain he has made and will be liable to indemnify the company for any loss arising from the transactions.

There are also criminal penalties (see Casenotes).

12.5 **Disqualification of Directors**

(For a treatment of this subject in the context of the personal liability of directors, see L. S. Sealy, *Disqualification and Personal Liability of Directors*, CCH, 4th edition, 1993.)

The standard of care set out in *Re City Equitable Fire Insurance Co. Ltd* [1925] Ch 407 should mean that unless the appointment of a director has been manifestly foolish the rules set out in that case will work together to provide a sliding scale of responsibility which will weigh heaviest on those most able to do the job, and whose expectations of reward from the job are probably highest. If the standard set in *D'Jan* becomes established an objective standard of case has been introduced.

Under the Company Directors Disqualification Act 1986 the courts must under s. 6 disqualify a director from managing a company if he has been a director of a company which has become insolvent (either while he was acting for it or later) and the court finds that his conduct 'makes him unfit to be concerned in the management of a company'. By s. 6(4) the minimum period of disqualification is two years and the maximum fifteen years. Although this legislation raises many questions the major issue relevant to the standard of director's duties is what is meant by 'unfitness'. Unfitness also seems to have an objective content and this will be discussed in detail later. There are other grounds for disqualification which must also be examined.

Under the Disqualification of Directors Act 1986 ss. 2–5 a court may make a disqualification order against a person for the following reasons.

Conviction of indictable offence

He is convicted of an indictable offence in connection with the promotion, formation, management or liquidation of a company or with the receivership or management of a company's property (s. 2). The offence need only be capable of being prosecuted on indictment. The relevant conviction could be obtained in a magistrates' court. Actual misconduct of a company's affairs need not be proved. In *Re Georgiou* (1988) 4 BCC 322 the offence was carrying on an unauthorised insurance business. There was no allegation that it was a badly-managed insurance business. In *R v. Goodman* [1994] BCLC 349 a chairman and major shareholder of a public company 'gave' his shares to a friend who sold them three days before it became public knowledge that the company was in trouble. He was later convicted of insider dealing and disqualified for 10 years under s. 2 of the Company Directors Disqualification Act 1986. He appealed on the grounds that the insider trading was not an offence committed in connection with the management of a company. It was held that it was. The correct test was whether the offence had some relevant factual connection with the management of the company, not whether it had been committed in the course of managing the company (such as not filing returns). Here there was a clear connection. There is no minimum period of disqualification under this section and disqualification is discretionary. If the offence is dealt with by a magistrates' court the maximum disqualification period is five years. If the offence is dealt with on indictment the maximum period is fifteen years.

Persistent default

He appears to the court to have been persistently in default in relation to any requirement under the companies' legislation for the filing, delivery or sending of any return, account or other document or the giving of any notice with or to the Registrar of Companies (s. 3). There is a presumption that a person has been 'persistently in default' if he has been convicted of a default, or has been required by court order to make good a default, three times in the preceding five years (sections 3(2) and (3)). This does not prevent an application for an order being made under this section when neither of those matters can be shown. In *Re Arctic Engineering Ltd* [1986] 1 WLR 686 'persistently' was held to require some degree of continuance or repetition. There is no need to show a wilful disregard of statutory requirements, although the absence of fault will be important when the exercise of the discretion not to disqualify is in question. Under this section any court having jurisdiction to wind up the company has jurisdiction to make the order. Section 5 gives jurisdiction in precisely the same circumstances to a magistrates' court. This will usually be the court which actually convicts the director. Under both sections disqualification is discretionary and there is a maximum period of five years.

Fraud discovered in winding up

He appears to the court in the course of winding up the company:

(i) to have been guilty of an offence (whether convicted or not) of fraudulent trading.

(ii) to have otherwise been guilty, while an officer or liquidator of the company or receiver or manager of its property, of any fraud in relation to the company or of any breach of his duty as such officer, liquidator, receiver or manager (s. 4).

This section applies to fraud, and so on, whenever it occurred. It is the revelation that must be in the course of the winding-up, not the fraud. The court with jurisdiction to make the order is 'any court having jurisdiction to wind up the company'. Disqualification is discretionary and the maximum period is fifteen years. It is not necessary for the purposes of s. 4 that the company should be insolvent. Under s. 4(1)(a) anyone guilty of fraudulent trading may be disqualified. This offence may be committed by any person who was knowingly a party to the carrying on of the fraudulent business. By contrast, those liable to be disqualified under s. 4(1)(b) are more uncertain. Sealy (*Disqualification and Personal Liability of Directors* CCH, 1989) lists the officers caught and possibly caught under s. 4(1)(b). They are:

(i) certainly caught:
a director
a shadow director
a secretary
a 'manager'.

(There is a great deal of uncertainty surrounding the definition of a 'manager'. In *Re A Company No. 00996 of 1979* [1980] Ch 138, at p. 144, Shaw LJ said:

> 'any person who in the affairs of the company exercises a supervisory control which reflects the general policy of the company or which is related to the general administration of the company is in the sphere of management. He need not be a member of the board of directors. He need not be subject to specific instructions from the board.')

    a liquidator
    a receiver

(ii) Those less certainly included (depending on the construction of the term 'officer') are:
    an auditor
    the supervisor of a voluntary arrangement (made under the Insolvency Act 1986 ss. 1–7)
    an administrator (appointed under the Insolvency Act 1986 s. 8).

Note that the disqualification order under the above provisions is discretionary. The court does not have to make such an order even if the facts that would enable it to do so are proved.

Duty to disqualify

There is a duty to disqualify imposed on the court under s. 6 of the Company Directors Disqualification Act 1986, which reads as follows:

> 'The court shall make a disqualification order for a period of not less than two years nor more than fifteen years against a person if, on application by the Secretary of State or at his discretion by the Official Receiver where a company is being wound up by the court in England and Wales, the court is satisfied that –
>
> (a) such person is or has been a director of a company which has at any time become insolvent (whether while he was a director or subsequently); and
> (b) his conduct as a director of the company (taken alone or together with his conduct as a director of any other company or companies) makes him unfit to be concerned in the management of a company.

Insolvency

This is defined by s. 6(2). A company becomes insolvent if:

(a) it goes into liquidation at a time when its assets are insufficient to pay its debts, liabilities and winding-up expenses; or

(b) an 'administration order' is made (irrespective of the solvency or otherwise of the company at any relevant time) or;

(c) an 'administrative receiver' is appointed (irrespective of the company's financial state).

The net is spread wide as every liquidator (or administrator and so on), must report on the conduct of those possibly caught by the statute to a special enforcement unit which then takes the decision whether or not to ask the court for a disqualification order.

Possible effect on directors' duty of care

If the courts are expecting directors to live up to a high standard in order to escape being adjudged 'unfit' it is possible that this legislation will have the effect of raising the standards expected of directors generally. It would seem strange to the courts if a position is reached where a director has been found unfit and disqualified and yet is not liable to account for irregularities under the rule in that case. There may well be a tendency to adopt a similar standard by which to judge directors. What has been the standard to determine unfitness? There has been a considerable amount of case law on the subject but as yet no very clear conclusion can be drawn. The statute itself gives some guidance on matters which are to be considered by the court, but gives no further explanation of what is meant by 'unfit'. Thus by s. 6 the conduct that must be taken into account is conduct in relation to the company that has become insolvent and any other company. By s. 9 the matters referred to in Parts I and II of Schedule 1 must be considered to determine unfitness. The court is directed to have regard 'in particular' to those matters. It is clear that these are the matters considered important by Parliament when an assessment of a director's fitness is made. The matters include: breaches of duty by the director, misuse of company funds, responsibility for and/or misconduct in the insolvency of the company; failure to comply with a number of administrative obligations, such as failing to keep proper accounts and other records required by the Companies Act 1985; and failure to communicate the contents of the accounts and records (where required to do so) to the Registrar of Companies.

Judging from the extensive case law on the subject, the courts have taken these matters into account. They have also had regard to other matters not on this list, some of which appear to have become important. There is also an unfortunate confusion as to the meaning of the final overall standard of unfitness. Some of the confusion is caused by the fact that a number of the relevant decisions were decided when s. 300 of the Companies Act 1985 was still in force. This was very similar to the Company Directors Disqualification Act 1986 s. 6, but required the director's involvement in the insolvency of two companies. The disqualification under this section was discretionary. Under s. 6 the court *must* make a disqualification order for a minimum of two years if a relevant company has gone into liquidation and there is a finding of unfitness. However, this is apparently mitigated by the ability of the court to permit the disqualified director to act as a director during the period of disqualification (imposing terms if the court deems it appropriate (see page 216). (Section 1 defines a disqualification order as an order that '[the defendant] shall not, *without leave of the court* be a director . . . ') (emphasis supplied).

Unfitness

Apart from the factors set out in the statute which the court is directed to take into account, other facts have been considered important in determining unfitness. In particular, there has been some debate as to the importance of the existence of outstanding debts for VAT, PAYE and NIC.

In *Re Dawson Print Group* [1987] BCLC 601 and *Re Stanford Services* [1987] BCLC 607 different views were taken about the importance of using 'Crown debts' to finance the company. What was happening in both cases was that the directors had withheld VAT, National Insurance and PAYE money which ought to have been paid by the company to the government. This money was used in order for the company to continue trading. In *Stanford* the misuse of this money was seen as a clear indication of unfitness, whereas in *Dawson* similar misuse was not seen as being particularly significant. The Court of Appeal in *Re Sevenoaks Stationers* [1991] Ch 164 made no distinction between 'Crown debts' and others unless especial suffering had been caused by non-payment of Crown debts.

Breach of what standard of care makes a director unfit?

As far as the overall standard is concerned, various alternatives have been considered by the courts. In
Dawson and *Stanford* alone the following explanations of 'unfitness' appeared:

(i)   a breach of commercial morality
(ii) really gross incompetence
(iii) recklessness
(iv) the director would be a danger to the public if he were allowed to continue to be involved in the management of companies.

Consideration (iv) seems now to be ruled out by the Court of Appeal's decision in *Secretary of State for Trade and Industry* v. *Gray and another* [1995] 1 BCLC 276 where the court found that only the behaviour alleged to make the defendant unfit could be considered. The future protection of the public was not a relevant consideration. The Court of Appeal approved the decision of Vinelott J in *Re Pamstock Ltd* [1994] 1 BCLC 736 where a disqualification order was made even though 'The respondent seemed to me . . . to be a man who today is capable of discharging his duties as director honestly and diligently.'

In *Re Bath Glass* [1988] BCLC 329 and *AB Trucking and BAW Commercials* Ch D, 3 June 1987, unreported an objective standard was imposed. A director was unfit if his actions were very far from that of a reasonably competent director. Until a generally agreed interpretation of unfitness has emerged from the decisions it is impossible to tell whether this legislation will have an effect on the standard imposed on directors under *Re City Equitable Fire*. The willingness of the court to disqualify where the director is incapable of understanding his duties may indicate that the excuse of incompetence which is available under *Re City Equitable Fire* is ripe for review and may have a limited life. This willingness is illustrated by *AB Trucking and BAW Commercials*. The respondent was said to be 'incapable of understanding the commercial reality of accounts' and thus 'incapable of discharging his duty to the public'. Nevertheless Harman J imposed a disqualification order for four years.

A very high standard of behaviour seems to have been required the court in *Re New Generation Engineers Ltd* [1993] BCLC 435. The factors said to merit disqualification were keeping inadequate accounting records so that it was not possible to monitor the financial position of the company and adopting a policy of only paying those creditors who pressed for payment or who needed to be paid in order to keep the company's business going. Each of these were said to provide grounds for disqualification although the eventual order was only for three years.

Important factors in determining unfitness

1. The amount of debts outstanding and the practice of not paying debts as a method of continuing to trade (see *Secretary of State for Trade and Industry* v. *McTighe and another* (No. 2) [1996] 2 BCLC 477 although Crown debts do not now seem to be particularly significant; see *Re Sevenoaks stationers* [1991] BCLC 325.

2. The number of companies that the director has been involved in, in particular the number of liquidations that he has been concerned with.

3. The way in which the companies have been managed, in particular to what extent accounts have been kept up to date and returns made to the Companies' Registry.

4. The personal circumstances of the director. Here the cases are confusing. Sometimes the youth and inexperience of a director are held to mitigate against a disqualification. The idea of this presumably is that he is growing up. On the other hand in *Re Majestic Recording Studios Ltd* the court was quite adamant that a person could be unfit when they were incompetent. Fraudulent behaviour did not need to be shown. What seems to be happening is that the court is assessing the degree of moral blame to be attached to the director for the company's failures. This will be less if incompetence was the cause of failure rather than fraud. This does not

mean that there will be no finding of unfitness but it will be a factor which the court will take into account when deciding to exercise its discretion as to length of disqualification.

5. The state of mind of the defendant. The relevance of this factor is closely tied to the debate as to the true nature of disqualification. There are two clearly opposed approaches. One is that the imposition of a disqualification order is a penal sanction which may well have the effect of removal of the livelihood of the director in question. The other approach regards disqualification as the removal of a licence to trade using limited liability. Passages in judgments can be found clearly supporting either approach. In *Re Civicia Investments Ltd* [1983] BCLC 456, Nourse J said:

'It might be thought that [consideration of the appropriate period of disqualification] is something which, like the passing of sentence in a criminal case, ought to be dealt with comparatively briefly and without elaborate reasoning . . . no doubt in this, as in other areas, it is possible that there will emerge a broad and undefined system of tariffs for defaults of varying degrees of blame . . . the longer periods of disqualification are to be reserved for cases where the defaults and conduct of the person in question have been of a serious nature, for example, where defaults have been made for some dishonest purpose.'

The quasi-penal nature of disqualification under this section was clearly acknowledged in *Re Crestjoy Products Ltd; Secretary of State for Trade and Industry* v. *Goddard and Others* Ch D, 18 Oct 1989 (Lexis). In that case the judgment of Browne-Wilkinson VC in *Lo-Line Electric Motors Ltd* [1988] Ch 477 was cited as a 'most useful encapsulation of the current authority'. The passage cited reads:

'The primary purpose of the section is not to punish the individual but to protect the public against the future conduct of companies by persons whose past records as directors of insolvent companies have shown them to be a danger to creditors and others. Therefore, the power is not fundamentally penal. But, if the power to disqualify is exercised . . . disqualification does involve a substantial interference with the freedom of the individual. It follows that the rights of the individual must be fully protected.'

The court went on to hold that

'since the making of a disqualification order involves penal consequences for the director, it is necessary that he should know the substance of the charges that he has to meet'.

The judge in *Crestjoy* agreed with this analysis but nevertheless went on to say:

'It seems to me, however, that when I am faced with a mandatory two-year disqualification if facts are proved, the matter becomes more nearly penal, or, at least, more serious for the individual faced with it than under the former situation where a judge could, in the exercise of his discretion, say that although the conduct had been bad yet he was now convinced that a disqualification should not be made because, for example, the respondent had learnt his lesson.'

In view of the seriousness of the matter, an application to bring an action seeking a disqualification order out of time was refused.

The approach in Crestjoy has been disapproved by the Court of Appeal in *Secretary of State for Trade and Industry* v. *Gray* where the Court held that only past behaviour could be considered. Mitigating factors which arose after the events alleged would not be relevant. However, both in that case (see further discussion below) and in subsequent cases the quasi-penal nature of the proceedings have been acknowledged. In *Re Living Images Ltd* [1996] 1 BCLC · 348 the court determined that although the proceedings were civil proceedings and the standard of proof was therefore on a balance of probabilities, the seriousness of both the allegations and the consequences meant that the court would 'require cogent evidence as proof', thus presumably setting a higher standard than the 'more likely than not' test.

Although it seems that this reason for regarding the matter as serious is less convincing in view of the possibility of permitting the director to continue as such under licence (see p. 216), nevertheless it is still a significant interference with the freedom of the individual if that licence has to be obtained from the court. The disqualification remains mandatory, not discretionary.

The debate as to the nature of disqualification may be one of the reasons for the difficulty that has been experienced by the court in determining whether 'unfitness' can be judged according to an objective standard or whether it requires an element of moral culpability. This is an important distinction because if an objective standard of competence is set, this legislation may well have an impact on the general duty for directors' liability.

Objective (negligence) standard or subjective fault?

In *Re Bath Glass* (1988) 4 BCC 130 Peter Gibson J said:

'To reach a finding of unfitness the court must be satisfied that the director has been guilty of a serious failure or serious failures, whether deliberately or through incompetence, to perform those duties of a director which are attendant on the privilege of trading through companies with limited liability. Any misconduct of the respondent *qua* director may be relevant.'

Since the 'serious failure' could occur because of the incompetence of the director, this means that the test imposed is an objective one, in that the standard can be breached by someone, who through no fault of his own, is incapable of performing the duties of a director. This is a clear divergence from the *Re City Equitable Fire* approach.

A similar view was taken by Harman J in *AB Trucking and BAW Commercials* Ch D 3 June, unreported. The respondent was said to be 'incapable of understanding the commercial reality of accounts' and thus 'incapable of discharging his duty to the public'. Harman J imposed a disqualification order for four years.

It seems clear that an objective standard of 'fitness' is being imposed. The exact nature of the test is still unclear. As we have seen, various tests appear in the cases (see Dine, *Company Lawyer* vol. 9, no. 10, p. 213 and the list set out on pp. 201–2).

All or any of these could be at least partially objective in nature. Analysis of the standard has been poor. The view that 'incompetence' is sufficient seems to be growing, but in the absence of a definition of the ability to be expected of a 'reasonable director' such a standard is still necessarily vague. The one thing that does seem clear is that this mythical creature can both understand and keep accounts. If he cannot, he is unfit. Even if he employs a professional who should be competent to deal with the necessary paperwork, this will only be a matter to take into consideration when determining the length of disqualification.

This approach was taken by Harman J in *Re Rolus Properties Ltd & Another* (1988) 4 BCC 446. He said:

'The privilege of limited liability is a valuable incentive to encourage entrepreneurs to take on risky ventures without inevitable personal total financial disaster. It is, however, a privilege which must be accorded upon terms and some of the most important terms that Parliament has imposed are that accounts be kept and returns made so that the world can, by referring to those, see what is happening. Thus, a total failure to keep statutory books and to make statutory returns is significant for the public at large and a matter which amounts to misconduct if not complied with and is a matter of which the court should take account in considering whether a man can properly be allowed to continue to operate as a director of companies, or whether the public at large is to be protected against him on the grounds that he is unfit, not because he is fraudulent but because he is incompetent and unable to comply with the statutory obligations attached to limited liability. In my view that is a correct approach and the jurisdiction does extend and should be exercised in cases where a man has by his conduct revealed that he is wholly unable to comply with the obligations that go with the privilege of limited liability.'

The disqualification order was reduced from a four-to-six-year period to two years because of the reliance by the director on professional advice.

In *Re Continental Assurance Co of London plc, Secretary of State for Trade and Industry* v. *Burrows and others* [1997] 1 BCLC 48 the court held that 'the degree of competence required . . . extended at least to a requirement that a director who was a corporate financier should be prepared to read and understand the statutory accounts of the holding company'.

One thing seems clear. An unfit director is worse than merely incompetent. He is guilty of 'gross negligence or total incompetence' *Re Lo-Line Electric Motors* (1988) 4 BCC 415, or being 'wholly unable to comply with the obligations which go with the privilege of limited liability' *Re Rolus Properties* (see above). The merely incompetent or those guilty of commercial misjudgment will not be considered unfit *Re McNulty's Interchange Ltd & Another* (1988) 4 BCC 533. In *Secretary of State for Trade and Industry* v. *Hickling and others* [1996] BCC 678 the court held that directors who had been guilty of naivety, over-optimism and misplaced trust should not, in the absence of dishonesty, commercial immorality or gross incompetence, be disqualified. There is, however, a rather opaque reference to disqualification being nearer to a 'negligence' standard than a determination of 'reasonable financial provision' in *Secretary of State for Trade and Industry* v. *Gray and another* [1995] 1 BCLC 276. However the reference was in the context not of setting the standard for disqualification but of determining whether or not the Court of Appeal should interfere with the judge's findings. It seems to indicate that there is a discoverable standard for disqualification which the Court of Appeal can impose rather than set that standard which remains obscure. Until the courts have settled the standard of competence of a 'reasonable' director, it will continue to be uncertain whether a particular director has been incompetent. Further uncertainty is added by the requirement that the director should have been totally or wholly incompetent. It would be helpful if the courts addressed the definition of the degree of competence required of a 'fit' director. However, discussion of the meaning of 'unfitness' may be discouraged by the Court of Appeal's dicta in *Re Sevenoaks Stationers* [1991] BCLC 325, where they held that such 'judicial paraphrases should not be construed in lieu of the words of the statute'. Unfitness was to be regarded as a 'jury question'.

As mentioned above the Court of Appeal had a further chance to consider the setting of standards in *Secretary of State for Trade and Industry* v. *Gray and another* [1995] 1 BCLC 276 but again failed to determine the relationship between moral culpability and incompetence or to set some measure of competence. In view of the latter failure it is the more surprising that the Court felt able to overturn the lower court's finding that the directors were not unfit and should therefore be disqualified. The Court held that the respondent's conduct fell below the 'standard appropriate' for directors. The three allegations in this case were that the companies involved had (i) been trading while insolvent, (ii) failed to keep proper accounting records and (iii) failed to file accounts on time. This behaviour had also involved the giving of preferences. Other remedies had been pursued in respect of the preferences, so that the judge discounted them. The Court of Appeal held that she was wrong to do so. The language in the case gives support to the argument that this is a penal measure. As described above, the Court held that only the past conduct was relevant. The present state of affairs was irrelevant to the issue of disqualification, as was the future protection of the public. This attitude certainly seems to indicate that the thrust is punishment for past misdeeds. Deterrence is also an aim. Thus Hoffman LJ approved the statement by Sir Donald Nicholls VC in *Secretary of State for Trade and Industry* v. *Ettinger, Re Swift* [1993] BCLC 899: 'Those who make use of limited liability must do so with a proper sense of responsibility. The directors' disqualification procedure is an important sanction introduced by Parliament to raise standards in that regard.'

The length of the disqualification and 'mitigating factors'

In *Re Sevenoaks Stationers* [1991] BCLC 325, the Court of Appeal held that in determining the length of a disqualification under s. 6 of the Company Directors Disqualification Act the top bracket of disqualification should be reserved for serious cases. This would involve disqualification of 10 years or more. The Court of Appeal suggested that cases in this bracket might well include cases of imposition of a second disqualification order on a director. Unhelpfully, Dillon LJ suggested that the 'middle bracket of disqualification from 6–10 years should apply for serious cases which do not merit the top bracket' [1991] BCLC 325, at p. 328. The minimum bracket of 2 to 5 years of disqualification 'should be applied where, though disqualification is mandatory, the case is, relatively, not very serious'. Unfortunately the Court did not analyse or discuss the matters which were likely to place a case within one of the 'brackets' with the exception of Crown debts. These were said only to be of especial significance where they had caused suffering over and above that caused by other creditors. It is unfortunate that the Court of Appeal did not seize the opportunity to carry out a more comprehensive review of the matters which would cause a case to fall within each bracket. More particularly, the matters which may be viewed as 'mitigating factors' are even more unclear.

There are a number of factors which have caused the court to impose a shorter order than would otherwise be the case. In cases decided under s. 300 of the Companies Act 1985 the same factors led the court to exercise its discretion not to disqualify. Among those factors are:

Effect on employees
The court may be reluctant to impose a disqualification order where jobs are at stake. In *Re Majestic Recording Studios* [1989] BCLC 1, the judge made a clear finding that the director was unfit but then went on to permit him to continue to be director of one company under certain conditions, partly because of the hardship that this would otherwise cause to employees.

Acting on professional advice
This was a significant factor in reducing the period of disqualification in
Re Rolus Properties Ltd & Another.

The youth of the director
The youth of the director at the time of the failure of the company and
evidence that he has learnt from past mistakes (see *Re Chartmore*, 12 Oct.
1989, [1990] BCLC 673. However, the status of these cases and factors
seems very doubtful in view of the Court of Appeal's clear ruling in
Secretary of State for Trade and Industry v. *Gray* that only past behaviour
should affect the decision to disqualify. Hoffman LJ, however, recognised
that 'whether or not he has shown himself unlikely to offend again' will be
relevant to whether or not there will be a grant of leave to act whilst
disqualified. He went on to say: 'it may also be relevant by way of
mitigation on the length of disqualification, although I note that the
guidelines in *Re Sevenoaks Stationers Ltd* [1991] BCLC 325 are solely by
reference to the seriousness of the conduct in question.'

Leave to act while disqualified

A curious light is thrown on the mandatory nature of the disqualification
under s. 6 by the power of the court to exercise a discretion to permit a
director to act as such during the period of disqualification. This could
amount to a reversal of the duty to impose a disqualification order, but it
seems that the court will often impose quite stringent conditions on the
grant of such permission see *Re Lo-Line Electric Motors*, [1988] BCLC
698. A recent example is *Re Chartmore* (see above). In that case a
disqualification for two years for 'gross incompetence' was imposed.
However, the director was permitted to continue to act for a named
company for one year despite these misgivings expressed by Harman J:

> 'The only matter that bothers me is that the failure of the company for
> which I have disqualified Mr Buckingham, Chartmore Limited, was
> primarily due to Mr Buckingham having started it with quite
> inadequate capitalisation and having carried it on unrealising that he
> was in effect trading on the creditors' backs in such a manner as to show
> that degree of inadequacy warranting disqualification.
>   This new company has one hundred pounds paid up share capital and
> no other equity on its balance sheet at all. There are no other directors'
> loan accounts which could be subordinated to the trade and other
> creditors or converted into equity. There is a statement by Mr
> Buckingham that he and his fellow director have paid fifteen thousand
> pounds into the company. That worries me because the accounts show
> no trace of the sum and they therefore cast considerable doubt on Mr
> Buckingham's sworn statement.'

It is to be hoped that the courts will exercise caution in using this
discretion.

Disqualification after investigation

Section 8 of the Company Directors Disqualification Act 1986 gives power to the court to make a disqualification order, on the application of the Secretary of State, if it appears from a report made to him or from information or documents obtained by him that it is expedient in the public interest that an order should be made against a director or former director of any company. The court must be satisfied that the conduct of the director in relation to the company makes him unfit to be concerned in the management of a company.

It would have been under this section that the Secretary of State could have made an application for disqualification following the House of Fraser enquiry. It is to be noted that not only the unfitness test must be satisfied but that the Secretary of State may only make the application if it appears to be expedient in the public interest that a disqualification order should be made. This gives a very wide discretion to the Secretary of State as to whether he should apply. Presumably he may take into account all such matters as would be considered by the Director of Public Prosecutions when considering whether to exercise his discretion to prosecute. Such matters may well include the wisdom of prolonging an already drawn-out affair as well as the chances of the application being successful. It must be noted that the power of the Secretary of State is limited to application to the court. Contrary to the thrust of some press reports at the time of publication of the House of Fraser report, the power to disqualify lies with the court and not with the Secretary of State. There is a discretion to disqualify under this section. The maximum disqualification period is fifteen years.

Conclusion

The legislation has been widely used and disqualification is made more significant because a register of disqualified directors is kept and can be consulted. Two major difficulties remain in the operation of s. 6, the first is the exact degree to which the penal nature of the provisions should lead to care in protecting the rights of director defendants, the second is the definition of the standard of care to be expected from a reasonable director. The latter needs to be ascertained in order to more clearly identify deviancy. It is to be hoped that care will be taken to define this standard in future cases.

12.6 Insider Dealing

The practice of 'insider dealing' or 'insider trading' occurs when a person with information makes use of that information for his own gain or to enable another to gain. Opinions differ as to whether the defendant should have gained the information in some privileged capacity. This aspect makes a fundamental difference to the philosophical basis of the laws forbidding the practice and is discussed below. First the content of the European Community and United Kingdom rules will be examined.

In respect of insider dealing or insider trading the United Kingdom law applies penal sanctions. There may be other constraints on company directors who contravene insider trading legislation using information gained as a director. They will be in breach of their duties to their company. Company law duties which may be used to control this type of behaviour are also examined below. The United Kingdom legislation, as well as much of the legislation in force in other Member States will be driven by the EC Insider Trading Directive which was implemented in the United Kingdom by the Criminal Justice Act 1993 which came into force on 1 March 1994.

The implementation of the EC Insider Trading Directive in the UK

The EC Insider Dealing Directive should have been implemented by the Member States by 1 June 1992. The United Kingdom Government have implemented the Directive by the Criminal Justice Act 1993 of which the relevant provisions came into force on 1 March 1994.

Part V of the Act contains the implementation of the EC Directive on Insider Dealing (89/592/EEC) s. 54 and Schedule 2 defines the securities to which the insider trading provisions apply.

Securities
There is a double test. The relevant securities must appear in the list in Schedule 2 (which the Treasury may amend by order (s. 54(2)) and must satisfy such other condition as shall be laid down by Treasury order. Schedule 2 currently lists: stocks and shares, debt securities, warrants, depositary receipts, options, securities futures and contracts for differences.

In the absence of the relevant orders it is difficult to comment on the double test save to say that it will involve complications. It does not appear from the face of the section that the Treasury approach will be to issue a simple list of securities which are caught and it would be almost impossible to do so. The introduction of any 'condition' to be satisfied must inevitably cause uncertainty although the approach is perhaps preferable to the approach in the Company Securities (Insider Dealing) Act 1985 which differentiates between deals on a stock exchange and off-market deals. It provides that the prohibitions apply to dealing –

'(i) through an off-market dealer who is making a market in those securities, in the knowledge that he is an off-market dealer, that he is making a market in those securities and that those securities are advertised securities.'

The burden of proving the three necessary elements of *mens rea* to satisfy this test was clearly considerable. However under the proposed provisions the prosecutor must still show that the defendant knew that the securities fell within the orders to be issued by the Treasury under s. 54 since it is only in that case that information relating to them becomes 'inside information' and so subject to restriction (ss. 56, 57).

Having established that the securities in question are within the definition and that the defendant knew this the prosecutor must show that the defendant knew that the information was inside information and that the defendant 'has [the information] and knows that he has it, from an inside source (s. 57(1)(b)).

'Inside information'

'Inside information' must be information relating to securities as defined for the purposes of this Part (as discussed above). It must also relate to particular securities or a particular issuer of securities and not to securities or issuers in general. It must be specific or precise, must not have been made public and would be likely to have had a significant effect on the price of securities if made public.

This section replaces s. 10 of the current statute which provides that inside information:

(1) relates to specific matters relating or of concern (directly or indirectly) to the company in question, that is to say, is not of a general nature relating or of concern to that company; and

(2) is not generally known to those persons who are accustomed or who would be likely to deal in the securities to which the information relates, but which would, if it were generally known, be likely materially to affect the price of those securities.

Whether the new sections are an improvement must be doubted. Uncertainty must exist over the meaning of 'specific or precise' and 'significant effect' on price. Whether or not the facts of an individual case fit within these definitions will be for the jury to decide. They may well be in considerable difficulties in determining these matters which may involve considerations outside their normal day-to-day experience.

Further difficulties may arise concerning the moment of 'publication' since information may well become available in widening circles rather than to everyone simultaneously. This problem is addressed in s. 58. This provides a non-exhaustive definition of the meaning of 'made public'. Information is made public if it is published in accordance with the rules of a regulated market for the purpose of informing investors and their professional advisers, is in any record open to public inspection, can readily be acquired by those likely to deal in relevant securities or is derived from information which has been made public. The section goes on to permit a wide construction of 'made public' in that information may be treated as made public even though it can only be acquired by persons exercising diligence or expertise, it has only been communicated to a section of the public, it can be acquired only by observation, is communicated on payment of a fee or it is published only outside the United Kingdom.

'Insider'

It will be remembered that the prosecutor must prove not only knowledge that the information was inside information but also that the defendant has the information from an inside source and knows that he has it from an inside source (s. 57).

An insider is defined by s. 57 as a person who has the information through –

'(a) being a director, employee or shareholder of an issuer of securities; or

(b) having access to the information by virtue of his employment, profession, office or profession or the direct or indirect source of his information is a person within para. (a).'

This definition replaces the notion of a person 'knowingly connected with a company' under s. 9 of the Company Securities (insider Dealing) Act 1985 and those abusing information obtained in an official capacity (s. 2 of that Act). The wording follows Article 2 of the EC Insider Dealing Directive which defines the persons prohibited from trading as any person who:

'(i) by virtue of his membership of the administrative, management or supervisory bodies of the issuer,

(ii) by virtue of his holding in the capital of the issuer, or

(iii) because he has access to such information by virtue of the exercise of his employment, profession or duties in the exercise of his employment, profession or duties, possesses inside information.'

This formulation may catch the waiter who gleans the information from overheard conversation as he serves a meal to insiders since he gains the information by virtue of his employment. The loosening of the 'connection' with the company may make the offence too wide. It also puts in doubt the philosophical basis of making this behaviour a criminal offence. If the 'connection' was important an argument based on breach of trust by individuals was credible. A widening of the offence reduces this credibility. However, it is also arguable that the wording imports a causal link between the employment, etc. and the acquisition of the information. (On this point see Takis Tridimas, 'Insider Trading in Europe' 40 ICLQ 919.) By requiring that the 'access' to the information was 'by virtue' of the employment, etc. The link required is stronger than in the Commission proposal which defined an insider as any person who 'in the exercise of his employment, profession or duties acquires inside information'. The wording of the Act follows the wording of the adopted text. However, the wording of both the Directive and the Act is ambiguous and the necessity for a causal link may well fall to be determined by the European Court of Justice at some future date.

One possible improvement on the present law is the absence of the need to prove an 'obtaining' of the information. The defendant must know that he 'has' the information as insider or that the direct or indirect source of the information was an insider s. 57. It is clear that unsolicited information is covered. Under the present law it was unclear whether positive action by the defendant was necessary until the decision in *Attorney General's Reference (No. 1) of 1988* ([1989] BCLC 193) determined that it was not.

Liability of individuals
The offence set out in s. 52 makes it plain that only individuals can be liable.

The exclusion of criminal liability for companies can be explained by reference to the provisions of the Directive which clearly contemplates that companies can be insiders but also expressly provides (Article 2(2)) that when the status of insider is attributable to a legal person, the prohibition applies to the natural persons who decided to carry out the transaction for the account of the legal person concerned. It was therefore not possible to exclude companies from the definition of insiders but they can and will be excluded from liability as they are not considered to be in a position to commit the offence.

Next the prosecution must show that there was a 'dealing' in the securities, a disclosure of the information or an encouragement of another to deal (s. 52). It should be noted that unlike the other matters we have examined these are three alternative methods of committing the offence. All other matters pose cumulative hurdles for the prosecution.

(i) Dealing or encouraging dealing
Dealing is further defined by s. 55 and includes acquisition and disposal as principal or agent or the direct or indirect procurement of an acquisition or disposal by any other person. In *Attorney General's Reference (No. 1) of 1975* ([1975] 2 All ER 684 at p. 686) 'procure' was held to mean 'produce by endeavour'. The defendant must therefore have caused the prohibited result by his actions. In that case the defendant charged with the procurement had added alcohol to the drink of another without his knowledge. It was held that if the defendant knew that the other man intended to drive and that the ordinary and natural result of the added alcohol was to cause him to have an alcohol concentration above the limit for drivers, the defendant had procured him to commit the drink–driving offence.

The meaning of an 'indirect procurement' must therefore remain rather obscure, particularly so far as the *mens rea* to be proved. Must it be proved that the defendant foresaw or that it was reasonably foreseeable that the defendant's actions would lead to another acquiring or disposing of securities? The relationship between this section and s. 52(2)(a) which prohibits the encouragement of another to deal is also somewhat obscure.

Could there be an indirect procurement which was not an encouragement to deal or vice versa?

Dealing will only amount to an offence if it takes place in the circumstances set out in s. 52(3). They are

'that the acquisition or disposal in question occurs on a regulated market or that he relies on or is himself acting as a professional intermediary'.

This wording follows Article 2(3) of the EC Directive which permits Member States to exempt deals not involving a professional intermediary.'

'Professional intermediary' is defined in s. 59. Essentially it is a person who holds himself out to a section of the public as being someone willing to engage in the acquisition or disposal of securities or act as an intermediary between persons taking part in any dealing in securities.

(ii) Disclosing
Section 52(2)(b) provides that it is an offence to disclose information to another 'otherwise than in the proper performance of the functions of his employment, office or profession'. This section deals with the simple disclosure of information and is perhaps the most likely offence to be limited by the concept of 'taking advantage' discussed below.

(iii) Encouraging others to deal
The third way of committing the offence is by encouraging others to deal. It must be shown that the defendant must know or have reasonable cause to believe that the deal will occur on a regulated market or would be effected through a professional intermediary.

Finally the concept of 'taking advantage' has been used in a limited way in the provision of specific defences.

The defences
If the factors discussed so far can be proved, the defendant is guilty of insider dealing unless he can take advantage of the defences set out in s. 53 or specific defences which appear in Schedule 1. The Act is specific about the burden of proof in that each defence requires that the defendant should 'show' the relevant facts. This will presumably mean that a defendant must establish the defences on a balance of probabilities. The defences available on a dealing charge are that:

(a) he did not at the time expect the dealing to result in a profit attributable to the fact that the information in question was price-sensitive information in relation to the securities, or

(b) that at the time he believed on reasonable grounds that the information had been disclosed widely enough to ensure that none of those taking part in the dealing would be prejudiced by not having the information, or

(c) that he would have done what he did even if he had not had the information.

This exception replaces s. 3 of the 1985 Act and is apt to cover the situation where the profit motive is present but is not a primary purpose. The problem posed by the Directive was to retain this and other exceptions while implementing the Directive which contains no parallels. Use has been made of the 'taking advantage' approach in the Directive to achieve this.

The special trustee exceptions (s. 7 Insider Dealing Act 1986), will also be covered by this exception in the Act.

Section 52(2) provides exactly similar defences for the offence of encouraging another to deal and s. 53(3) provides a defence to the disclosure provision. It is a defence for a defendant accused of insider dealing by disclosure of information to show either that he did not expect anyone to deal as a result of the disclosure or that he did not expect the dealing to result in a profit attributable to the fact that the information was price-sensitive. In all cases the notion of profit includes avoidance of a loss (s. 53(6)).

There are also specific defences for market makers dealing in good faith in the course of business or employment, dealers whose information is market information concerning acquisition or disposal of certain securities who deal in good faith in circumstances where it was reasonable for him to deal; and price stabilisation operations provided that the individuals carrying them out have acted in conformity with price stabilisation rules made under s. 48 of the Financial Services Act 1986.

Article 2(4) of the Directive provides an exemption for transactions carried out by Member States or their agents 'in pursuit of monetary, exchange rate or public debt-management policies'.

This general exemption is reflected in s. 63 of the Act.

One concern which may be felt is the reversal of the burden of proof in all the above circumstances save for the general exemption in s. 63. The presumption against a defendant and the defence based on motive may of little comfort where criminal charges are in prospect.

Jurisdiction

By Article 5 of the Directive the Member States are to apply the prohibitions 'at least' to actions undertaken within their territory 'to the extent that the transferable securities concerned are admitted to trading on a market of a Member State'. This provision appears to be of impenetrable obscurity but an attempt has been made to reflect the Directive in s. 62 which restricts jurisdiction to acts done within the United Kingdom or markets declared by Treasury order to be a market regulated in the United Kingdom. It is not necessary that the dealing should have occurred within the United Kingdom, 'any act constituting or forming part of the alleged dealing' will be sufficient to found jurisdiction.

Conclusion

Article 13 of the Directive provides that the Member States shall determine the penalties to be applied for infringement of the prohibitions.

The only proviso to this discretion is that the 'penalties shall be sufficient to promote compliance'. The maximum penalty provided for in the Act is seven years imprisonment and an unlimited fine for a conviction on indictment. The United Kingdom would seem to have ignored both the criticism of the use of the criminal law and the possibility of substituting civil remedies. (See Tridimas, 'Insider Trading in Europe', [. 933 and J. Naylor, 'The Use of Criminal Sanctions by the UK and US authorities for Insider Trading' (1990) 11 Co Law 53.) Although the implementation provisions reflect the Directive well, the use of the criminal law probably does not promote compliance with the prohibitions as it is well known to be ineffective.

The sum total of the matters which the prosecution must prove has been set out above and it is plain that the offence is still complex and difficult to prove. It is arguable that putting in place an ineffective convoluted criminal offence is at the same time a misuse of the criminal law and an ineffective implementation of the EC Directive.

Should insider dealing be a crime?

Some argue that this is a 'victimless crime' in that it is not clear if there is actually a loser; others claim that the practice of insider trading increases the volume of sales on a market, so that overall the market gains:

Theories behind control of insider trading
In the United States regulation of insider dealing dates from the 1930s. A comprehensive ban on dealing passed into UK law in the 1980s. Prior to this, insider dealing by directors might have given rise to an action for breach of fiduciary duties provided that the misfeasance was not ratified by the company's general meeting.

Misappropriation The controversy surrounding the regulation of insider trading starts from a number of theoretical standpoints. Perhaps the simplest is the misappropriation theory which regards non-public price-sensitive information as a valuable commodity which is the property or akin to the property of a company. The information does not belong to the individuals who make up the company. It is therefore inequitable and akin to theft for those individuals to make use of that information for their own gain. This theory does not require any loss to have been suffered in real terms – the offensive behaviour is seen as the unjustifiable gain or avoidance of loss. This equation of insider trading with misappropriation is perhaps the strongest argument in favour of criminal sanctions. It is to be noted, however, that at this stage practical considerations have not been taken into account. The most compelling practical consideration is that both the offence and the transactions which constitute the actus reus are complicated. This makes proof of all of the elements of an offence to the criminal standard extremely difficult. There have been less than 20 convictions in the United Kingdom since the offence was introduced. Some of these followed pleas of guilty.

Fairness and confidence in the market This argument in favour of the regulation of insider trading rests on the perception that if, of two potential players in a market, one has price-sensitive information available and the other has not, that is unfair.

This argument may be bolstered by, or include reference to, the misappropriation theory and its proponents may or may not assert that the 'victims' suffer loss as opposed to making a profit. The unfairness is said to lead to loss of confidence by investors in the markets and will lead to a diminution in trading.

In fact, there are three closely related approaches which may overlap. The inherent unfairness approach, the misappropriation theory and the idea that insider trading may lead to loss of confidence in the market are all distinct reasons for regulating insider trading. They may be used together as above but the loss of confidence in the market may not necessarily be related to the perception that the market is unfair.

Market efficiency If it could be shown that insider dealing created a more efficient market, then there would be a benefit to all investors at the expense of no one. Manne ('Insider Trading and Property Rights in New Information' (1985) Cato J. 933) sought to establish that the effect of insider dealing is to produce a gradual change in prices as more and more people receive and rely on the information in question. Only speculative dealers on the market would suffer from insider dealing. The long-term investor will not be interested in the timing of the disclosure but will reap his reward in due course. When such an investor sells, Manne argues that even if he sells in ignorance of information which is causing insiders to trade, the very fact that they are trading increases the price he receives for his shares. Suter (*The Regulation of Insider Dealing in Britain*, Butterworths, 1989, p. 22) has the following to say about that proposition:

> 'Arguments as to the seller's gain will be of little comfort to a seller who argues that had he known what the insider knew, he would not have sold. In deciding to sell, he sells at a lower price than if the information had been disclosed. He is also deprived of information relevant to his investment decision. The fact that the seller's loss is contingent does not mean that the insider's gain is not made at the expense of anyone.'

The gap between the two positions can perhaps be explained by the difference between the economists' approach which focuses on the efficiency of the market and would regard the improved efficiency of the market and the consequent gain to all investors as outweighing any notions of inequities between individual participants. This attitude leads to the extreme theory which holds that the ability to use price-sensitive information before it is made public is a legitimate reward for those in a position to be able to do so.

The government's view However, the view current at present in official circles in the United Kingdom is that insider trading undermines confidence in the probity of the market and is unfair. It is a practice also condemned on the ground that it has parallels with those who use information or property belonging to a company to make gains on their own account.

Summary

1 The general fiduciary duties of directors are backed up by specific duties and prohibitions set out in the statutes.

2 These prohibitions include limitations on transactions between the company and directors or their families.

3 There is also a general prohibition on the misuse of price sensitive information about shares obtained by or from a person in a privileged position. The rule against insider dealing attracts criminal penalties.

Casenotes

Sections 320, 322–30 CA 1985 as amended

320. Substantial property transactions involving directors, etc.

(1) With the exceptions provided by the section next following, a company shall not enter into an arrangement –

 (*a*) whereby a director of the company or its holding company, or a person connected with such a director, acquires or is to acquire one or more non-cash assets of the requisite value from the company; or

 (*b*) whereby the company acquires or is to acquire one or more non-cash assets of the requisite value from such a director or a person so connected,

unless the arrangement is first provided by a resolution of the company in general meeting and, if the director or connected person is a director of its holding company or a person connected with such a director, by a resolution in general meeting of the holding company.

 (2) For this purpose a non-cash asset is of the requisite value if at the time the arrangement in question is entered into its value is not less than £1,000 but (subject to that) exceeds £50,000 or 10 per cent of the company's asset value, that is –

 (*a*) except in a case falling within paragraph (b) below, the value of the company's net assets is determined by reference to the accounts prepared and laid under Part VII in respect of the last preceding financial year in respect of which such accounts were so laid; and

 (*b*) where no accounts have been so prepared and laid before that time, the amount of the company's called-up share capital.

 (3) For purposes of this section and sections 321 and 322, a shadow director is treated as a director.

Section 321 provides for some exceptions to s. 320.

322. Liabilities arising from contravention of s. 320

(1) An arrangement entered into by a company in contravention of s. 320, and any transaction entered into in pursuance of the arrangement (whether by the company or any other person) is voidable at the instance of the company unless one or more of the conditions specified in the next subsection is satisfied.

(2) Those conditions are that –

    (a) restitution of any money or other asset which is the subject-matter of the arrangement or transaction is no longer possible or the company has been indemnified in pursuance of this section by any other person for the loss or damage suffered by it; or

    (b) any rights acquired bona fide for value and without actual notice of the contravention by any person who is not a party to the arrangement or transaction would be affected by its avoidance; or

    (c) the arrangement is, within a reasonable period, affirmed by the company in general meeting and, if it is an arrangement for the transfer of an asset to or by a director of its holding company or a person who is connected with such a director, is so affirmed with the approval of the holding company given by a resolution in general meeting.

(3) If an arrangement is entered into with a company by a director of the company or its holding company or a person connected with him in contravention of s. 320, that director and the person so connected, and any other director of the company who authorised the arrangement or any transaction entered into in pursuance of such an arrangement, is liable –

    (a) to account to the company for any gain which he has made directly or indirectly by the arrangement or transaction, and

    (b) (jointly and severally with any other person liable under this subsection) to indemnify the company for any loss or damage resulting from the arrangement or transaction.

(4) Subsection (3) is without prejudice to any liability imposed otherwise than by that subsection, and is subject to the following two subsections; and the liability under subsection (3) arises whether or not the arrangement or transaction entered into has been avoided in pursuance of subsection (1).

(5) If an arrangement is entered into by a company and a person connected with a director of the company or its holding company in contravention of s. 320, that director is not liable under subsection (3) if he shows that he took all reasonable steps to secure the company's compliance with that section.

(6) In any case, a person so connected and any such other director as is mentioned in subsection (3) is not so liable if he shows that, at the time the arrangement was entered into, he did not know the relevant circumstances constituting the contravention.

322A. Invalidity of certain transactions involving directors, etc.

This section applies where a company enters into a transaction to which the parties include –

(*a*) a director of the company of its holding company, or

(*b*) a person connected with such a director or a company with whom such a director is associated,

and the board of directors, in connection with the transaction, exceed any limitation on their powers under the company's constitution.

(2) The transaction is viodable at the instance of the company.

(3) Whether or not it is avoided, any such party to the transaction as is mentioned in subsection (1)(*a*) or (*b*), and any director of the company who authorised the transaction, is liable –

(*a*) to account to the company for any gain which he has made directly or indirectly by the transaction, and

(*b*) to indemnify the company for any loss or damage resulting from the transaction.

(4) Nothing in the above provisions shall be construed as excluding the operation of any other enactment or rule of law by virtue of which the transaction may be called in question or any liability to the company may arise.

(5) The transaction ceases to be voidable if –

(*a*) restitution of any money or other asset which was the subject-matter of the transaction is no longer possible, or

(*b*) the company is indemnified for any loss or damage resulting from the transaction, or

(*c*) rights acquired bona fide for value and without actual notice of the directors' exceeding their powers by a person who is not party to the transaction would be affected by the avoidance, or

(*d*) the transaction is ratified by the company in general meeting, but ordinary or special resolution or otherwise as the case may require.

(6) A person other than a director of the company is not liable under subsection (3) if he shows that at the time the transaction was entered into he did not know that the directors were exceeding their powers.

(7) This section does not affect the operation of section 35A in relation to any party to the transaction not within subsection (1)(*a*) or (*b*).

But where a transaction is voidable by virtue of this section and valid by virtue of that section in favour of such a person, the court may, on the application of that person or of the company, make such order affirming, severing or setting aside the transaction, on such terms, as appear to the court to be just.

(8) In this section "transaction" includes any act; and the reference in subsection (1) to limitations deriving –

(*a*) from any resolution of the company in general meeting or a meeting of any class of shareholders, or

(*b*) from any agreement between the members of the company or of any class of shareholders.".

(2) In Schedule 22 to the Companies Act 1985 (provisions applying to unregistered companies), in the entries relating to Part X, insert –

"section 322A Invalidity of certain Subject to section 718(3)."
transactions involving
directors, etc.

323. Prohibition on directors dealing in share options

(1) It is an offence for a director of a company to buy –

   (a) a right to call for delivery at a specified price and within a specified time of a specified number of relevant shares or a specified amount of relevant debentures; or
   (b) a right to make delivery at a specified price and within a specified time of a specified number of relevant shares or a specified amount of relevant debentures; or
   (c) a right (as he may elect) to call for delivery at a specified price and within a specified time or to make delivery at a specified price and within a specified time of a specified number of relevant shares or a specified amount of relevant debentures.

(2) A person guilty of an offence under subsection (1) is liable to imprisonment or a fine, or both.

(3) In subsection (1) –

   (a) 'relevant shares', in relation to a director of a company, means shares in the company or in any other body corporate, being the company's subsidiary or holding company, or a subsidiary of the company's holding company, being shares as respects which there has been granted a listing on a stock exchange (whether in Great Britain or elsewhere);
   (b) 'relevant debentures', in relation to a director of a company, means debentures of the company or of any other body corporate, being the company's subsidiary or holding company or a subsidiary of the company's holding company, being debentures as respects which there has been granted such a listing; and
   (c) 'price' includes any consideration other than money.

(4) This section applies to a shadow director as to a director.

(5) This section is not to be taken as penalising a person who buys a right to subscribe for shares in, or debentures of, a body corporate or buys debentures of a body corporate that confer upon the holder of them a right to subscribe for, or to convert the debentures (in whole or in part) into, shares of that body.

324. Duty of director to disclose shareholdings in own company

(1) A person who becomes a director of a company and at the time when he does so is interested in shares in, or debentures of, the company or any other body corporate, being the company's subsidiary or holding company or a subsidiary of the company's holding company, is under obligation to notify the company in writing –

(*a*)   of the subsistence of his interests at that time; and

(*b*)   of the number of shares of each class in, and the amount of debentures of each class of, the company or other such body corporate in which each interest of his subsists at that time.

(2) A director of a company is under obligation to notify the company in writing of the occurrence, while he is a director, of any of the following events –

(*a*)   any event in consequence of whose occurrence he becomes, or ceases to be, interested in shares in, or debentures of, the company or any other body corporate, being the company's subsidiary or holding company or a subsidiary of the company's holding company;

(*b*)   the entering into by him of a contract to sell any such shares or debentures;

(*c*)   the assignment by him of a right granted to him by the company to subscribe for shares in, or debentures of, the company; and

(*d*)   the grant to him by another body corporate, being the company's subsidiary or holding company or a subsidiary of the company's holding company, of a right to subscribe for shares in, or debentures of, that other body corporate, the exercise of such a right granted to him and the assignment by him of such a right so granted;

and notification to the company must state the number or amount, and class, of shares or debentures involved.

(3) Schedule 13 has effect in connection with subsections (1) and (2) above; and of that Schedule –

(*a*)   Part I contains rules for the interpretation of, and otherwise in relation to, those subsections and applies in determining, for purposes of those subsections, whether a person has an interest in shares or debentures;

(*b*)   Part II applies with respect to the periods within which obligations imposed by the subsections must be fulfilled; and

(*c*)   Part III specifies certain circumstances in which obligations arising from subsection (2) are to be treated as not discharged;

and subsections (1) and (2) are subject to any exceptions for which provision may be made by regulations made by the Secretary of State by statutory instrument.

(4) Subsection (2) does not require the notification by a person of the occurrence of an event whose occurrence comes to his knowledge after he has ceased to be a director.

(5) An obligation imposed by this section is treated as not discharged unless the notice by means of which it purports to be discharged is expressed to be given in fulfilment of that obligation.

(6) This section applies to shadow directors as to directors; but nothing in it operates so as to impose an obligation with respect to shares in a body corporate which is the wholly-owned subsidiary of another body corporate.

(7) A person who –

(*a*)   fails to discharge, within the proper period, an obligation to which he is subject under subsection (1) or (2), or (*b*)   in purported discharge of an obligation to which he is so subject, makes to the company a statement which he knows to be false, or recklessly makes to it a statement which is false,

is guilty of an offence and liable to imprisonment or a fine, or both.

(8) Section 732 (restriction on prosecutions) applies to an offence under this section. [324]

325. Register of directors' interests notified under s. 324

(1) Every company shall keep a register for the purposes of s. 324.

(2) Whenever a company receives information from a director given in fulfilment of an obligation imposed on him by that section, it is under obligation to enter in the register, against the director's name, the information received and the date of the entry.

(3) The company is also under obligation, whenever it grants to a director a right to subscribe for shares in, or debentures of, the company to enter in the register against his name –

(*a*)   the date on which the right is granted,

(*b*)   the period during which, or time at which, it is exercisable,

(*c*)   the consideration for the grant (or, if there is no consideration, that fact), and

(*d*)   the description of shares or debentures involved and the number or amount of them, and the price to be paid for them (or the consideration, if otherwise than in money).

(4) Whenever such a right as is mentioned above is exercised by a director, the company is under obligation to enter in the register against his name that fact (identifying the right), the number or amount of shares or debentures in respect of which it is exercised and, if they were registered in his name, that fact and, if not, the name or names of the person or persons in whose name or names they were registered, together (if they were registered in the names of two persons or more) with the number or amount of the shares or debentures registered in the name of each of them.

(5) Part IV of Schedule 13 has effect with respect to the register to be kept under this section, to the way in which entries in it are to be made, to the right of inspection, and generally.

(6) For purposes of this section, a shadow director is deemed a director.

326. Sanctions for non-compliance

(1) The following applies with respect to defaults in complying with, and to contraventions of, s. 325 and Part IV of Schedule 13.

(2) If default is made in complying with any of the following provisions –

(*a*)   s. 325(1), (2), (3) or (4), or

(*b*)   Schedule 13, paragraph 21, 22 or 28,

the company and every officer of it who is in default is liable to a fine and, for continued contravention, to a daily default fine.

(3) If an inspection of the register required under paragraph 25 of the Schedule is refused, or a copy required under paragraph 26 is not sent within the proper period, the company and every officer of it who is in default is liable to a fine and, for continued contravention, to a daily default fine.

(4) If default is made for 14 days in complying with paragraph 27 of the Schedule (notice to register of where register is kept), the company and every officer of it who is in default is liable to a fine and, for continued contravention, to a daily default fine.

(5) If default is made in complying with paragraph 29 of the Schedule (register to be produced at annual general meeting), the company and every officer of it who is in default is liable to a fine.

(6) In the case of a refusal of an inspection of the register required under paragraph 25 of the Schedule, the court may by order compel an immediate inspection of it; and in the case of failure to send within the proper period a copy required under paragraph 26, the court may by order direct that the copy be sent to the person requiring it.

327. Extension of s. 323 to spouses and children

(1) Section 323 applies to –

- (a)   the wife or husband of a director of a company (not being herself or himself a director of it), and
- (b)   an infant son or infant daughter of a director (not being herself or himself a director of the company),

as it applies to the director; but it is a defence for a person charged by virtue of this section with an offence under section 323 to prove that he (she) had no reason to believe that his (her) spouse or, as the case may be, parent was a director of the company in question.

(2) For the purposes of this section –

- (a)   "son" includes step-son, and "daughter" includes step-daughter ("parent" being construed accordingly),
- (b)   "infant" means, in relation to Scotland, pupil or minor, and
- (c)   a shadow director of a company is deemed a director of it.

328. Extension of s. 324 to spouses and children

(1) For the purposes of s. 324 –

- (a)   an interest of the wife or husband of a director of a company (not being herself or himself a director of it) in shares or debentures is to be treated as the director's interest; and
- (b)   the same applies to an interest of an infant son or infant daughter of a director of a company (not being himself or herself a director of it) in shares or debentures.

(2) For those purposes –

    (*a*) a contract, assignment or right of subscription entered into, exercised or made by, or a grant made to, the wife or husband of a director of a company (not being herself or himself a director of it) is to be treated as having been entered into, exercised or made by, or (as the case may be) as having been made to, the director; and

    (*b*) the same applies to a contract, assignment or right of subscription entered into, exercised or made by, or grant made to, an infant son or infant daughter of a director of a company (not being himself or herself a director of it).

(3) A director of a company is under obligation to notify the company in writing of the occurrence while he or she is a director, of either of the following events, namely –

    (*a*) the grant by the company to his (her) spouse, or to his or her infant son or infant daughter, of a right to subscribe for shares in, or debentures of, the company; and

    (*b*) the exercise by his (her) spouse or by his or her infant son or infant daughter of such a right granted by the company to the wife, husband, son or daughter.

(4) In a notice given to the company under subsection (3) there shall be stated –

    (*a*) in the case of the grant of a right, the like information as is required by s. 324 to be stated by the director on the grant to him by another body corporate of a right to subscribe for shares in, or debentures of, that other body corporate; and

    (*b*) in the case of the exercise of a right, the like information as is required by that section to be stated by the director on the exercise of a right granted by him by another body corporate to subscribe for shares in, or debentures of, that other body or corporate.

(5) An obligation imposed by subsection (3) on a director must be fulfilled by him before the end of 5 days beginning with the day following that on which the occurrence of the event giving rise to it comes to his knowledge; but in reckoning that period of days there is disregarded any Saturday or Sunday, and any day which is a bank holiday in any part of Great Britain

(6) A person who –

    (*a*) fails to fulfil, within the proper period, an obligation to which he is subject under subsection (3), or

    (*b*) in purported fulfilment of such an obligation, makes to a company a statement which he knows to be false, or recklessly makes to a company a statement which is false,

is guilty of an offence and liable to imprisonment or fine, or both.

(7) The rules set out in Part I of Schedule 13 have effect for the interpretation of, and otherwise in relation to, subsection (1) and (2); and subsections (5), (6) and (8) of section 324 apply with any requisite modification.

(8) In this section 'son' includes step-son, 'daughter' includes step-daughter, and 'infant' means, in relation to Scotland, pupil or minor.

(9) For purposes of s. 325, an obligation imposes on a director by this section is to be treated as if imposed by section 324.

329. Duty to notify stock exchange of matters notified under preceding sections

(1) Whenever a company whose shares or debentures are listed on a [recognised investment exchange other than an overseas investment exchange within the meaning of the Financial Services Act 1986] is notified of any matter by a director in consequence of the fulfilment of an obligation imposed by section 324 or 328, and that matter relates to shares or debentures so listed, the company is under obligation to notify [that investment exchange] of that matter; and [the investment exchange] may publish, in such manner as it may determine, any information received by it under this subsection.

(2) An obligation imposed by subsection (1) must be fulfilled before the end of the day next following that on which it arises; but there is disregarded for this purpose a day which is a Saturday or a Sunday or a bank holiday in any part of Great Britain.

(3) If default is made in complying with this section, the company and every officer of it who is in default is guilty of an offence and liable to a fine and, for continued contravention, to a daily default fine.

Section 732 (restriction on prosecutions) applies to an offence under this section.

NOTES

Sub-s. (1): amended by the Financial Services Act 1986, s. 212(2), Sch. 16, para. 20, as from 29 April 1988.

Restrictions on a company's power to make loans, etc, to directors and persons connected with them

330. General restriction on loans etc to directors and persons connected with them

(1) The prohibitions listed below in this section are subject to the exceptions in sections 332 to 338.

(2) A company shall not –

 (a) make a loan to a director of the company or of its holding company;
 (b) enter into any guarantee or provide any security in connection with a loan made by any person to such a director.

(3) A relevant company shall not –

 (a) make a quasi-loan to a director of the company or of its holding company;

(*b*) make a loan or a quasi-loan to a person connected with such a director;

(*c*) enter into a guarantee or provide any security in connection with a loan or quasi-loan made by any other person for such a director or a person so connected.

(4) A relevant company shall not –

(*a*) enter into a credit transaction as creditor for such a director or a person so connected;

(*b*) enter into any guarantee or provide any security in connection with a credit transaction made by any other person for such a director or a person so connected.

(5) For purposes of sections 330 to 346, a shadow director is treated as a director.

(6) A company shall not arrange for the assignment to it, or the assumption by it, of any rights, obligations or liabilities under a transaction which, if it had been entered into by the company, would have contravened subsection (2), (3) or (4); but for the purposes of sections 330 to 347 the transaction is to be treated as having been entered into on the date of the arrangement.

(7) A company shall not take part in any arrangement whereby –

(*a*) another person enters into a transaction which, if it had been entered into by the company, would have contravened any of subsections (2), (3), (4) or (6); and

(*b*) that other person, in pursuance of the arrangement, has obtained or is to obtain any benefit from the company or its holding company or a subsidiary of the company or its holding company.

Exercises

1 Would the transactions prohibited by statute be a breach of directors' duties according to the case law?

2 Should insider dealing be a criminal offence?

13 Suing the Company, Suing for the Company, Enforcing Director's Duties

13.1 Suing the Company

One of the reasons for conferring a legal personality on a company was to make it able to sue and be sued in its own name. Consequently a company can be sued for a wrong perpetrated by it, either by a member or by a third party who has been aggrieved by the company's action. Difficulties may sometimes arise when the capacity of the member to sue is in doubt (see the discussion of the articles as a contract in Chapter 5). As a general rule, however, where the wrong has been done to or by a company, the company can sue or be sued. Thus, if a director is in breach of his duties to the company, the company can sue him for redress. However, corporate personality causes problems as well as solving them. If the majority of the shares in a company are held by those controlling that company (and they often are) those controllers can perpetrate all kinds of wrongdoing to the detriment of the minority and then vote that the company should not take legal action to gain compensation. Suppose, for example, that a director sells to the company land worth £10,000. He and his cronies who together hold a majority of the shares in the company, pay £20,000 for the land. They then pass a resolution to the effect that the company should not take action to get back the money that has been taken unnecessarily from the company. The minority shareholders in the company have had the assets of the company diminished and thus the value of there shareholding in the company go down. What can they do? In theory it is the company's money to give away and it has done so. This is the type of situation in which the court has had to make an exception to the corporate personality rule. This exception is known as the exception to the rule in *Foss* v. *Harbottle* (1843) 2 Hare 461.

13.2 Suing for the Company (the exceptions to the rule in *Foss* v. *Harbottle* and derivative actions)

The duties which a director owes to the company are only useful if they can be effectively enforced. If a right has been infringed which is in law a right belonging to a company (for example, the misapplication of company property – *Foss* v. *Harbottle*, or indeed any other breach of directors' duties) the only proper plaintiff is the company itself (see p. 252 for a more detailed explanation of this rule). This rule has come to be known as the rule in *Foss* v. *Harbottle* (see Casenotes) because this is the case in which the rule was first clearly established. In *Bamford* v. *Bamford* [1970] Ch 212, Lord Justice Russell said:

> 'it would be for the company to decide whether to institute proceedings to avoid the voidable allotment: and again this decision would be one for the company in general meeting to decide by ordinary resolution. To litigate or not to litigate, apart from very special circumstances, is for decision by such a resolution.'

As a general principle this is admirable because it has the advantage of avoiding the problem of many actions being commenced simultaneously by all members that believed themselves to be aggrieved by a particular action of the management. However, real problems occur when the alleged perpetrators of the wrong against the company also control the general meeting. In those circumstances, of course, it is most unlikely that the members of the general meeting will resolve to sue themselves. When this happens, if the wrong done is serious enough a shareholder may be permitted to sue on behalf of the company. Four major difficulties confront such a plaintiff:

1. The standing of the plaintiff and his entitlement to sue must be settled as a preliminary matter before the substantive complaint has been heard. This involves the plaintiff in establishing that the alleged wrongdoers are 'in control' of the company. Further, the action must be brought *bona fide* for the benefit of the company for wrongs to the company for which no other remedy is available and not for an ulterior purpose. In *Barrett* v. *Duckett and others* [1995] 1 BCLC the action was brought to harass an ex-son-in-law and thus was not permitted.
2. The plaintiff must show that the company suffered a wrong of such an order that it would be unfair to permit the general meeting to ratify the wrong. The ambit of this requirement is most uncertain. It seems clear that actions wholly outside the power of the company to perform cannot be ratified by ordinary resolution, only by the special procedure under s. 35 Companies Act 1985 (see p. 45). It is certain that minor wrongs against the company can be ratified. There remains an enormous area of uncertainty providing a potential pitfall to a plaintiff in this sort of action.
3. The plaintiff must prove the actual commission of the serious wrong against the company by those controlling it. This in itself is a difficult task since the plaintiff is not, by definition, a controller of the company and so he will in all likelihood have limited access to information concerning the internal management of the company.
4. If the plaintiff can surmount these three not inconsiderable hurdles he will have succeeded in his action. During the course of the case he is always at peril as to costs. Even if he succeeds, the principal beneficiary of

the action is the company in whose favour judgment will be given. The actual gain to the plaintiff may thus be very small. His only gain may be the right to participate in the fortunes of a better-managed company. It is perhaps not surprising that this type of action is infrequently brought, particularly in view of the remedy introduced in 1980 and now to be found at ss. 459–461 of the 1985 Act. When a company is in liquidation the liquidator will be able to bring an action in the company's name and thus breaches of duty may more easily be made the subject of court proceedings. Nevertheless a 'derivative' action (that is, an action permitted because the court decides that an exception should be made to the rule in *Foss* v. *Harbottle*) is still an option open to a plaintiff who wishes to complain about the mismanagement of his company while it is still in business. The action is termed 'derivative' because the right that the plaintiff seeks to have enforced is not his own: it 'derives' from the company. The four difficulties faced by such a plaintiff must be examined in more detail.

13.3 **Ratification – The Improper Elevation of Majority Rule**

A number of the practical difficulties facing shareholders seeking to enforce the directors' duty is caused by an imperfect understanding of the rights which are being exercised. A shareholder gains two separate rights with ownership of a share. One right is to the value of that share as a piece of property. The other is a right to participate in the value generated by the commercial entity which is the company itself. Where the harm is done to the company by a *mala fide* act of directors the majority have no standing and should be unable to release the director from his duty. The company is bigger than 100% of the shareholders. Unless a duty to vote unselfishly in the interests of the company is imposed on shareholders, all a vote will tell us is how they would like their rights in the value of the share to be protected.

In the other situation where shareholders' property rights are being infringed the majority also has no role since a vote by such a majority is merely an assertion that their personal interests lie in one course of action being taken not that their derivative interests lie in that course. This tells us nothing about the legitimate or illegitimate impact on the minority's rights. The protection of minority rights should therefore focus not on balancing majority and minority rights since this does no more than pit one set of personal interests against another. Instead the concentration should be on ensuring that no shareholder's property interest is unfairly damaged when directors move forward acting in the best interests of the company whether the disadvantaged shareholder is in the minority or majority. Such an approach would eliminate the complex calculations which now determine the *locus standi* of a plaintiff and whether there has been a fraud on the minority. It is therefore arguable that ratification can only provide evidence of whether the directors are acting in the best interests of the company (because a number of shareholders agree with their actions), or that the course of action pursued is not an unfair infringement of the property rights of others. In either case a ratification by an 'independent' majority would provide the best evidence. However, ratification provides no justification for depriving a shareholder of *locus standi* to sue, because the votes cast by others can never be conclusive evidence that the company's benefit has been regarded or that an unfair course of action is not being pursued. Ratification ought therefore to be a matter taken into account by the court when determining what, if any, remedies are appropriate but should be irrelevant to the standing of the plaintiff.

The confusion which has arisen in the case-law stems from these misunderstandings as to the true value of a ratification.

Locus standi – who is in control of the company?

In *Birch* v. *Sullivan* [1958] 1 All ER 56 the court said that when an individual plaintiff institutes a derivative action to enforce a right belonging to the company, he must specifically allege in his pleadings, and be prepared to prove, that those in control of the company would prevent the company from suing in its own name. If there is any challenge to that allegation the matter must be determined as a preliminary issue (*Prudential Assurance Co. Ltd* v. *Newman Industries Ltd (No. 2)* [1982] Ch 204). The great difficulty is in determining an effective test which will embrace all circumstances in which the persons complained about are 'in control' of a company. In *Prudential Assurance Co. Ltd* v. *Newman Industries Ltd (No. 2)* [1981] Ch 257, the judge who first heard the case believed that the court should examine the realities of the situation. He said:

'if the defendants against whom relief is sought on behalf of the company control the majority of votes, the action will be allowed to proceed whether a resolution that no action should be brought by the company has been passed or not; so also, if the persons against whom relief is sought do not control a majority of the votes but it is shown that a resolution has been passed and passed only by the use of their votes. . . But there are an infinite variety of possible circumstances . . . If shareholders having a majority of votes in general meeting are nominees, the court will look behind the register to the beneficial owners to see whether they are the persons against whom relief is sought: see *Pavlides* v. *Jensen* [1956] Ch 565. There seems no good reason why the court should not have regard to any other circumstances which show that the majority cannot be relied upon to determine in a disinterested way whether it is truly in the interests of the company that proceedings should be brought.'

The judgment of the Court of Appeal in that case left matters most unclear. The suggestion was made that if 'control' was an issue the court should grant an adjournment 'to enable a meeting of shareholders to be convened by the board, so that he can reach a conclusion in the light of the conduct of, and proceedings at, that meeting'. This would seem to imply rejection of the idea that all matters which might in fact affect control of the company should be investigated. The approach suggested by the Court of Appeal would to some extent confine the court to taking into account matters which appeared, so to speak, 'on the face of' the meeting. However, the judgment offers no very clear guidance as to what matters should be taken into account. Even if it did, the Court of Appeal's words would be of doubtful value, since the issue of the *Foss* v. *Harbottle* rule had become irrelevant to the outcome of the case by the time it was heard in that court. The judges had refused to hear counsel's arguments on the proper scope of *Foss* v. *Harbottle* and were careful to point out that they were not expressing a 'concluded' view on the scope of the rule in *Foss* v. *Harbottle*. The extent to which a court can probe the reality of the situation to determine control thus remains uncertain. What is clear from *Smith* v. *Croft (No. 2)* [1988] Ch 114 (see Casenotes) is that a minority shareholder who would otherwise be able to sue on behalf of the company, under an established exception to the rule in *Foss* v. *Harbottle*, may nevertheless be prevented from doing so if a majority of the members, independent of the wrongdoers, is opposed to the litigation. If a majority of the oppressed minority is not prepared to support the action it cannot go ahead.

Two other restrictions are that a defendant may raise not only defences which would be valid against an action by the company, but also defences that would only be valid against the plaintiff personally (*Nurcombe* v. *Nurcombe* [1985] 1 All ER 65 (see Casenotes)). It has also been held that a minority shareholder may not bring a derivative action when a company has gone into liquidation. Only the liquidator can represent the company after that moment (*Fargo Ltd* v. *Godfroy* [1986] 3 All ER 279)

Serious wrongdoing by those in control

An essential distinction that is made in company law is between actions by the controllers of the company which cannot be 'ratified' by the majority of the company voting in a general meeting and those that can be ratified. Ratification is a concept borrowed from agency law where it is used to describe the process of retrospective validation of an agent's acts. If an agent acts outside the authority conferred upon him by his principal, the principal can at a later date approve the action of the agent and agree to be legally bound by any transaction entered into by that agent. In company law, if the directors of the company have acted in breach of their duties it is open to the shareholders on some occasions but not on others to vote that such directors will not be sued in respect of those breaches of duty. The major difficulty is in identifying what breaches are ratifiable and can be forgiven and which are not ratifiable and will therefore found an action provided the wrongdoers are in control of the company in the sense discussed above. However, there is another curious feature of ratification which must be noted. Where a breach of duty *is* ratifiable it may be so ratified by a majority vote *notwithstanding that the wrongdoers make up part or all of the vote in favour of ratification.* It is argued at the beginning of this chapter that the courts have made a fundamental mistake as to the value of ratification. However, as matters stand the distinction that is crucial to the ratification issue is the type of wrongdoing that has occurred.

What actions make up a wrong which cannot be ratified?

The categories that are identifiable from the cases are:

1. Where the act complained of is *ultra vires* or illegal (see s. 35 CA 1985).
2. Where there is a 'fraud on the minority'.

It is clear in the aftermath of the *Prudential* case that there is to be no exception to the rule in *Foss* v. *Harbottle* simply 'where the interests of justice so require'.

Ultra vires and illegal acts
It was for some time unclear whether an *ultra vires* or illegal act was a wrong done to individual shareholders as well as a wrong done to the company. If it could be regarded as infringing the personal rights of shareholders, each shareholder would have a personal right to sue on his own behalf and would not need to invoke the derivative action. However, it now seems clear, following *Smith* v. *Croft*, that all cases in which compensation is sought on behalf of the company for past *ultra vires* or illegal acts are to be regarded as cases brought on behalf of the company. They will therefore have to be in the derivative form. This does not affect the personal right of a shareholder to sue to restrain an action which is about to occur and which will be *ultra vires* or illegal. The role of *ultra vires* will be much diminished in the future because of the Companies Act 1985 s. 35. An example of illegality and *ultra vires* is *Smith* v. *Croft* itself (see Casenotes). *Ultra vires* acts may now be ratified by a special resolution of the company (s. 35 Companies Act 1985) but another special resolution will be required to relieve directors or others from any liability incurred because of their involvement in the *ultra vires* transaction.

Fraud on the minority
It should be noted that 'fraud' in this context has a special meaning unconnected with any considerations of deceit or of criminal law notions of fraud. Some actions may involve crimes, others may not. Over the years commentators have discerned various categories of fraud on the minority from the cases but all agree that the cases are difficult to reconcile with one

another and in some cases behaviour can be found which fits more than one of the categories. Perhaps the proper way to regard the cases is to extract the total wrongdoing of the controllers and ask whether this is behaviour that can be condoned by a (possibly partial) majority vote? Categories which have been identified are:

1. Expropriation of the company's property.
2. *Mala fide* breaches of duty.
3. Negligent acts from which the directors benefit.
4. Use of powers for an improper purpose.

To some extent these categories are merely a way of saying that where there has been a breach of duty by directors the court will examine all the facts to determine whether it is such a serious matter that it cannot be 'forgiven' by ratification. Obviously, taking the company's property is the clearest example of such a situation, so that is an identifiably separate category. With regard to the other instances of breach of duty it is doubtful whether there is value in attempting to do more than look at the sum total of the behaviour of the controllers in order to assess whether a proper case can be made for *Foss* v. *Harbottle* to be disapplied. For that reason breaches of duty not involving expropriation of company property are divided into non-ratifiable acts which are then distinguished from ratifiable acts. Amongst the latter are: *bona fide* incidental profit making; use of powers for an improper purpose; and negligence which does not benefit the directors.

Expropriation of company property
In *Menier* v. *Hooper's Telegraph Works* (1874) LR 9 Ch D 350 a rival company had a controlling interest in the company concerned. They used this controlling interest to settle an impending action between the two companies in their favour. The judge said that the majority had 'put something into their pockets' at the expense of the minority. This fell squarely within the fraud on the minority exception and would not be permitted. Similarly, in *Cook* v. *Deeks* [1916] 1 AC 544, the directors diverted to themselves contracts which they should have taken up on behalf of the company. It was held that directors holding a majority of votes would not be permitted to make a present to themselves.
  A case falling on the other side of the line, where the behaviour was held to be mere incidental profit-making by the directors so that the breach of duty could have been ratified is *Regal Hastings Ltd* v. *Gulliver* [1942] 1 All ER 378. In that case, Regal Hastings Ltd owned a cinema. The directors decided to acquire two other cinemas with a view to the sale of the whole concern. They formed a subsidiary company. The owner of the cinemas demanded that the subsidiary should have a paid up capital of £5,000 before he would grant a lease. The directors subscribed for £3,000 of the shares and Regal Hastings for £2,000. The concern was then sold and the directors ultimately made a profit on their shares. The court said that the

directors were in breach of their duties. As this had involved making a profit out of the fiduciary relationship in which they stood to the company they were bound to repay the profits they had made.

Breaches of duty

Here, as elsewhere, the only clear distinction between breaches of duty which are ratifiable and those which are not lies in the extent to which the behaviour is regarded as villainous. In *Atwool* v. *Merryweather* (1867) 5 Eq 464, a company was formed to acquire a mine from Merryweather. In fact the mine was worthless and the formation of the company and its subsequent flotation was nothing more than a conspiracy to defraud the public. It was held that the company could get back the money it had paid for the worthless mine despite the fact that the majority had voted against this course of action.

Other examples include *Alexander* v. *Automatic Telephone Co.* [1900] 2 Ch 56, where the directors holding the majority of the shares tried to avoid paying the full price for their shares, while requiring all other members to do so; and *Estmanco (Kilner House) Ltd* v. *GLC* [1982] 1 WLR 2. The latter case is interesting, since the judge seemed to take an overall view of the wrongdoing without seeking to put it carefully into categories. The court came to the conclusion that a derivative action would lie where the end result of the breaches of duty was to 'stultify the purpose' for which the company had been formed (see Casenotes).

Negligent acts which benefit a director

In *Daniels* v. *Daniels* [1978] Ch 406 (see Casenotes) the court held that a minority shareholder who has no other remedy may sue where directors use their powers intentionally or unintentionally, fraudulently or negligently in a manner which benefits themselves at the expense of the company.

This last case shows that benefit to themselves provides a dividing line between ratifiable and non-ratifiable actions because it was held in *Pavlides* v. *Jensen* [1956] Ch 565 that an individual plaintiff would not be permitted to sue where the claim was based on negligence alone. No exception to the rule in *Foss* v. *Harbottle* would be made in such a case.

Use of powers for an improper purpose

Clear instances of actions that are ratifiable occur where powers given to the directors for one purpose are misused. An example of this is when shares are issued to fend off a take-over or otherwise to alter the balance of voting power within a company. The courts have held that the power to issue shares must only be used where the primary purpose of the issue is to raise capital (*Bamford* v. *Bamford* [1970] Ch 212). However, where the directors have misused these powers the courts have consistently allowed ratification by a majority vote at a general meeting provided that the holders of the newly-issued shares were not allowed to exercise votes attached to the new shares (*Bamford* v. *Bamford* (as above); *Hogg* v. *Cramphorn Ltd* [1967] Ch 254).

One last category of cases must be mentioned. They are the cases concerned with the alteration of articles (see Chapter 5). It has been held that an individual may prevent the alteration of articles of association where that alteration was not made *bona fide* for the benefit of the company. However, the cases do not make it clear on what basis the action is brought. If it is brought on the basis that a personal right has been infringed, then it could be argued that the preservation of the integrity of the articles is the concern of every shareholder and any breach of those articles could be remedied by a personal action. This would allow the multiplicity of suits to prevent which the rule in *Foss v. Harbottle* was invented. However, that rule is rarely mentioned in that series of cases so it may be the case that the upholding of the articles can be achieved by a personal action. However, if that is not the case another category must be added to the 'fraud on the minority' cases. That is where alteration of the articles is attempted by a majority in control of the company but that alteration is not *bona fide* for the benefit of the company (see cases discussed in Chapter 5).

13.4 The Statutory Remedy in Section 459

Section 459 of the Company's Act 1985 provides a remedy for a member when 'the company's affairs are being or have been conducted in a manner which is unfairly prejudicial to the interests of its members generally or of some part of its members'. The 1985 text referred to 'the interests of some part of the members'. The new text was substituted by s. 145 Companies Act 1989 and Schedule 19, para. 11 (for the full text, see Casenotes). The extension may have the effect of including nearly all behaviour which could be litigated under a derivative action although it is as yet not clear that the two are co-extensive. However, in *Lowe* v. *Fahey and others* [1996] 1 BCLC 262 a claim was brought under s. 459 for repayment to the company of funds wrongly diverted elsewhere by directors. This would, of course be a classic derivative action situation. Nevertheless, Charles Aldous QC held that there was an arguable case under s. 459 and refused to strike out the action. Section 459 first appeared in statutory form as s. 75 of the Companies Act 1980 and is, of course, referred to as such in the earlier decisions regarding its interpretation. The courts have been reluctant to restrict the width of discretion given by the sections, and guidelines to its application tend to be in general terms.

13.5 Unfair Prejudice

Consideration was given to the meaning of unfair prejudice in *Re Bovey Hotel Ventures* (1981) unreported, quoted in *Re R.A. Noble & Son*

(Clothing) Ltd [1983] BCLC 273. Slade J said: 'a member of a company will be able to bring himself within the section if he can show that the value of his shareholding in the company has been seriously diminished or at least seriously jeopardised by reason of a course of conduct on the part of those persons who do have *de facto* control of the company, which was unfair to the member concerned'. He suggested that the test should be an objective one: would the reasonable bystander observing the consequences of their conduct . . . regard it as having unfairly prejudiced the petitioner's interest? This test was adopted by the court in the *R. A. Noble* case. In that case a clear distinction was drawn between the prejudice which was held to have occurred and the unfair element which was not shown. In that case one of the directors had been deliberately and systematically excluded from the running of the affairs of the company. This was conduct which the judge found could have come within the section. However, the circumstances of each particular case had to be examined and in this case the director had brought his exclusion upon himself by disinterest. The conduct was therefore not unfair. This approach was adopted in *Re London School of Electronics Ltd* [1986] Ch 211. In *Re Macro (Ipswich) Ltd* [1994] 2 BCLC 354 the court held that where conduct was unfairly prejudicial to the financial interests of the company then it would also be unfairly prejudicial to the interests of its members. In assessing the fairness of the conduct the court had to perform a balancing act in weighing the various interests of different groups within the company. The court did not interfere in questions of commercial management but where the mismanagement was sufficiently significant and serious to cause loss to the company then it could constitute the basis for finding unfair prejudice. The concept of unfairness is thus capable of being a very broad one indeed. A number of possible limitations have been raised:

1. What is the 'conduct of the company's affairs'?
2. Must there be infringement of a legal right in order to show unfair prejudice?
3. What interest in the company must the petitioner have?
4. In what capacity must the defendant be complaining?

Conduct of Company Affairs

In *Re A Company (No. 001761 of 1986)* [1987] BCLC 141 the court held that the acts of a shareholder in a personal capacity outside the conduct of the company's affairs were irrelevant. Thus the court was not interested in 'an attempt to blacken the respondent's name and to make the court look on her with disfavour as an immoral and attractive woman'. See also *Re Leeds United Holdings plc* (discussed below).

The infringement of legal rights

The concept of unfair prejudice is larger than the idea of infringement of legal rights. In *Re A Company* [1986] BCLC 376, Hoffman J said that in a small company 'the member's interests as a member may include a legitimate expectation that he will continue to be employed as a director and his dismissal from that office and exclusion from the management of the company may therefore be unfairly prejudicial to his interests as a member'. The same view was taken in *Re Sam Weller & Sons Ltd (Re A Company (No. 823 of 1987))* [1990] BCLC 80, where the court refused to strike out a petition alleging unfair prejudice by a failure to declare an adequate dividend. The court emphasised that 'interests' should be considered as wider than 'rights'. It should be noted that this wide view seems to be more easily adhered to in cases where a small company is involved (see *Re Carrington Viyella PLC* (1983) 1 BCC 98) but it has recently been litigated in a number of sporting contexts. In *Re Tottenham Hotspur plc* [1994] 1 BCLC 655 Terry Venables, the chief executive of Tottenham Hotspur, and Alan Sugar, its chairman, originally had a 50/50 interest in the company. Sugar later obtained control and Venables was removed as chief executive. Venables claimed that this removal was contrary to a legitimate expectation that Venables would be involved in managing the company. The court found that there was little if any evidence to support the allegation and did not make any order. In *Re Leeds United Holdings plc* [1996] 2 BCLC 545 the court held that 'The legitimate expectations which the court has to have regard to under s. 459 must relate to the conduct of the company's affairs, the most obvious and common example being an expectation of being allowed to participate in the affairs of the company.' However, the court went on to dismiss the s. 459 action in that case because it was based on an expectation that a particular shareholder would not sell his shares without the consent of the other shareholders. This was held not to relate to the company's affairs and therefore fell outside s. 459.

The important case of *Re Saul D Harrison & Sons plc* [1995] 1 BCLC 14 contains an extensive analysis of the operation of s. 459 to protect 'legitimate expectations'. Hoffman LJ said:

'In deciding what is fair or unfair for the purposes of s. 459, it is important to have in mind that fairness is being used in the context of a commercial relationship. The articles of association are just what their name implies: the contractual terms which govern the relationships of the shareholders with the company and each other. . . Since keeping promises and honouring agreements is probably the most important element of commercial fairness, the starting point an any case under s. 459 will be to ask whether the conduct of which the shareholder complains was in accordance with the articles of association. . . Although one begins with the articles and the powers of the board, a finding that conduct was not in accordance with the articles does not necessarily mean that it was unfair, still less that the court will exercise its discretion to grant relief. There is often sound sense in the rule in *Foss* v. *Harbottle* (1843) 2 Hare 461. In choosing the term 'unfairly prejudicial', the Jenkins Committee para. 204) equated it with Lord Cooper's understanding of 'oppression in *Elder* v. *Elder and Watson*

(1952) SC 49: 'A visible departure from the standards of fair dealing and a violation of the conditions of fair play on which every shareholder who entrusts his money to a company is entitled to rely' So trivial or technical infringements of the articles were not intended to give rise to petitions under s. 459.'

Hoffman LJ goes on to point out that technically lawful actions may also be unfair:

'the personal relationship between a shareholder and those who control the company may entitle him to say that it would in certain circumstances be unfair for them to exercise a power conferred by the articles upon the board or the company in general meeting. I have in the past ventured to borrow from public law the term 'legitimate expectations' to describe the correlative 'right' in the shareholder to which such a relationship may give rise. It often arises out of a fundamental understanding between the shareholders which formed the basis of their association but was not put into contractual form, such as an assumption that each of the parties who has ventured his capital will also participate in the management of the company and receive the return on his investment in the form of salary rather than dividend.'

The judgement emphasises that the fact that the company is small is not sufficient to find that there are legitimate expectations above and beyond those in the articles. 'Something more' was needed and was absent in this case. It is clear that some evidence must be brought of an understanding between the parties separate from the articles. In *Re BSB Holdings* [1996] 1 BCLC 155 the Court made it clear that Saul D. Harrison did not mean that s. 459 was limited to cases of breaches of the articles or other agreements and that the categories of behaviour for which relief could be given were not closed. However, the court followed Saul D. Harrison in emphasising that 'fairness' meant fairness in a commercial context, which meant that directors had a duty to exercise their powers fairly between different classes of shareholders.

What interest in the company must the petitioner have?
In *R & H Electric and another* v. *Haden Bill Electrical Ltd* [1995] 2 BCLC 280 the court held that a broad view should be taken of the capacity in which a petitioner complained for the purposes of s. 459. In that case a company controlled by P was a major creditor of Haden Bill Electrical (HB), P was a director and chairman of HB until relationships broke down and he was removed at short notice. The court held that P could rely on his interest in having been instrumental in raising the loan through his company and the understandings that flowed from that and was not just confined to his interest as a shareholder.
Section 459 (2) of the Act allows those to whom shares have been transferred or transmitted by operation of law (for example, by

inheritance) to petition. Section 460 gives the same right to the Secretary of State. These powers have not apparently been used. In *Re A Company* (1986) 2 BCC 98 & 952 it was held that those who were not registered as shareholders but who were entitled to the benefit of owning the shares (beneficial owners) could not petition.

In what capacity must the complaint be made?
Under the predecessor section to s. 459 a member had to make his complaint 'in his capacity as member'. This meant that if his real complaint was, for example, that he had been excluded from the office of director, his complaint would not found an action. The same difficulty arose as that discussed in Chapter 5 concerning the enforcement of the articles as a contract. In *Re A Company* [1983] Ch 178 the court seemed at first sight to adopt this line. However, the contrast that was being made in that case was between the interests of a person as a shareholder in a company, and totally incidental interests that the same shareholder might have which could be affected by the company's actions. An example might be if the company gained permission to establish a rubbish tip in close proximity to the private house of someone who happened to own shares in that company. It seems that in the light of the number of cases which have taken into account the 'legitimate expectations' of the members to partake in the management of the company that the courts will be most reluctant to return to the strict division between a member's interest as a member and his interest as an active participant in the management of the company.

Which members?
In a number of cases (*Re Carrington Viyella PLC* (1983) 1 BCC 98; *Re A Company* (1988) 4 BCC 506) the court ruled that the behaviour would adversely affect all shareholders. There was therefore no 'part' of the shareholders affected so that the petition could not succeed. This curious approach has been reversed by the Companies Act 1989, s. 145, Schedule 19 article 11 which substituted the words 'unfairly prejudicial to the interests of its members generally or of some part of its members' for the words found in the 1985 Act which referred only to behaviour 'unfairly prejudicial to the interests of some part of the members' (see Casenotes).

13.6 The Relief That Can be Granted

Section 461 of the statute provides that if a court is satisfied that a petition on the ground of unfairly prejudicial conduct is well founded 'it may make such order as it thinks fit for giving relief in respect of the matters complained of'. Sub-section 2 of s. 461 particularises a number of actions which the court might take (see Casenotes). The particularisation of these potential actions is expressly 'without prejudice' to the general discretion contained in sub-section 1 and so in no way limits the court's powers. The court has freely used its power to order the sale of shares. This has the virtue of breaking the deadlock in a company where the behaviour complained of is exclusion from management which has caused the shares held by the complainant to lose value. In *Re Brenfield Squash Racquets Club Ltd* [1996] 2 BCLC 184 the court even ordered the majority to sell their shares to the minority shareholders where that (exceptionally) seemed to be the best solution for the company. In such cases the valuation will be back-dated to the time before the behaviour complained of commenced.

Evaluation and reform

The Law Commission has recently considered the whole range of shareholder remedies and their consultation paper (Law Commission Consultation Paper No. 142) is an invaluable source of legal learning on all the topics covered in this chapter as well as containing a comparison with a number of commonwealth jurisdictions. The final report will be published in 1997. Pointing to the disadvantages of the derivative action, the Commission suggests replacement by a statutory derivative action. This would be available to any member if the case fell within the situation: 'that, if the company were the applicant, it would be entitled to any remedy against any person as a result of threatened breach by any director of the company of any of his duties to the company.' The Commission also recommend far-reaching changes in the case management by the courts of both derivative and s. 459 actions. It has long been felt that s. 459 actions, as well as derivative actions are over long and very costly because multiple allegations can be and are made. The case management regime seeks to limit the scope of the case which will eventually be heard. Because the Commission's final report is not available it is not possible to be very specific about the detail which will be included, so sight of this final report is highly recommended for students studying this area of law.

13.7 **Winding up orders**

Section 122 (1)(g) of the Insolvency Act 1986 provides that a company may be wound up by the court if the court is of the opinion that it is just and equitable that the company should be wound up. This is qualified by s. 125(2) of the Insolvency Act 1986 that the company should not be wound up if some other remedy is available to the petitioners, and the court is of the opinion that they are acting unreasonably in seeking to have the company wound up instead of pursuing that other remedy. This proviso is likely to be of much greater importance in the light of the wide jurisdiction exercised by the courts under s. 459 (CA 1985). It is a drastic move to destroy the company completely as a remedy for unfairness. Far better to allow an aggrieved party to buy his way out at a fair valuation.

The cases prior to 1980 can only therefore afford guidance about the availability of the winding up remedy now. In the light of s. 459, petitioners might be prevented by s. 125(2) of the Insolvency Act 1986 from obtaining a winding up order which they could have obtained before a s. 459 remedy appeared on the statute book. Nor need the 'alternative remedy' necessarily be a s. 459 remedy. In *Re A Company* [1983] 1 WLR 927, the court emphasised that the power to grant a winding up order on the just and equitable ground was discretionary and should certainly be refused where a reasonable offer to buy the petitioner's shares had been refused.

A petition for s. 459 relief can be combined with a petition to wind up on the just and equitable ground. It should be noted that unfair prejudice or malpractice need not be alleged in order to show that there is a case for winding up (see, for example, *Re German Date Coffee Co.* (1882) 20 Ch D 169, where the purpose for which the company was formed was no longer attainable). In *Re R.A. Noble & Son (Clothing) Ltd* [1983] BCLC the judge held that malpractice need not be shown provided that the conduct of those in control had been the 'substantial cause' of the lack of mutual confidence between the parties. In that case the judge dismissed the petition for s. 459 relief and made an order for the winding up of the company on the just and equitable ground.

13.8 When a Winding up Order is Likely to be Made

The leading case on 'just and equitable' winding up is *Re Ebrahami* v. *Westbourne Galleries Ltd* [1973] AC 360. In that case the petition was brought by a Mr Ebrahami, who for many years had been an equal partner with Mr Nazar in a business dealing in Persian carpets. In 1958 it was decided to incorporate the business and Ebrahami (E) and Nazar (N), who were both appointed directors, each held 500 shares. Soon after this N's son was made a director and E and N each transferred 100 shares to the son. After this the Nazars held a majority of the votes. In 1965, the relationship between the Nazars and E began to break down. In 1969, the Nazars used their majority to remove E from his directorship. Thereafter he was unable to take any part in the management of the business and he received no money since all payments were made to the participants in the business by way of directors' salaries rather than dividends. The court held that the removal of E had been lawful. Nevertheless, because the company was in essence an incorporated partnership, the Nazars had abused their power and were in breach of the good faith partners owed to one another. E was therefore entitled to a winding up order.

This may well now be a situation in which s. 459 relief could be granted and thus a winding up order would be refused. (For a detailed look at the judgment in this case see the Casenotes.)

Other situations in which the remedy has been granted are where deadlock has been reached because shares were equally divided between two factions at odds with each other: *Re Yenidje Tobacco Co. Ltd* [1916] 2 Ch 426 and where the whole purpose or substratum of the company had failed. An instance of the latter is *Re German Date Coffee Co.* (1882) 20 ChD 169 where the company (mercifully?) failed to obtain the patent to make coffee from dates. That activity had been the major purpose for which the company was formed.

In order for a petition to succeed a shareholder must show that he has an interest in the winding up: that is, that there is a probability that the company is solvent and so, after the winding up, there will be assets to be distributed to the shareholders (*Re Expanded Plugs Ltd* [1960] 1 WLR 514).

13.9 **Department of Trade Investigations**

The Department of Trade and Industry is the government department concerned with the conduct of companies and the law which governs them. By legislation the department is given various powers to investigate the affairs of companies. One way that this can be done is by the appointment of an inspector to look into the affairs of a company. The appointment can be instigated in a variety of ways:

1. On the order of the court
The Department of Trade must appoint an inspector to investigate the affairs of a company if the court so orders (s. 432(1) Companies Act 1985).

2. On the application of the company
Section 431(2)(c) provides that inspectors may be appointed on the application of the company. The application must be accompanied by evidence showing a good reason why the company's affairs should be investigated and even then the department have a discretion as to whether or not an inspector will be appointed. Few inspectors have been appointed under this power.

3. Fraud, unfair prejudice or withholding of information
The department also has a discretion to appoint inspectors where there is evidence of a company's affairs being conducted in a fraudulent or unfairly prejudicial way, that it proposes to act unlawfully or that 'its members have not been given all the information with respect to its affairs which they might reasonably expect' (s. 432(1)(b)).

Although some inspectors have been appointed under this section, there is grave danger that the mere announcement of the appointment of inspectors will bring lasting damage to the reputation of the company which cannot be reversed even if the allegations prove to be unfounded at the end of the day. Because of this difficulty the Companies Act 1967 introduced a wide range of powers which the Department of Trade and

Industry could use more discreetly to determine whether allegations of misconduct were soundly based. ss. 447–452 CA 1985 now enable the department to require the production of books and papers, to ask for a search warrant if there are grounds for suspecting that articles requested have not been forthcoming and to search premises in respect of which a warrant is issued. Criminal penalties are available for providing false statements and for falsifying, mutilating or destroying documents. It is a defence to show that there was no intention to conceal the state of affairs of the company or to defeat the law. The department's officers are acting in a police capacity when they require the production of books and papers. They are not acting in a way similar to judges. The court will therefore not exercise its power to review decisions taken by those who act in a judicial or quasi-judicial capacity. However the notice requiring the production of books and papers must not be unreasonably or excessively wide (*R* v. *Secretary of State for Trade, Ex Parte Perestrello* [1981] QB 19).

13.10 **When Inspectors Have Been Appointed**

In *Re Pergamon Press* [1970] 3 WLR 792 the Court of Appeal held that inspectors were not acting in a judicial or quasi-judicial way. Nevertheless they have a duty to act fairly. This is important as they have very wide-ranging powers to examine on oath the officers and agents of the company to require documents and even to require a person who is not connected with the company to attend before them and assist in their enquiry (ss. 433–435 CA 1985). By s. 436, obstruction of officers is treated as contempt of court. Following the investigation the inspectors make a report which will be admissible as evidence in any subsequent legal proceedings (s. 441(1). The report is only evidence of the opinion of the inspectors with regard to matters investigated by them, not as to the existence of facts.)

13.11 **Following Investigations**

After an investigation by inspectors or by the department using its powers to require books and documents, the DTI must decide if it is in the public interest to take legal proceedings. If it decides that the public interest will be best served by so doing, it can bring any action the company itself might bring including petitioning for a winding up order (ss. 438, 440).

13.12 **Power to Investigate Share Ownership**

Part XV of the Companies Act gives the Department of Trade wide powers to investigate the ownership of shares in any company and to impose restrictions on the transfer of those shares while it does so.

Summary

1 Directors owe their duties to the company and the company is therefore the proper plaintiff in an action to enforce such duties. This is usually known as the rule in *Foss* v. *Harbottle*.

2 If such a rule was absolute, the majority would have an absolute right to defraud the minority.

3 Exceptions to the rule have therefore been made. Whether the individual shareholder can sue or, on the other hand, whether the majority can prevent the action and forgive the directors (ratification of the directors' actions) depends on the depravity of the wrongdoing in question.

4 An oppressed minority have a wide and flexible action which is procedurally simpler in ss. 459–461 Companies Act 1985 as amended by Companies Act 1989.

5 An aggrieved member may also petition the court to wind up a company on the ground that it would be just and equitable to do so.

6 The DTI have wide powers to inspect the books of companies where malpractice is suspected.

Casenotes

1 *Foss* v. *Harbottle* (1843) 2 Hare 461
The Vice Chancellor [Sir James Wigram] said:

'It was not, nor could it successfully be, argued that it was a matter of course for any individual members of a corporation thus to assume to themselves the right of suing in the name of the corporation. In law the corporation and the aggregate members of the corporation are not the same thing for purposes like this; and the only question can be whether the facts alleged in this case justify a departure from the rule which, prima facie, would require that the corporation should sue in its own name and in its corporate character, or in the name of someone whom the law has appointed to be its representative.'

2 *Smith* v. *Croft* [1987] Ch 114
The plaintiff's action claimed that certain payments to directors had been excessive and were therefore *ultra vires*. The court held:

(i) that although excessive remuneration paid to directors might be an abuse of power, where the power to decide remuneration was vested in the board, it could not be *ultra vires* the company;

(ii) that although a minority shareholder had *locus standi* to bring an action on behalf of a company to recover money paid away wrongfully, the right was not indefeasible even if the transaction was *ultra vires*. It was proper to have regard to the views of the independent shareholders, and their votes should be disregarded only if the court was satisfied that they would be cast in favour of the defendant directors in order to support them rather than for the benefit of the company, or if there was a substantial risk of that happening; accordingly since the majority of the independent shareholders' votes would be cast against allowing the action to proceed, the statement of claim should be struck out.

3 *Nurcombe* v. *Nurcombe* [1985] 1 All ER

The husband and wife were respectively the majority and minority shareholders in a company. They were divorced in 1974 and in the course of matrimonial proceedings it was disclosed that the husband had breached the fiduciary duty which he owed as a director to the company. The wife continued the matrimonial proceedings after that information came to light and the improper profit made by the husband was taken into account in the matrimonial proceedings. The wife subsequently sought to bring a derivative action. The court would not permit her to do so on the grounds that it would be inequitable to permit the wife to pursue the derivative action when the amount of improper profit had been taken into account in other proceedings.

4 *Estmanco (Kilner House) Ltd* v. *GLC* [1982] 1 WLR 2

A block of flats was in the process of being sold by the Greater London Council (GLC). Once a flat had been sold, the purchasers of the flats became shareholders of the Esmanco company. When all the flats had been sold the company would function to manage the flats and the shareholders would have voting rights. The policy of selling the flats was discontinued after the political control of the Council changed. Twelve flats had been sold. The new Council resolved upon a new housing policy and decided to break the terms of the agreement and use the unsold flats to accommodate the needy. A shareholder sought to bring a derivative action on the company's behalf against the Council to enforce the covenant. The Council held the only voting shares in the company at that time and had voted that no action should be taken in respect of the breach of the agreement. The action succeeded. Megarry vc said:

'There can be no doubt about the twelve voteless purchasers being a minority; there can be no doubt about the advantage to the Council of having the action discontinued; there can be no doubt about the injury to the applicant and the rest of the minority, both as shareholders and as purchasers, of that discontinuance; and I feel little doubt that the Council has used its voting power not to promote the best interests of the company but in order to bring advantage to itself and disadvantage to the minority. Furthermore, that disadvantage is no trivial matter, but represents a radical alteration in the basis on which the Council sold the flats to the minority. It seems to me that the sum total represents a fraud on the minority in the sense in which 'fraud' is used in that phrase, or alternatively represents such an abuse of power as to have the same effect.'

5 *Daniels* v. *Daniels* [1978] Ch 406

A husband and wife were the two directors of a company and also the majority shareholders. They caused the company to sell to the wife land owned by the company. Four years later she sold the land for over twenty-eight times what she had paid for it. The judge permitted minority shareholders to claim against the directors. He said:

'a minority shareholder who has no other remedy may sue where directors use their powers, intentionally or unintentionally, fraudulently or negligently, in a manner which benefits themselves at the expense of the company'.

Sections 459-461 CA 1985 as amended

PART XVII

PROTECTION OF COMPANY'S MEMBERS AGAINST UNFAIR PREJUDICE

459. Order on application of company member

(1) A member of a company may apply to the court by petition for an order under this Part on the ground that the company's affairs are being or have been conducted in a manner which is unfairly prejudicial to the interests of its members generally or of some part of its members (including at least himself) or that any actual or proposed act or omission of the company (including an act or omission on its behalf) is or would be so prejudicial.

(2) The provisions of this Part apply to a person who is not a member of a company but to whom shares in the company have been transferred or transmitted by operation of law, as those provisions apply to a member of the company; and references to a member or members are to be construed accordingly.

[(3) In this section (and so far as applicable for the purposes of this section, in s. 461(2)) 'company' means any company within the meaning of this Act or any company which is not such a company but is a statutory water company within the meaning of the Water Act 1989.]

460. Order on application of Secretary of State

(1) If in the case of any company–

- (a) the Secretary of State has received a report under s. 437, or exercised his powers under s. 447 or 448 of this Act or s. 44(2) to (6) of the Insurance Companies Act 1982 (*inspection of company's books and paper*), and
- (b) it appears to him that the company's affairs are being or have been conducted in a manner which is *unfairly prejudicial to the interests of some part of the members*, or that any actual or proposed act or omission of the company (including an act or omission on its behalf) is or would be so prejudicial, he may himself (in addition to or instead of presenting a petition *under s. 440* for the winding up of the company) apply to the court by petition for an order under this Part.

(2) In this section (and, so far as applicable for its purposes, in the section next following) 'company' means any body corporate which is liable to be wound up under this Act.

NOTES
Sub-s (1): amended by CA 1989, ss. 145, 212, Sch. 19, para 11, Sch. 24 post.

---

461. Provisions as to petitions and orders under this Part

(1) If the court is satisfied that a petition under this Part is well founded, it may make such order as it thinks fit for giving relief in respect of the matters complained of.

(2) Without prejudice to the generality of subsection (1), the court's order may –

    (*a*) regulate the conduct of the company's affairs in the future,

    (*b*) require the company to refrain from doing or continuing an act complained of by the petitioner or to do an act which the petitioner has complained it has omitted to do,

    (*c*) authorise civil proceedings to be brought in the name and on behalf of the company by such person or persons and on such terms as the court may direct,

    (*d*) provide for the purchase of the shares of any members of the company by other members or by the company itself and, in the case of a purchase by the company itself, the reduction of the company's capital accordingly.

(3) If an order under this Part requires the company not to make any, or any specified, alteration in the memorandum or articles, the company does not then have the power without leave of the court to make any such alteration in breach of that requirement.

(4) Any alteration in the company's memorandum or articles made by virtue of an order under this Part is of the same effect as if duly made by resolution of the company, and the provisions of this Act apply to the memorandum or articles as so altered accordingly.

(5) An office copy of an order under this Part altering, or giving leave to alter, a company's memorandum or articles shall, within 14 days from the making of the order or such longer period as the court may allow, be delivered by the company to the register of companies for registration; and if a company makes default in complying with this subsection, the company and every officer of it who is in default is liable to a fine and, for continued contravention, to a daily default fine.

[(6) The power under [section 411 of the Insolvency Act] to make rules shall, so far as it relates to a winding-up petition, apply for the purposes of a petition under this Part.]

NOTES

    Commencement: 1 July 1985 (sub-ss. (1)–(5)); 1 March 1986 (sub-s (6)).
    Sub-s (6): substituted by the Insolvency Act 1985, s. 109, Sch. 6, para 24, and further amended by the Insolvency Act 1986, s. 439(1), Sch. 13, Pt I.

Protection of company's members against unfair prejudice

11. In Part XVII of the Companies Act 1985 (protection of company's members against unfair prejudice) –

    (a) in s. 459(1) (application by company member), and
    (b) in s. 460(1)(b) (application by Secretary of State),

for 'unfairly prejudicial to the interests of some part of the members' substitute 'unfairly prejudicial to the interests of its members generally or of some part of its members'.

6 *Ebrahami* v. *Westbourne Galleries* [1973] AC 360
Lord Wilberforce said:

> 'the foundation of it all lies in the words 'just and equitable' and, if there is any respect in which some of the cases may be open to criticism, it is that the courts may sometimes have been too timorous in giving them full force. The words are a recognition of the fact that a limited company is more than a mere legal entity, with a personality in law of its own: that there is room in company law for recognition of the fact that behind it, or among it, there are individuals, with rights, expectations and obligations *inter se* which are not necessarily submerged in the company structure. That structure is defined by the Companies Act and by the articles of association by which shareholders agree to be bound. In most companies and in most contexts, this definition is sufficient and exhaustive, equally so whether the company is large or small. The 'just and equitable' provision does not, as the respondents suggest, entitle one party to disregard the obligation he assumes by entering a company, nor the court to dispense him from it. It does, as equity always does, enable the court to subject the exercise of legal rights to equitable considerations, that is, of a personal character arising between one individual and another, which may make it unjust, or inequitable, to insist on legal rights, or to exercise them in a particular way.
>
> It would be impossible, and wholly undesirable, to define the circumstances in which these considerations may arise. certainly the fact that a company is a small one, or a private company, is not enough. There are very many of these where the association is a purely commercial one, of which it can safely be said that the basis of association is adequately and exhaustively laid down in the articles. The superimposition of equitable considerations requires something more, which typically may include one, or probably more, of the following elements: (i) an association formed or continued on the basis of a personal relationship, involving mutual confidence – this element will often be found where a pre-existing partnership has been converted into a limited company; (ii) an agreement, or understanding, that all, or some (for there may be 'sleeping' members), of the shareholders shall participate in the conduct of the business; (iii) restriction upon the transfer of the members' interest in the company – so that if confidence is lost, or one member is removed from management, he cannot take out his stake and go elsewhere.'

Table 13.1 shows current director control mechanisms.

Exercises

1 Discuss the advantages and disadvantages of the courses of action open to an aggrieved minority shareholder.

2 What purpose did the rule in *Foss* v. *Harbottle* serve? To what extent has s. 459 replaced derivative actions?

Table 13.1 *Current director control*

Control Mechanism	Legal Source	Advantages	Disadvantages	Reform
Shareholder democracy	S303 CA 1985 Bushell v Faith (but see SE rules) S319 CA 1985	Simple mechanism	Doesn't work: because: 1) information flow 2) power in management hands – Art 70 Table A. Automatic self-cleansing. 3) Concentration of power leads to entrenched management – golden parachutes, poison pills etc.	Cadbury says strengthen by improved information flow (?). Suggest limit limited liability – 3 share types. Share A – Aunt Agatha – no voting rights – limited liability. Share B – institutions voting rights – lose limited liability if not exercised. Share C – Directors lose limited liability on S.2141A basis and/or outvote Share B on constitutional issues.
Directors' duties of care and skill	Re City Equitable Fire Re D'Jan	Clever sliding scale – so long as appointment OK – all level of company management catered for – not too strict Smith v Van Gorkum	? Too low a standard ? Has D'Jan introduced objectivity	Use disqualification idea of unfitness or S.2141A to encourage introduction of objective standard. ? Different categories of company – see SMES.
Directors' fiduciary duties	Regal Hastings/Movitex/ Island export/Industrial developments v Cooley/ Howard Smith/Contrast Teck Corp v Miller	Imposes strict trust-like duties Practitioners believe these bring certainty	? Does anyone really understand the muddle caused by Foss v H + ratification. ? Does S.459 cover all this ground.	Abolish? Just S.459?
Directors' statutory duties	SS 320-33 CA 1985 and many others insider trading	Attempt to bring in objective definition of unfitness?	Very technical and probably 100% overlap with fiduciary duties	Abolish?
Disqualification	Company directors (disqualification) Act 1986 Re Sevenoaks stationers		Badly blurs distinction between civil and criminal laws Courts don't know how to handle it.	Qualify directors? Revert to City Equitable Fire. Just decide whether civil or criminal.

14 Shares

A share does not confer on its owner a right to the physical possession of anything. It confers a number of rights against the company (for example, the limited right to enforce the articles – see Chapter 5). The face value of the share is also a measure of the shareholder's interest in the company. In the event of the distribution of the company's assets the amount that will come to any particular shareholder will be proportionate to the face value of the shares owned by him.

The interest of the shareowner in the company and his right to uphold the constitution of the company distinguish the shareholder from the owner of a debenture. The holder of a debenture has lent money to the company, so he, as well as a shareholder, has provided money for the company's operations. A debenture holders rights are, however, restricted to the remedies given to him by his contract of loan with the company. He has no *interest* in that company.

However, companies have found that to attract different types of investor it is useful to have different types of shares. The various 'classes' of shares all enjoy different rights, which are usually set out in the articles. However, where these rights have not been clearly defined, the law lays down rules which fill in the gaps and determine the rights of the different classes of shareholders. Where the company wishes to alter the rights of any of the classes, strict rules have to be complied with. The alteration of such rights is known as a 'variation' of rights.

14.1 **Ordinary Shares**

Unless the memorandum, articles or the documents describing the shares when they were issued otherwise provide, ordinary shareholders are entitled to receive dividends when they are declared (they cannot force a declaration), and to be paid a proportion of the company's assets after payment of the creditors when the company is wound up. The amount will be proportionate to the size of his shareholding and if the amount to be distributed exceeds the nominal value of the company's shares, each shareholder will participate in this 'surplus' in proportion to the nominal value of his shareholding.

An ordinary shareholder will also normally have the right to exercise one vote for each share he holds at the general meetings of the company.

These rights only subsist if there is nothing to the contrary in the document describing the original issue of the shares, in the articles or memorandum. The rights otherwise given by law to shareholders are often varied by those documents. For example, it is common for a company to have more than one class of ordinary shareholders with different voting rights.

14.2 **Preference Shares**

The holders of preference shares are entitled to have some of a payment out by the company paid to them before the ordinary shareholders are paid. Again, the terms of issue or the memorandum and articles can determine the rights of the holders but the courts have had to provide a network of rules which make up possible gaps in the description of the shareholder's rights which appear in these documents. Rules are usually expressed in terms of 'presumptions', that is, the courts will presume that a particular right does or does not attach to a share unless it can be shown that this cannot be the case because of the way in which the shares are described in one of the documents mentioned. The alternatives are that the preference shares can be preferred over the ordinary shares in respect of:

(i)   dividend; or
(ii) return of capital; or
(iii) both dividend and return of capital.

In all these cases matters are further complicated by the fact that the preferences may be 'cumulative' or 'non-cumulative'. A cumulative right means that if the dividend in one year was less than the shareholder was entitled to expect, the arrears must be made up in a subsequent year before the ordinary shareholders receive anything. Unlike the ordinary shareholders, the preference shareholders do know what sum they should receive because the dividend due to a preference shareholder is generally expressed as a fixed percentage of the par value of the share.

Preference as to dividend

There is a presumption that a fixed preferential dividend is cumulative, that is, arrears from previous years must be made good before any amount is paid to the ordinary shareholders. The presumption may be rebutted by the terms of the documents describing shareholders' rights. The right to have any money paid to them by way of dividend only becomes a right when the directors exercise their discretion to pay a dividend at all. Neither the preference shareholders nor the ordinary shareholders can force the declaration of a dividend, even when the company is doing well.

When the company goes into liquidation a difficult question which sometimes needs to be settled is whether the preference shareholders are entitled to arrears of dividend before anyone else is paid. A number of cases have determined that unless there is an express right to the arrears in the documents, the preference shareholders are not entitled to have these arrears made up (see, for example, *Re Crichton's Oil* [1902] 2 Ch 86; *Re*

Wood Skinner & Co. [1944] Ch 323). The 'express' right need not be very clear, however, as the presumption that they will not be made up is easy to displace.

The other presumption that applies here is that the rights stated in any of the relevant documents are exhaustive. The preference shareholders will have a right to what is expressly stated but no more.

Capital

Just because preference shareholders have a right to be paid dividends before ordinary shareholders does not give them preference when the company is being wound up and the capital of the company is being distributed amongst the shareholders. A further question that arises is whether the preference shareholders are entitled to participate on an equal footing with the ordinary shareholders if there is a surplus after:

(i)   the preference shareholders have had their capital returned (if they have a preference as to return of capital); and
(ii) the ordinary shareholders have had their capital returned.

If after those two operations there is still a surplus for distribution, there is a question as to whether the preference shareholders may participate in the distribution of the surplus.

These two dilemmas are solved by:

(a) the presumption that all shareholders should be treated equally so that unless there is a specific right spelled out in the documents giving the preference shareholders a preference as to the repayment of capital then they have no such preference; and
(b) the rule that where a preference as far as the repayment of capital is expressed, the rights set out in the document describe the totality of the rights as far as capital is concerned. The description of rights is said to be 'exhaustive'. Where a preference as to capital is given to preference shareholders, they will therefore not participate in any surplus remaining after capital has been repaid unless an express right to do so is written into the issue documents, the memorandum or articles.

14.3 Voting Rights

Section 370(6) Companies Act 1985 provides:

'(6) In the case of a company originally having a share capital, every member has one vote in respect of each share or each ten pounds of stock held by him; and in any other case every member has one vote.'

This provision is, however, subject to the memorandum or articles which may provide for as complicated a structure of voting rights as may be desired. The idea of non-voting shares has been attacked from time to time. An example of the case against non-voting shares is to be found in a Note of Dissent to the 'Jenkins Committee' report. The note of dissent was signed by Mr L. Brown, Sir George Erskine and Professor L. C. B. Gower.

> 'Feeling as we do, that the development of non-voting equity shares is undesirable both in principle and practice, we find ourselves unable to concur in the failure to make stronger recommendations for their control.
>
> 2. In our opinion the growth of non-voting and restricted voting shares (a) strikes at the basic principle on which our Company Law is based (paragraph 3 below), (b) is inconsistent with the principles underlying our Report and the Reports of earlier Company Law Committees (paragraphs 4,5 and 6) and (c) is undesirable (paragraphs 7 *et seq.*).
>
> 3. The business corporation is a device for enabling an expert body of directors to manage other people's property for them. Since these managers are looking after other people's money it is thought that they should not be totally free from any control or supervision and the obvious persons to exercise some control are the persons whose property is being managed. Hence the basic principle adopted by British Company Law (and, indeed, the laws of most countries) is that ultimate control over the directors should be exercised by the shareholders. This control cannot be exercised in detail and from day to day, but shareholders retain the ultimate sanction in that it is they who 'hire and fire' the directorate.
>
> When the directors own the majority of the equity they are free from outside control, but here they are managing their own money. Hence the interests of the directors and the shareholders are unlikely to conflict, and self-interest should be a sufficient curb and spur (subject to certain legal rules to protect the minority against oppression). When, however, the directors have no financial stake in the prosperity of the company, or only a minority interest, the outside control operates. [Paras 4 & 5 showed that the thrust of most Company Law reports was to increase effective shareholder control.]
>
> 6. In recent years, however, control by shareholders has been stultified in two ways: firstly in a few cases by cross-holdings and circular-holdings within a group of companies, [see Chapter 1] and secondly by non-voting equity shares. The first method has already received the attention of the legislature and an attempt has been made to control it by section [23 of the Companies Act 1985]. In our discussion of this section . . . we recognize that it is improper for directors to maintain themselves indefinitely in office, against the wishes of the other shareholders. We also recognize that section [23 Companies Act 1985] does not go far enough in preventing this mischief and we reject an extension of the section with reluctance and only because of the

complexity and arbitrary nature of the provisions which would be necessary . . . The second method of maintaining control by the existing directors, by utilising non-voting shares, is not as yet controlled in any way; it is only of recent years that it has become a major issue. Today non-voting shares are the simplest and most straightforward method whereby directors can render themselves irremovable without their own consent, notwithstanding that they only own or control a fraction of the equity.

7. It is said that shareholder control is ineffective because of the indifference of shareholders. Everyone would probably agree that shareholders are apathetic while all goes well. But, while all goes well, there is no reason why they should not be apathetic; their intervention is only required when things go ill. No doubt it is true that the small individual shareholder has little power even then, but, as we point out . . . the institutional investor has considerable influence; and even non-institutional shareholders are collectively powerful so long as they have votes. It can hardly be doubted that the possibility that a take-over bidder will obtain control by acquiring those votes has caused directors to pay greater heed to the interests of shareholders.

8. It is also said that shareholder control is inefficient, since directors, as a class, know better what is good for business and for the shareholders than the shareholders themselves. In the normal case this is usually true. But if shareholder control is destroyed and nothing put in its place we have to go still further and say that business efficiency is best ensured by allowing the directors to function free from any outside control, except that of the Courts in the event of fraud or misfeasance, and by making themselves irremovable, without their own consent, however inefficient they may prove to be.'

Despite this cogent criticism, nothing has been done to curb the use of non-voting shares. Indeed, the Stock Exchange accepts non-voting shares provided it is made clear at the outset that this is what they are.

Preference shareholders may have restricted voting rights but they often have a right to vote on issues when their dividend is a certain amount in arrears. By statute they have voting rights when the company is trying a 'variation' of their rights. However, we shall see that 'variation' has in this context a special and narrow definition (see p. 255).

14.4 The Exercise of Voting Powers

There are two restrictions imposed by the courts on the exercise of the right to vote. The vote must be exercised in a way that is 'bona fide for the benefit of the company as a whole' in situations where the courts permit a challenge to a resolution on that basis (this question principally arises where there is an attempt to alter the articles – see Chapter 5). Secondly, where the member voting belongs to more than one class of shareholder, and he is exercising a vote in the context of a 'class vote', he may not vote with his holdings in another class principally in mind. Both of these principles are aptly illustrated by *Re Holder's Investment Trust Ltd* [1971] 1 WLR 583. In that case, the court was considering an unopposed petition for the confirmation by the court of a reduction of capital. Megarry J said:

> 'The resolution was carried by the requisite majority because nearly 90% of the preference shares are vested in the trustees of three trusts set up by Mr William Hill, and they voted in favour of the resolution. These trustees . . . also hold some 52% of the ordinary stocks and shares . . . .[counsel] contends that the extraordinary resolution of the preference shareholders was not valid and effectual because the supporting trustees did not exercise their votes in the way that they ought to have done, namely, in the interests of preference shareholders as a whole. Instead, being owners of much ordinary stock and many shares as well, they voted in such a way as to benefit the totality of the stocks and shares that they held . . . In the *British America* case [*British America Nickel Corporation Ltd* v. *M.J. O'Brien Ltd* [1937] AC 707], Viscount Haldane, in speaking for a strong board of the Judicial Committee, referred . . . to 'a general principle, which is applicable to all authorities conferred on majorities of classes enabling them to bind minorities; namely, that the power given must be exercised for the purpose of benefiting the class as a whole, and not merely individual members only' . . . I have to see whether the majority was honestly endeavouring to decide and act for the benefit of the class as a whole, rather than with a view to the interests of some of the class and against that of others . . . [the] exchange of letters seems to me to make it perfectly clear that the advice sought, the advice given, and the advice acted upon, was all on the basis of what was for the benefit of the trusts as a whole, having regard to their large holdings of the equity capital . . . From first to last I can see no evidence that trustees ever applied their minds to what under company law was the right question, or that they ever had the *bona fide* belief that is requisite for an effectual sanction of the reduction. Accordingly, in my judgment there has been no effectual sanction for the modification of class rights.'

14.5 Variation of Class Rights

If a company wishes to vary the rights attaching to a class of shares or act contrary to the interests of a class of shareholders, special rules must be observed.

Class rights

The protection of the special regime extends to 'rights attached to any class of shares' and it is only when these rights are under threat that it applies. The question as to the meaning of this phrase arose in *Cumbrian Newspapers Group Ltd* v. *Cumberland & Westmorland Herald Newspaper & Printing Co. Ltd* [1987] Ch 1. In that case, a wide definition of the phrase was adopted. Scott J said:

> 'In my judgment, if specific rights are given to certain members in their capacity as members or shareholders, then those members become a class. The shares those members hold for the time being, and without which they would not be members of the class, would represent, in my view, a 'class of shares' for the purposes of s. 125.'

In that case the right in issue was a right given to the plaintiff under the defendant's articles, including a pre-emptive right regarding the transfer of any shares in the defendant and the right to nominate a director to the board of the defendant so long as it held 10 per cent of the issued ordinary shares of the defendant. These rights were held to be class rights, only alterable in accordance with the special procedure set out in s. 125. This decision means that where particular rights are granted to an individual shareholder they would not be alterable without the consent of that shareholder. In those circumstances the individual concerned would constitute a class of one. It might in some cases be possible to say that the right had not been granted to the individual 'in his capacity as shareholder' but in some other capacity. If that is not so, provisions very common in the articles of private companies will become, for all practicable purposes, unalterable. For the time being it is clear that 'class rights' is to be widely defined.

Variation or abrogation

The special procedures apply where class rights are to be 'varied' or 'abrogated'. The courts have, in general, taken a narrow view of what is meant by these words. In general there will be a variation if the alteration directly affects the way the rights are described, but not if the value of the shareholding has been altered in some other way, for example, by varying the rights of another class of shares.

The attitude of the courts can only be understood properly by examining some of the relevant cases.

In *Greenhalgh* v. *Arderne Cinemas Ltd* [1946] 1 All ER 512, the company, by resolution, subdivided some 10s. (50p) ordinary shares into five 2s. (10p) ordinary shares. The votes created by this were used to pass a resolution for increasing the capital of the company. The effect of this was explained by Greene MR as follows:

> 'As a result of those two resolutions, if they are valid, the voting power of the appellant, which previously gave him a satisfactory measure of voting control, is liable to be completely swamped by the votes of the other ordinary shareholders.'

Despite this, the resolution was held not to have varied the rights of the appellant:

> 'the effect of this resolution is, of course, to alter the position of the . . . 2s. shareholders. Instead of Greenhalgh finding himself in a position of control, he finds himself in a position where control has gone, and to that extent the rights of the . . . 2s. shareholders are affected, as a matter of business. As a matter of law, I am quite unable to hold that, as a result of the transaction, the rights are varied; they remain what they always were – a right to have one vote per share *pari passu* with the ordinary shares for the time being issued which include the new 2s. ordinary shares resulting from the subdivision.'

In *Re Old Silkstone Collieries* [1954] Ch 169 it was held that a reduction of capital by repaying preference shareholders so that they would lose their right to compensation which would have been due to them under the government's compensation scheme did constitute a variation of their rights. However, by no means any elimination of a class of shares will constitute a variation. Where capital is repaid in accordance with the par value of the shares, and no well-defined right is taken away, the special procedure need not be invoked. The most usual of these will be a clearly defined right to participate in surplus assets on a winding up.

The protection intended by the statute has not been forthcoming in the following cases:

1. *Re Mackenzie & Co. Ltd* [1916] 2 Ch 450, where a reduction of capital was carried out by the cancellation of paid-up capital in two cases to an equal extent. The practical result was to reduce the amount payable under the fixed preferential dividend to the preference shareholders, while the ordinary shareholders could share the larger remainder of any declared dividend. Because the percentage of the dividend was not affected, that is, the actual description of the rights on the face of it, were not altered, there was held to be no variation.

2. In *Re Schweppes Ltd* [1914] 1 Ch 322, an issue of shares ranking equally with existing shares was held not to be a variation.

3. In the *Greenhalgh* case (see page 265) subdivision of shares and consequent dilution of voting rights was held not to be a variation.

4. In *White* v. *Bristol Aeroplane Company* [1953] Ch 65, an issue of bonus shares to one class which greatly increased their voting power as opposed to another class was held not to be a variation.

5. In *Dimbula Valley (Ceylon) Tea Co.* v. *Laurie* [1961] Ch 353, an issue of bonus shares to one class which would substantially reduce the amount which they would receive when participating in surplus assets on a winding up was held not to be a variation.

Thus, it is only in the most obvious cases, usually when the rights attaching to shares have been altered by alteration of the actual wording describing those rights, where the special protection afforded by s. 125 comes into play. This seems to be an unnecessarily technical and legalistic approach to interpretation of legislation. It seems particularly strange when deciding what is meant by a law operating in the business sphere that a hard distinction should be drawn between 'affecting rights as a matter of business' and 'varying rights as a matter of law'. One reason for this cautious approach which can be discerned from the cases is the fear that by using a wide definition of 'variation' the courts would be allowing one class a veto over a scheme which might benefit the company as a whole. It would seem, however, that in this instance the courts have been rather over-cautious.

Where there is a true 'variation'

Once it has been determined that a class right will be varied by a scheme put forward by a company, the correct procedure depends on (i) where the rights in question are set out, and (ii) whether the constitution of the company has a provision permitting the variation.

Rights set out in the memorandum – no variation clause
Where the rights of the various classes of shareholder are described in the memorandum and there is no variation of rights clause either in the memorandum or the articles, then the rights can only be varied:

(a) if all the members of the company agree (see *Ashbury* v. *Watson* (1885) 30 ChD 376);
(b) by a scheme of arrangement under s. 425 (see Chapter 16);
(c) by alteration of the articles by a special resolution passed *bona fide* for the benefit of the company and then proceeding as for the situation where the rights are described in the memorandum but there is a variation clause in the articles. In s. 17 Companies Act 1985 there is a provision which enables 'a condition contained in a company's memorandum which could lawfully have been contained in articles of association instead' to be altered by special resolution. However, by s. 17(2)(b) this power does not exist (i) where the memorandum prohibits the alteration of the conditions in question or (ii) where exercise of the power would involve any variation or abrogation of the special rights of any class of members.

This section does not prohibit alteration of the memorandum to insert a variation of rights clause except where the rights are protected specifically from change by the memorandum itself. However, it is doubtful whether the insertion of such a clause is covered by the section which permits alteration of 'conditions' which could have been contained in the articles. It seems highly doubtful whether the absence of a variation of rights clause can be seen as a 'condition'.

Rights set out in the memorandum – with variation clause in memorandum
Where rights are set out in the memorandum and there is a variation of
rights clause in the memorandum then the procedure is that the clause
must be followed. However, in particular circumstances there is also a
statutory restriction on such a variation which must also be complied with.
This occurs where:

(a) the variation proposed is concerned with the giving, variation,
revocation or renewal of an authority to issue securities for the purpose
of s. 80 Companies Act 1985 (see Chapter 7).
(b) the variation is concerned with a reduction of capital under s. 135 (see
Chapter 9).

In those circumstances s. 125(3) applies and requires that, in addition to
compliance with the variation of rights clause in the memorandum and
any other conditions imposed by the company's constitution, two other
conditions must be met:

(a) the holders of three-quarters in nominal value of the issued shares of
that class consent in writing to the variation; or
(b) an extraordinary resolution passed at a separate general meeting of
the holders of that class sanctions the variation.

Rights set out in the memorandum – with variation clause in the articles
In this case s. 125(4) of the Companies Act 1985 applies and provided that
the variation of rights clause was included in the articles at the time of the
company's original incorporation then those rights may be varied if the
procedure set out in the variation clause is followed unless:

(a) the variation proposed is concerned with the giving, variation,
revocation or renewal of an authority to issue securities for the purpose
of s. 80 Companies Act 1985 (see Chapter 7); or
(b) the variation is concerned with a reduction of capital under s. 135 (see
Chapter 9).

In those circumstances s. 125(3) applies and requires that, in addition to
compliance with the variation of rights clause in the memorandum and
any other conditions imposed by the company's constitution, two other
conditions must be met:

(a) the holders of three-quarters in nominal value of the issued shares of
that class consent in writing to the variation; or
(b) an extraordinary resolution passed at a separate general meeting of
the holders of that class sanctions the variation.

If the variation clause was not included in the original articles then it
would seem that it must be ignored and a variation carried out as if it did
not exist (see p. 267).

Rights set out in articles – no variation clause
In this case s. 125(2) Companies Act 1985 applies:
•

(2) Where the rights are attached to a class of shares otherwise than by the company's memorandum, and the company's articles do not contain provision with respect to the variation of those rights, those rights may be varied if, but only if –

    (a) the holders of three-quarters in nominal value of the issued shares of that class consent in writing to the variation; or

    (b) an extraordinary resolution passed at a separate general meeting of the holders of that class sanctions the variation;

and any requirement (howsoever imposed) in relation to the variation of those rights is complied with to the extent that it is not comprised in paragraphs (a) and (b) above.

Rights in articles (or elsewhere except in memorandum) – variation clause in articles
Here again s. 125(4) Companies Act 1985 applies. The rights can only be varied in accordance with the variation of rights clause in the articles except when:

(a) the variation proposed is concerned with the giving, variation, revocation or renewal of an authority to issue securities for the purpose of s. 80 Companies Act 1985 (see Chapter 7).
(b) the variation is concerned with a reduction of capital under s. 135 (see Chapter 10).

In those circumstances s. 125(3) applies and requires that, in addition to compliance with the variation of rights clause in the memorandum and any other conditions imposed by the company's constitution, two other conditions must be met:

(a) the holders of three-quarters in nominal value of the issued shares of that class consent in writing to the variation; or
(b) an extraordinary resolution passed at a separate general meeting of the holders of that class sanctions the variation.

14.6 Class Meetings

If a class meeting is held to comply with any of the arrangements explained above, s. 369 Companies Act 1985 governs the length of notice which must be given, s. 370 governs the conduct of meetings and votes, and ss. 376 and 377 cover circulation of members' resolutions. In addition to these provisions any provisions of the articles relating to general meetings must be observed (s. 125(6) Companies Act 1985) with the necessary modifications and subject to these provisions found in s. 125(6):

(a) the necessary quorum at any such meeting other than an adjourned meeting shall be two persons holding or representing by proxy at least one-third in nominal value of the issued shares of the class in question and at an adjourned meeting one person holding shares of the class in question or his proxy;

(b) any holder of shares of the class in question present in person or by proxy may demand a poll (see Chapter 10).

14.7 Alteration of Articles to Insert a Variation Clause

Section 125(7) provides: 'Any alteration of a provision contained in a company's articles for the variation of rights attached to a class of shares, or the insertion of any such provision into the articles, is itself to be treated as a variation of those rights.'

14.8 Statutory Right to Object

Section 127 Companies Act 1985 gives a right to apply to the court to have a variation cancelled. The right to apply is surprisingly limited. One inbuilt limitation is the very narrow definition of 'variation' which was discussed above (see p. 265). As well as that, the statute requires that the application must be made by the holders of not less than 15 per cent of the issued shares of the class of shares whose rights are being varied, provided that they did not consent to or vote for the alteration. An application must be made to the court within twenty-one days after the variation was apparently made and may be made by one of the shareholders who must be appointed in writing (s. 127(3) Companies Act 1985). If such an application is made the variation has no effect until it is confirmed by the court. On hearing the application the court has a discretion to disallow the variation if it is satisfied, having regard to all the circumstances of the case, that the variation would unfairly prejudice the shareholders of the class represented by the applicant.

The narrow ambit of this minority right may account for the fact that the courts have indicated that a minority shareholder affected by a variation would have a common law right to challenge a variation on the grounds that the resolution to achieve the variation was not passed in good faith (see *Carruth* v. *ICI* [1937] AC 707 at 756, 765). There would be no necessity for the holders of 15 per cent of the shares of the class to agree on such an action. The matter could also come before the court in an action under ss. 459–461 for unfairly prejudiced shareholders (see Chapter 13).

Summary

1 Shares confer on a shareowner a number of rights in a company. Shares are often divided into different classes, ordinary and preference shares being commonplace.
2 The rights attaching to shares are usually to be found in the articles of association. Any lacunae in the description of share rights are made good by various presumptions of law.
3 Shares may or may not have voting rights.
4 Changing class rights will be considered a 'variation' only if the description of the rights is changed.
5 Where there is a true variation the correct procedure must be followed or the variation will be open to challenge. The procedure is largely set out in s. 125 Companies Act 1985.

Exercises

1 What are the arguments for and against non-voting shares?
2 Are the courts too restrictive in their definition of variations?
3 What are the usual differences between ordinary and preference shares?

15 Lending Money and Securing Loans

A company can finance its activities by selling shares or by raising money from banks or other money-lending institutions. If the company is granted a loan, the lender may become a debenture-holder. A debenture has never been satisfactorily defined. In *Levy* v. *Abercorris Slate and Slab Co.* (1883) 37 Ch D 260, Chitty J said 'In my opinion a debenture means a document which either creates a debt or acknowledges it, and any document which fulfils either of these conditions is a 'debenture'.' Shareholders are members of the company and their rights have been described elsewhere in this book. Debenture-holders are creditors of the company and their rights are normally defined in the contract made between them and the company. It is interesting to note that, unlike shares, debentures can be issued at a discount unless they are convertible into shares, when such an issue at a discount would be an invitation to evade the rule that shares may not be issued at a discount (*Moseley* v. *Koffyfontein* [1904] 2 Ch 108). The lender may wish to secure his position by taking a charge over the property of the company, that is, creating a legal relationship between himself and the company which will ensure he is paid in priority at least to some of the other claimants against the company.

15.1 Debenture-Holder's Receiver

The power of a debenture-holder to appoint a receiver will be determined by the terms of the debenture itself. If the circumstances in which a receiver may be appointed arise, he will be appointed to collect the assets of the company with a view to the repayment of the debt due to the debenture-holder. He must, however, pay creditors whose claim should be paid before his, for example a preferential creditor under s. 196 Companies Act 1985 (*CIR* v. *Goldblatt* [1972] Ch 498).

15.2 Fixed and Floating Charges

It may be important for the purposes of determining the priority of charges to decide whether a particular charge is a 'fixed' or 'floating' charge. Essentially a fixed charge gives the holder the right to have a particular asset sold in order to repay the loan that he has given the company. This means that the company may not deal with the property subject to the fixed charge without the consent of the holder of the charge.

A floating charge gives the holder the right to be paid in priority to others after the sale of the assets subject to the charge, but in this case the assets over which the charge floats are not specified. The company may continue to deal with them without the permission of the holder of the charge and it is only on the happening of certain events (such as non-payment of an instalment of interest or repayment of capital) that the charge will become fixed. On the happening of the event in question (which will be specified in the contract for the loan) the charge is said to 'crystallise' and will become fixed on the particular assets that the company holds at that moment which answer to the general description of the property over which the charge originally 'floated' it then becomes indistinguishable in form from a floating charge. Thus, if the original charge 'floated' over all stock-in-trade and a crystallising event occurred, the goods subject to the crystallised charge would be the stock the company owned on that particular day.

The court in *Re Yorkshire Woolcombers Association* [1903] 2 Ch 284 (see Casenotes) grappled with the definition of floating charges. In the Court of Appeal, Romer J said:

'I certainly do not intend to attempt to give an exact definition of the term 'floating charge' nor am I prepared to say that there will not be a floating charge within the meaning of the Act, which does not contain all the three characteristics that I am about to mention, but I certainly think that if the charge has the three characteristics that I am about to mention it is a floating charge: (1) if it is a charge on a class of assets of a company present and future; (2) if that class is one which, in the ordinary course of the business of the company, would be changing from time to time; and (3) if you find that by the charge it is contemplated that, until some future step is taken by or on behalf of those interested in the charge, the company may carry on its business in the ordinary way as far as concerns the particular class of assets I am dealing with.'

Thus, the idea of a 'floating' charge is that the company is unhindered from dealing with its assets despite the fact that an outsider has a legal interest in those assets.

When the charge is created, the nature of the charge as a fixed or floating charge depends on its characteristics and not on whether the parties have described it as a fixed or floating charge. Thus in *Re Armagh Shoes Ltd* [1982] NI 59, the charge being considered by the court was described in the document that created it as a 'fixed' charge but was held by the court to have been a floating charge. The document included the following:

'the mortgagor pursuant to every power and by force of every estate enabling it in this behalf and as beneficial owner hereby charges in the favour of the bank by way of fixed charge all receivables debtors plant machinery fixtures fittings and ancillary equipment now or at any time hereafter belonging to the mortgagor.'

Hutton J said:

'the authorities establish that the description of a charge as a fixed or specific charge does not, in itself, operate to prevent the charge from being a floating charge; and the deed in this case contains no express provision restricting the company from dealing with the assets charged. In my judgment in the present case it is a necessary implication from the deed that the company was to have the right or licence to deal with the assets, comprised within the ambit of the charge, in the ordinary course of its business until the bank decided to enforce the charge. I can see no basis for the implication that it was the intention of the company and the bank that the company would deal with the charged assets in breach of its contract with the bank, to which breaches the bank would turn a blind eye, and that if a third party asked the company if it was entitled to transfer some of the charged assets to him the company would have to tell him to obtain the bank's consent to the transfer.'

In *Re Keenan Brothers Ltd* [1986] BCLC 242 the parties tried to create a fixed charge on money that was due to be paid to the company in the future, that is, 'book debts'. Two questions arose: (i) whether it was possible in law to create a fixed charge on future book debts – the court answered in the affirmative; and (ii) whether the charge that had in fact been created in this case was a fixed charge or a floating charge. On this point, McCarthy J, giving judgment in the Irish Supreme Court, emphasised the term in the agreement that read:

'The company shall pay into an account with the Bank designated for that purpose all moneys which it may receive in respect of the book debts and other debts hereby charged and shall not without the prior consent of the Bank in writing make any withdrawals or direct any payment from the said account.'

He said:

'In my view, it is because it was described as a specific or fixed charge and was intended to be such, that the requirement of a special bank account was necessary; if it were a floating charge payment into such an account would be entirely inappropriate and, indeed, would conflict with the ambulatory nature of the floating charge . . . In *Yorkshire Woolcombers Association Ltd* Romer LJ postulated three characteristics of a floating charge, the third being that, 'if you find that by the charge it is contemplated that, until some future step is taken by or on behalf of those interested in the charge, the company may carry on its business in the ordinary way as far as concerns the particular class of assets I am dealing with. Counsel for the banks has argued that this latter characteristic is essential to a floating charge and that the banking provision in the instruments here negatives such a characteristic; I would uphold this view.'

This case can be contrasted with *Re Brightlife Ltd* [1987] Ch 200, where Hoffman J held that the charge in question was a floating charge. It was a charge over (among other things) future book debts. Hoffman J held that the existence of a floating charge is not dependant on the company over whose property it floats having complete freedom of action. He said:

'It is true that clause 5(ii) does not allow Brightlife to sell, factor or discount debts without the written consent of Norandex [who had the benefit of the charge]. But a floating charge is consistent with some restriction on the company's freedom to deal with its assets. For example, floating charges commonly contain a prohibition on the creation of other charges ranking prior to or *pari passu* with the floating charge. Such dealings would otherwise be open to a company in the ordinary course of its business. In this debenture, the significant feature is that Brightlife was free to collect its debts and pay the proceeds into its bank account. Once in the account, they would be outside the charge over debts and at the free disposal of the company. In my judgment a right to deal in this way with the charged assets for its own account is a badge of a floating charge and is inconsistent with a fixed charge.'

See also *New Bullas Trading Ltd* [1993] BCC 251, in which the Court of Appeal found that the debenture in question in that case had created a fixed charge over book debts which would become a floating charge over the proceeds once they had been collected and paid into a specified account. The debenture holder had power to give directions as to the application of the money once it had been received but had not exclusive control over that money unless a direction had actually been given. There were thus circumstances in which the company could dispose of the money and the charge was a floating charge. Before the money was collected the company had an absolute obligation to pay any proceeds of book debts into a particular account. At this stage there was therefore a fixed charge over the book debts. In *William Gaskell Group* v. *Highley* [1994] 1 BCLC 197 the issue of whether the charge was fixed or floating turned on whether a clause requiring payment of the proceeds of debts into an account which could not be drawn on without the consent of the Midland Bank remained valid after the Midland assigned the debenture. The court held that it was still commercially viable to require the Midland's consent, the clause remained valid and the restriction meant that the charge was a fixed charge.

The court will look carefully at the substance of the charge and will not be bound by the wording adopted by the parties. In *Re G. E. Tunbridge Ltd* [1995] 1BCLC 409 a charge described as a fixed charge which purported to be over all the assets of the company except those covered by a floating charge was held not to create a fixed charge over intangible assets such as book debts or tangible assets which were likely to be changed or sold over time. This was despite the fact that the company was not permitted to dispose of the assets subject to the fixed charge without the consent of the chargee. However, in *Re Climex Tissues* [1995] 1 BCLC 409 a charge was held to be properly described as a fixed charge despite the fact that the company was apparently permitted to deal with the property subject to the charge 'in the ordinary course of business'. The court held that this wording must be taken to refer to the stock (toilet rolls) and not the capital machinery but also held that the existence of a limited power to deal with property was not necessarily inconsistent with a fixed charge. Each case therefore turns on its precise facts and the degree of liberty with which the company is able to deal with the property which is subject to the charge. See also *Re Cosslett (Contractors) Ltd, Clark* v. *Mid Glamorgan County Council* [1996] 1 BCLC 407, *Royal Trust Bank* v. *National Westminister Bank plc and another* [1996] 2 BCLC 682.

15.3 **The Characteristics of Fixed and Floating Charges**

The cases examined above show that the greater the interference with the freedom to use and dispose of the assets affected by the charge the more likely it is the courts will hold the charge to be a fixed charge, however the parties have described it. Because of the huge variety of clauses to be found in documents creating charges, it is impossible to arrive at an exhaustive definition of the difference between the two types of charges; the whole of the nature of the restrictions must be examined. The difference is important when the priority of various claimants has to be decided.

15.4 **Crystallisation of the Floating Charge**

A charge will certainly crystallise on the happening of the following:

- the appointment of an administrative receiver by the chargeholder,
- the appointment of an administrater,
- the commencement of liquidation,
- the cessation of business.

The document which creates the floating charge will provide for certain events which will cause the floating charge to become a fixed charge. Prior to the Companies Act 1989 there was much discussion as to whether this 'crystallisation' could be 'automatic', that is, could occur without any action on behalf of the debenture-holders or their agents, merely because an event specified in the debenture had occurred. There was some authority to the effect that this could occur (*obiter* in *Re Brightlife*, see above). In *Re Woodroffes (Musical Instruments) Limited* [1986] Ch 366, it was held that the crystallisation of a first floating charge did not occur automatically when a subsequent charge was crystalised. However, it was also held that a floating charge did automatically crystallise on the cessation of a company's business. Whether the cessation of business and the moment at which a business ceases to be a going concern are different was unclear to Nourse J. He said: 'My own impression is that these phrases are used interchangeably in the authorities '. . . but whether that be right or wrong, I think it clear that the material event is a cessation of business and not, if that is something different, ceasing to be a going concern'. The moment of crystallisation in that case was important, because if the floating charge had crystallised before the appointment of a receiver, the preferential creditors would have lost the priority that they enjoy under s. 175 over the holders of a 'floating charge' created by the company. The charge would be a fixed charge at the relevant date. This effect was confirmed in *Re ELS Ltd; Ramsbottom* v. *Luton Borough Council* [1994] BCC 449. the court held that on crystallisation the goods subject to the charge ceased to be goods of the company and became the goods of the chargee. Consequently it was not possible for bailiffs acting for the local authority to seize the goods because of rates owed by the company to the local council.

In the Companies Act 1985, s. 410 gives power to the Secretary of State to make regulations concerning the automatic crystallisation of floating charges. This appears to be statutory recognition of automatic crystallisation. However, until regulations are made there remains a degree of uncertainty in the law. See 15.12 below for a discussion of the effects of crystallisation.

15.5 **Legal and Equitable Charges**

The order in which competing claims against company property will be paid will depend on whether the creditor holds a legal or equitable charge. A legal charge will commonly only occur:

(i) when there is a charge by way of legal mortgage of land under the Law of Property Act 1925, s. 85(1) or 86(1), or
(ii) where the legal interest in the charged property is transferred to the chargee by way of security for an obligation, on condition that the interest will be transferred back to the surety if and when the secured obligation is met.

All other charges are equitable charges. In the absence of registration, equitable charges take priority in order of creation. However, a legal charge created after an equitable charge will take priority over it unless the chargee had notice of the prior charge. For the effects of registration, see p. 280.

15.6 **Floating Charges and Other Claims Against the Company**

Subsequent fixed charges

Section 464(4) provides that in Scotland a fixed charge has priority over a floating charge, although the document creating a floating charge may contain a restrictive clause which will prevent a subsequent charge ranking higher in priority if it is known to the subsequent chargee (s. 464(1)). For a comprehensive survey of these provisions see *AIB Finance Ltd* v. *Bank of Scotland* [1995] 1 BCLC 185. The same result is achieved in England by the case law (see *Wheatley* v. *Silkstone and Haigh Moor Coal Company* (1885) 29 ChD 715). In the absence of actual notice of a restriction on the creation of later charges (sometimes called a negative pledge clause) the fixed charge will take priority over a previous floating charge. This, of course, is subject to the effects of non-registration of registrable charges. The legislation appears to produce an odd result in that the registration rules affect priority as against those subsequently acquiring an interest in the same property. It would seem that a subsequent fixed charge will rank in priority over a registered floating charge, even if the fixed charge is not registered.

Subsequent floating charges

A company will not be able to create a second floating charge ranking equally or having priority over an existing floating charge, in the absence of words permitting this in the instrument creating the first floating charge (*Re Benjamin Cope & Sons* [1914] 1 Ch 800). However, a permission to create a subsequent charge ranking equally or in priority to an earlier one may be construed out of a clause reserving power to create charges over specific property. The theory seems to be that reserving a general power to charge property when a first charge is created will not permit the erosion of the value of the first charge by creation of a second charge. However, such erosion is permitted where the reservation of the right to charge is confined to specific property. In *Re Automatic Bottle Makers Ltd* [1926] Ch 412, Sargant LJ said:

> 'Great stress has, however, been laid for the respondents on a decision of my own as a judge of first instance in *Re Benjamin Cope & Sons* [1914] 1 Ch 800, and it has been argued that that case decides that a general floating charge is necessarily incompatible with the subsequent creation under a special charging power of a floating charge to rank in priority or *pari passu* with the earlier floating charge. I have examined that decision with great care, and have no reason to think that it was wrong, particularly in view of the fact that it appears to be in accord with an earlier decision of Vaughan-Williams J in *Smith* v. *England and*

Scottish Mercantile Investment Trust [1896] WN 86 and not to have been questioned since. But the facts in that case were very different. There the original charge was on the whole undertaking and property for the time being of the company, and the reservation of a power to mortgage was in quite general terms; and it was held that such a power could not have been intended to authorise a competing charge on the entirety of the property comprised in the earlier charge. Here the reservation of the power to mortgage is precise and specific in its terms, and extends only to certain particular classes of the property of the company.'

In certain circumstances charges can be overturned when a company is liquidated. For a discussion of this see Chapter 17.

Set offs

If an outsider has a right which is enforceable against the company at the time when a floating charge crystallises, he can resist any claim which the receiver has against him to the extent of his right against the company, that is, he can set-off his right against the amount being claimed by the receiver (*Robbie* v. *Whitney Warehouses* [1963] 3 All ER 613).

Judgment creditors

Once a receiver has been appointed by debenture-holders, the claim of the debenture holders will take priority to the claim of the creditor despite the fact that he has obtained judgment in his favour (*Cairney* v. *Black* [1906] 2 KB 746).

15.7 Retention of Title Clauses

These clauses are sometimes known as *Romalpa* clauses after the case of *Aluminium Industrie Vaassen BV* v. *Romalpa Aluminium Ltd* [1976] 1 WLR 676, which established their validity. A clause is inserted in a sale of goods contract which provides that the goods purchased shall remain the property of the seller until the purchase price is paid. If a receiver is appointed under the terms of a floating charge before the purchase price is paid, an unpaid purchaser would be able to recover 'his' goods from the company, the receiver may not treat them as the property of the company. The unpaid seller's rights continue only until the goods are identifiable and in the possession of the buyer. Thus in the case of *Borden (UK) Ltd* v. *Scottish Timber Products* [1979] 3 WLR 672, the material sold under the contract was resin. This was processed with other materials into chipboard. The unpaid seller had no rights over the chipboard. A simple retention of title clause does not at present require registration (See also *Clough Mill Ltd* v. *Geoffrey Martin* [1985] 1 WLR 111; *Specialist Plant Services Ltd* v. *Braithwaite Ltd* [1987] BCLC 1).

However where more complicated clauses have been used a registerable charge may be created. See *Re Bond Worth* [1980] Ch 228, *Re Curtain Dream plc* [1990] BCLC 925.

15.8 Registration of Company Charges

The law in this area is in a state of flux. The 1989 Companies Act contains new rules but it is possible that these changes to the law on the registration of company charges either will not come into force or will themselves be temporary. Many hope that the Diamond Report's recommendations (Prof. Diamond *A Review of Security Interests in Property* (HMSO, 1989)) will receive full implementation in the not-too-distant future. The Diamond Report's radical proposals for a review of the whole of the law relating to security over property other than land are still under consideration. If implemented there would be a single register of security interests created by companies, partnerships and sole traders in the course of business. Determination of priority would be by date of filing. The register would cover retention of title clauses, hire purchase and chattel leases for more than three years. It would replace the present scheme and create a single register for these charges. This chapter examines the law as it will be when the 1989 Act is fully in force with references back to the law before that implementation. At the time of writing consultations on the content of regulations to be made under this part of the Act were proceeding. The sections will be referred to by the number that they will bear when the 1989 Act is fully in force. For the first time the provisions provide a single system for England, Wales and Scotland.

15.9 Basic Definitions

New s. 395(2) provides that a 'charge' means any form of security interest (fixed or floating) over property, other than an interest arising by operation of law. As before, charges such as repairer's liens or unpaid vendor's liens are outside the registration scheme.

Section 419(1) provides that 'chargee' means the person for the time being entitled to exercise the security rights conferred by the charge.

By s. 396(1) a charge only requires registration if it falls within the list of registrable charges set out in the Act. This is the same approach as was previously adopted, but there are some changes to the list of registrable charges. Before that list is examined it is worth noting that s. 420 sets out a useful index of the defined expressions in this part of the Act.

15.10 **Which Charges are Registrable?**

1 s.396(1)(a) Land

'a charge on land or any interest in land other than (i) in England and Wales, a charge for rent or any other periodical sum issuing out of the land; or
(ii) Scots equivalent.'

It is notable that s. 396(2)(a) provides that a charge on a debenture is not caught by s. 396(1)(a) by reason of the fact that the debenture is secured by a charge on land or goods (or an interest in land or goods). This reverses the previous rule in *Re Molton Finance* [1968] Ch 325 as to submortgages of debentures secured on land or goods or interests therein.

2 s. 396(2)(b) Goods

'a charge on goods or any interest in goods, other than a charge under which the chargee is entitled to possession either of the goods or of a document of title to them.'

This provision extends the category to a wider class of goods than before. The charge does not have to be evidenced in writing. The exclusion of a charge giving the chargee possessory rights has the effect of excluding pledges and liens from registration.

Matters not included in the registration system include retention of title clauses, hire purchase contracts and other forms of conditional sale agreement. The implementation of the Diamond report in full would cause all these categories to become registrable.

s.396(2)(b) 'Goods' means any tangible moveable property other than money.

Section 396(2)(c) includes charges on goods where chargee is entitled to take possession in case of default or on the occurrence of some other event.

3 s.396(1)(c) Intangible moveable property

This is, a charge on

  (i) goodwill
  (ii) intellectual property, i.e.,
           by s. 396(2)(d);
      (i) patents, trade marks, service marks, registered designs, copyright or design right or
      (ii) any licence under or in respect of such right.
  (iii) Book debts (of the company or assigned to it)
           excluding
      (i) s. 396(2)(f) the deposit by way of security of a negotiable instrument given to secure payment of a book debt.

(ii) s. 396(2)(g) a shipowner's lien on subfreights. This reverses
the rule in *Re Welsh and Irish Ferries* [1986] Ch 471.
(iii) s. 396(2)(e) a debenture which is part of an issue or a series.
(iv) Uncalled Share capital of the company or calls made but not
paid.

4 s.396(i)(d) Securing an issue of debentures

By s. 419(1) 'issue of debentures' means a group of debentures each
containing or giving by reference to another instrument a charge to the
benefit of which the holders of debentures of the series are entitled *pari
passu.*

5 s.396(1)(e) A floating charge on the whole or part of the company's
property.

By ss. 396(2)(g) excluding a shipowner's lien on subfreights.

15.11 **Salient Points**

Of these complicated provisions the most notable factors are:

(i) The category of charges on goods or interest in goods is wider than it
used to be but not as wide as to include pledges, liens, retention of title
clauses, hire purchase contracts or conditional sale agreements, although
the last three may well be included in the registration system if the
Diamond Report is implemented in full.
(ii) There is as yet no definition of book debt, but one will be made by
regulations pursuant to s. 396(4).
(iii) The *Re Brightlife* [1987] Ch 200 controversy will not be solved until
the definition of book debts is arrived at. In that case, Hoffman J decided
that a bank account fell outside the definition of book debts so that a
charge over a bank account did not require registration. The Registrar
has, however, accepted such charges for registration. Because of the
changed role of the Registrar it will still be possible in the future to register
such charges. However, whether the registration of them should become
obligatory will depend on the definition of book debts adopted by the
government. The Diamond report contains the view that it is unnecessary
to include such charges, at least until the implementation of Part II of his
recommendations. Because bank accounts are usually secret, other
creditors will not be misled by the existence of an undisclosed charge
over one. This controversy does not affect the situation where the charge
over the bank account is registrable in its own right, for example as a
floating charge.
(iv) The rule in *Re Welsh and Irish Ferries* [1986] Ch 471 has been
reversed. Because the existence of liens on subfreights is well known it was
not thought necessary, and was very inconvenient to register them.
(v) Section 396(2)(f) exempts from registration the common practice
whereby a company sells goods on credit to *x*, thus creating a book debt of

the company. To pay the debt, x gives the company a post-dated cheque, which the company deposits with a bank in return for an advance.

(vi) The act contains nothing to reverse *Paul & Frank Ltd* v. *Discount Bank (Overseas) Ltd* [1967] Ch 348, in which it was held that a charge on an insurance policy before a claim arose was not a book debt. The Diamond report recommended registration of such charges (para 23.5) but this might be done when book debts are defined.

(vii) Charges over shares are, as before, not registrable *per se.*

15.12 **Notice of Crystallisation of Floating Charges**

New s. 410 gives power to the Secretary of State to make regulations requiring the registration of the occurrence of crystallising events, or action taken to crystallise a charge. Regulations may also be made to provide for the consequences of failure to give such notice which may include treating the crystallisation as ineffective. If such regulations are made this will amount to statutory recognition of automatic crystallisation of floating charges. The worst problem caused by this concept was the possible evasion of statutory rules by automatic crystallisation. This danger has been partly removed by s. 251 Insolvency Act 1986 which defines a floating charge as a charge which, as created, was a floating charge. However, other creditors of the company might be unaware of a crystallising event. This problem would be solved by such regulations as envisaged here. The DTI have suggested (in Consultation Document, July 1988) that registration should be within seven days of the crystallisation, crystallisation then to be valid from the date when the crystallising event occurred. If notification was not given within seven days the crystallisation would be invalid until it was notified when it would be valid against all save for those acquiring an interest in or security over the relevant property between the crystallising event and notification, including a liquidator or administrator.

15.13 **Delivery of Particulars and Priorities**

Prescribed particulars must be delivered to the Registrar within twenty-one days of the creation of the charge (s. 398(1)). This is unchanged. However, the charge itself need not be produced (unlike the old law) so that the rule that in the case of property situated abroad, the twenty-one days ran from the date when the relevant documents could have arrived in the UK has gone. Section 414(4) provides for the twenty-one-day rule to apply to property situated abroad.

The date of creation of a charge is the date of execution of the instrument creating the charge or of fulfilment of conditions if executed conditionally or the date of an enforceable agreement conferring a security interest forthwith or on the acquisition by the company of property subject to the charge.

15.14 **Priorities Under the Registration System**

No change has been made to the fundamental rule regarding priority, which still give priority in accordance with the date of creation. This is despite the inadequate protection which is given by a system which bases priority on the date of creation of a charge and then permits registration within twenty-one days. The Diamond report recommendations for a system of registration based on date of registration, coupled with a provisional registration system or for a certificate of guarantee from the Registrar were both rejected.

15.15 **The Register and Certification**

Section 397 deals with the register and the certificate of filing. The certificate is conclusive evidence that specified particulars or other information were delivered to the Registrar no later than the stated date. By s. 397(5) it is presumed that they were not delivered earlier unless the contrary is proved.

The prescribed particulars which must be delivered to the Registrar in order to register a charge will be laid down by regulations s. 415(1). The regulations will almost certainly require inclusion of a negative pledge, that is, whether a company has undertaken not to create other charges ranking equally or ahead of it.

15.16 **Effect of Registration**

Section 398(4) provides that the Registrar will merely file the statement of particulars delivered by the parties. The charge will not be produced so there is no question of checking the particulars. Registration of a charge will continue to be sufficient to give notice of the charge to anyone subsequently taking a charge over the company. Although the doctrine of constructive (deemed) notice has been generally abolished by s. 711A(1), s. 711A(4) provides that it is subject to s. 416. Section 416(1) provides:

'A person taking a charge over a company's property shall be taken to have notice of any matter requiring registration and disclosed on the register at the time the charge is created.'

Section 416(2) provides thus:

'Otherwise, a person shall not be taken to have notice of any other matter by reason of its being disclosed on the register or by reason of his having failed to search the register in the course of making such inquiries as ought reasonably to have been made. This is clear so far as additional information which is not discovered by the person taking the charge. It is also clear that where such a person has in fact discovered the additional information he is not deemed to know it merely because it is on the register. The section does not seem to preclude proof of actual knowledge of such information.'

15.17 Duty to Register and Effect of Non-registration

Section 398 provides that it is the duty of a company which creates a charge, or acquires property subject to a charge, to deliver particulars of the charge to the Registrar within twenty-one days of the creation of the charge. Anyone interested in the charge may deliver the particulars but if no one does so the company and any officer of the company in default commits an offence and will be liable to a fine.

The most important consequence of failure to deliver, however, is that by s. 399(1) it becomes void on the happening of a 'relevant' event against (a) an administrator or liquidator of the company, and (b) any person who for value acquires an interest or right over property subject to the charge. This happens even where the relevant event occurs within the twenty-one-day period so long as the relevant event occurs after the creation of the charge and no particulars are delivered within the twenty-one-day period.

The relevant events are set out in s. 399(2):

'In the Part "the relevant event" means –
- (a) in relation to the voidness of a charge as against an administrator or liquidator, the beginning of the insolvency proceedings, and
- (b) in relation to the voidness of a charge as against a person acquiring an interest in or right over property subject to a charge, the acquisition of that interest or right.'

By s. 399(3) where a relevant event occurs on the same day as the charge is created there is a presumption that it occurred after the creation of the charge.

Section 419(5) provides that the beginning of insolvency proceedings means the presentation of a petition on which an administration order or winding up order is made or the passing of a resolution for voluntary winding up.

This means that, as under the old law, a subsequent chargee can ignore an unregistered charge even if he has actual notice of it, unless such subsequent chargee has expressly agreed to be subject to the unregistered charge. These provisions change the situation of a purchaser from the company of the property subject to the charge. Such a purchaser will now take the property free of the charge even if he knew of the charge provided he has not agreed to take the property subject to the charge.

15.18 Payment of Money Secured by Unregistered Charge

Section 407(1) provides that money secured by an unregistered demand becomes repayable on demand when the charge becomes void to any extent. This would occur on the happening of a 'relevant event'. Under the old law such money became automatically repayable at the end of the twenty-one-day period.

15.19 Late Delivery of Particulars

Section 400 disapplies s. 399(1) so that if particulars are delivered late the charge will be perfected and the subsequent happening of a 'relevant event' will not have the consequences provided for in s. 399. The system of late registration will not require a court order and will be available regardless of the reasons for failure to deliver within the twenty-one days. This does not affect rights acquired by the happening of a 'relevant event' before the late registration.

In any event the late delivery of particulars does not perfect the charge completely. Section 400(2) provides that the late registered charge will become void against a liquidator or administrator if insolvency proceedings begin within a certain period of time after the delivery of particulars and at the time the particulars were delivered the company was unable to pay its debts or becomes unable to pay its debts as a result of the transaction in question. The periods are: two years in the case of a floating charge created in favour of a connected person; one year in the case of any other floating charge; and six months in any other case.

15.20 Varying or Supplementing Registered Particulars

Section 401 permits the delivery to the Registrar of 'further particulars of a charge' at any time. These will then be filed by the Registrar and copies sent to the company, the chargee and, if the particulars were filed by a third interested party, to that party. This procedure is available for the rectification of errors or omissions or for extending the scope of an existing charge. In the latter case it might be better to create a new charge as, if the particulars are then delivered within twenty-one days the charge will be valid and have priority from the date of its creation. Correction will run from the date the further particulars are received by the Registrar. The procedure is a considerable advance on the old law which required a court order for rectification.

15.21 Effect of Errors and Omissions

Where the particulars of a charge that has been registered are not complete or are inaccurate, the charge will be void to the extent that 'rights are not disclosed by the registered particulars which would be disclosed if they were complete and accurate' (s. 402). The charge is void to that extent where a 'relevant event' occurs at a time when the particulars are incomplete or inaccurate as against an administrator or liquidator of the company or any person who has for value acquired an interest in or right over property subject to the charge.

The court may order that the charge is effective against an administrator or liquidator if it is satisfied:

'(a) that the omission or error is not likely to have misled materially to his prejudice any unsecured creditor of the company, or
(b) that no person became an unsecured creditor of the company at a time when the registered particulars were incomplete or inaccurate in a relevant respect' (s. 402(4)).

So far as a person acquiring a right or interest in the property subject to the charge, the court may order that the charge is effective as against them 'if it is satisfied that he did not rely, in connection with the acquisition, on registered particulars which were incomplete or inaccurate in a relevant respect' (s. 402(5)).

Inaccuracy as to the name of the chargee is not equivalent to a failure to disclose the rights of the chargee (s. 402(6)).

15.22 **Registration of Discharge**

Section 403 provides that a memorandum to the effect that a registered charge has ceased to affect the company's property may be delivered to the Registrar. This does not effect a change in the law. The memorandum must be signed by both company and chargee. The Registrar will send a copy of the memorandum and a note as to the date of delivery to the company, the chargee and, if the memorandum was filed by another interested party, to that person (s. 403(3)). If the memorandum is not correct and the charge continues to affect the company's property, the charge becomes void to the extent that it would be void were it unregistered, that is, void against the administrator, liquidator or person taking interest in property subject to the charge for value after a 'relevant event' occurs at a later date than delivery of the memorandum.

15.23 **Oversea Companies**

New ss. 703A–703N are inserted into the CA 1985 by Schedule 15 of the Companies Act 1989. The most important change is that the obligation on oversea companies to register charges applies only if they have registered a place of business in Great Britain under the CA 1985 s. 691. This reverses the effect of *Slavenburg's Bank NV* v. *Intercontinental Natural Resources Ltd* [1980] 1 All ER 955.

A company which registers under s. 691, and has at that time property in Great Britain subject to a registrable charge, must deliver particulars relating to the charge at that time (s. 703D(1)). A company which is already registered under s. 691 and which creates a registrable charge on property in Great Britain or acquires such property subject to an existing registrable charge, must deliver particulars relating to the charge within twenty-one days of the acquisition or creation of the charge unless the property is no longer in Great Britain at the end of twenty-one days (s. 703D(2)).

If a company registered under s. 691 brings property subject to a registrable charge to Great Britain and keeps it here continuously for four months, particulars relating to the charge must be delivered before the end of the four-month period (s. 703D(3)).

A ship, aircraft or hovercraft is treated as being in Great Britain if it is registered here; other vehicles are treated as in Great Britain if they are managed from a place of business in Great Britain (s. 703L(1)).

15.24 **The European Company Statute**

The Commission of the EU have proposed that there should be a new form of company available to the business community. It would be governed partly by a Regulation which would operate at a European level and thus be common to all Member States. Where the Regulation did not provide answers, the relevant law would be supplied by the Member State where the company was registered, which must be where it also has its head office. The company must be formed by participants from at least two Member States and it is envisaged that it will carry on cross-border operations by setting up branches in various Member States. The Regulation makes no provision for a central registry so that, at present, the law of the State of registration would govern the registration of charges over such a company's property. There would seem to be no obstacle to thus extending the UK system, but it may well be a matter for debate whether other Member States will have systems which can readily be adapted to enable sufficient information to be available to lenders and whether there needs to be a central European Registry to deal with this problem if the European Company becomes a reality.

15.25 **Effect of Registrar's Certificate**

The certificate will no longer be conclusive evidence that the requirements as to registration have been satisfied. By s. 397(3) the certificate issued by the Registrar will be conclusive evidence that the particulars were not delivered later than the date stated, and there is a rebuttable presumption that the particulars were not delivered earlier.

Summary

1 Money lent to a company will normally be secured by a fixed charge over definite property or by a floating charge which will enable the company to deal with the assets involved until crystallisation of the floating charge turns it into a fixed charge.

2 Crystallisation of a floating charge will normally occur when the lender (debenture-holder intervenes to assert his rights, often at the appointment of a receiver.)

3 It is still unclear whether a floating charge can 'automatically' crystallise on the happening of an event specified in the debenture or whether intervention by the debenture holder is required. The 1989 Act contains the power to make regulations on the subject.

4 Charges must be registered if they are to be valid against others taking security from a company. They must be registered within twenty-one days of creation but priority is in order of creation rather than order of registration.

5 The registration provisions cover the situations where there is late delivery of particulars of a charge or errors or omissions in particulars.

Casenotes

Re Yorkshire Woolcombers' Association Ltd [1903] 2 Ch 284
By a trust deed of 23 April 1900, the Yorkshire Woolcombers Association Ltd specifically mortgaged all its freehold and leasehold properties to trustees to secure its debenture stock, and, as beneficial owner, charged in favour of the trustees 'by way of floating security all its other property and assets both present and future, and its undertaking, but not including capital for the time being uncalled'. The deed contained a power enabling the association to deal with the property and assets which were subject to the charge. The question before the court was whether the charge was a fixed or floating charge, since it had not been registered and, if it was a floating charge, it would be void as against the receiver. Farwell J said at first instance:

'The very essence of a specific charge is that the assignee takes possession, and is the person entitled to receive the book debts at once. So long as he licenses the mortgagor to go on receiving the book debts and carry on the business, it is within the exact definition of a floating security.'

The Court of Appeal upheld this judgment; part of the speech of Romer J is reproduced in the text.

Exercises

1 Would a system of priority of charges depending on order of registration be better?

2 If a floating charge is created does (i) a subsequent fixed charge; (ii) a subsequent floating charge expressed to rank equally have priority over it?

16 Takeovers, Reconstructions, Amalgamations

A great number of company reconstructions occur as a result of the take-over of one company by another. This will often be achieved by the company which is effecting the takeover offering to buy the shares held by the shareholders in the target company. Such reconstructions are governed by a mixture of rules, some found in the statutes and others to be found in the City Code on Takeovers and Mergers. The Stock Exchange's rules (Admission of Securities to Listing), known as the 'Yellow Book' also require disclosure of a number of matters when a take-over is attempted and a company listed on the Exchange is involved. Such a company must disclose detailed information concerning the company making the offer and the precise terms of the offer in the document which sets out the takeover proposal. This document is known as the 'offer document'.

16.1 **Public Offers**

If the offeror company proposes an exchange of its shares for the target company's shares, that is, the price for the shares of the target company is shares in the offeror company, this will be a public issue of shares and will be governed by the rules given in Chapter 7.

16.2 **Monopolies**

Some takeover bids may be regarded as bad for the general public because the end result would be a company which had such a large share of the market as to be able to dominate that market and set the terms on which the items it dealt with changed hands. If a company was alone in a particular market it would have a monopoly of that market. In fact, the authorities normally intervene some time before a monopoly situation is reached. A number of the rules in this area have been made under the Fair Trading Act 1973 and Article 86 of the EEC Treaty. If the matter is one affecting the UK market, the Secretary of State has the power to refer certain takeovers to the Monopolies Commission which will consider the possible effect of the takeovers on the relevant market. If a takeover has implications for the EC market, the EC Commission will assess its probable effect.

16.3 **The Takeover Panel**

The Panel which supervises takeovers of public and other large companies is not a body created by statutory authority and the Code it issues and the decisions made by the Panel do not have the force of law. This situation may be threatened by the EC Takeover Directive (see Chapter 18). Proponents of the Panel argue that the present system enables the Panel to respond flexibly and quickly to situations as they arise. However, adherence to the Code and the rulings of the Panel is voluntary, although it is universally accepted that the Panel is widely effective. Because of the wide acceptance of the Panel's decisions, the court has recently held that the court should have the power to review such decisions. In *R* v. *Panel on Takeovers Ex Parte Datafin* [1987] 2 WLR 699, the Court of Appeal held that the decisions of the Panel should be reviewable by the court, although a review was refused in that particular case. The court was reluctant to hinder the work of the Panel and so held that resort to the court should not be made during the course of the events on which the Panel was ruling. The court should allow the Panel to make decisions and allow events to take their course, intervening, if at all, later, in retrospect, by declaratory orders. In *R* v. *Panel on Takeovers and Mergers Ex Parte Guinness PLC* [1989] BCLC 255 the Court of Appeal confirmed that the Panel's decisions would only be subject to judicial review where something had gone wrong with its procedure so as to cause real injustice and require the intervention of the court.

16.4 **General Principles and Rules**

The Code sets out general principles 'of conduct to be observed in take-over and merger transactions'. There are also more detailed rules and notes which provide guidance as to the way in which the rules should operate. The Code requires that the spirit of the general principles and rules as well as the precise wording should be observed. The Code seeks to ensure fair treatment of all shareholders, including equal treatment of different classes of shares, as well as equal treatment of members of each class. To this end there is a requirement of disclosure of the financial soundness of the offeror company; a duty on directors of both companies to consider their shareholders' interests and not to have regard to their personal interests; a requirement that information given to shareholders is sufficient to enable a properly informed decision to be made; and a requirement that any information supplied must be available to all shareholders. There are also rules preventing the use of tactics by an offeree board which would tend to frustrate a takeover bid.

16.5 **Partial Offers**

One of the key rules of the Code requires that where 30 per cent or more of the shares in a company have been acquired by some one concern or by a number of concerns or persons 'acting in concert', then, except in exceptional circumstances and with the permission of the Panel, an equivalent offer must be made for the remainder of the shares. This seeks to prevent the situation where there is acquisition of sufficient shares to ensure control of the company, followed by a much lower offer to remaining shareholders. This rule is backed up by the Rules in Part VI Companies Act 1985 which require the disclosure of interests in shares in certain circumstances. These rules have required minor modification as a result of the EC Directive on the Disclosure of Interests in Shares (see Chapter 18 and Disclosure of Interests in shares (Amendment) Regulations SI 1993/1819 and SI 1993/2689.

16.6 Compulsory Purchase Provisions

If the takeover bid has as its object the acquisition of all the shares in a company, a small dissentient minority could prevent this by refusing to sell their shares. The Companies Act 1985 as amended by the Financial Services Act 1986 therefore provides (ss. 428–430F Companies Act 1985 as amended by Schedule 12 Financial Services Act 1985) that if the offeror has acquired or contracted to acquire not less than nine-tenths in value of the shares to which the takeover offer relates, he may give notice to the holder of any other such shares that he desires to acquire those shares (s. 429(1)). The notice can only be given if the offeror acquires the necessary nine-tenths in value of the shares within four months from the date of the offer and must be given within two months of his acquiring that proportion of the shares (s. 429(3)). If a notice is served under these provisions the offeror can and must purchase the shares unless an application is made to the court by a shareholder under s. 430C for an order that the offeror may not exercise his power of compulsory acquisition. In fact, the court is unlikely to look upon such an application with favour. In *Re Grierson, Oldham and Adams Ltd* [1968] Ch 17, Plowman J said:

'The first, general observation is that the onus of proof here is fairly and squarely on the applicants, and indeed they accept that that is so. The onus of proof is on them to establish, if they can, that the offer was unfair . . . I notice . . . that at first instance in *Re Bugle Press Ltd* [1961] Ch 270, Buckley J, whose decision was upheld by the Court of Appeal, said:

'In the ordinary case of an offer under this section, where the 90% majority who accept the offer are unconnected with the persons who are concerned with making the offer, the court pays the greatest attention to the views of that majority. In all commercial matters, where commercial people are much better able to judge of their own affairs than the court is able to do, the court is accustomed to pay the greatest attention to what commercial people who are concerned with the transaction in fact decide.'

This view was confirmed in *Re Lifecare International PLC* [1990] BCLC 222.

This scheme for compulsory purchase may not be used in a situation which is not a true take-over situation and which therefore ought to proceed under one of the other schemes discussed below (*Re Bugle Press*, see Casenotes).

16.7 **Reconstructions**

Ss.425–7 Companies Act 1985 sets out a procedure which envisages major reconstruction of a company. One of the situations in which these sections may be used is where a merger of two companies is proposed. Such a reconstruction will affect the rights of members and creditors. Care must be taken to ensure that all interests are taken into account. The schemes of compromise or arrangement set out in these sections provide a somewhat cumbersome procedure involving two applications to the court, one to enable meetings to take place so that interested parties can vote on the scheme, the second to obtain approval of the court for the scheme if the reaction of the meetings has been favourable.

A s. 425 scheme needs the consent of three-quarters 'in value of the creditors or class of creditors or members . . . present and voting either in person or by proxy at the meeting' before the court can approve the scheme and make it binding on all members and creditors.

Application is made to the court by the company, its liquidator, a creditor or member. The court then directs meetings to be held of all the classes concerned. If there are conflicting interests within a class, meetings of 'sub-classes' must be held. In *Re Hellenic and General Trust Ltd* [1976] 1 WLR 123 the shares which belonged to the wholly-owned subsidiary of the offeror company were held to belong to a different class from those which belonged to independent shareholders. It was held that where different shareholders have different interests they must be regarded as belonging to a separate class.

16.8 **Meetings**

Following the application to the court, the court may order meetings to be held. The court has a discretion whether or not to order meetings and will not do so if the scheme is not feasible (see *Re Savoy Hotel Ltd* [1981] Ch 351).

If the court orders meetings, notices summoning the meetings will be sent out to shareholders and creditors. The notices must explain the scheme and the material interests of the directors of the company (s. 426). At the meeting of each class a majority in number representing three-quarters in value of those present and voting in person or by proxy must approve the scheme if it is to go further. If the necessary approval is achieved, the approval of the court may be sought.

16.9 **Approval of the Court**

The court will normally accept the verdict of the substantial majority required at the meetings and approve the scheme. However, the principle that at the meetings the votes must be cast 'with a view to the class as a whole' has evolved to prevent the scheme being approved because of the vote of someone who had a special interest to protect or further. If such a person is not neutralised by the requirement that persons with different interests should have different class meetings, the scheme may fail at the approval stage because the vote was carried by a voter seeking to further his own interests at the expense of the class as a whole. Thus in *Re English, Scottish and Australian Chartered Bank* [1893] 3 Ch 385, Lindle LJ said:

> 'If the creditors are acting on sufficient information and with time to consider what they are about and are acting honestly, they are, I apprehend, much better judges of what is to their commercial advantage than the Court can be. I do not say it is conclusive because there might be some blot on a scheme which had passed that had been unobserved and which was pointed out later. If, however, there should be no such blot, then the court ought to be slow to differ from [the creditors].'

However, in *Carruth v. Imperial Chemical Industries Ltd* [1937] AC 707, Lord Maugham said: 'The Court will, in considering whether a scheme ought to be approved, disregard a majority vote in favour of it if it appears that the majority did not consider the matter with a view to the interests of the class to which they belong only.'

The situation appears to be that the court has an unfettered discretion to upset a vote if it is unhappy about whether the outcome is fair to the minority.

16.10 **Reconstruction in a Liquidation**

Under ss. 110–111 Insolvency Act 1986 a company which is in a member's voluntary liquidation (see Chapter 17) may empower its liquidator by special resolution to transfer a whole or part of its business or property to another company in return for shares in that company. The shares must be distributed amongst the shareholders of the original company in strict accordance with their rights to share in the assets in a winding up. Such a scheme does not require the approval of the court. However, if shareholders with one-quarter of the voting power do not agree with the scheme, they may express their dissent to the liquidator and require him either to abstain from carrying out the scheme or to purchase their shares at a price agreed or fixed by arbitration. This right cannot be excluded by the memorandum of association (see *Bisgood v. Henderson's Transvaal Estates* [1908] 1 Ch 743). The relationship between the s. 425 procedure and the Insolvency Act procedure was explained in *Re Anglo Continental Supply Co.* [1922] 2 Ch 723, where Astbury J said [current section numbers inserted]:

'(1) When a so-called scheme is really and truly a sale etc under s. 110 *simpliciter* that section must be complied with and cannot be evaded by calling it a scheme of arrangement under s. 425.

(2) Where a scheme cannot be carried through under s. 110 though it involves (*inter alia*) a sale to a company under that section . . . the Court can sanction it under s. 425 if it is fair and reasonable . . . and it may, but only if it thinks fit, insist as a term of its sanction, on the dissentient shareholders being protected in a manner similar to that provided for in s. 110.

(3) Where a scheme of arrangement is one outside s. 110 entirely the Court can also and *a fortiori* act as in proposition 2, subject to the conditions therein mentioned.'

Summary

1 Takeovers by the purchase of shares are regulated by a voluntary code: the City Code on Takeovers and Mergers, administered by the Panel on takeovers and mergers.

2 Submission to the rulings of the Panel is voluntary but it is generally an effective system.

3 The Panel seeks to protect shareholders, in particular by requiring equal treatment of the shareholders in a target company.

4 If 90 per cent of the shares in a company have been acquired, the remainder of the shares may be purchased compulsorily (s. 459).

5 The minority whose shares may be purchased in this way may object to the scheme but will generally receive an unsympathetic hearing.

6 S.425 Companies Act 1985 provides a cumbersome scheme for the reconstruction of a company, requiring two applications to the court and the holding of separate meetings of shareholders. There is some doubt as to whether, at meetings, those entitled to vote have a duty to vote otherwise than in their own selfish interests.

7 Sections 110-111 Insolvency Act 1986 provide a method of reconstruction of a company through liquidation.

Casenotes

Re Bugle Press Ltd [1961] Ch 270
Two majority shareholders in a company formed a new company and put forward an arrangement simply for the purpose of getting a 90 per cent majority and getting rid of a dissentient minority by way of compulsory purchase under what is now s. 459. The court would not permit this.

Exercises

1 To what extent should takeovers be subject to statutory control?
2 What are the advantages and disadvantages of the methods of reconstructing a company?
3 Do shareholders have a duty to others when exercising a vote in a shareholders' meeting?

17 Insolvency and Corporate Reconstruction

The Insolvency Act 1986 revised and updated the law in this area, introducing two new procedures with a view to encouraging corporate rescues. These new procedures are the Administration and Voluntary Arrangement processes.

17.1 Administration

The idea behind the introduction of this procedure is to encourage the identification of financial problems at an early stage so that a company which has a sound financial base but has encountered cash-flow difficulties can avoid liquidation. The commencement of the administration procedure imposes a freeze on proceedings against the company and therefore provides a period of calm within which arrangements can be made with the company's creditors for rescheduling of debts or restructuring of ownership and control of the company. The administrator is an insolvency practitioner who will have overall control of the process and who has wide powers to assist him to achieve his aims.

17.2 Limitation on Jurisdiction

A major limitation of the administration process is that the holder of a valid floating charge can veto the making of the order.

17.3 When an Order Can Be Made

S.8(1) Insolvency Act 1986 provides that the court may make an administration order if:

(1) It is satisfied that the company is, or is likely to become, unable to pay its debts within the meaning of s. 123 Insolvency Act 1986 (see p. 298)
(2) It considers that the making of an administration order would be likely to achieve:

   (a) the survival of the company and the whole or any part of its undertaking as a going concern;

(b) the approval of a voluntary arrangement under Part I of the Act (see p. 302).
(c) the sanctioning under s. 425 CA 1985 of a compromise or arrangement between the company and any of its creditors or members (see Chapter 16).
(d) a more advantageous realisation of the company's assets than would be effected on a winding up.

Section 123 deems a company to be unable to pay its debts:

(a) if a creditor who is owed a sum exceeding £750 which is due to be paid to him has served a written demand on the company requiring it to pay the amount due and the company has failed to pay such a sum for a period of three weeks or to come to some other arrangement to the reasonable satisfaction of the creditor; or
(b) if execution or other process issued on a judgment or other court order in favour of the creditor of the company is returned unsatisfied in whole or in part; or
(c) if it is proved to the satisfaction of the court that the company is unable to pay its debts as they become due; or
(d) it is proved to the satisfaction of the court that the value of the company's assets is less than the amount of its liabilities taking into account its contingent and prospective liabilities.

17.4 The Application

An application may be made by:

(i) the company
(ii) the directors
(iii) a creditor

The application is made by a petition supported by an affidavit stating that the preconditions for the making of an order are satisfied and giving details of the financial position of the company (s. 9(1) Insolvency Act 1986 and Rule 2.1(2) and (3) of the Insolvency Rules 1986).

17.5 Service of Petition

Once issued, the petition must be served on:

(1) any person who has appointed an administrative receiver or has power to do so (usually the holder of a valid floating charge);
(2) an administrative receiver, if appointed;
(3) a petitioner who has presented a winding-up petition (if any) and a provisional liquidator, if any;

(4) the proposed administrator; and
(5) where the petition is presented by the company's creditors, the company (s. 9(2) Insolvency Act 1986 and Rule 2.4 (2)).

The Rules provide for the petition to be served not less than five days before the day fixed for the hearing. However, the court may shorten that period (*Re A Company No. 00175 of 1987* [1987] BCLC 467). In that case Vinelott J said:

> 'the legislature must, I think, have intended that a person with power to appoint an administrative receiver should have an adequate opportunity of considering whether to exercise his power before it is extinguished. However, what constitutes an adequate opportunity – whether the period of service of the petition should be abridged or at the other extreme whether the hearing of a petition for which five clear days' notice has been given should be further adjourned – must depend upon the circumstances of each individual case.'

Speed of action is often important as the condition of a company is very likely to worsen if knowledge of the proceedings becomes widespread. The court may therefore require a quick decision from the holder of a floating charge who is entitled to appoint an administrative receiver. If such a person consents to the making of an administrative order the court will dispense with the need to serve notice on him and the order can be made very quickly.

17.6 **Hearing**

At the hearing of the petition any of the following may appear or be represented:

(1) the petitioner;
(2) the company;
(3) any person who has appointed an administrative receiver or has the power to do so;
(4) an administrative receiver, if appointed;
(5) a person who has presented a winding-up petition;
(6) the proposed administrator; and
(7) with the leave of the court any other person who appears to have an interest justifying his appearance (Rule 2.9).

The court has a general discretion to make any order it thinks fit (s. 9(4)). However, where the court is satisfied that there is an administrative receiver of the company then the court is required to dismiss the petition unless it is also satisfied that either:

(1) the person by whom or on whose behalf the administrative receiver was appointed has consented to the making of the order; or

(2) if an administration order were made, any security by virtue of which the administrative receiver was appointed would be liable to be upset by virtue of the provisions which permit the avoidance of antecedent transactions (see p. 306) (s. 9(3) Insolvency Act 1986).

17.7 **Effect of Presentation of a Petition**

By s. 10 of the Insolvency Act 1986, after a petition for an administration order has been presented:

(i) no resolution may be passed or order made for the winding up of the company;

(ii) no steps may be taken to enforce any security over the company's property or to repossess goods in the company's possession under any hire-purchase agreement except with the leave of the court and subject to such terms as the court may impose; and

(iii) no other proceedings and no execution or other legal process may be commenced or continued and no distress may be levied against the company or its property except with the leave of the court and subject to such terms as the court may impose.

The intention behind these provisions is to preserve the company's assets and business in order to assist the task of the administrator if one is appointed. However, after the presentation of a petition for an administration order an administrative receiver may be appointed or a winding-up petition may be presented. The latter course might well be taken by creditors who consider that an administration order would not be appropriate.

17.8 **Notice of Order**

The administrator must give the company notice of the order as soon as it is granted. Notice must also be given to all known creditors within twenty-eight days and the order must be published in appropriate newspapers (IA s. 21, IR 2.10).

17.9 **Effect of Administration Order**

By ss. 11(1) and 14(4), once the administration order is made:

(i) any winding up petition is dismissed; and

(ii) any administrative receiver must vacate office.

(iii) the director's powers are suspended since all powers which could be exercised in such a way as to interfere with the exercise of the administration are not exercisable except with the consent of the administrator.

17.10 **Powers of the Administrator**

Harry Rajak, in *Company Liquidations* (CCH publications, 1988) describes the powers given to an administrator thus;

> 'The administrator is given comprehensive powers so as to be able to exercise virtually total control over the company. Two different schemes can be identified in the Insolvency Act 1986. The first, which is explicit, is to give to the administrator and the administrative receiver certain common powers. These are set out in Schedule I to the Act, and conferred, in the case of an administrator, by s. 14(1)(b) [see Casenotes]). The Act then confers on the administrator other powers which are not given to an administrative receiver and which, by and large, reflect the fact that the administrator is expected to adopt a wider public role more akin to that of official receiver, rather than the narrower, more partisan position of the administrative receiver.'

The powers are extremely widely drafted including a power to deal with property which is the subject of a floating charge.

17.11 **Duties of the Administrator**

The general duties of an administrator are set out in s. 17 Insolvency Act 1986. They are:

(i) to take into custody or control the company's property;
(ii) to manage the affairs, business and property of the company until proposals for the company's future are approved;
(iii) to summon meetings if directed by the court, or if required by the Rules.

It is the specific duty of an administrator to prepare a statement of the company's affairs and proposals as to the future management of the company. The proposals are considered by a creditor's meeting. This meeting determines whether the administration is to continue (Insolvency Act 1986, s. 23). If agreement is not reached the court may discharge the administration order, make an interim order or 'any other order that it thinks fit' (Insolvency Act 1986, s. 24(5)).

The result of failure to agree will usually be the liquidation of the company, but it has been argued that the court will not have the power under s. 24 Insolvency Act 1986 to make a winding-up order (Rajak, *Company Liquidations* p. 77). In that case the procedure set out in s. 124 would probably have to be adhered to.

Voting at the meeting is according to the amount of each creditor's outstanding claim. A resolution is passed when approved by a majority (in value) of those present and voting, whether by person or proxy (IR r.2.28(1)) except, however, where those who voted against the resolution included 'more than half in value of the creditors to whom notice of the meetings was sent and who are not, to the best of the chairman's belief, persons connected with the company' (IR, r.2.28 (1A)).

17.12 Unfairly Prejudicial Management

Section 27 Of the Insolvency Act 1986 establishes for creditors and members of a company in administration a remedy similar to that for shareholders under s. 459 of the Companies Act 1985 (see Chapter 13).

17.13 Application to Discharge the Order

The administrator may apply to the court at any time for the administration order to be discharged and must make an application for the discharge or variation of the order if it appears to him that the purpose specified in the order either has been achieved or has become incapable of achievement (s. 18 Insolvency Act 1986). On such an application the court has a wide discretion to discharge or vary the administration order and make such consequential provision as it thinks fit.

17.14 Voluntary Arrangements

This is a scheme for making arrangements with creditors which will be legally binding on all creditors, even if not all of them agree. This has the advantage that where a company has sensible plans which are likely to avoid a liquidation, those plans cannot be upset by a single creditor insisting on a liquidation of the company. The disadvantage of the scheme under the Insolvency Act 1986 is that the scheme may not be approved for some weeks and there is nothing, until creditor approval is gained, to prevent such a liquidation from occurring.

17.15 Proposal

The first step towards approval of an arrangement is a proposal to the company and the creditors. The proposal is made by the directors unless the company is in administration or liquidation, when it is made by the administrator or liquidator (Insolvency Act 1986, s. 1). A receiver or administrative receiver is not empowered to propose a voluntary arrangement. The arrangement must be supervised by a qualified insolvency practitioner. The most likely proposals will be the acceptance by each creditor of a percentage of their claim, or a moratorium on enforcement of claims for a certain period.

17.16 The Involvement of the Court

If the supervisor of the scheme is someone other than the liquidator or administrator, he must report to the court within twenty-eight days as to whether the proposal should be considered and, if so, the dates and times when he would call the relevant meetings (IA, s. 2(2)). He is then obliged to summon those meetings.

17.17 Contents of the Proposal

The rules lay down the matters which must be set out in the proposal. As might be expected, the company's assets and liabilities must be set out in detail, as must the proposed arrangement itself.

17.18 Meetings

Meetings of the company members and the creditors must be summoned. For the members' meeting the requisite majority for any resolution is more than one-half of the members present in person or by proxy and voting (IR r.1.20(1)).

As far as the creditors' meeting is concerned, there are two requisite majorities – more than 75 per cent for the resolution to pass any proposal or any modification of the proposal, and more than 50 per cent for other resolutions. The percentages are of votes of creditors present in person or by proxy and voting. There are detailed rules by which certain votes must be ignored in order to prevent the majorities being made up of persons connected with the company. If the arrangement is approved it binds everyone who was entitled to have notice of and vote at the meeting.

17.19 Challenges

An arrangement can be challenged on the grounds of unfair prejudice or material irregularity at either of the meetings (IA s. 6(1)).

17.20 **Administrative Receivership**

An administrative receiver is appointed by a secured creditor. The court does not normally need to be involved in the procedure. An administrative receiver will take control of the whole of the company's property in order to realise it so that the creditor who was responsible for her appointment will be paid. Theoretically this procedure does not involve the liquidation of the company, but in practice the receiver will not be appointed unless there are serious concerns as to the solvency of the company and the appointment of the receiver will often be the last straw for the company.

From the time of his appointment the receiver has authority to deal with the property which is the subject matter of the charge. The authority of the directors to deal with that property disappears. However, the directors remain in office for other purposes, for example to fulfil the company's duty to provide the registrar with information. The directors also retain their power to bring legal proceedings in the company's name. *Newhart Developments Ltd* v. *Co-operative Commercial Bank Ltd* [1978] QB 814 provided that their exercise of that power does not interfere with the receiver in realising the charged assets.

The powers of the receiver will be found in the contract which creates the charge. However, all receivers will also have the powers conferred by s. 42(1) and Schedule 1 of the Insolvency Act 1986.

17.21 **Liquidations**

A company will cease to exist by being liquidated and struck off the register of companies. A company may be wound up by the court or voluntarily by the members.

A company may be wound up by the court if:

(i) the company has by special resolution resolved that the company be wound up by the court;

(ii) the company was originally registered as a public company but has not been issued with a certificate under CA 1985, s. 117, that it satisfies the minimum capital requirement, and more than a year has passed since its registration;

(iii) it is an old public company within the meaning of the Consequential Provisions Act;

(iv) the company does not commence its business within a year from its incorporation, or suspends its business for a whole year;

(v) the number of members is reduced below two (unless the company converts itself into a single member company in accordance with the Companies (Single Member Private Limited Companies) Regulations 1992 (see Chapter 1));

(vi) the company is unable to pay its debts;

(vii) the court is of opinion that it is just and equitable to wind up the company (see Chapter 13).

The court will wind up a company after the successful presentation of a winding-up petition which may be presented by the company, the directors, any creditor or any person liable to contribute to the assets of the company in the event of a winding-up (contributory), the supervisor of a voluntary arrangement, or in some circumstances by a receiver. All shareholders are contributories even if they have no further money to pay on their shares and are not actually liable to contribute to the assets of the company.

A member's petition will only succeed if he can show that he has a tangible interest in the winding-up. He must show that he would gain an advantage or avoid or minimise a disadvantage.

A creditor, contributory, the Official Receiver or the Department of Trade and Industry may seek a compulsory winding-up order even if the company is in voluntary liquidation.

17.22 Voluntary Winding-up

A company may be wound up voluntarily when the members resolve by special resolution to wind it up or if it resolves by extraordinary resolution that it cannot, by reason of its liabilities, continue its business and that it is advisable to wind it up (s. 84 IA 1986). If the directors, after a full investigation, believe that the company will be able to pay its debts in full (with interest) within twelve months from the commencement of the winding-up the liquidation is a 'members' voluntary winding-up' (s. 89 IA 1986). If no declaration of solvency is made the liquidation becomes a creditors' voluntary winding-up. In this case a creditors' meeting must be summoned and the liquidator must attend the creditors' meeting and give a report on any exercise of his powers. Section 107 provides that in a voluntary winding-up, the property of the company is to be applied first in paying the preferential debts, then in satisfaction of its liabilities, and lastly it is to be distributed amongst the members according to their rights and interests as determined by the articles.

The directors of the company can petition for its winding up as can a receiver. The Secretary of State may also petition for a winding up if it appears that it may be in the public interest to do so (s. 124A Insolvency Act 1986).

17.23 The Liquidator

With the commencement of the winding-up of the company, the directors cease to control its affairs and the liquidator manages the company with a view to collecting all the assets of the company. The winding up will normally commence at the time of the presentation of the petition for winding up. However where a resolution for voluntary winding up has been passed the date of the resolution will (in the absence of fraud or mistake) be the relevant date (s. 129 IA 1A 1986). The liquidator must be an insolvency practitioner (s. 390(1) IA 1986). His eventual aim will be to pay the costs of the winding-up, pay the debts of the company and distribute any surplus amongst the members (ss. 107, 143 IA 1986). He has a considerable array of powers conferred for this purpose (see Rajak, *op. cit.*, para. 903, *et seq.*).

In a winding-up by the court the liquidator is subject to the control of the court. All liquidators are subject to substantial duties both equitable and statutory (see Rajak, *Company Liquidations* para. 922 *et seq.*).

If, during a members' voluntary winding-up the liquidator forms the opinion that the company will be unable to pay its debts within the period specified in the directors' declaration of solvency, he is obliged to summon a creditor's meeting and from the date of that meeting the liquidation becomes a creditors' voluntary winding-up (ss. 95, 96 IA 1986).

17.24 Order of Payment of Debts

The assets (which will be diminished by the enforcement of any fixed charge) are applied in the following order:

1. The proper expenses of the winding up;
2. The preferential debts. These appear in IA 1986 s. 386 and Schedule 6 (see Casenotes); If the company has not enough money to meet these debts in full, preferential creditors take priority over the holders of floating charges (s175 IA 1986)
3. Floating charge holders.
4. Ordinary creditors;
5. Members.

17.25 Avoiding Antecedent Transactions

The liquidator may be able to avoid certain transactions entered into by a company in order to increase the fund available to the general body of creditors.

Transactions at an undervalue

An administrator or liquidator may apply to the court where the company has entered into a transaction at an undervalue (s. 238 IA 1986). The court has an unfettered discretion to make such order as it thinks fit. The Act lays down the time limits within which the transaction must have occurred for it to be vulnerable to this application. So far as a company going directly into liquidation is concerned these periods are: The period is counted back from the date of the resolution to wind-up or the date of the presentation of the winding-up petition. The liquidator must establish that at the time of the transaction the company was unable to pay its debts. Under s. 241 the court has a wide discretion to make orders to transfer property in order to correct the situation but may not affect the rights of a *bona fide* purchaser of property (section 241(IA) 1986). This latter restriction has been clarified and extended by the Insolvency (No. 2) Act 1994 which came into force on 26 July 1994 in relation to interests acquired and benefits received by third party purchasers after that date. It applies both to transactions at an undervalue and to preferences and protects a subsequent purchaser if he has acted in good faith for value. This extends protection to those who knew that there has been a transaction at an undervalue or a preference at some time but nevertheless acted in good faith at the time of the transaction. However, where the purchaser has knowledge both of the preference or undervalue transaction and 'relevant proceedings' there is a rebuttable presumption that the purchaser is not in good faith. Lack of good faith is also presumed where the subsequent purchaser is connected with or is an associate of the company. 'Relevant proceedings' means administration or liquidation within certain time-scales set out in the Act.

Preferences

There are similar provisions for the upsetting of a preference, which is the doing of anything by the company which has the effect of putting either one of its creditors, or someone who is a surety or guarantor of one of its debts, in a position which, in the event of the company going into insolvent liquidation, will be better than the position he would have been in if that thing had not been done (IA s. 239(4)(b)). The relevant periods during which preferences can be upset are (i) two years if the other party to the transaction was connected with the company; or (ii) six months if the other party was not connected.

The court has the same discretions here as it has with regard to transactions at an undervalue. In *Re M.C. Bacon Ltd* [1990] BCLC 324 the court (Chancery Division) gave some guidance on the interpretation of the Insolvency Act sections concerning transactions at an undervalue and preferences. In that case a company had carried on business as a bacon importer and wholesaler. It had been profitable until it had lost its principal customer. The company continued trading on a smaller scale for some time but eventually had to go into liquidation. During the time when it was trading on a small scale a debenture was granted to the bank. At this time the company was either insolvent or nearly so. The validity of the debenture was challenged . Miller J held that the debenture was not invalid as a preference under s. 239 (IA) 1986 because the directors in granting it had not been motivated by a desire to prefer the bank but only by a desire to avoid the calling in of the overdraft and their wish to continue trading. Nor was the debenture invalid as a transaction at an undervalue under s. 238 because the giving of the security had neither depleted the company's assets nor diminished their value.

In coming to the conclusion about the preference under s. 239 Miller J drew a clear distinction between the 'desire' of the directors and their 'intention'. The section requires desire and this was interpreted as synonomous with motive. If intention had been the test the debenture would surely have been invalid as the court would have needed only to be satisfied that the directors knew that the bank would be put in a better position than before by the debenture. In view of the introduction of objective tests elsewhere (e.g. s. 214 (IA) 1986, see below), this extremely subjective approach is perhaps surprising.

Transactions defrauding creditors

A transaction at an undervalue may also be challenged under s. 423 IA 1986. Under this provision there are no time limits and the company need not be in liquidation or even insolvent. It is necessary to show that the transaction was entered into *for the purpose of* putting assets beyond the reach of a creditor or potential creditor or of prejudicing the interests of such a person. In *Arbuthnot Leasing International Ltd* v. *Havelet Leasing Ltd (No. 2)* [1990] BCC 636 a company's business and assets had been transferred on legal advice to an off-the-shelf company shortly before it went into receivership. The court ordered the reversal of the transaction. In *Chohan* v. *Saggar and another* [1994] 1 BCLC 706 the court held that the proper purpose of an order under s. 423 was both to restore the position to what it would have been if the transaction had not been entered into and to protect the interests of the victims of the transaction.

Extortionate credit transactions

Section 244 Insolvency Act 1986 permits companies to set aside credit transactions which are deemed to be extortionate. This can only occur when the company is in liquidation or administration. The transaction must have been entered into at any time during the three-year period ending with the day on which an administrator was appointed or the day on which the company goes into liquidation (either the date on which the winding-up resolution is passed or the date on which a winding-up order is granted).

A credit transaction is extortionate if it either:

(1) requires grossly exorbitant payments to be made whether unconditionally or only in certain events in exchange for credit; or

(2) it grossly contravenes ordinary principles of fair dealing.

The court must, however, take account of the risk that was taken by the creditor in providing credit. This may be important as companies in this situation may have been bad risks even some considerable time previously.

The court may set such an agreement aside in whole or in part, or vary the terms.

Avoidance of floating charges

A floating charge can be successfully challenged by a liquidator or administrator under s. 245 of the Insolvency Act 1986 if:

(1) It was a floating charge within s. 251 Insolvency Act 1986. This defines a floating charge as 'a charge which, as created, was a floating charge'. (This definition prevents crystallisation by notice converting the charge into a fixed charge and giving debenture-holders priority over preferential creditors.)

(2) If it was created within two years of the commencement of the winding-up or administration where it was created in favour of a connected person; one year where it was in favour of a person unconnected with the company and if it was created in favour of an unconnected person only if it was created when the company was unable to pay its debts.

(4) To the extent that the company has received nothing in exchange. This means that a charge which would otherwise be invalid under s. 245 Insolvency Act 1986 will be valid to the extent of any value in money paid, or goods and services supplied to the company or in discharge or reduction of the company's debts provided this was done by the chargee at the time of or after the creation of the charge. Thus a new loan to pay off and replace an old loan will not be exempt under this section unless made in good faith to enable the company to carry on business (see *Re Destone Fabrics* [1941] Ch 319; *Re Matthew Ellis* [1933] Ch 458).

Connected persons

For the purposes of the provisions which may result in the avoidance of prior transactions, s. 249 Insolvency Act 1986 provides a definition of persons 'connected with' a company. It reads:

a person is connected with a company if –
   (a) he is a director or shadow director of the company or an associate of such a director or shadow director, or
   (b) he is an associate of the company.

'Associate' has the meaning given by s. 435 of the IA 1985. This is reproduced in the Casenotes to this chapter and it can clearly be seen that the net is spread very widely indeed.

17.26 Fraudulent Trading

Fraudulent trading is actionable both as a civil offence (Insolvency Act 1986, s. 213 and as a criminal offence (Companies Act 1985, s. 458). In both cases it is necessary to establish trading with 'intent to defraud'. This requires the court to find that the directors were acting dishonestly, not just that they were acting unreasonably (*Re L. Todd (Swanscombe) Ltd* [1990] BCC 125). The difficulty of establishing this has made this remedy little used. It is wider than wrongful trading, however, in that it is available against 'any persons who were knowingly parties to the carrying on of the business' of the company. For a comprehensive recent discussion of the law concerning fraudulent trading see *R* v. *Smith* [1996] 2 BCLC 109.

Only a liquidator may apply under the civil remedy, but criminal proceedings can be instituted for fraudulent trading outside the insolvency context, regardless of whether a company is wound up or not. The court has power under the civil remedy to make an order that the respondent 'make such contribution (if any) to the company's assets as the court thinks proper'.

17.27 Summary Remedy against Delinquent Directors

S.212 Insolvency Act 1986

S.212 Insolvency Act 1986 provides a means by which any person concerned in the management of a company may be made liable if it can be shown that he has

'misapplied or retained, or become accountable for, any money or other property of the company, or been guilty of any misfeasance or breach of any fiduciary or other duty in relation to the company'.

This section was given a wide interpretation by Hoffman LJ in *Re D'Jan of London Ltd* [1993] BCC 646 where he held a director liable for a breach of the duty of skill and care, using as a standard that imposed in respect of wrongful trading. For the possible effect of this judgment on directors' duties see Chapter 11.

17.28 Wrongful Trading

This is only a civil remedy. In essence it consists of continuing to trade when the company is known to be insolvent. It may, if successful, lead to the same order for a contribution as an order under the fraudulent trading provisions (see above). As with fraudulent trading, an application may only be made by the liquidator.

In the case of wrongful trading, an application can only be made when the company has gone into an insolvent liquidation (Insolvency Act 1986, s. 214(2)), that is, going into liquidation at a time when its assets are insufficient for the payment of its debts, other liabilities and the expenses of its winding up. An application can only be made against a director or shadow director. In *R* v. *Farmizer (Products) Ltd* [1995] 2 BCLC 462 it was held that an action under s. 214 was subject to s. 991 of the Limitation Act 1980 which imposes a six-year limitation period for bringing a claim. Time runs from the time when the company goes into insolvent liquidation.

Standard

The contrast with fraudulent trading is clear when it is realised that the director is judged by what he ought to have known as well as by what he did know and there is no question of having to establish dishonesty. Thus, wrongful trading applies at a time when a director at some time prior to the commencement of the winding-up, knew or ought to have concluded that there was no reasonable prospect that the company would avoid going into insolvent liquidation. There is a defence: the relevant person escapes where by the standard of the 'reasonably diligent person' he satisfies a court that he took *every step* with a view to minimising the potential loss to the company's creditors after he had the first knowledge of the insolvent state of the company.

The standard of knowledge and skill required is a cumulative blend of the subjective and objective, and includes:

(a) the general knowledge, skill and experience that may reasonably be expected of a person carrying out the same functions as are carried out by that director in relation to the company; and
(b) the general knowledge, skill and experience that director has (Insolvency Act 1986, s. 214(5)).

The thinking of the courts was well explained by Knox J in *Produce Marketing Consortium Ltd* [1989] 1 WLR 745. He said:

'It is evident that Parliament intended to widen the scope of legislation under which directors who trade on when the company is insolvent may in appropriate circumstances be required to make a contribution to [a company's creditors] . . . the test to be applied by the Court has become one under which the director in question is to be judged by the standards of what can reasonably be expected of a person fulfilling his functions and showing reasonable diligence in doing so. . .The general knowledge, skill and experience postulated will be much less extensive in a small company in a modest way of business with simple accounting procedures and equipment than it will be in a large company with sophisticated procedures. Nevertheless certain minimum standards are assumed to be attained . . . [Wrongful trading is] an enhanced version of the right which any company would have to sue its directors for breach of duty – enhanced in the sense that the standard of knowledge skill and experience required is made objective.'

Although much academic discussion has focussed on wrongful trading it is not used frequently by practitioners who usually consider that the money which will be clawed back will not be worth the time and effort involved in proceedings.

17.29 **The Destination of the Money**

Assets recovered by the liquidator in connection with transactions at an undervalue, voidable preferences, extortionate credit transactions, wrongful and fraudulent trading and misfeasance proceedings under s. 212 IA 1986 are paid into the general pool of the company's assets. They are not available for the payment of particular creditors. However, where a floating charge is invalidated the effect will often be to give priority to another charge which has been validly created over the same assets (*Capital Finance Co Ltd* v. *Stokes* [1968] 1 All ER 573).

17.30 **Dissolution**

A company ceases to exist when it is dissolved. This can only happen when its affairs are completely wound up.

In a winding-up by the court, the liquidator sends notice of the final meeting of creditors and vacation of office by him to the Registrar of Companies, the notice is registered and the company is normally dissolved at the end of the period of three months from the date of registration.

On completion of a voluntary winding-up the liquidator presents his final accounts to meetings of the company's creditors and/or members. Within a week after that has been done the liquidator must send copies of the accounts and a return of the holdings of the meetings to the Registrar of Companies. The Registrar registers them and the company is normally deemed to be dissolved three months later (IA ss. 94, 205).

Ss.201 and 205 contain provisions which permit delaying dissolution on the application of an interested party. By s. 651 the court has a discretion to declare a dissolution void at any time within twelve years. Section 652 provides that dissolution does not affect the liability of officers and members of the company to be sued.

Summary

1 There is a fairly new procedure known as administration which has the aim of saving companies which are otherwise in danger of liquidation. An administrator is appointed to propose a scheme which will assist the company out of its difficulties. Debenture-holders with a power to appoint a receiver also have a power to veto an administration procedure. The making of an order preserves the property by preventing proceedings against the company for the recovery of debts and preventing the making of a winding-up order.

2 Voluntary arrangements are schemes for coming to an arrangement with creditors. By a majority agreeing to the scheme, it becomes binding on all the creditors. The purpose is to prevent a minority of creditors from precipitating a liquidation where there is a hope that the company can be saved.

3 A company may be wound up by a court or by a voluntary creditors' or members' winding-up. The last course is only available where the company is solvent.

4 So far as the distribution of property is concerned, holders of fixed charges have a right to enforce their security. After that other property is distributed as follows:

  (i)   The proper expenses of the winding up;
  (ii) Preferential creditors, who take priority over floating chargeholders where there is not enough money to satisfy them in full;
  (iii) Creditors with floating charges by way of security;
  (iv) Ordinary creditors;
  (v)   Members.

5 There are a number of provisions for avoiding transactions which took place before the liquidation. In certain circumstances the following can be avoided:

  (a)   Transactions at an undervalue;
  (b)   Preferences;
  (c)   Extortionate credit transactions;
  (d)   Floating charges;

6 Anyone may be liable to criminal or civil penalties if they have been involved in fraudulent trading. Directors or shadow directors may be liable for wrongful trading if they continued to trade when they knew or ought to have concluded that the company was insolvent.

Casenotes

Insolvency Act 1986

14. General powers

(1) The administrator of a company –

  (a)   may do all such things as may be necessary for the management of the affairs, business and property of the company, and
  (b)   without prejudice to the generality of paragraph (a), has the powers specified in Schedule 1 to this Act;

and in the application of that Schedule to the administrator of a company the words 'he' and 'him' refer to the administrator.

(2) The administrator also has the power –

  (a)   to remove any director of the company and to appoint any person to be a director of it, whether to fill a vacancy or otherwise, and
  (b)   to call any meeting of the members or creditors of the company.

(3) The administrator may apply to the court for directions in relation to any particular matter arising in connection with the carrying out of his functions.

(4) Any power conferred on the company or its officers, whether by this Act or the Companies Act or by the memorandum or articles of association, which could be exercised in such a way as to interfere with the exercise by the administrator of his powers is not exercisable except with the consent of the administrator, which may be given either generally or in relation to particular cases.

(5) In exercising his powers the administrator is deemed to act as the company's agent.

(6) A person dealing with the administrator in good faith and for value is not concerned to inquire whether the administrator is acting within his powers.

SCHEDULES

SCHEDULE 1

Section 14,42

Powers of Administrator or Administrative Receiver

1. Power to take possession of, collect and get in the property of the company and, for that purpose, to take such proceedings as may seem to him expedient.

2. Power to sell or otherwise dispose of the property of the company by public auction or private contract or, in Scotland, to sell, feu, hire out or otherwise dispose of the property of the company by public roup or private bargain.

3. Power to raise or borrow money and grant security therefor over the property of the company.

4. Power to appoint a solicitor or accountant or other professionally qualified person to assist him in the performance of his functions.

5. Power to bring or defend any action or other legal proceedings in the name and on behalf of the company.

6. Power to refer to arbitration any question affecting the company.

7. Power to effect and maintain insurances in respect of the business and property of the company.

8. Power to use the company's seal.

9. Power to do all acts and to execute in the name and on behalf of the company any deed, receipt or other document.

10. Power to draw, accept, make and endorse any bill of exchange or promissory note in the name and on behalf of the company.

11. Power to appoint any agent to do any business which he is unable to do himself or which can more conveniently be done by an agent and power to employ and dismiss employees.

12. Power to do all such things (including the carrying out of works) as may be necessary for the realisation of the property of the company.

13. Power to make any payment which is necessary or incidental to the performance of his functions.

14. Power to carry on the business of the company.

15. Power to establish subsidiaries of the company.

16. Power to transfer to subsidiaries of the company the whole or any part of the business and property of the company.

17. Power to grant or accept a surrender of a lease or tenancy of any of the property of the company, and to take a lease or tenancy of any property required or convenient for the business of the company.

18. Power to make any arrangement or compromise on behalf of the company.

19. Power to call up any uncalled capital of the company.

20. Power to rank and claim in the bankruptcy, insolvency, sequestration or liquidation of any person indebted to the company and to receive dividends, and to accede to trust deeds for the creditors of any such person.

21. Power to present or defend a petition for the winding up of the company.

22. Power to change the situation of the company's registered office.

23. Power to do all other things incidental to the exercise of the foregoing powers.

SCHEDULE 6

Section 386

THE CATEGORIES OF PREFERENTIAL DEBTS

Category 1: Debts due to Inland Revenue

1. Sums due at the relevant date from the debtor on account of deductions of income tax from emoluments paid during the period of 12 months next before that date.
The deductions here referred to are those which the debtor was liable to make under section [203 of the Income and Corporation Taxes Act 1988] (pay as you earn), less the amount of the repayments of income tax which the debtor was liable to make during that period.

2. Sums due at the relevant date from the debtor in respect of such deductions as are required to be made by the debtor for that period under section [559 of the Income and Corporation Taxes Act 1988] (sub-contractors in the construction industry).

Category 2: Debts due to Customs and Exercise

3. Any value added tax which is referable to the period of 6 months next before the relevant date (which period is referred to below as 'the 6-month period').
For the purposes of this paragraph –

   (a)   where the whole of the prescribed accounting period to which any value added tax is attributable falls within the 6-month period, the whole amount of that tax is referable to that period; and
   (b)   in any other case the amount of any value added tax which is referable to the 6-month period is the proportion of the tax which is equal to such proportion (if any) of the accounting reference period in question as falls within the 6-month period;

and in sub-paragraph (a) 'prescribed' means prescribed by regulations under the Value Added Tax Act 1983.

4. The amount of any car tax which is due at the relevant date from the debtor and which became due within a period of 12 months next before that date.

5. Any amount which is due –

(a)   by way of general betting duty or bingo duty, or

(b)   under s. 12(1) of the Betting and Gaming Duties Act 1981 (general betting duty and pool betting duty recoverable from agent collecting stakes), or

(c)   under s. 14 of, or Schedule 2 to, that Act (gaming licence duty),

from the debtor at the relevant date and which became due within the period of 12 months next before that date.

Category 3: Social security contributions

6. All sums which on the relevant date are due from the debtor on account of Class 1 or Class 2 contributions under the Social Security Act 1975 or the Social Security (Northern Ireland) Act 1975 and which became due from the debtor in the 12 months next before that date.

7. All sums which on the relevant date have been assessed on and are due from the debtor on account of Class 4 contributions under either of those Acts of 1975, being sums which –

(a)   are due to the Commissioners of Inland Revenue (rather than to the Secretary of State or a Northern Ireland department), and

(b)   are assessed on the debtor up to the 5th April next before the relevant date,

but not exceeding, in the whole, any one year's assessment.

Category 4: Contributions to occupational pension schemes, etc

8. Any sum which is owed by the debtor and is a sum to which Schedule 3 to the Social Security Pensions Act 1975 applies (contributions to occupational pension schemes and state pension scheme premiums).

Category 5: Remuneration, etc, of employees

9. So much of any amount which –

(a)   is owed by the debtor to a person who is or has been an employee of the debtor, and

(b)   is payable by way of remuneration in respect of the whole or any part of the period of 4 months next before the relevant date,

as does not exceed so much as may be prescribed by order made by the Secretary of State.

10. An amount owed by the way of accrued holiday remuneration, in respect of any period of employment before the relevant date, to a person whose employment by the debtor has been terminated, whether before, on or after that date.

11. So much of any sum owed in respect of money advanced for the purposes as has been applied for the payment of a debt which, if it had not been paid, would have been a debt falling within paragraph 9 or 10.

12. So much of any amount which –

    (a) is ordered (whether before or after the relevant date) to be paid by the debtor under the Reserve Forces (Safeguard of Employment) Act 1985, and

    (b) is so ordered in respect of a default made by the debtor before that date in the discharge of his obligations under that Act,

as does not exceed such amount as may be prescribed by order made by the Secretary of State.

Interpretation for Category 5

13.–(1) For the purposes of paragraphs 9 to 12, a sum is payable by the debtor to a person by way of remuneration in respect of any period if –

    (a) it is paid as wages or salary (whether payable for time or for piece work or earned wholly or partly by way of commission) in respect of services rendered to the debtor in that period, or

    (b) it is an amount falling within the following sub-paragraph and is payable by the debtor in respect of that period.

(2) An amount falls within this sub-paragraph if it is –

    (a) a guarantee payment under s. 12(1) of the Employment Protection (Consolidation) Act 1978 (employee without work to do for a day or part of a day);

    (b) remuneration on suspension on medical grounds under s. 19 of that Act;

    (c) any payment for time off under s. 27(3) (trade union duties), 31(3) (looking for work, etc) or 31A(4) (ante-natal care) of that Act; or

    (d) remuneration under a protective award made by an industrial tribunal under s. 101 of the Employment Protection Act 1975 (redundancy dismissal with compensation).

14.–(1) This paragraph relates to a case in which a person's employment has been terminated by or in consequence of his employer going into liquidation or being adjudged bankrupt or (his employer being a company not in liquidation) by or in consequence of –

    (a) a receiver being appointed as mentioned in s. 40 of this Act (debenture-holders secured by floating charge), or

    (b) the appointment of a receiver under s. 53(6) or 54(5) of this Act (Scottish company with property subject to floating charge), or

    (c) the taking of possession by debenture-holders (so secured), as mentioned in s. 196 of the Companies Act.

(2) For the purposes of paragraphs 9 to 12, holiday remuneration is deemed to have accrued to that person in respect of any period of employment if, by virtue of his contract of employment or of any enactment that remuneration would have accrued in respect of that period if his employment had continued until he became entitled to be allowed the holiday.

(3) The reference in sub-paragraph (2) to any enactment includes an order or direction made under an enactment.

15. Without prejudice to paragraphs 13 and 14 –
    (a) any remuneration payable by the debtor to a person in respect of a period of holiday or of absence from work through sickness or other good cause is deemed to be wages or (as the case may be) salary in respect of services rendered to the debtor in that period, and
    (b) references here and in those paragraphs to remuneration in respect of a period of holiday include any sums which, if they had been paid, would have been treated for the purposes of the enactments relating to social security as earnings in respect of that period.

[Category 6: Levies on coal and steel production

15A. Any sums due at the relevant date from the debtor in respect of:
    (a) the levies on the production of coal and steel referred to in Articles 49 and 50 of the ECSC Treaty, or
    (b) any surcharge for delay provided for in Article 50(3) of that Treaty and Article 6 of Decision 3/52 of the High Authority of the Coal and Steel Community.]

Orders

16. An order under paragraph 9 or 12 –

    (a) may contain such transitional provisions as may appear to the Secretary of State necessary or expedient;
    (b) shall be made by statutory instrument subject to annulment in pursuance of a resolution of either House of Parliament.

NOTES

Paras 1,2: amended by ICTA 1988, s. 844, Sch. 29, para. 32 Table.
Para 15A: inserted by the Insolvency (ECSC Levy Debts) Regulations 1987, SI 1987 No. 2093, reg. 2(1), (3).

PART XVIII

INTERPRETATION

435. Meaning of 'associate'

(1) For the purposes of this Act any question whether a person is an associate of another person is to be determined in accordance with the following provisions of this section (any provision that a person is an associate of another person being taken to mean that they are associates of each other).

(2) A person is an associate of an individual if that person is the individual's husband or wife, or is a relative, or the husband or wife of a relative, of the individual or of the individual's husband or wife.

(3) A person is an associate of any person with whom he is in partnership, and of the husband or wife or a relative of any individual with whom he is in partnership; and a Scottish firm is an associate of any person who is a member of the firm.

(4) A person is an associate of any person whom he employs or by whom he is employed.

(5) A person in his capacity as trustee of a trust other than –

   (a) a trust arising under any of the second Group of Parts or the Bankruptcy (Scotland) Act 1985, or

   (b) a pension scheme or an employees' share scheme (within the meaning of the Companies Act),

is an associate of another person if the beneficiaries of the trust include, or the terms of the trust confer a power that may be exercised for the benefit of, that other person or an associate of that other person.

(6) A company is an associate of another company –

   (a) if the same person has control of both, or a person has control of one and persons who are his associates, or he and persons who are his associates, have control of the other, or

   (b) if a group of two or more persons has control of each company, and the groups either consist of the same persons or could be regarded as consisting of the same persons by treating (in one or more cases) a member of either group as replaced by a person of whom he is an associate.

(7) A company is an associate of another person if that person has control of it or if that person and persons who are his associates together have control of it.

(8) For the purposes of this section a person is a relative of an individual if he is that individual's brother, sister, uncle, aunt, nephew, niece, lineal ancestor or lineal descendant, treating –

   (a) any relationship of the half blood as a relationship of the whole blood and the stepchild or adopted child of any person as his child, and

   (b) an illegitimate child as the legitimate child of his mother and reputed father;

and references in this section to a husband or wife include a former husband or wife and a reputed husband or wife.

(9) For the purposes of this section any director or other officer of a company is to be treated as employed by that company.

(10) For the purposes of this section a person is to be taken as having control of a company if –

   (a) the directors of the company or of another company which has control of it (or any of them) are accustomed to act in accordance with his directions or instruction, or

   (b) he is entitled to exercise, or control the exercise of, one third or more of the voting power at any general meeting of the company or of another company which has control of it;

and where two or more persons together satisfy either of the above conditions, they are to be taken as having control of the company.

(11) In this section 'company' includes any body corporate (whether incorporated in Great Britain or elsewhere); and references to directors and other officers of a company and to voting power at any general meeting of a company have effect with any necessary modifications.

Exercises

1 Describe the roles of liquidators and administrators.
2 Consider the possible liabilities of directors on a winding-up of a company (see Chapters 11, 12 and 13 as well as this chapter).
3 In what circumstances and on what time-scale can transactions prior to a liquidation be avoided?

18 The Effect of the EU on English Company Law*

The Member States of the European Community (EU) have agreed to move towards a 'single European Market'. This means that as many as possible of the barriers to trading freely across national frontiers will be removed. One difficulty of trading internationally occurs when companies involved in trading are themselves subject to different rules. They are more likely to be suspicious of each other and require complicated legal safeguards in their contracts. These will have to be drawn up with reference to several systems of law. Because of this the EU has tried to harmonise a number of rules relating to companies. This has generally been done by 'Directives'. These are laws which have been adopted by the Council of the European Community. After this adoption they become part of UK law by *implementation*. This is achieved by the relevant government department (in this case almost always the Department of Trade and Industry) drafting a statute which translates the provisions of the Directives into terms which will be understood in the United Kingdom. The statute is then dealt with by the UK Parliament in the ordinary way except that, because there is an obligation to implement the Directive, the scope for making amendments to the legislation is necessarily limited.

18.1 The Making of a Directive

The procedure followed for making a Directive is as follows. The Commission (the EU's civil servants) discuss the proposal with officials from Member States and other interested parties (such as, in this country, the Confederation of British Industry, the Institute of Directors, the Chartered Accountants' professional bodies, the Stock Exchange, and the Law Society). During this period the Commission will issue a number of drafts and receive comments on those drafts from the interested parties. The Commission will then adopt the final draft as a formal proposal.

*The author and publishers wish to thank the Commission of the European Communities for permission to reproduce copyright material in this chapter.

The formal proposal is then submitted to the Council, the European Parliament and the Economic and Social Committee (ECOSOC). The Council will not normally start considering the proposal until the European Parliament and ECOSOC have delivered formal opinions on it. Once these opinions have been received, the Commission may amend the proposal before resubmitting to the Council.

A Council working group, made up of officials from Member States, then discusses the proposal in detail before referring it to the Committee of Permanent Representatives (COREPER) which in turn refers it to the Council. Depending on the Article of the original Treaty on which the proposal is based, the Council will either simply adopt the proposal or agree a common position by majority voting in accordance with the constitution of the EU. In the latter case the European Parliament then has an opportunity to give a second opinion before the proposal returns to the Council for final adoption. It is after the final adoption of the measure that the Member States must go through the implementation process described above. The Maastricht Treaty resulted in increased powers for the Parliament which has resulted in active co-operation between it and the other institutions rather than Parliament merely giving reports on proposed legislation.

Rarely, company law may be also affected by an EU Regulation. This is a method of making law which is different from passing Directives, because a Regulation will apply directly throughout the Community. It will not require a statute to implement it but may need legislation to translate its effect into ideas which are familiar in the UK, and to fill in gaps.

18.2 **The Extent of the Influence of EU Rules**

The changes brought about by the EU mostly become law in this country by passing a statute in the usual way. Many people do not realise that a large number of the recent changes to our law are in fact 'Directive-driven', that is, they were only included in company law reform measures because of an obligation to implement a Directive. The extent of the EU's influence has therefore been partially hidden. Because these measures are now part of general company law, it is not necessary to deal with them in detail here. More discussion of them will be found in the chapters dealing with the particular topics involved. However, the importance of EU measures can be seen from the summary of those Directive-driven measures already introduced. The continuing and increasing influence of the EU is shown by the number of measures which are progressing through the steps towards becoming Community law. The time taken to complete the procedure depends on many things: the more complex and controversial the measure the longer it will take. The progress of some measures may also depend on whether an influential figure, such as the

President of the Commission, is particularly keen to see the measure adopted during his term of office.

It is also important to note that many Directives have been held by the European Court of Justice to be of 'direct effect' and where this has happened the terms of the Directive will take precedence over the law of the United Kingdom or other Member State if they are different.

Note: Because this is an area where law is changing, this text will quickly become out of date. The Department of Trade are usually able to help enquirers with information about the latest position in respect of any particular Directive.

18.3 Sources of EU Law

Primary Sources

The primary source of EU law is the Treaty of Rome, signed by the original six member States in 1957 and to which the UK became a party in 1972 by signing one of the Acts of Accession. The Treaty contains a large number of Articles, some of which have in themselves the content of the relevant law, e.g. Arts 85 and 86 concerning competition law, and others which lay down the framework of laws, the detail of which is made by secondary community legislation.

The scope of the Treaty of Rome was enlarged by the Single European Act (SEA) signed in 1986. In line with the desire to speed up European integration and achieve a common internal market, the SEA also introduced a number of important procedural changes, in particular allowing for more measures to be passed by the Council of Ministers (see p. 313) by majority vote. The Treaty of Maastricht, which came into force from 1 November 1993, also makes significant amendments from the original Treaty as already amended by the SEA. One of the more obvious changes is that the community is now generally known as the European Union. It is important to note, however, that the European Union does not replace the European Community. The European Union is the collective name for the governments of the member States, whereas the power to initiate and enforce community-wide legislation remains with the institutions of the European Community.

Secondary EU legislation

Article 189 of the EU Treaty specifies a number of ways in which the council and the Commission can legislate. These are collectively referred to as 'acts'. They are:

(1) Regulations

These are binding from the time of agreement and are 'directly applicable' in a member State; in other words they have the force of law in all member States from the time of making.

(2) Directives

These are addressed to the member States, which are bound by them as to the results to be achieved, but have a discretion as to how they achieve the results. In other words, they have to be implemented by domestic legislation. A period of time is usually specified within which the member States are obliged, so far as is necessary, to change their domestic laws. The UK has implemented directives by means of both Acts of Parliament and secondary legislation (a general power to implement by statutory instrument is given under the European Communities Act 1972, s. 2).

Sometimes directives have been regarded as directly effective or directly applicable in the law of a member State. For example, in Joined Cases C-19 and C20/90, *Karella* v. *Minister of Industry, Energy and Technology* (1991 OJ C166/12), it was held that certain provisions of the Second Company Law Directive were of direct effect. It is also possible that failure to implement a directive may give rise to an action by an individual, resulting in the award of damages against the member State in default. This was the situation in Joined Cases C-6 and 9/96, *Francovich and Boniface* v. *Italian Republic* ([1992] ECR 133, discussed on p. 331). Where there is a relevant EU directive which has not been correctly implemented, specialist legal advice needs to be sought as to whether it is effective to override the UK law on the particular point or might give rise to a remedy in damages.

(3) Decisions

These may be addressed to a member State or to an individual, and are directly binding on the addressee.

(4) Recommendations and Opinions

These are not binding, but of persuasive authority.

Regulations, directives and some decisions are published in the *Official Journal*.

18.4 The Institutions of the EU

The principal institutions provided for in the Treaty of Rome, as amended, are the Parliament, the Council, the Commission, the Court of Justice and the Economic and Social Committee.

The European Parliament

The Parliament is not a true legislative body, although in recent years it has played a more important role and it does have some negative control over the EU's budget.

It must be consulted by the Council of Ministers over proposed legislation, including the legislation relating the internal market, and, since the SEA, it has had the chance, having once disagreed with proposed legislation, to have a second look at the draft. If it maintains its objection, the Council can still proceed but must do so unanimously. Following the Maastricht Treaty, there is a provision for acts to be jointly adopted by the European Parliament and the Council and provision for the intervention of a Conciliation Committee where Parliament and Council differ. The Commission also reports regularly to the Parliament. The Treaty of Maastricht has increased the powers of the Parliament, but it will not become a legislative body with powers equivalent to that of the UK legislature.

The Council of Ministers

The Council is the primary law-making body of the EU, although it can act only on the basis of a recommendation from the Commission and must consult the Parliament and the Economic and Social Committee. It consists of representatives from the governments of each Member State, with different representatives for different sorts of business. Thus the UK government may for different purposes be represented by, for example, the Prime Minister, the Foreign Secretary or the Secretary of State for Trade and Industry.

Originally, and for many years, the Council could proceed only by unanimous agreement. However, the SEA and the Maastricht Treaty now allows the Council to act by what is called a 'qualified majority' in respect of many items of legislation relating to the completion of the internal market. For this purpose, member States have 'weighted' voting rights according to their size and legislation can be passed by a majority which works out at just over two-thirds. By itself, the UK cannot veto legislation requiring only a qualified majority.

In practice, much of the work of the Council is delegated to the Committee of Permanent Representatives or to Management Committees.

The European Commission

There are 17 Commissioners chosen from the member States to act essentially as the guardians of the Community interest. The Commission has three primary functions. First, it brings forward proposals for legislation in the form of draft regulations, directives etc. Secondly, it is charged with enforcing community law against member States, if necessary by bringing proceedings before the Court of Justice. It is also the sole policeman of EU competition law. Thirdly, the Commission acts as the EU executive or civil service, implementing decisions of the Council.

The European Court of Justice

The Court of Justice is the ultimate arbiter of European Law. Over many years of interpreting the Treaty of Rome and other EU legislation, it has revealed itself to be almost as much of a law-making body as the other institutions. It is clear that it works in a radically different way from the courts in the UK, in particular in its willingness to make law and in not regarding itself bound by its previous decisions.

Litigation can reach the Court in a number of ways. The most relevant for the purposes of this work are: (1) actions taken against other member States by the Commission or by a fellow member State, for example alleging a failure to implement or an outright breach of EU legislation and (2) issues of Community law referred to the Court by a national court under Art 177 of the Treaty. The latter is particularly important because individuals (and companies) have very limited rights to bring direct actions in the Court of Justice against member States or the EU institutions, and no right to bring actions alleging breach of EU law against other individuals. Their best remedy is to try to raise EU law indirectly in proceedings in the national court. Any national court has the power to refer the point to the Court of Justice for a preliminary ruling. Courts of last resort have a *duty* to refer.

The Court of First Instance is part of the European Court of Justice. It hears most competition cases and cases concerning the staff of the European Community institutions but its jurisdiction has recently been extended to cover all cases except those of constitutional significance and anti-dumping cases.

The Economic and Social Committee

This body consists of persons appointed by the Council to represent a variety of sectional interests throughout the community. Essentially it plays a consultative role.

Community Jurisprudence and Community Law

Recent cases show that it is not possible to ignore any area of EC law. The Treaty articles dealing with such diverse matters as competition law and free movement may be relevant in a company law context. Three cases make the point. In *Alpine Investments BV* v. *Minister van Financien* [1995] 2 BCLC 214 the issue was whether Dutch rules preventing cold calling of clients in another member state were contrary to Article 59 of the EC Treaty which prohibits restrictions on the free movement of services between Member States, *Oakdale (Richmond) Ltd* v. *National Westminister Bank plc* [1997] 1 BCLC 63 concerned the compatibility of loan arrangements with Articles 85 and 86 of the EC Treaty (prohibition of anti-competitive measures). *Chequepoint SARL* v. *McClelland and another* [1997] 1 BCLC 117 concerned the compatability of orders for security for costs made against companies in another Member State of the Community with Community prohibitions preventing discrimination against nationals of another Member State.

18.5 The EU Company Law Harmonisation Programme

The following is a summary of legislation which has been passed, and the most important of the proposals currently being considered by the EU legislators. The programme is considered in sections according to their format or subject matter. The sections are:

(1) Regulations;
(2) Company law directives;
(3) Securities regulation;
(4) Insolvency; and
(5) Competition and latest development.

Regulations

European Economic Interest Grouping (OJ 28 L199/1)
This creates a new instrument for business which may be formed by persons from at least two member States. It must not have as its primary purpose the making of profits, and it may only employ 500 employees. When it was a proposal it was envisaged that one of the purposes for which it would be most used was joint research and development, but it is being utilised for a wide variety of purposes (see Anderson, *European Economic Interest Groupings* (Butterworths, 1990), p. 9).

The European Company Statute (OJ 1991 C176/1 and COM (91) 174)
The Commission of the European Economic Community has published a proposal for a regulation and a directive, together known as the European Company Statute (ECS). If passed, this legislation would create a new business organisation which will be governed partly by the European law contained in the Statute and partly by the law of the member State in which it registers. It will create a new option for businesses – no company need convert into a European company, nor would the proposal require any alteration to current company law, save to add a European company as an extra choice for businesses.

This type of company would also be formed by persons from more than one member State, but there is no restriction on its profit-making capacity, nor on the number of employees it may have. All European companies would, however, be obliged to have a system of worker involvement in the important decisions made by the company. This requirement is contained in a draft directive linked to the regulation which contains the company's structural provisions.

18.6 **Company Law Directives**

Implemented Directives

It should be noted that the European Court of Justice appears to be increasingly vigilant in detecting poor implementation of directives and will not hesitate to substitute its interpretation of the directive for a member State provision which it regards as a defective interpretation of EU law.

The First Directive (OJ 1968 spec ed 41–45).   This provides a system of publicity for all companies. Member countries must ensure disclosure of the following:

(1) The memorandum and articles;
(2) officers of the company;
(3) paid-up capital;
(4) balance sheet and profit and loss account;
(5) winding-up; and
(6) appointment of liquidators.

The Directive also provides that a third party who enters into a contract with the company may presume that the act is within the objects of the company. This latter provision was badly implemented by s. 9 of the European Communities Act 1972, and re-enacted as s. 35 of the Companies Act 1985. A further measure in this field has been introduced by the Companies Act 1989, s. 108 which inserted a new s. 35 into the Companies Act 1985 (see pp. 44–5). Many of the other provisions were implemented by the Companies Act 1980, a statute which was almost entirely directive-driven, and are now consolidated in the 1985 Act. All member States have implemented this directive. Its major achievement is the introduction of a uniform disclosure system of company information in all member States. Article 11 was the subject of an important ECJ decision in Case 16/89, *Marleasing SA* v. *La Comercial International de Alimentation SA* ((1990) ECR 1–4135).

The Second Directive (OJ 1977 L 26/1).   This applies to public companies and lays down minimum requirements for the formation of the company and the maintenance, increase and reduction of capital. Companies must disclose their corporate form, name, objects, registered office, share capital, classes of shares and the composition and powers of the various organs of the company. The minimum subscribed capital of a public limited company must exceed 25,000 ECU. Capital subscribed in kind must be valued by an independent expert. There are other maintenance of capital provisions, and the Directive provides for pre-emptive rights for shareholders. Like the First Directive, the Second Directive was part of the driving force behind the Companies Acts of 1980 and 1981, now consolidated. All member States have implemented this directive.

The interpretation of the Second Directive was the subject of examination by the European Court of Justice. Two cases came before the court: Joined cases C-19 and 20/90, *Karella* v. *Minister for Industry and the Organisation for the Restructuring of Enterprises* (1991 OJ C166/12, judgement of 30 May 1991) [1994] 1 BCLC 774 and Case 381/89, *Syndesmos EEC, Vasco et al* v. *Greece et al.* (ECR, (1992) ECR 1-2111, judgement on 24 March 1992). In these cases the Court held that Arts. 25 and 29 of the Second Directive which relate to the increase of capital had direct effect in the laws of the member States and applied not only when a company was functioning normally, but also when the company was the subject of a rescue operation. The effect of the decisions was to prevent the allocation of new shares without taking into account the rights of existing shareholders and to prevent an increase in share capital before consideration of the scheme to do so by the general meeting. The Greek government could not override the interests of shareholders by pleading reasons of social policy.

This case of dubious value to company law, since it relies heavily on the idea of shareholder democracy which seems to be bolstered at the expense of the 'revitalisation of companies of particular social and economic importance'. Further, in case C-441/93, *Panagis Pafitis and Others* v. *Bank of Central Greece and Others* (12 March 1996, nyr), an increase in the capital of a bank which was made by the Greek government without the approval of the general meeting was held to be contrary to Articles 25 to 29 of the Second Directive. The Court rejected the argument that banks were not subject to the directive.

The Third Directive 1978 (OJ 1978 L 295/36). This regulates mergers between public companies where the assets and liabilities of the acquired company are transferred to the acquiring company. The shareholders of the acquiring and acquired companies receive an equivalent stake in the merged company. The necessary valuations are carried out by an independent expert. The rights of employees are covered by Directive 77/197, part of EEC Social Affairs and Employment law. This has been implemented in the UK by the Companies (Mergers and Divisions) Regulations 1987 ((SI 1987) No. 1991). A study by BDO Binder Hamlyn at the behest of the Commission shows that merger and division activity is not very common.

The Fourth Directive (OJ 1978 L 222/11). This contains detailed rules regarding the drawing up of the accounts of individual companies, and was implemented by statutes which are now to be found in Part VII of the

Companies Act 1985, but which were mostly introduced into our law by the Companies Acts of 1980 and 1981. There are amendments to this directive and the Seventh Directive, which go some way to lift the burden from small companies, but also include partnerships within the ambit of these directives (Directive 90/605/EEC, OJ 1990 L317/60 and Directive 90/604/EEC, OJ 1990 L317/57, for which see below). The directive has been implemented in all Member States, although there is increasing doubt as to whether the 'true and fair' provisions in particular bear the same meaning in different Member States; however, the ECJ has had an opportunity to set out some general principles in *Tomberger* v. *Gebruder von der Wettern GmbH (Case C-234/94)* [1996] 2 BCLC 457.

The Sixth Directive (OJ 1982 L 378/47).   This covers the division of an existing public company into entities. Member countries are not obliged to introduce this form of reconstruction but, if it is used, the process must be in conformity with the directive. The allocation of assets and liabilities among the various beneficiary companies require specific provisions to protect creditors. On any increase in capital, the existing shareholders must be given pre-emptive rights. This directive has also been implemented by the Companies (Mergers and Divisions) Regulations 1987 ((SI 1987/1991). This directive has also been implemented in all member States.

The Seventh Directive (OJ 1983 L 193/1).   The Seventh Directive specifies how and in what circumstances consolidated accounts are to be prepared and published by companies with subsidiaries. In the UK, the Companies Act 1989 has implemented this directive. The provisions of the directive were considered in *Tomberger* v. *Gebruder von der Wettern GmbH (Case C-234/94)* [1996] 2 BCLC 457 (see above).

The Seventh Directive has been implemented by France, Germany, Greece, Luxembourg and the Netherlands.

Amendments to the Fourth and Seventh Directives.   There are amendments to the Fourth and Seventh Directives. The first (Directive 90/605/EEC, OJ 1990 L317/60) seeks to prevent avoidance of the provisions of those directives by the use of partnerships. The preamble makes clear the aims. Noting that the Fourth and Seventh Directives apply only to companies, it continues:

'Whereas, within the Community there is a substantial and constantly growing number of partnerships and limited partnerships all of the fully liable members of which are constituted either as public or as private limited companies;

Whereas these fully liable members may also be companies which do not fall within the law of a Member State but which have a legal status comparable to that referred to in Directive 68/151/EEC [First Directive];

Whereas it would run counter to the spirit and aims of those Directives to allow such partnerships and partnerships with limited liability not to be subject to Community rules . . .'

To this end, the amending directive requires a name, head office and legal status of any undertaking of which a limited liability company is a fully liable member to be indicated in the accounts of such member, and imposes the obligation to draw up accounts on the members of partnerships, and to have them audited and published. The directive also attempts to fit such partnerships into the consolidated account framework and provides jurisdictional rules for this purpose. This directive has been amended by the Partnership and Unlimited Companies Regulations 1993 (SI 1993/1820).

The second amendment is to the rules for small and medium enterprises with the aim of lessening the burdens placed on small enterprises by burdensome accounting requirements. The amending directive (SI 1992/2452) changes the definition of enterprises which may qualify for exemption from the full requirements of the directive. It does this by amending Art 11 of the Fourth Directive, which was further amended in 1994 when the European Council adopted Directive 94/8 on 21st March 1994. This revision constitutes the third five yearly revision provided for under Article 53(2) of the Fourth Directive. After amendment that Article will read:

'The Member States may permit companies which on their balance sheets dates do not exceed the limits of two of the three following criteria:
- balance sheet total 250,000 ECU (replacing 200,000 ECU)
- net turnover: 5,000,000 ECU (replacing 4,000,000 ECU)
- average number of employees during the financial year: 50 to draw up abbreviated balance sheets . . .'

The article also permits member States to waive the application of Arts 15(3)(a), 15(4) to the abridged accounts. These paragraphs require that movements in the various fixed asset items by shown in the balance sheet or in the notes on the accounts.

This directive has been implemented in the UK by the Companies (Accounts of Small and Medium-Sized Enterprises and Publication of Accounts in ECU's) Regulations 1992 (90/604 EEC, OJ 1990 L317/57).

Eighth Directive (OJ 1984 L126/20). The Eighth Directive places an obligation on member States to ensure that auditors are independent and properly carry out their task of vetting company accounts. It lays down minimum requirements for the education and training of auditors. This has also been implemented by the Companies Act 1989.

Eleventh Directive on the disclosure requirements of branches of certain types of company (Directive 89/666/EEC, OJ 1989 L124/8). This directive deals with disclosures to be made in one member State by branches of companies registered in another member State or a non-EEC countries (i.e. in UK terms – an 'oversea company'). The directive recognises that a branch does not have a legal personality of its own, and it would therefore require disclosure of information concerning the company of which the branch is part, including its accounts, drawn up in accordance with the Fourth and Seventh Directives, ie in a manner consonant with ss. 228 to 230 of the Companies Act 1985, that company accounts must give a true and fair view of the state of affairs within that company or group of companies. This directive has been implemented in the UK by the Oversea Companies and Credit Financial Institutions (Branch Disclosure) Regulations 1992.

The Twelfth Directive (Directive 89/667/EEC). The Twelfth Company Law Directive embodies a proposal adopted by the European Council in December 1989 (OJ 1989 L395/40). The idea was to introduce legislation in member States to permit single member companies with limited liability. This Directive has now been implemented in the UK by the Companies (Single Member Private Limited Companies) Regulations 1992 (SI 1992/1699).

The idea is simple in essence. The single shareholder company will be introduced throughout the Community. The Commission believes that the availability of company status without the need to find another shareholder will encourage individuals to set up businesses. There is also the advantage that such businesses will have a separate legal personality, thus allowing continuity of the business even if the owners change.

The effect of the directive is to require member States to allow private limited companies to have a single member who could be either a natural person or a legal person, i.e. a company. All the shares will have to show the name of the person owning them and be held by a single shareholder.

The sole member will have to: exercise personally the powers of the general meeting; record in minutes the decisions taken under those powers; draw up in writing any agreement between the sole member and the company. Otherwise, the company will be subject to the restraints of company law in the usual way.

An alternative scheme is provided for in Article 7 of the directive. Member States are given the option of introducing legislation which would enable an individual businessman to set up an undertaking whose liability was limited to 'a sum devoted to a stated activity'. This appears to be similar to a company limited by guarantee. The detailed rules will be found in the Companies (Single Member Private Limited Companies) Regulations 1992.

Directive on the information to be published when a major holding in a listed company is acquired or disposed of. The effect of this directive on UK law will be minimal as the current UK disclosure requirements are more stringent than those contained in the directive. This Directive has been welcomed by interested UK parties as a harmonisation measure which will 'pull up' other systems towards the UK standard. This directive has been implemented by the Disclosure of Interests in Shares (Amendment) Regulations 1993, which came into force on 18 September 1993 (SI 1993/ 1819), and the Disclosure of Interests in Shares (Amendment) (No 2) Regulations 1993, which came into force on 29 October 1993.

Proposals under consideration by the Council

The Fifth Directive. This proposal has caused a great deal of controversy. In the original proposal the structure of companies would be changed so that there would be two boards of directors, an executive board and a supervisory board. That proposal has now been modified so that there can be a single board, provided that it is divided into executive and supervisory members. Further controversy has been caused by the employee participation provisions. Originally, employee participation by appointment to the board was the only model in the proposed directive. This has subsequently been modified, and employee participation can also be by way of informed consultation or by having the power of veto in certain limited circumstances over those appointed to the board. There is, nevertheless, considerable opposition to this measure, not least from the UK. The position of the UK delegation is that these types of provision are irrelevant to company law. This is a position hard for Dutch and German delegations to understand, since the division between company law and labour law is not clear-cut in those countries. Apart from these fundamental difficulties, the directive has also been criticised for the degree of detail it contains, and the complicated and rigid procedures for informing and consulting employees. UNICE, the CBI and the Law Society all fear that the enactment of the Fifth Directive would increase the burden of regulation on companies, without a commensurate increase in benefits either to the company or to employees. Unless agreement can be reached on the issues of board structure and employee participation, it is unlikely that the Fifth Directive will proceed further, and the Commission's proposal for a European Company Statute may remain blocked. In an attempt to unblock the progress of the Directive the Commission is consulting on the possibility of unblocking the participation provisions and perhaps relying on the European works council Directive. However the Parliament is opposed to this course and, in a resolution of 17 January 1997 sets out its position, arguing that the establishment of a works council is not equivalent to participation at board level and suggesting that the minimum standards should be:

'for the dual board system a seat for workers on the supervisory board and in the single board system an institution which will agree, with the management of the firm, on opportunities for participation in economic matters and on the obligation of employers to negotiate in respect of decisions concerning the workers'.

According to the preamble to the Directive, the main objectives of the proposal are (a) to ensure that the laws of Member States regarding the structure of public companies and the function of their organs are co-ordinated in order that they shall give equivalent protection to members and others; and (b) to require Member States to observe common principles regarding employee participation in the management of those companies. Originally this objective was to be achieved by introducing a compulsory two-tier system of management consisting of separate management and supervisory boards. However, the latest drafts of the directive permit the adoption of a 'one-tier' system of management. Two aspects of the current draft call for close analysis in order to assess the probable impact of the Directive on UK law, although there are a number of other problems not within these categories. For example, the application of the draft directive on groups is most uncertain. If the Directive remains unchanged there will also be difficulties in implementing the provisions with regard to the liability of directors (discussed in more detail under 'Directors' Duties', Chapter 11) and the provisions permitting action by members in a way which will make considerable inroads on the rule in *Foss* v. *Harbottle* (discussed in 'Minority Rights', Chapter 13). The two major aspects of the Directive are:

1. The provisions concerning the management structure of the Company.
2. The provisions for the involvement of employees.

The structure of the company
The Directive is limited to public companies (Article 1). It sets out two basic models for company management. Within these two models various alternatives are available.

(a) *The two-tier model*   The basic structure is set out in Article 3(a) which provides that 'The company shall be managed by a management organ under the supervision of a supervisory organ'. The idea of this provision is that the supervisory organ should appoint and supervise the work of a management organ, which would in turn run the day to day affairs of the PLC. A member of the management must be specifically appointed to be in charge of personnel matters and employee relations. The members of the management organ are to be appointed by the supervisory organ where employees may elect some of the members of the supervisory organ. Where one of the alternative forms of employee participation is adopted, the members of both organs may be elected by the general meeting.

Only natural persons (i.e. humans as opposed to companies) may be members of the management organ (Article 5), and where a company is appointed to a supervisory board it must designate a 'permanent' (immortal?) representative who will be subject to the same conditions and obligations as if he were personally a member of the supervisory organ.

No person may be a member of both boards. Article 7 provides that the first appointments may last for three years only, the remainder for a maximum of six years. Neither board may fix the pay of its members and the management organ may not fix the pay of the supervisory board (Article 8). A member of the management organ is prohibited from carrying on any professional activity outside the company without the prior authorisation of the supervisory organ. In the case of the supervisory organ, members may not be appointed until full disclosure of other posts held has been made to the appointing body and those entitled to object to the appointment. Any professional activity taken up after appointment must be disclosed to the management and supervisory bodies.

The supervisory board must authorise all transactions not within the normal business of the company if the transaction is one in which a member of either board has an interest, even if only an indirect interest (Article 10). The interested party must not take part in the decision to go ahead with the transaction.

These conflict-of-interest provisions could be cumbersome and restrictive if 'normal business' were narrowly defined and 'indirect interest' widely defined. While not in principle different from English law in that a director must not put himself into a situation where his duty and interest are in conflict, this method of dealing with such situations shows a degree of inflexibility.

There are currently two alternative drafts which cover the situation where a transaction has been concluded with a third party without the necessary authorisation by the supervisory board. Both would prevent the company relying on lack of authorisation in order to avoid the consequences of the transaction. The first alternative contains an exception which would permit the company to avoid the transaction, where the company proves that the third party was aware of the absence of authorisation 'or could not have been unaware thereof'. The second draft would not in any event allow the company to avoid the transaction because of absence of authorisation.

Article 10.a provides that the members of each board are to be considered as having equal duties and responsibilities. It is difficult to see exactly what this means when the some of the members in the 'single board' system will be managers and others will be supervisors. It may be that this Article only means that there can be no 'sleeping' directors who take no part in the running of the company but lend their name to the company to increase its respectability in the eyes of the public. This Article also provides that the members of the board act in the interests of the company 'having regard in particular to the interests of its shareholders and employees'. The members of the board have a duty of confidentiality (Article 10.3). This could cause difficulties where employee directors wished to give information to the people who elected them. If they give the information they may be in breach of their duty of confidentiality. If they do not they may irritate those who elected them and lose the next election.

The management organ is required to report to the supervisory board at least every three months and the supervisory board has the power to require a report by the management board at any time. The supervisory board also has extensive rights to require information and undertake investigations (Article 11).

One of the most important powers held by the supervisory board is the power to dismiss the management board (Article 13). Where employees do not elect the supervisory board and have no power to object to appointments to that board, Member States may provide that the general meeting may also dismiss the members of the management organ. Article 13.2 provides that the members of the supervisory board (other than those appointed by employees) may be dismissed by the people who appointed them or by a court or tribunal for a stated reason. It also provides that members of either organ have a right to speak in their own defence prior to any decision to dismiss them. If dismissal is not for a good reason the dismissed member will be entitled to compensation. The prominence of the supervisory board in dismissal of the management organ would require a fundamental revision of the English law principle that the management are accountable only to the shareholders. Whether a supervisory board would be a more effective watchdog than the shareholders is a matter for speculation.

(b) *The one-tier model*   In this model only one board, 'the administrative organ', governs the company and its affairs. In companies employing on average less than 1000 members the administrative organ is to be appointed by the general meeting and the executive member of the board (who will run the company's day-to-day affairs – a managing director) is to be elected from the appointed board by the administrative body acting by a majority. Member States may allow the general meeting to both appoint the members of the board and elect the executive member. Apart from the formal division into executive and non-executive members, a division which occurs in practice in any event, small PLCs would seem to be little affected by the advent of the Directive. Power to dismiss the executives would lie with the general meeting as well as with the board (Articles 21.a.2 and Article 21.t) but it may be questioned if this will in fact change the balance of power within companies.

The basic one-tier system is set out in Article 21.a. This provides that the minimum number of members of the administrative organ is three. The management of the company is to be delegated to executive members of the board, the number of executive members being less than the number of the other members and the member particularly responsible for personnel being specified. This provision, coupled with the power of dismissal of the executive members by the administrative organ means that the non-executives will have the power to dismiss the executive members of the board. How real the threat of dismissal would be must be a matter for debate. The United States experience seems to be that hiring and firing remains the province of the Chief Executive Officer, whatever the theoretical powers of the 'outside directors'.

As with the two-tier scheme, where members of the administrative organ are companies, they must designate a permanent delegate whose potential liability is unlimited. There is also a limit of three years on the duration of the appointment of members of the first board and six years thereafter, members being eligible for re-election.

The members of the administrative organ may not fix their own pay but may fix the extra pay that the executive members will receive for managing the day-to-day affairs of the company (Article 21.n). The Directive does not make it clear who is to fix the basic pay, presumably this will be a matter for the shareholders.

The provisions requiring disclosure and authorisation of outside professional activities are similar to those detailed above in relation to the two-tier structure.

Where a member of the board has an interest in a transaction the whole board must authorise it (Article 21.o). This obviously provides less of a safeguard than the two-tier system, where the authorisation of the supervisory board is required when the interested party is a member of the management organ. As with the two-tier structure, there are provisions prohibiting a member from taking part in a decision in which he has an interest, and a requirement that all decisions to go ahead with transactions where a member of the board is interested must be communicated to the next general meeting (Article 10). Similarly, there are still alternative texts relating to the effect of lack of authorisation on where the company enters into a transaction with a third party. Text 2 would absolutely prevent lack of authorisation having any effect on a contract with a third party. Text 1 provides for an exception to that rule in a situation where the company proves that the third party was aware of the lack of authorisation or could not be unaware of it.

Article 21.q is in the same terms as Article 10.a so far as the duties and potential liabilities of the members of the administrative organ are concerned. Similarly, the duties of reporting, the rights of investigation and the rights to documents and information are in terms similar to the provisions for the two-tier system. Throughout, the difference is that the duties lie on the executive members of the board and the rights belong to the whole board and each of its members (Article 11 and Articles 21.q and r).

The dismissal provisions are similar to provisions in the two-tier schemes (Articles 12 and 13), and the same provisions as to civil liability apply to both schemes (Article 9 and Article 21.u applying Articles 14–21).

The Directive has been opposed partly because the imposition of compulsory structures has been seen as a restriction on the current right of the shareholders to choose a system of management. A partial answer to this is that the role of shareholders of a large public corporation in influencing management may be a very limited one, particularly where there has been a wide dissemination of shares. In fact, as the Directive now stands, it is questionable whether the structure of many corporations would have to be altered at all. Compliance with the Directive would merely mean that the status quo had been legally recognised. Many companies have boards divided into executive and non-executive directors, and in the one-tier system the roles of the directors are defined only by the requirement that the management of the company is to be delegated to the executive members of the board (Article 21). The other members of the board may fulfil the roles currently played by non-executive directors, who may be supervisors or consultants. It seems that the amendments made to the original proposal (which would have made the two-tier board compulsory) have reflected UK practice if not UK law. There seems to be little objection in bringing the law into step with practice.

The provisions for the involvement of employees
Article 4 sets out the alternative schemes for employee participation. Member States have a discretion as to the application of the scheme to small companies. They can decide how large a company must be before schemes become compulsory. However, that discretion is limited by the provision in Article 4.1, that where companies employ on average over 1000 people, Member States must make the adoption of one of the schemes compulsory. The discretion given is a discretion to fix a lower figure of employees as a trigger to the adoption of the employee participation schemes. The number of employees is calculated as an average over two consecutive years (Article 4.3). There is also a discretion permitting Member States to provide that employee participation shall not be implemented in respect of a company when a majority of the employees has expressed its opposition to such participation.

The employee participation schemes
(a)   Employee participation in the appointment of the members of the supervisory organ (Article 4.b).
In this scheme, between one third and one half of the supervisory board are to be appointed by the employees of the company. Where employees appoint one half of the members of the supervisory board, the way votes are calculated must ensure that decisions are ultimately taken by the members appointed by the general meeting (Article 4.b(2)).
   An alternative method of appointment of the supervisory organ permits the appointment of members by co-optation by that board. In this case the general meeting (or a designated committee of the general meeting) or the representatives of the employees will have a right to object to the appointment of a proposed candidate either because he lacks the ability to carry out his duties or because if he were appointed the supervisory body would 'having regard to the interests of the company, the shareholders and the employees, be "improperly constituted"'. The meaning of this

phrase is unclear. Because of the context in which it appears it would seem to have a meaning beyond simply a board whose constitution contravenes the letter of the Directive. In such cases the appointment is not to be made unless the objection is declared unfounded by an independent body existing under public law (Article 4.c).

(b) Employee participation through a body representing company employees (Article 4.d).

In this case, a body representing the employees will have a right to regular information and consultation on the administration, situation, progress and prospects of the company together with its competitive position, credit situation and investment plans. The body representing the employees will also have the same right to information as is conferred on the supervisory body by Article 11. These include a right to a three-monthly report by the management on the progress of the company's affairs, in particular on 'the turnover and the state of the company'. As well as the regular report, the employees will be able to require a report from the management organ at any time on 'certain aspects' of the company's affairs and may require from the management organ the production of all information and documents 'necessary in the exercise of its duties'.

The body representing the employees would also have to be consulted by the supervisory organ before it granted authorisation for certain actions (to be specified under Article 12). Where the supervisory organ does not comply with the opinion of the employees it must provide reasons for its failure to do so. The body representing employees must meet regularly, at least immediately before every meeting of the supervisory board; must be given all the documentation and information connected with the agenda of the supervisory board 'needed for its deliberations'; and may require the attendance of the chairman of the supervisory board, his deputy or a member of the management organ.

(c) Employee participation through collectively agreed systems.

By this, alternative employee participation is to be regulated in accordance with collective agreements concluded between the company and organisations representing employees. The minimum contents of such agreements are specified (Article 4.e). Such agreements are to provide for one of the following:

(i) appointment of between one third and one half of the supervisory organ by the employees;

(ii) appointment of the supervisory board by co-optation but with the employee representatives having a right to object, which will prevent the appointment unless the objection is declared unfounded by an independent body existing under public law.

(iii) employee representatives to have the rights explained in (b) (employee participation through a body representing company employees – see above).

These, then, are the alternative models, one of which must be adopted by companies with an average of over 1,000 employees. Principles to govern the election of employee representatives are also laid down (Article 4.i). Both the members of bodies representing employees and, where the employees are electing members of the supervisory board, those members, are to be elected using a system of proportional representation 'ensuring that members are protected'. All employees must be able to participate in the election which must be by secret ballot. Further, free expression of opinion must be guaranteed.

So far as the option providing for the co-optation of members and the employees' right to object is concerned, the Law Society's Standing Committee on Company Law commented as follows: 'This does not offer an option equivalent to the other methods of participation which are made available by the Directive. The employees are given no right to nominate candidates and, while their representatives can object to an appointment, they have no right to object to any member of the supervisory board remaining in office.' The comment goes on to point out the lack of a definition of the expression 'improperly constituted'. It is one of the two grounds which enable an employee to object to an appointment, that the appointment would cause the board to be 'improperly constituted'. The other ground is 'lack of ability'.

The Committee is right to conclude that this method of participation is not equivalent to the others, but for that reason it might be of particular interest to some who have objected to the Directive on the grounds that it would cause a radical restructuring of the whole system of company law. In fact Article 4.c provides for only a negative and minimum degree of interference. A company would, of course, also have to comply with the restructuring provisions detailed above, but this could be done simply by separation of executive and non-executive members of the board (there need only be one board). These provisions might not be a major problem in practice.

It may also be argued that the 'representative body' option would not need any far-reaching changes in company law. However, while this option could be easily accommodated in the present company law structure it might be difficult to reconcile with present trade union practices. It would, however, be interesting to know if there are companies which already comply with the Directive in respect of the provision of information, particularly where there has been a single union agreement signed.

The CBI object to the inclusion of the employee participation proposals in the draft Directive on several grounds. In particular it believes that employee participation should not be the subject of legislation, as the likely outcome of such intervention will be loss of flexibility. As for these particular proposals the CBI point to the potential delays that will occur in decision-making if the consultation procedures are followed. They also point to the possible conflict between employees concerned with the short-term welfare of the company and the long-term future of the company. So far as employees actually elected to the board are concerned, a serious conflict-of-interests problem could arise since they would, with other board members, be bound to act 'in the interests of the company having regard in particular to the interests of its shareholders and employees' (Article 21.q, one-tier board). This will prevent an employee member from solely representing the interests of those whose votes put him on the board, a matter which may well cause resentment. Further, the duty of confidentiality imposed on board members may still further distance an employee board member and his constituents.

While all the criticisms detailed above have some force, it may well be that the overall problem with implementing such proposals in the UK will be the lack of will to comply. However, if the consultation and provision of information provisions were made a little less formal and rigid, this Directive could be implemented here with the minimum upheaval and, by standardising the expectation of employees, could be of assistance in labour relations.

The implementation of the draft Fifth Directive would not be a major disaster as some have feared, nor, indeed, would it cause a major upheaval if companies chose to take the 'lowest common denominator' approach and keep a single-tier board, involving employees only by providing information and consultation. However, it must be questioned whether the whole exercise will not merely be a case of encouraging red tape and the feeling that if the letter of the regulations is observed, no effort needs to be put into the true improvement of labour relationships. The major criticism of both the management and the employee provisions is that they restrict the freedom of companies to manoeuvre and could prevent swift and effective response to changing conditions. The calculation that must be made is to determine whether benefits to labour relations are real or ephemeral and balance any real benefits against the possibility of stultification of freedom of manoeuvre. The alterations to the structure of boards of large PLCs are likely to be minimal.

The Tenth Directive (OJ 1985 C23 28/11). This directive concerns cross-border mergers and is progressing no further because fears have been expressed that a cross-border merger could be a way of escaping from worker participation provisions. Thus it awaits agreement on that issue.

Draft Proposal for a Ninth Directive (not formally adopted by the Commission). In 1984 a draft of a proposal which would be concerned with the conduct of groups of companies was circulated. There is no immediate prospect of work on this project resuming.

18.7 **Securities Regulation**

Implemented directives

Directive of 5 March 1979 co-ordinating the conditions for the admission of securities to stock exchange listing (OJ 22 L66/21). This directive forbids the admission of securities to a stock exchange listing unless the conditions laid down in the directive are satisfied. The conditions include requirements as to the legal position and minimum size of the company, the free negotiability of the shares, and the proportion of the shares that must be held by the public (usually 25 per cent or more).

Directive of 15 March 1980 on the listing particulars to be published for the admission of securities to official stock exchange listing (OJ 23 L100/1, OJ L185/81). This lays down detailed requirements as to the information which must be published in the form of 'listing particulars' before a company's securities may be admitted to trading on a stock exchange. The directive also requires the listing particulars to be approved before publication by a competent authority. Once the listing particulars have been approved by the competent authorities in one member State, the directive requires other member States to recognise the listing particulars as sufficient, with the exception that each member State may require additional information specific to the market within its jurisdiction. The directive also provides for the recognition of a prospectus as listing particulars, where a prospectus meets the requirements of the directive.

Directive on the continuing disclosure of information (OJ 25 L48/26). As its name implies, this directive provides for the publication of information by companies after an initial listing on an exchange.

Directive co-ordinating the requirements for drawing up, scrutiny and distribution of the prospectus to be published when transferable securities are offered to the public (OJ 32 L124/8).This directive requires a prospectus to be published when securities are to be offered to the public for the first time by a company not seeking a listing on a recognised stock exchange at that time. The details of the information which is to be made public appear in the directive. The directive also provides for the mutual recognition of prospectuses drawn up in accordance with Directive 80/390, both as prospectuses and listing particulars (see p. 000). This regime will be extended by:

The directive amending Directive 80/390 EEC in respect of mutual recognition of prospectuses as listing particulars. The Council adopted this directive on 23 April 1990. It requires that a public offer prospectus which has been approved in the issuer's home Member State, and which complies with the conditions laid down for listing particulars, will be recognised as listing particulars in other member States. It also extends the mutual recognition of listing particulars and prospectuses. This directive has been implemented in the United Kingdom by the Public Offers of Securities Regulations (1995 SI 1995 No. 1537 – see Chapter 7).

The Insider Dealing Directive (OJ 32 L334/30).
This directive creates a detailed set of rules which will impose liability on legal or natural persons if they misuse information about companies, if that information is price-sensitive. The directive is a minimum standards measure, ie member States are free to go further than the directive requires. It requires member States to make insider dealing unlawful, and to co-operate in obtaining and exchanging information about it for enforcement purposes.

Implementation was by the Criminal Justice Act 1993 which came into force in March 1994 (see Chapter 12). The new law is extremely complex and only a few prosecutions have been brought under its provisions.

Directives adopted by the Council

The Investment Services Directive. This directive was adopted in July 1993 (OJ 19898 L386/32).

The idea is that 'investment firms' should gain authorisation from their 'home' State. This authorisation would then act as a passport to enable them to carry on that investment business in other Member States (Articles 1, 4). The service in question could be provided on a cross-border basis within the Community, or the investment firm in question will be permitted to set up branches in the other member States without needing to be authorised again.

Proposals being considered by the Council

The Thirteenth Directive on Takeovers (OJ 32 C64/8). An original proposal was adopted by the Commission at the end of 1988. It has raised fears in the UK that the Takeover Panel may have to be established on a statutory footing, although the current wording does not make this certain. It contains a number of rules to be found in the City Code on Takeovers and Mergers, but many commentators believe that it will increase litigation and prevent the authority overseeing takeovers from acting with as much flexibility as the Panel. In February 1996 the Commission issued a new proposal (COM (95) 655 final) which is described as a 'framework' directive. It relies on general principles, most of which are to be found in the City Code on Takeovers and Mergers, but the DTI still believes that it will increase litigation and prevent the authority overseeing takeovers from acting with as much flexibility as the Panel. A DTI consultative document dated April 1996 invited views on the new draft directive and the House of Lords Select Committee on the European Communities has produced a report on the directive (Session 1995–6, 13th Report, HL paper 100).

The Barriers to Takeovers Initiative.   In 1989 a comprehensive analysis of barriers to takeovers in the Community was undertaken at the behest of the UK Department of Trade and Industry. Identification of a number of barriers has led to the Commission submitting a number of proposals to the Council in order to assist the removal of a number of the perceived difficulties. The proposals consist of amendments to the Second Company Law Directive and to the draft Fifth and Thirteenth Company Law Directives. The effects would be to extend the rules on the acquisition of own shares by a company to the situation where the shares are acquired by a subsidiary of that company, to reduce the possibility of frustrating action after the announcement of a takeover bid by restricting the power of the board of an offeree company to acquire the company's own shares after a bid has been announced, to strengthen the rights of shareholders to nominate, appoint and dismiss directors, and to strengthen the provision in the Fifth Directive which provides for equal voting rights for shareholders.

18.8 Insolvency

The Council of Europe Bankruptcy Convention

This is not an EU initiative but emanated from the Council of Europe. The intention of the Convention is to provide a framework for insolvencies where assets are situated within the territory of more than one signatory. The idea is to establish a primary liquidation or bankruptcy conducted by a 'liquidator' with powers to act in other States where assets are situated. If the need arises for a 'secondary' bankruptcy proceeding in another State, this could be established but would normally be subordinate to the main procedure.

The EC Bankruptcy Convention (Adopted October 1995 and signed by all Member States save the UK which withheld signature because of the 'beef crisis')

Based on Article 220 of the Treaty, this Convention will apply to insolvency proceedings involving the disinvestment of the debtor. This will exclude rescue procedures such as Administration in the UK. Both this proposal and the Council of Europe Convention deal with company insolvency as well as the insolvency of individuals.

Jurisdiction

Jurisdiction to open insolvency proceedings is given to the contracting State in whose territory the centre of the debtor's main interests is situated. There is a presumption that the centre of main interests of a company or other legal person is at the place of registered or statutory office.

Applicable Law

The law applicable is to be the law governing insolvency in the State where the proceedings are opened. There is a reference to national law as opposed to internal law in the relevant Article, so it is presumed that conflict of laws rules will apply. Nevertheless, the Convention permits the opening of secondary bankruptcies in certain situations and thus opens the possibility of proceedings being started in two or more jurisdictions with differing laws applying to the whole bankruptcy. This means that the principle of universality (i.e. a single law applying to the whole proceeding) has been abandoned and conflicts between different priority rules will inevitably arise.

Recognition of insolvency proceedings

The Convention provides that an insolvency proceeeding, once validly commenced, shall be recognised in all other contracting States. The insolvency proceeding is to have the effect which it has in the State where the proceeding was commenced. If this had been unqualified it would have imported true universality. However, as already mentioned, it is subject to the right to open secondary insolvency proceedings.

Liquidator's powers

The liquidator is to have in all contracting States the powers which are conferred on him by the State where the proceedings are opened. further, the liquidator will have the power to remove assets from any jurisdiction which is a signatory State to the Convention.

Relationship between main and secondary jurisdictions

Having strayed fron the principle of universality, the Convention has the difficult task of determining the relationship between the two sets of proceedings. There is a duty laid on the primary and secondary liquidators to communicate promptly with one another. Further, a secondary liquidation can be stayed for up to three months at the request of the liquidator in the main proceedings provided that interest is paid to preferential or secured creditors. A composition in the secondary proceedings may not become final without the consent of the liquidator in the main proceeding. Such consent cannot be witheld if the financial interests of the creditors in the main proceeding are not affected by the composition. Any surplus remaining in a secondary bankruptcy after payment of all claims must be passed to the main liquidator.

The Francovich Directive (Directive 80/987/EEC)

This directive concerns the protection of employees in the event of the insolvency of their employer (OJ L283/23). It was the non-implementation of this directive that led to the European Court of Justice's decision in Joined Cases C-6 and 9/90, *Francovich and Boniface* v. *Italian Republic* ([1992] ECR 133). An Italian company went into insolvent liquidation leaving the plaintiff and others with unpaid arrears of salary. Italy had not set up a compensation scheme to cover this situation. It was required to do so by the terms of Council Directive 80/987/EEC of 20 October 1980 on the approximation of the laws of the member States relating to the protection of employees in the event of the insolvency of their employer (OJ 1980 L283/23).

According to Art 11 of the directive, member States were bound to bring into force the laws, regulations and administrative provisions necessary to comply with the directive by 23 October 1983. The Commission, in its role as Community policeman brought an enforcement action against Italy under Art. 169 of the EEC Treaty. In its judgment in that case (*Commission* v. *Italy*) the ECJ found that the Italian Republic had failed to comply with its obligations under the directive.

From the plaintiff's point of view the situation remained unsatisfactory. He had still received no money. He brought proceedings in Italy claiming compensation from the Italian State for failure to implement properly Directive 80/897/EEC. The Italian courts submitted the question of Mr Francovich's entitlement to damages to the ECJ by way of a preliminary reference under Art 177 of the EEC Treaty. The ECJ held that in these circumstances the plaintiff was entitled to compensation.

The Money Laundering Directive (Directive 91/308 EEC OJ 1991 L166/77)

This is a Council directive on the prevention of the use of the financial system for the purpose of money laundering.

Money laundering is the intentional:

(a) conversion or transfer of property, in the knowledge that such property is derived from criminal activity, for the purpose of concealing or disguising the illicit origin of the property, or of assisting any person who is involved in such activity to evade the legal consequences of his action;

(b) concealment or disguise of the nature, source, location, disposition, movement, rights with respect to, or ownership of, property, in the knowledge that such property is derived from criminal activity, or from an act of participation in such activity;

(c) acquisition, possession or use of property in the knowledge, at the time of receipt, that such property was derived from criminal activity, or from an act of participation in such activity; and

(d) participation in, association or conspiracy to commit, attempts to commit and aiding, abetting, facilitating and counselling the commission of any of the actions established in the previous paragraphs.

Implementation in the UK is by the Criminal Justice Act 1993 and regulations made in accordance with the Act (The Money Laundering Regulations 1993 SI 1993 No, 1933).

The directive for informing and consulting employees of groups

This directive has been adopted by the Council (OJ 254/64)

Based on Art 100 of the EEC Treaty, the proposal has its roots in the Social Charter. Indent 5 of the preamble provides:

'Whereas point 17 of the Community Charter of Fundamental Social Rights of Workers provides, inter alia, that information and consultation for workers must be developed along appropriate lines, taking account of the practices in force in the various Member States; whereas the Charter states that "this shall apply especially in companies having establishments in two or more Member States . . ."'

The preamble also stresses the likelihood of increased merger and cross-border activity and continues:

'if economic activities are to develop in a harmonious fashion, this situation requires that undertakings and groups of undertakings operating in more than one Member State must inform and consult the representatives of their employees affected by their decisions.'

The directive is historically linked to the 'Vredling Directive', which laid down procedures for informing and consulting employees of undertakings with 'complex structures' (OJ Vol 26C 217/3). The directive lays down requirements for informing and consulting employees in all undertakings, or groups of undertakings, which operate in more than one Member State and employ more than 1000 employees within the Community, including at least 100 employees at two different establishments in different Member States.

Such undertakings must set up a European works council which will be the channel for informing and consulting employees. The directive does not yet apply to UK companies because of the opt-out negotiated by the previous government but following the election of the Labour government reversal of this position is expected. In any event, a number of UK companies have chosen to form European works councils.

18.9 **Conclusion**

It is clear from the above summary that a great deal has been done. Company law harmonisation is aimed at the realisation of a complete freedom of establishment. It is said to be necessary in order to avoid distortions in the market, which may result from the use of freedom of establishment in such a way that member States which have a well-developed company law are put into a disadvantageous position. Unless a minimum degree of harmonisation has taken place, a 'Delaware effect' is feared, ie companies will prefer to incorporate in a member State because of the liberal company law in that State, in the same way that a majority of public companies incorporate in the State of Delaware in the USA. However, it is by no means clear that freedom of establishment can be achieved by harmonisation of the sort described above. A significant difficulty is the failure to harmonise tax regimes. There has been some progress in this field recently (Council Directive of 23 July 1990 on the Common System of Taxation Guidelines in the Case of a Parent Company and Subsidiaries of Different Member States and Council Directive 91/308 EEC OJ 1991 L166/77). Even leaving that problem aside, the mode of harmonisation by directive will not create a completely uniform set of laws and a completely 'level playing field'. The importance of companies, and the importance of increasing their freedom of establishment, are undeniable. Two problems have arisen from the directives which have sought to achieve harmonisation. First, in order to make sure that implementing legislation has a harmonising effect, the directive must itself be detailed and inflexible. It has been argued that the directives are too detailed, and that they risk petrifying company law. Even so, it is likely that there will be minor differences in member States after implementation. The detailed provisions may lead to a 'blocking effect'. The procedure for modifying an adopted directive is burdensome. the danger that the law will not accord with business practice is therefore very real. Despite the detail in the directives, there remain significant differences between company regimes in member States. The burden of regulations on companies has also increased.

Secondly, the harmonisation programme has been unable so far to create a 'European outlook' for companies. Harmonisation by directive is unlikely to do so, as implementation is by incorporation into national laws. An alternative approach has, as a herald, the introduction of the EEIG. This cross between a small company and a partnership with non-profit motives is remarkable as it is a supra-national 'European' institution. It may be that a European Company Statute introduced by regulation could achieve harmonisation, in the sense that all countries would have available the same basic structure for a company. The current proposal for a European company is unlikely to achieve this aim, however, as the laws of the member States are relied on heavily to fill in gaps left by the Statute. There is a grave danger of creating 15 different 'European companies'.

Summary

1 The EU harmonisation programme is composed of a number of measures designed to create a uniform company law throughout Europe.
2 Although a number of measures have become law, the harmonisation that has been achieved is not considerable because a number of obstacles have become apparent.
3 The most significant of these has been the inability of the Member States to agree on taxation of companies, the treatment of groups of companies and worker participation provisions.
4 Other problems have appeared because the programme has consisted mostly of Directives which need implementation in each of the Member States. Some of them contain options which means that even after implementation of the Directives there is no consistency in company law throughout the Member States.
5. In other cases there have been differences in implementation measures with the same result. Much still needs to be done to remove the obstacles to companies operating easily throughout the Member States.

Exercises

1 Describe the process by which a Directive becomes law in this country.
2 Identify three major changes which have been or will be brought about by the harmonisation programme.
3 What are the advantages and disadvantages of the worker participation schemes contained in the Fifth Directive?
4 What new forms of business organisations will be available when the harmonisation programme is complete?

19 The New Company Laws of Eastern Europe

In Chapter 3 various possible models of companies were discussed. As Eastern European States emerge from economies where property was state-owned and no vehicles existed for private enterprise, they are having to invent their own versions of company law. It is interesting to examine some of the strucures which are emerging. This chapter examines the company law in Kazakhstan, Hungary, Poland, and the Czech Republic.

The models in the various jurisdictions are not clear cut, however, and distinct differences exist between the various types of enterprise in each country and across the jurisdictions. The way in which the law treats the property of the enterprise affords significant clues to the way in which the company is viewed.

19.1 The Property of the Enterprise

In Kazakhstan the property of an enterprise is defined as:

'the basic funds and the circulating assets derived from the capital put in by the founders as well as revenues received from bank loans and from economic activity as well as from "any other source not prohibited by law".'

In Hungary and Poland the law protects the right of a company to acquire property in its own right but does not provide an insight into the relationship between the entity and its property, whereas the original Czech definition of an enterprise in relation to its property revealed much about the model of company envisaged as it included 'all its tangible and intangible assets and the skills applied by its staff to its business activity' (this has now been changed; see below). The attitude to company property thus revealed would seem to indicate that, in 1991, only the Czech law envisaged an enterprise or associative model, the others complied much more closely to ownership or contractual models. The subsequent amendment of the Czech Commercial Code gives further credence to this analysis. It appears to bring Czech law into line with the others by introducing a more limited definition of a commercial concern. New s. 5 of the Czech Commerical Code reads:

'for the purposes of this Code, an enterprise is understood to be the aggregate of the tangible, personal, and intangible components of business activity. Things, rights and other property values belonging to the entrepreneur which are used, or because of their nature are intended for use, in the operation of the enterprise, belong to the enterprise.'

It is arguable that this wide definition of a company still includes staff and their skills, but the deliberate excising of them from the previous definition points to a contrary view.

19.2 **Structures of Boards and Shareholders**

Close examination of other factors such as the structure of boards and the rights and duties of shareholders reveals a more diverse picture.

Poland

The Polish models both for private and public companies give much power to the shareholders, providing for the appointment and removal of the management and supervisory boards by them. However, the wide powers of control given to the shareholders meeting in private companies is not reflected in the rules for public companies, which are much more closely controlled by additional financial and accounting control. This would indicate that the closely held corporations are seen as corresponding to the contractual model, to be controlled by their private owners, whereas public companies are to be much more to be the province of external state control, closer to the idea that state property is being administered, remote from idea of private contractual shareholder ownership.

Hungary

The Hungarian limited liability company gives similar powers to the shareholders to elect and dismiss the members of the boards but some interesting provisions point away from the conclusion that a simple ownership or contractual model has been adopted. Thus, members may not vote on any resolutions in which they have an interest (Art. 187 of the Hungarian Commercial Code). Article 188 of the Hungarian Commercial Code imposes a duty of care on members exercising their vote:

> 'Members who adopt a resolution which they knew, or could have reasonably been expected to have known, would obviously impair the major interests of the company, bear unlimited and joint liability for any damage so arising'.

Such duties placed on shareholders significantly depart from the idea that the company belongs to the shareholders and thus from the notion that they can manipulate it according to their own wishes. In this version the interests of the company are paramount when important issues are at stake. The denial of the shareholders' right to act selfishly on all occasions indicates a rejection of the simple contractual ownership model in favour of making the company's own rights paramount. In determining the company's rights and interests more factors are important than simply the shareholders' wishes. This accords with the idea that shareholders have two rights as a result of their ownership of shares. This idea is at the root of the associative model discussed above, and has been analysed by Leader (1995), who describes the two property rights which shareholders gain through share ownership as being (a) personal right, which is essentially an ordinary contractual right permitting the shareholder to act selfishly to protect the value of shares, and (b) a further derivative right to be exercised in the interests of the company. This right may be exercised in order to make sure that the company is properly run in its own best interests. This author has argued that there has been increasing acceptance in the United Kingdom of the paramount importance of the company's interests which is seen in the acceptance of the importance of the interests of constituency groups other than shareholders. It may be argued that UK company law is moving towards a model of a company in which shareholders must take account of more than their own immediate interests when determining policy. Increasingly the company is recognised as an entity quite separate from its owners. There is clear recognition of other interests which must be taken account of when decisions are made by management. There is increasing acceptance of the inability of majorities to drive the company in whichever direction they wish. The point is reinforced by the attitude of the courts to the question of alteration of the articles of association. The UK and Hungarian models may therefore not be as dissimilar as might be expected.

Kazakhstan

In Kazakhstan the General Provisions provide that the appointment of managers is primarily a matter to be determined by the charter of each enterprise. However, some emphasis is laid on the 'right of the owner' of the enterprise to determine the managers either directly or through the bodies to whom such power is delegated. The 'director' of an enterprise has full powers to represent the enterprise.

So far as Kazak joint stock companies are concerned Article 70(2) provides that the general meeting is to be the highest management organ. The establishment of a supervisory board is optional. Article 70 contains a fairly extensive list of decisions which are to be within the exclusive competence of the general meeting. These rights include changes to the Charter. It would be the Charter which would set out the rights and responsibilities of any supervisory board. Employee rights are governed by laws separate to those setting out the corporate structures. This model would seem to give very considerable power (in theory at least) to the shareholders and may fall into the commonly identified pitfall for this contractual model of in fact giving too much power to the executive. In a partnership with limited liability a wholly different management is the rule, providing for an executive body which is controlled by an audit commission. Participants (partners) have voting rights and a right to apply to the court to nullify decisions of the executive. The details of how this skeleton structure is to work is left to the individual partnership agreements. In view of this and the lack of detailed consideration of the constitutional workings of these structures by the courts, it is difficult to clearly identify the relevant model. It appears, however, that the participants or shareholders are powerful, but in the case of a limited partnership are to be controlled by an audit commission. Control of the management by the shareholders of a joint stock company is the clear intention, thus probably falling into the contractual model category and the trap of unsupervised management.

19.3 **The Czech Example**

In a Czech limited liability company the general meeting has wide powers, including the amendment of both the memorandum and articles of association and the appointment and dismissal of the executives and members of the supervisory board. Where there is a supervisory board it does not therefore follow the classic German model, which is an option in the EU Fifth Directive and European Company Statute. Both these latter models give power to the supervisory board to hire and fire executives. The supervisory board may be elected partly by the general meeting, partly by a 'person named in the articles' and partly by the general meeting. In the Czech model the power remains with the general meeting, which may effectively exercise it because of the maximum of 50 members. Further, s. 126 provides that it is a duty of a participant to attend the general meeting either in person or by proxy and that a member of either the executive or the supervisory board cannot act as a proxy.

A quorum is representation of half of the votes with one vote per 1000 crowns unless the memorandum specifies a different allocation of votes. There must be a meeting annually. For most decisions a simple majority is sufficient. The memorandum may require a greater majority on any issue, but changes to articles and memorandum, increase or reduction of capital, approval of promoter's actions or the winding up the company require at least a two-thirds majority. Participants with 10 per cent or more of the registered capital may convene a general meeting.

Executives

Limitations on the authority of executives to bind the company may be present in the memorandum or articles but will not affect third parties (s. 133(2) Czech Commerical Code). The executives have a duty to arrange for the keeping of proper files and accounts and an express duty to keep participants informed.

Section 136 prohibits competitive conduct. The company may demand the return of profits made by a wide range of competitive actions including concluding in the executive's own name and for his/her own account 'business transactions which are related to the business activity of the company'. Further, the executive must not negotiate company business for other persons, be a partner with unlimited liability in another business or be on the board of another company unless the companies are related by one having a business interest in the other.

Supervisory Board

A supervisory board must be established if the memorandum so provides. It must have at least three members and its job is essentially to supervise the executives and submit reports on the company's documentation to the general meeting. The provisions on anti-competitive conduct apply equally to members of the supervisory board and one of their duties is to convene a general meeting 'if the interests of the company so requires'.

Amendment of the Memorandum of Association

Section 141 seems to require unanimity for amendments but ss. 125 and 127(4) permit alteration of both articles and memorandum by a special majority of the general meeting.

Shareholder Rights and Obligations

The share must be fully paid no later than one year after the company's entry on to the Commercial Register (earlier if the articles so require). The general meeting has power to determine whether a dividend shall be paid and the shareholder will be entitled to a share in the profits proportional to the proportion of his/her shares to the total shareholder capital (unless the articles contain a different ratio). Votes of shareholders depend on the nominal value of shares, though the articles may lay down a maximum number of votes per shareholder. A general meeting may be called by those holding one-tenth of the capital (s. 181).

General Meeting

As with the limited liability company, the general meeting is the most important body, described by s. 184 as the 'supreme body'. Many of the provisions mirror these of the limited liability company but a quorum is defined as comprising representatives of 30 per cent of the capital (articles may provide that less is sufficient), and class rights may only be altered where agreement of two-thirds of the class is forthcoming, and there are a number of detailed provisions concerning the taking, preparation and publicity of the minutes of the meeting.

Board of Directors

The powers and duties of this board mirror the powers and duties of the executives of a limited liability company but it is notable that there must be at least three members, the board must exercise their range of powers with due care without disclosure of confidential information to third parties and it is specifically provided that breach of duties will lead to personal liability in the case of insolvency of the company (s. 194(6)).

Prohibition of Competitive Conduct

These provisions mirror those which relate to limited liability conduct but there are new provisions regarding contracts with directors 'or with persons close to them' providing for such a contract to be permissible only where there has been prior approval of the general meeting (s. 196a). The description of 'connected persons' in this way is admirable and avoids the complex lists to be found in many legislative attempts at anti-avoidance.

Supervisory Board

Similarly the supervisory board has the same range of duties as that of a limited liability company. Here, though, the German/EU model is more evident as two-thirds of the supervisory board are to be elected by the general meeting and one-third by employees where there are more than 50 full-time employees. The ratio may be altered in favour of employees but only to 50 per cent being elected by employees. Different opinions of employee board members must be reported to the general meeting. The Czech model is therefore a mixture of the constituency and enterprise models familiar in Western Europe.

19.4 **Employment Laws**

It is noteworthy that in the Polish laws employment provisions do not appear in the same code which deals with the structure of companies, giving a further indication that ownership rather than enterprise is the driving force behind this legislation.

In Hungary, although detailed provisions regarding labour law are not present in the statutes concerned with the structure of companies, the provisions of the Labour Code are to serve 'as guidelines' for trade union rights (Art. 12). More specifically, where full-time employees exceed 200, there is a requirement that employees should participate through a supervisory board in the activities of the company (Art. 13). They are to elect one-third of the members of such a board. It is clear that one of the constituents whose interests are to be taken seriously are employees, and it may be that such a degree of involvement by employees makes the Hungarian company closer reflecting an enterprise model rather than a constituency one.

As detailed above, it is the Czech laws which most closely weave the rights of employees into the corporate structure, though in Kazakhstan the equivalent of works councils are important. There, the General Provisions provide for the establishment by all enterprises of a labour collective. A labour collective consists of all the workers in the enterprise. Its main organ is the general meeting, which considers the need for and terms of a collective contract with the enterprise and empowers a relevant organ to sign the contract. All enterprises must conclude a collective contract which covers both social and production questions. Difficulties are to be settled in the first instance by a collective committee formed by equal representation of workers and management. Otherwise a judicial settlement will determine the terms of the contract. Employment relations are further controlled in Kazakhstan by Article 16 of the Commercial Code which sets out the minimum requirements for a contract of employment which must include the obligations of the enterprise towards the worker relating to conditions of employment and social guarantees.

19.5 **Foreign Investors**

Much attention is paid in the countries discussed in this chapter to the status of the foreign investor and the security of private investment generally and foreign investment in particular. The concern about the status of the foreign investor has two aspects. The first is clearly the possibility that wealth will be systematically siphoned away from the relevant countries. The second, which gives us some clues to the models of companies envisaged, is a wish to attact foreign investment. The laws reflect these concerns by an equivocal approach to the ownership of property by the company. Thus in Kazakhstan the 1993 constitution provides that ownership is inviolable and legislation contains extensive safeguards against expropriation by nationalisation or otherwise. For example, Article 10(3) of the Law of Enterprises guarantees the property of an enterprise. However, this must be qualified by the restrictions placed on state enterprises. These restrictions reflect the difficulties in transition from a wholly state-owned enterprise to one where a private 'owner' must now figure. An enterprise will normally carry on business according to the powers transferred to it by the owner but state enterprises are restricted in that they must not, without the consent of the owner or the relevant state agency:

> ' – sell and transfer to other persons, exchange, grant for temporary use, or loan buildings and installations, equipment, and other basic funds of the enterprise belonging to it: – create branches and subsidiary enterprises, found enterprises and joint production entities jointly with private entrepreneurs, contribute their production and monetary capital to them.' (Art. 2).

Similarly, the move to private ownership appears to have caused some confusion in Hungary. The aim of the Business Organisations Law of Hungary is set out in its preamble. Some confusion is evident in parts of the statement of aims, notably that:

> 'The law should promote a more efficient utilisation of social property, and in particular state property.'

This is followed by Article 1(2), which provides the ability of companies to acquire rights, in particular property rights, of their own. It is unclear whether a notion of 'state property' still underlies the ability of companies to acquire rights for themselves.

19.6 **Conclusion**

The above analysis is inevitably extremely tentative, depending as it does on the bare legislative bones. A much clearer picture will emerge when companies under the various regimes have been functioning for a longer time and an accretion of practice and case law has appeared. It seems that the models have characteristics which are identifiable from a Western European perspective, but that they vary from a fairly narrow contractual model to something identifiably similar to an enterprise model in the Czech public limited company. When there have been further developments it may be that some of the hybrid characteristics will cause the emergence of identifiably distinctive models which will inform and enrich the development of company laws elsewhere.

Bibliography and Further Reading

General

Cheffins, *Company Law*, OUP, 1996.
Dine, *Criminal Law in the Company Context*, Dartmouth, 1995.
Farrar, *Company Law*, 3rd edn, Butterworths, 1991.
Gore-Brown on Companies, 44th edn, Jordans, 1986.
Gower, *Principles of Modern Company Law*, 6th edn, Sweet & Maxwell, 1996.
Mayson, French and Ryan, *Company Law*, 13th edn, Blackstone Press, 1996.
Rajak, *A Sourcebook of Company Law*, 2nd edn, Jordans, 1996.
Sealy, *Cases and Materials in Company Law*, 6th edn, Butterworths, 1996.

Chapter 1 The reasons for forming companies

Fraser, 'The Corporation as a Body Politic' (1983) *Telos*, no. 57, 5.
Rajak, *A Sourcebook of Company Law*, 2nd edn, Jordans, 1996.
Wedderburn, 'The Social Responsibility of Companies' (1985) 15, *Melbourne U L Rev*, 4.
Wolff, 'On the Nature of Legal Persons' (1983), 54 *LQR* 494.

Chapter 2 Starting a company

Secretarial Administration, Jordans (looseleaf).
Sealy, *Cases and Materials in Company Law*, pp. 1–10.

Chapter 3 Corporate personality

Fraser, 'The Corporation as a Body Politic' (1983) *Telos*, no. 57, 5.
Hart, 'Definition and Theory in Jurisprudence' (1954) 70 *LQR* 37.
Kahn-Freud, 'Some Reflections on Company Law Reform' (1944) 7 *MLR* 54.
Pickering, 'The Company as a Separate Legal Entity' (1968) 31 *MLR*.
Twining (ed.) *Legal Theory and Common Law*, Oxford, 1996.
Wedderburn, 'The Social Responsibility of Companies' (1985) 15, *Melbourne U L Rev*, 4.
Wolff, 'On the Nature of Legal Persons' (1938) 54 *LQR* 494.

Chapters 4 and 5 The memorandum and articles of association

Drury, 'The Relative Nature of the Shareholder's Rights to Enforce the Company Contract' (1986) *CLJ* 219.
Gregory (1981) 44 *MLR* 526.
Leader and Dine in *Perspectives on Company Law, I*, Patfield (ed.), Kluwer, 1995.
Wedderburn, 'Shareholders' Rights and the Rule in *Foss* v. *Harbottle*' (1958) *CLJ* 193.

Chapter 6 Promoters

Green (1987) 37 *ICLQ* 109.

Chapters 7 and 8 Public issue of securities and regulation of investment business

Andenas and Kenyon-Slade (eds) *Financial Market Regulation*, Sweet & Maxwell, 1993.
Gore-Brown on Companies, 44th edn, Jordans, 1986, ch. 12.
Page and Ferguson, *Investor Protection*, Butterworths, 1992.
Pennington (1984) 5 Co Law.
Plender and Wallace, *The Square Mile: A Guide to the New City of London*, Century Publishing, 1985.
Review of Investor Protection, Part I (Cmnd 9125, 1984).
Rider, Chaikin and Abrams, *Guide to the Financial Services Act* 1986, CCH editions, 1987.
Streight, *Futures Markets*, Blackwell, 1983.
Welch (1985) 6 Co. Law 246.

Chapter 9 Maintenance of capital

Green Paper, *The Purchase by a Company of its Own Shares*, Cmd 7944, 1980.
Sealy, *Cases and Materials in Company Law*, ch. 7.

Chapter 10 The balance of power inside the company: corporate governance

Berle and Means, *The Modern Corporation and Private Property*, New York, 1932.
Boyle, 'The Minority Shareholder in the Nineteenth Century' (1965) 28 *MLR* 317.
Wedderburn, 'Shareholders' Rights and the Rule in *Foss* v. *Harbottle*' (1958) *CLJ* 193.

Chapters 11 and 12 Director's duties

Dine, 'Disqualification of Directors' (1991) 12 Co Law 6.
Dine, *Criminal Law in the Company Context*, Dartmouth, 1995.
Gore-Brown on Companies, ch. 27.
Guidelines for Directors, Institute of Directors, 1990.
Sealy, *Company Law and Commercial Reality*, Sweet & Maxwell, 1984.
Sealy, *Disqualification and the Personal Liability of Directors*, CCH, 4th edn, 1992.
Suter, *Insider Dealing in Britain*, Butterworths, 1989.
Hopt and Wymeersch, *European Insider Dealing*, Butterworths, 1991.

Chapter 13 Suing the company

Boyle (1980) 1 Co Law 3.
Boyle (1965) 28 *MLR* 317.
Prentice (1973) 89 *LQR* 107.
Rider (1978) *CLJ* 270.
Wedderburn (1957) *CLJ* 194 and (1958) *CLJ* 93.

Chapter 14 Shares

Gore-Brown on Companies, ch. 14.
Gower, *Modern Company Law*, 4th edn, Stevens, 1979, pp. 562–3.

Chapter 15 Lending money and securing loans

Boyle, 'The Validity of Automatic Crystallisation Clauses' (1979) JBL 231.
Farrar, 'The Crystallisation of a Floating Charge' (1976) 40 *Conveyancer* 397.
Robbie and Gill, 'Fixed and Floating Charges: A New Look at the Banks' Position'
    (1981) JBL 95.

Chapter 16 Takeovers, reconstructions, amalgamation

Deakin and Hughes (eds), *Corporate Governance*, Blackwell, 1997.
Gore-Brown on Companies, ch. 29.
Patfield and Snaith, 'Regulating the City', ch. 5 of *The Changing Law*, Leicester
    University, 1990.
Weinburg and Blank, *Takeovers and Mergers*, 4th edn, Sweet & Maxwell, 1979.

Chapter 17 Insolvency and corporate reconstruction

Gore-Brown on Companies, part VII.
McCormack, *Proprietary Claims and Insolvency*, Sweet & Maxwell, 1996.
Rajak, *Company Liquidations*, CCH, 1988.
Rajak (ed), *Insolvency Law*, Sweet & Maxwell, 1993.

Chapter 18 The effect of the EU on English company law

Andersen, *European Economic Interest Groupings*, Butterworths, 1990.
Buxbaum and Hopt, *Legal Harmonisation and the Business Enterprise*, Walter de
    Gruyter, 1988.
Dine and Hughes, *European Community Company Law*, Jordans, looseleaf.
House of Lords Select Committee on the European Communities, *19th report on the*
    European Company Statute (HL Paper 71).
Israel (19??) 'The EEIG – a Major Step Forward for Community Law' 9 Co Law 14.
Van Gervan and Aalders, *European Economic Interest Groupings*, Kluwer, 1990.
Wachter, van Hulle, Lanau, Schaafsma and Raaijmakers, *Harmonisation of Company*
    and Securities Law, Tilbury University Press, 1989.
Wooldridge, *EC Company Law*, Athlone, 1991.

Index

364   *Index*

  and priority to debenture
      holders   279
  running the company   158
  secured and appointing an
      administrative receiver   304
  voluntary arrangements and
      insolvency   302
  voluntary winding-up   305
  winding-up and property
      distribution   313
  see also insolvency; liquidation;
      meeting

D
damages and articles of association
    alteration   68–9
Danckwerts (LJ)   49
debenture   21, 55, 97, 99, 171, 307
  definition of   272
debenture holder   275, 282
  appointing a receiver   272, 279,
      312
  crystallisation of the floating
      charge   276–7
  and floating charges   309
  rights   259
debts, bad   113
Denning, Lord Justice   31, 39, 41,
    75, 153, 183, 199
Department of Trade   283
  drafting statutes from
      Directives   321
  investigations   251–2; and share
      ownership   252
derivative action   *see* suing for the
    company
Diamond, A. L.   1
Diamond Report   280, 281–2, 283,
    284
Dickerson, Robert   2
Dillon, (LJ)   215
Diplock, Lord   73, 183
Directive
    68/151/EEC (article 9)   44, 70,
      72 EC   44, 70, 72
  amending prospectus, mutual
      recognition   342–3
  continuing disclosure   342
  defined   324
  on the Disclosure of Interest in
      Shares   292

influence of   322–3
Insider Dealing   217–26, 343;
    (Criminal Justice Act
    1993)   217–34
Investment Services   343
making of   321–2
money laundering   346–7
precedence over UK law   323
Prospectus   92–4
prospectus requirements   342
on publishing major holding EU
    company law   332–3
publishing particulars   342
stock exchange entry
    conditions   342
takeover   291
see also First, Second, Third, *etc.*
director   3, 5
age of   144
appointment   142–6; interests'
    regulations   172; retirement
    regulations   170–1
when board ceases to
    function   152–3
breach of duties   46
company alter ego   39
company first   67
company transactions involving
    (notes)   226–9
definition of   143–4
delegation regulations   169–70
disqualification   148, 196; and
    removal regulations   171
employment contract   149
executive and non-executive   179;
    Cadbury Report   180–2;
    rules of duty   186–8
expenses regulations   171
and family prohibited share
    dealings   232–4;
    shareholding disclosure   234
First Directive disclosure   328
general meeting
    relationship   150–2
gratuities and pensions
    regulations   172
invalid company
    transactions   227–9
liability for company
    damage   187
liability law, USA   188
limitation of powers   45
managing   149–50